"As people created in the image of God and called to ~~~~~~~~~~ ~~ ~~~~~~~, it is imperative for us to align how we live with what God has revealed and his purposes for us. Therefore, the gospel and the biblical witness should be the starting point for any understanding of spiritual formation. This volume does a superb job of grounding spirituality in the full range of biblical teaching. It lays an indispensable foundation."

> **Clinton E. Arnold,** Dean and Professor of New Testament Language and Literature, Talbot School of Theology, Biola University

"For some, spirituality is driven by technique; for others, it is the pursuit of direct and unmediated connection with the divine; for still others, it is a label that covers experiences of the ill-defined numinous. Indeed, today's 'take' on spirituality perfectly reflects the personal autonomy found in Judges: everyone does that which is right in his or her own eyes. To think clearly about spirituality as it emerges from serious Bible study, however, is to enter a world where one really does grow in knowledge of the living God, but by the means God has ordained, by the power of the Spirit, with transformed conduct the inevitable result. Christopher Morgan and his colleagues have enriched our grasp of biblical spirituality by their biblical, theological, and historical probings."

> **D. A. Carson,** Research Professor of New Testament, Trinity Evangelical Divinity School; Cofounder, The Gospel Coalition

"*Spirituality* is a contemporary buzzword. Surprisingly, even some atheists speak of their spirituality. There is even a book with the title *A Little Book of Atheist Spirituality*. How important, then, is this book which presents a biblically based, theologically deep, historically informed, and practically helpful Christian examination of spirituality. A galaxy of fine scholars take the reader through the Old and New Testaments, great themes such as holiness, and the heritage of evangelical spirituality, and explore the practical implications of biblical spirituality. A rich feast!"

> **Graham A. Cole,** Dean, Vice President of Education, and Professor of Biblical and Systematic Theology, Trinity Evangelical Divinity School; author, *He Who Gives Life* and *The God Who Became Human*

"Humans are deeply spiritual beings. It's why we seek out a greater sense of purpose and the meaning of our existence. All around us today, people are pursuing spirituality. Chris Morgan has compiled a timely and essential guidebook to true biblical spirituality that can be found only with Christ at the center. This is not an easy journey, but it is essential if we are to live a life that brings glory to God."

Kevin Ezell, President, North American Mission Board, The Southern Baptist Convention

"There are many books on spirituality, but this one stands out because it takes in the entire range of the biblical canon. Written with scholarly depth and a practical bent, this volume is a great addition to the growing literature in the field. I highly recommend it!"

Timothy George, Founding Dean, Beeson Divinity School, Samford University; general editor, Reformation Commentary on Scripture

"As Francis Schaeffer taught us, the Lord's work must be done in the Lord's way. In every generation, therefore, we face no more urgent question than the meaning of true spirituality. The excellent team of scholars writing in *Biblical Spirituality* combines academic gifts with personal wisdom to show us, from the whole of the Bible, how God has put his glory on the whole of life. Is there a more wonderful reality for us to consider together?"

Ray Ortlund, Lead Pastor, Immanuel Church, Nashville, Tennessee

"This is a biblical theology of biblical spirituality. And its the best I've read. If you want to see what biblical spirituality is, read this book."

Donald S. Whitney, Associate Dean and Professor of Biblical Spirituality, The Southern Baptist Theological Seminary; author, *Spiritual Disciplines for the Christian Life* and *Praying the Bible*

"As one who has spent my life helping people with the practical side of spiritual growth, I am deeply grateful for a strong and clear guide to the theology of growth! Your own growth and the growth of those you lead will be strengthened by the truths in *Biblical Spirituality*."

Tom Holladay, Teaching Pastor, Saddleback Church, Lake Forest, California; author, *Putting It Together Again* and *The Relationship Principles of Jesus*

BIBLICAL SPIRITUALITY

Other Crossway Books in the Theology in Community Series

The Deity of Christ (2011)

Fallen: A Theology of Sin (2013)

The Glory of God (2010)

Heaven (2014)

The Kingdom of God (2012)

The Love of God (2016)

Suffering and the Goodness of God (2008)

BIBLICAL SPIRITUALITY

Christopher W. Morgan, editor

WHEATON, ILLINOIS

Nathan A. Finn, "Spiritualities in the Christian Tradition" (chap. 8), adapted from *Spirituality for the Sent* edited by Nathan A. Finn and Keith S. Whitfield. Copyright © 2017. Used by permission of InterVarsity Press, P.O. Box 1400, Downers Grove, IL 60515, USA. www.ivpress.com.

Gregg R. Allison, "Spiritual and Embodied Disciplines" (chap. 9), adapted from *NorthStar Theology* by Gregg R. Allison. Copyright 2017 by Sojourn Community Church. Used by permission of Sojourn Community Church.

Cover design: Studio Gearbox

Cover image: *Magdalene in the House of Simon the Pharisee*, by Giuseppe Tortelli, oil on canvas / Mondadori Portfolio / Electa / Adolfo Bezzi / Bridgeman Images

First printing 2019

Printed in the United States of America

Trade paperback ISBN: 978-1-4335-4788-1
ePub ISBN: 978-1-4335-4791-1
PDF ISBN: 978-1-4335-4789-8
Mobipocket ISBN: 978-1-4335-4790-4

Library of Congress Cataloging-in-Publication Data

Names: Morgan, Christopher W., 1971- editor.

Title: Biblical spirituality / Christopher W. Morgan, editor.

Description: Wheaton : Crossway, 2019. | Series: Theology in community series | Includes bibliographical references and index.

Identifiers: LCCN 2018050404 (print) | LCCN 2019014496 (ebook) | ISBN 9781433547898 (pdf) | ISBN 9781433547904 (mobi) | ISBN 9781433547911 (epub) | ISBN 9781433547881 (tp)

Subjects: LCSH: Spirituality—Biblical teaching.

Classification: LCC BS680.S7 (ebook) | LCC BS680.S7 B525 2019 (print) | DDC 248—dc23

LC record available at https://lccn.loc.gov/2018050404

Crossway is a publishing ministry of Good News Publishers.

To Shelley and Chelsey,
I could not be more blessed as a husband and dad. I love you!

CONTENTS

LIST OF ABBREVIATIONS

AB	Anchor Bible
BBR	*Bulletin for Biblical Research*
BECNT	Baker Exegetical Commentary on the New Testament
BDAG	Bauer, W., F. W. Danker, W. F. Arndt, and F. W. Gingrich. *Greek-English Lexicon of the New Testament and Other Early Christian Literature*
BDB	Brown, F., S. R. Driver, and C. A. Briggs. *A Hebrew and English Lexicon of the Old Testament*
Bib	*Biblica*
BibInt	*Biblical Interpretation*
BSac	*Bibliotheca sacra*
CBQ	*Catholic Biblical Quarterly*
CTR	*Criswell Theological Review*
EvQ	*Evangelical Quarterly*
IBC	Interpretation: A Bible Commentary for Teaching and Preaching
Int	*Interpretation*
JBL	*Journal of Biblical Literature*
JBQ	*Jewish Bible Quarterly*
JETS	*Journal of the Evangelical Theological Society*
JSNTSup	Journal for the Study of the New Testament: Supplement Series
JTS	*Journal of Theological Studies*
LCL	Loeb Classical Library
LNTS	Library of New Testament Studies
LQ	*Lutheran Quarterly*
NAC	New American Commentary
NICNT	New International Commentary on the New Testament
NICOT	New International Commentary on the Old Testament
NIDOTTE	*New International Dictionary of Old Testament Theology and Exegesis*
NIGTC	New International Greek Testament Commentary
NIVAC	NIV Application Commentary
NSBT	New Studies in Biblical Theology

PNTC	Pelican New Testament Commentaries
SBET	*Scottish Bulletin of Evangelical Theology*
SBJT	*Southern Baptist Journal of Theology*
ThTo	*Theology Today*
TJ	*Trinity Journal*
TLOT	*Theological Lexicon of the Old Testament.* Edited by E. Jenni, with assistance from C. Westermann. Translated by M. E. Biddle. 3 vols.
VT	*Vetus Testamentum*
WBC	Word Biblical Commentary
WCF	Westminster Confession of Faith
ZECNT	Zondervan Exegetical Commentary on the New Testament

SERIES PREFACE

As the series name, Theology in Community, indicates, theology in community aims to promote clear thinking on and godly responses to historic and contemporary theological issues. The series examines issues central to the Christian faith, including traditional topics such as sin, the atonement, the church, and heaven, but also some which are more focused or contemporary, such as suffering and the goodness of God, the glory of God, the deity of Christ, and the kingdom of God. The series strives not only to follow a sound theological method but also to display it. Chapters addressing the Old and New Testaments on the book's subject form the heart of each volume. Subsequent chapters synthesize the biblical teaching and link it to historical, philosophical, systematic, and pastoral concerns. Far from being mere collections of essays, the volumes are carefully crafted so that the voices of the various experts combine to proclaim a unified message. Again, as the name suggests, theology in community also seeks to demonstrate that theology should be done in teams. The teachings of the Bible were forged in real-life situations by leaders in God's covenant communities. The biblical teachings addressed concerns of real people who needed the truth to guide their lives. Theology was formulated by the church and for the church. This series seeks to recapture that biblical reality. The volumes are written by scholars, from a variety of denominational backgrounds and life experiences with academic credentials and significant expertise across the spectrum of theological disciplines, who collaborate with each other. They write from a high view of Scripture with robust evangelical conviction and in a gracious manner. They are not detached academics but are personally involved in ministry, serving as teachers, pastors, and missionaries. The contributors to these volumes stand in continuity with the historic church, care about the global church, share life together with other believers in local churches, and aim to write for the good of the church to strengthen its leaders, particularly pastors, teachers, missionaries, lay leaders, students, and professors.

For the glory of God and the good of the church,

Christopher W. Morgan

ACKNOWLEDGMENTS

God has made us to love him and to love and live in community with one another. I am grateful for the people that God has placed in my life to shape me and my thinking. There are too many to mention all of them, but I want to express gratitude to those who have made an impact on this project:

- Dr. Tony Chute and Dr. Greg Cochran, for your friendship, partnership, and leadership in CBU's School of Christian Ministries.

- Gary McDonald, for sharing life together and excelling in grace and generosity.

- SoCal Baptist Ministries, Phil Kell, and the California Baptist Foundation, for your wonderful generosity and support.

- Dr. Milton Higgins, for your warm love, prayers, and generosity.

- Dr. Ron Ellis, Dr. Chuck Sands, Kent Dacus, the trustees, and the administration at California Baptist University, for your vision and support.

- CBU's School of Christian Ministries' faculty, for your friendship and your resolve to exalt the Lord, serve churches, and invest in students.

- Maigen Turner, my administrative assistant, for your positive attitude, proficient work, and eagerness to help.

- Students at California Baptist University, for your desire to grow in God's Word to serve his church.

- Lydia Brownback and Elliott Pinegar, for your superb editorial help.

- The whole Crossway team, for your encouragement, service, and work to bless God's people.

CONTRIBUTORS

Gregg R. Allison (PhD, Trinity Evangelical Divinity School), professor of Christian theology, The Southern Baptist Theological Seminary

Anthony L. Chute (PhD, Trinity Evangelical Divinity School), associate dean and professor of church history, School of Christian Ministries, California Baptist University

Gregory C. Cochran (PhD, The Southern Baptist Theological Seminary), director of applied theology and professor of theology and ethics, School of Christian Ministries, California Baptist University

Nathan A. Finn (PhD, Southeastern Baptist Theological Seminary), provost and dean of the university faculty, North Greenville University

George H. Guthrie (PhD, Southwestern Baptist Theological Seminary), professor of New Testament, Regent College

Paul R. House (PhD, The Southern Baptist Theological Seminary), professor of divinity, Beeson Divinity School, Samford University

Justin L. McLendon (PhD, Mid-America Baptist Theological Seminary), assistant professor of theology, Grand Canyon University

Christopher W. Morgan (PhD, Mid-America Baptist Theological Seminary), dean and professor of theology, School of Christian Ministries, California Baptist University

Charles L. Quarles (PhD, Mid-America Baptist Theological Seminary), research professor of New Testament and biblical theology, Southeastern Baptist Theological Seminary

Benjamin M. Skaug (PhD candidate, Gateway Seminary), senior pastor, Immanuel Baptist Church, Highland, California

A TRAJECTORY OF SPIRITUALITY

CHRISTOPHER W. MORGAN
AND JUSTIN L. MCLENDON

"A prominent feature of our times is the robust revival of spirituality."[1] Bruce Demarest is right, and we do not have to look far for reasons to explain this renewed interest. Whether it is a reaction to society's downward moral and ethical spiral, dissatisfaction with formal religion, the lingering residue of postmodernism, or a host of other factors, we are witnessing a renewed interest in all things spiritual. For some, spirituality means the latest self-help literature or a generic sense of self-improvement through diet, exercise, meditation, or some sort of spiritual contemplation. Others think of major religious traditions or, more commonly, a Western synthesis of these traditions into innumerable spiritualized alternatives that can be viewed in either religious or nonreligious terms and practices.

But what does the Bible say about spirituality? How should we begin discussing the matter of spirituality with biblical and theological focus? The answer is more difficult to ascertain than we might first suppose. Talk of spirituality can be vague and loose, detached from Scripture while appearing biblical, and so clarity is crucial as we consider formation and our spiritual journeys. D. A. Carson insightfully links true Christian spirituality to the gospel, urging us to work outward from that center.[2] Our understanding of spirituality must have its roots in the gospel, its moorings in biblical theology, and its focus in theology. These theological roots do not create a cold, lifeless orthodoxy unengaged with the Spirit's

---

[1] Bruce Demarest, *Four Views on Christian Spirituality*, ed. Bruce Demarest (Grand Rapids, MI: Zondervan, 2012), 11. Demarest's introductory essay cogently surveys current research and practices of the recent increase in spirituality.
[2] D. A. Carson, "When Is Spirituality Spiritual? Reflections on Some Problems of Definition," *JETS* 37 (Sept. 1994): 381–94.

active work in our daily lives but actually ground the life-transforming work of the Spirit in the Word while protecting the legitimacy of our spiritual longings and practices. Carson highlights the moral and ethical necessities of living by the Spirit (Gal. 5:16) and of understanding how the Spirit enables and empowers us to live purposefully so that we can approach what Carson calls an "all-of-life approach to spirituality—every aspect of human existence, personal and corporate, brought under the discipline of the Word of God, brought under the consciousness that we live in the presence of God, by his grace and for his glory."[3] J. I. Packer proposes similar bearings:

> I want to see a focused vision of spiritual maturity—the expansion of the soul is the best phrase I can use for it. That is, a renewed sense of the momentousness of being alive, the sheer bigness and awesomeness of being a human being alive in God's world with light, with grace, with wisdom, with responsibility, with biblical truth.[4]

Indeed, we seek *biblical* spirituality, "a renewed sense of the momentousness of being alive in God's world" as God's people led by God's Spirit through God's Word unto godly, Christlike character—all for God's mission by God's grace and for God's glory.

The Bible portrays this spiritual pilgrimage widely and often, referring to it as walking with God, walking in God's ways, worship, holiness, obedience, discipleship, following Christ, life in the Spirit, maturity, and sanctification. The Bible portrays our spiritual pilgrimage as requiring grace-given faith, love, growth, diligence, repentance, prayer, commitment, intentionality, and discipline. Our spiritual pilgrimage is depicted as personal and as life together in the body of Christ. Our spiritual growth is also gradual, as Paul prays that the love of Philippian believers would "abound more and more, with knowledge and all discernment, so that you may approve what is excellent, and so be pure and blameless for the day of Christ, filled with the fruit of righteousness that comes through Jesus Christ, to the glory and praise of God" (Phil. 1:9–11).

As the Bible relates these truths, it offers us something of a trajectory of our spiritual journey. Beginning with man's being created in the image of God and culminating in the ultimate glory of God, the trajectory of our spiritual journey develops

---

[3] Ibid., 394.
[4] Wendy Murray Zoba, "Knowing Packer: The Lonely Journey of a Passionate Puritan," *Christianity Today* (April 6, 1998), 40.

- the image of God: created for spirituality
- fallen man: the distortion of our spirituality
- Christ's saving work: the basis of our spirituality
- new life: the beginning of our spirituality
- the triune God: the source of our spirituality
- Christlikeness: the goal of our spirituality
- love: the focus of our spirituality
- the church: the community of our spirituality
- ordinary life: the context of our spirituality
- indwelling sin and temptation: obstacles in our spirituality
- the already and the not yet: tensions in our spirituality
- Word, prayer, and church: means for our spirituality
- reproducing disciples: the mission of our spirituality
- the glory of God: the ultimate end of our spirituality
- the grace of God: fuel for our journey.

The Image of God: Created for Spirituality

The story of our spirituality can be found only within the biblical story-line, which starts suddenly: "In the beginning, God created the heavens and the earth" (Gen. 1:1). Already in existence prior to matter, space, or time, the eternal, self-existent God creates the universe and all that exists. God "creates, says, sees, separates, names, makes, appoints, blesses, finishes, makes holy, and rests."[5] God creates out of nothing, forms it according to his purposes, and fills it with plants and animals. God is not like other gods of the ancient Near East. Gordon Wenham observes: "God is without peer and competitor. He does not have to establish his power in struggle with other members of a polytheistic pantheon. The sun and moon are his handiwork, not his rivals."[6] The true God is not the sky, sun, moon, water, trees, animals, or anything else created; God creates them, and they are subject to him. The creation is neither God nor a part of God; he is absolute and has independent existence, and creation has derived existence from him and continually depends on him as its sustainer (cf. Acts 17:25–28). The transcendent Creator is a king who accomplishes his will by his word and names the elements of his creation (Gen. 1:5).

The Creator is also personal. On each day of creation God is personally involved in every detail, crafting them in a way that pleases him and benefits his creatures. On the sixth day, he personally creates man in his own image, breathing life into him. The personal God has made

---

[5] C. John Collins, *Genesis 1–4: A Linguistic, Literary, and Theological Commentary* (Phillipsburg, NJ: P&R, 2006), 71.
[6] Gordon J. Wenham, *Genesis 1–15*, WBC (Waco, TX: Word, 1987), 37–38.

humans to be personal as well, with the ability to relate to him, live in community with one another, and have dominion over creation. As Carson reminds, "We are accorded with an astonishing dignity" and have "implanted within us a profound capacity for knowing God intimately."[7] By creating us in his image, God distinguishes us from the rest of creation and establishes that he is distinct from us—we are not gods but creatures made in his image.

God's goodness is reflected in the goodness of his creation and reinforced in the steady refrain, "And God saw that it was good" (1:10, 12, 18, 21, 25; see also 1:4), even "very good" (1:31). Material creation reflects God's goodness, which is evident also in his generous provisions of light, land, vegetation, animals, and "creeping" things. These are blessings given for humanity's benefit, as are the ability to relate to God, fertility to procreate, and authority to use the abundant provisions for man's own good. By the seventh day, God has finished his creative work, rests, and blesses and sanctifies the day as holy, as a Sabbath to be kept. In doing so, God displays his joy and satisfaction in his creation, his celebration of completion, and he commemorates this special event.[8]

Genesis 2:4–25 focuses on God's formation of man and woman and his provision of the garden of Eden as a place for them in which to live and work.[9] As Allen Ross summarizes, "God has prepared human beings, male and female, with the spiritual capacity and communal assistance to serve him and to keep his commands so that they might live and enjoy the bounty of his creation."[10] Man is formed from the dust of the ground but is more than dust—his life comes directly from the very breath of God (2:7). In planting the garden and moving man there, the Creator and covenant Lord provides a wonderful and sacred space for humans to enjoy a harmonious relationship with him, each other, the animals, and the land. The garden highlights God's presence with man. God establishes the terms for living in his presence and graciously puts forward only one prohibition: man shall not eat from the tree of the knowledge of good and evil. Contrary to what might be expected, man is allowed to eat of the tree of life (which confers immortality) but not of the tree of the knowledge of good and evil (which gives access to wisdom), "for that leads to . . .

---

[7] D. A. Carson, *The Gagging of God: Christianity Confronts Pluralism* (Grand Rapids, MI: Zondervan, 1996), 205.

[8] Allen P. Ross, *Creation and Blessing: A Guide to the Study and Exposition of Genesis* (Grand Rapids, MI: Baker, 1996), 114.

[9] Collins, *Genesis 1–4*, 39, 101.

[10] Ross, *Creation and Blessing*, 127.

an independence of the creator incompatible with the trustful relationship between man and his maker which the story presupposes."[11] Because God's generosity to man is so abundant, his prohibition would not seem difficult to accept.

God lovingly notices that "it is not good that the man should be alone" (2:18) and generously meets man's need by creating woman as a complementary and intimate companion united with him for life together. Genesis 2 ends positively and, given the beliefs of ancient Israel, surprisingly: "The man and his wife were both naked and were not ashamed" (2:25). In the garden, nakedness is not reason for shame but points to the man and woman's innocence and the unspoiled delight they have in each other.[12]

The good God creates a good world for the good of his creatures. Humans too are created good and blessed beyond measure, being made in God's image, with an unhindered relationship with God, and with freedom. In the beginning, God creates humans in his image and designs them for spirituality—to enjoy a loving and personal relationship with the covenant Lord, as well as holistic relationships with themselves, one another, and creation.

Fallen Man: The Distortion of Our Spirituality

Against this pristine backdrop, Genesis 3 recounts a tempter who calls into question God's truthfulness, sovereignty, and goodness. The tempter is "crafty" and deflects the woman's attention away from the covenantal relationship God has established.[13] Sadly, in 3:6 she saw, she took, she ate, and she gave, which culminates in "he ate." Wenham observes that the midpoint of 3:6–8, "and he ate," employs the key verb of the narrative, "eat," and is placed between the woman's inflated expectations for eating (good to eat, delight to the eyes, and giving insight) and its actual effects: eyes opened, knowing they were nude, and hiding in the trees.[14] The contrast is striking: the forbidden fruit did not deliver what the tempter promised but brought new dark realities warned of by the good and truthful covenant Lord.

This initial act of human rebellion brings divine justice: "They sinned by eating, and so would suffer to eat; she led her husband to sin, and so would be mastered by him; they brought pain into the world by their

---

[11] Wenham, *Genesis 1–15*, 87.
[12] Ibid., 88; Collins, *Genesis 1–4*, 139.
[13] Collins, *Genesis 1–4*, 171.
[14] Wenham, *Genesis 1–15*, 75.

disobedience, and so would have painful toil in their respective lives."[15] Collins adds:

> There are small ironic wordplays. . . . For example, in Genesis 3:5 the serpent promises that the humans' eyes will be *opened* and they will *know* something, while in verse 7 it is fulfilled: their eyes were *opened* and they *knew* something—but it was just that they were naked! . . . Similarly, there is a play between the use of the root *r-b-h* in 3:16 ("I will surely *multiply* your pain in childbearing") and its use in the commission of 1:28 ("Be fruitful and *multiply*"). Whereas procreation had previously been the sphere of blessing, now it is to be the area of pain and danger.[16]

The consequences of their sin are suitable and shattering. The couple feels shame, realizing they are naked (3:7). They sense their estrangement from God, even foolishly trying to hide from him (3:8–10). They are fearful of God and how he might respond (3:9–10). Their alienation from each other also emerges, as the woman blames the serpent, while the man blames the woman and, by insinuation, even God (3:10–13). Pain and sorrow also arise. The woman experiences pain in childbirth, the man toils in trying to grow food in a land with pests and weeds, and both discover conflict in their relationship (3:15–19). Even worse, the couple is banished from Eden and God's glorious presence (3:22–24).

How they wish they had listened to God's warning that if they ate of the tree of the knowledge of good and evil, they would "surely die" (2:17)! And die they do. They die spiritually, and their bodies also begin to experience gradual decay that will lead ultimately to their physical death, as God's judgment states: "To dust you shall return" (3:19).

Most devastating of all is that these consequences befall not only Adam and Eve but extend to their descendants as well. Robert Pyne describes the dismal scene:

> Standing together east of Eden [Adam and Eve] each felt alone—betrayed by the other, alienated from God, and confused about how it had all come apart so quickly. . . .
> The children were all born outside of Eden. . . . None of them ever saw the tree of life or had a chance to taste or reject the forbidden fruit. At the same time, none of them enjoyed marriage relationships without some degree of rivalry or resentment, and they inevitably ate bread pro-

---

[15] Ross, *Creation and Blessing*, 148.
[16] Collins, *Genesis 1–4*, 169, emphasis original.

duced by the sweat of their brow. Born in a fallen world, they knew only the curse, never Eden. Still they knew that this was not the way life was supposed to be. . . .

Adam and Even sinned alone, but they were not the only ones locked out of the Garden. Cut off from the tree of life, they and their descendants were all destined to die.[17]

So, in the beginning, God created a good cosmos with good humans who enjoyed good relationships with him, themselves, one another, and creation itself. But then sin entered the picture and brought disruption and alienation in each human relationship—with God, oneself, one another, and creation. Yet humans are still in the image of God, blessed by God, and commanded to be fruitful and multiply as recipients of God's presence, promise, and grace.

Nevertheless, in Adam sin entered the picture and has brought disruption and alienation in each of our human relationships—with God, self, one another, and creation. Adam sinned not merely as the first bad example but as the representative of all humanity. In its contrast of Adam's and Christ's representation of us, Romans 5:12–21 stresses that in Adam there was sin, death, and condemnation. In Adam was the old era, the dominion of sin and death. Note the outcomes of Adam's representative trespass:[18]

- "many died" because of his sin (v. 15);
- his sin "brought condemnation" to all (v. 16);
- "death reigned" over all human beings (v. 17);
- all people were condemned because of his one trespass (v. 18); and
- by virtue of his sin "many were made sinners" (v. 19).

Note also four particular effects resulting from Adam's sin and representation:

- many/all were made sinners (v. 19);[19]
- many/all died (v. 15);
- condemnation is upon all (v. 16, 18); and
- death reigned over all humans (v. 17).

Thus, in Adam all are sinners; all die; all are under the domain of death;

---

[17] Robert A. Pyne, *Humanity and Sin* (Dallas: Word, 1999), 162.

[18] Thomas R. Schreiner, *Romans*, BECNT (Grand Rapids, MI: Baker, 1998), 268.

[19] Paul does not set "many" in comparison with "all," nor vice versa. Rather, he contrasts Adam's one act with the widespread effects of that sin upon humanity, "many." Likewise, Paul contrasts Christ's act with its incalculable effects on "many." Paul uses "all" similarly here. For example, many die and all die.

all are condemned.[20] Because of the fall, our spirituality is distorted and our relationship with God is now characterized by hostility, guilt, and condemnation.

Christ's Saving Work: The Basis of Our Spirituality

Thankfully, sin is no match for God's grace, showcased especially in Christ's saving work.

"Christianity is a rescue religion," says John Stott, and the totality of Christ's work, from eternity past to our future hope, supports every aspect of our spirituality.[21] Christ's saving work refers to "all that Christ did when he came to this earth 'for us and our salvation,' all that he continues to do now that he is risen from the dead and at God's right hand, and all that he will do when he returns in glory at the end of the age."[22]

In the fullness of time, God the Son entered human history to "redeem those who were under the law, so that we might receive adoption as sons" (Gal. 4:5). Our advocate, Jesus Christ the righteous, knew no sin, yet he became sin so that "in him we might become the righteousness of God" (2 Cor. 5:21; cf. 1 Pet. 2:22). He offered himself as our propitiation, defeating our sin through his substitutionary death and triumphing over death through his victorious resurrection.[23] We are sons and daughters of the risen and exalted King, and "God has sent the Spirit of his Son into our hearts, crying, 'Abba! Father!'" Our collective cry is in praise to God for Christ's victory over sin and death; we are no longer slaves but sons and daughters, heirs of God (Gal. 4:5–7). As Paul claims, "Christ Jesus is the one who died—more than that, who was raised—who is at the right hand of God, who indeed is interceding for us" (Rom. 8:34). Paul's "more than that" acknowledges Jesus' work on both sides of the empty tomb. His sinless life, substitutionary death, bodily resurrection, exaltation, and more ground our spirituality, including such blessings as justification, forgiveness, righteousness, peace with God, and "access by faith into this grace in which we stand" (Rom. 5:2).

---

[20] Rom. 3:9–20 teaches similarly: we are all "under sin" (v. 9); "none is righteous, no, not one" (v. 10); every mouth will be stopped (v. 19); the whole world will be judged guilty before God (v. 19); and no human being will be justified by the works of the law (v. 20). Eph. 2:1–3 also underlines the universality of sin, guilt, and death. Apart from Christ, we all are in the state of spiritual death. This is characterized by the lifestyle that flows from this state as well as those who are mired in this state's being called "sons of disobedience" and "children of wrath." Sin and guilt are universal. Apart from Christ, spiritual death is our state. For more on our sin, see Christopher W. Morgan and Robert A. Peterson, eds., *Fallen: A Theology of Sin*, Theology in Community (Wheaton, IL: Crossway, 2013).

[21] John Stott, *Basic Christianity*, 2nd ed. (London: InterVarsity Press, 1971), 81.

[22] Robert Letham, *The Work of Christ*, Contours of Christian Theology (Downers Grove, IL: InterVarsity, 1993), 18–19.

[23] This section especially draws from Robert A. Peterson, *Salvation Accomplished by the Son: The Work of Christ* (Wheaton, IL: Crossway, 2011).

New Life: The Beginning of Our Spirituality

Christ died for us—the ungodly, sinners, his enemies—that we might be right with him and have spiritual life (Rom. 5:6, 8, 11). Note the outcomes of Christ's representative work:

- his grace and gift abounded for many (v. 15);
- his grace brought "justification" whereas Adam introduced "condemnation" (v. 16);
- instead of death's reigning, believers now "reign in life" by virtue of the grace of Jesus Christ (v. 17);
- the righteous act of Jesus Christ brought "justification and life" for all (v. 18);
- through Christ's obedience the many are now "made righteous" (v. 19).

In Christ there is righteousness, life, and justification. In Christ there is a new reign, marked by grace and life. In Christ, the spiritually guilty find righteousness; the spiritually dead find life. In Christ, grace abounds—in our justification (5:12–21) and in our sanctification (6:1–14).

All journeys have a beginning, and our Christian spirituality begins with this new life in Christ. Jesus assures that all who hear his word and believe have the eternal life he grants, which leads to a passing from death to life (John 5:25). Jesus' words to Nicodemus underline our need for this new life: "Unless one is born again he cannot see the kingdom of God. . . . Do not marvel that I said to you, 'You must be born again'" (John 3:3, 7). To be born again means to receive new life in Christ, as John Murray explains:

> God effects a change which is radical and all-pervasive, a change which cannot be explained in terms of any combination, permutation, or accumulation of human resources, a change which is nothing less than a new creation by him who calls the things that be not as they were, who spake and it was done, who commanded and it stood fast. This, in a word, is regeneration.[24]

Put similarly:

> Regeneration, or the new birth, is a work of God's grace whereby believers become new creatures in Christ Jesus. It is a change of heart wrought by the Holy Spirit through conviction of sin, to which the sinner responds in repentance toward God and faith in the Lord Jesus Christ. Repentance and faith are inseparable experiences of grace.[25]

---

[24] John Murray, *Redemption Accomplished and Applied* (Grand Rapids, MI: Eerdmans, 1955), 96.
[25] See "Salvation," in the *Baptist Faith and Message 2000*. See also Anthony A. Hoekema, *Saved by Grace* (Grand Rapids, MI: Eerdmans, 1989), 106–7.

With repentance from sin, and faith in Christ, comes our justification, in which God, through the sinless life, substitutionary death, and bodily resurrection of Christ, forgives us of our sin, grants Christ's righteousness to us, and judicially declares us righteous. In Christ, our sins are forgiven, our status is righteous, and our new identity is formed: we are the children of God, adopted into God's covenant family as heirs of the kingdom.[26]

The trajectory of our spirituality begins with our own spiritual death. God acts on our behalf, for our good and for his glory, to rescue us through Christ and his saving work. He gives us new life/birth in Christ, fosters our repentance and faith, declares us righteous in Christ, and adopts us into his family. But God's work on our behalf has not concluded. Using familial language, Peter expresses God's purpose to sanctify us: "As obedient children, do not be conformed to the passions of your former ignorance, but as he who called you is holy, you also be holy in all your conduct, since it is written, 'You shall be holy, for I am holy'" (1 Pet. 1:14–16).

This sanctification is both definitive and progressive. Definitive (or initial) sanctification is the Holy Spirit's work of setting sinful men and women apart as holy in Christ, constituting them as saints. Paul addresses the Corinthian church, certainly not the epitome of holiness, as "those sanctified in Christ Jesus, called to be saints" (1 Cor. 1:2). The Corinthian believers were "washed," "sanctified," and "justified"—past tense (6:11). We already are holy as saints. And yet we are growing in holiness and must rely on the Spirit to live up to our new identity. This is called "progressive sanctification." Thomas Schreiner relates the two:

> For Paul, then, sanctification usually refers to the definitive work by which God has set apart believers in the realm of the holy in Christ Jesus. This eschatological work is accomplished at conversion, so that believers can be said to be holy or sanctified in God's presence. Still, Paul recognizes the need for growth in holiness and that transformation is a process (cf. 2 Cor. 3:18), since complete sanctification and holiness will not be granted until Christ returns. Believers are already holy in Christ, and yet the fullness of that holiness will not be theirs until the day of redemption.[27]

So the trajectory of our spirituality begins with our new life in Christ, received by faith, in which we are born again; are justified, adopted, and

---

[26] J. I. Packer, *Knowing God* (Downers Grove, IL: InterVarsity Press, 1973), 207.
[27] Thomas R. Schreiner, *New Testament Theology: Magnifying God in Christ* (Grand Rapids, MI: Baker, 2008), 375–76.

made holy; and increasingly grow in holiness. This work, from first to last, is a triune work of love.

The Triune God: The Source of Our Spirituality

Ephesians 1 praises the Father for heaping spiritual blessings upon us: "Blessed be the God and Father of our Lord Jesus Christ, who has blessed us in Christ with every spiritual blessing in the heavenly places" (1:3). God is the source of all our spiritual blessings. He has blessed us to the praise of his "glorious grace" (1:6) and for his "glory" (1:12, 14). This passage celebrates the work of the three persons of the Trinity in salvation. The Father's election leads to our holiness and adoption (1:4–5). The Son's redemption brings our forgiveness (1:7). The Father seals believers' union with Christ by giving us the Holy Spirit as that seal, guaranteeing final salvation (1:13–14). All three persons work to save us, and they work in harmony. The result is continuity in God's people: the Father chooses, the Son redeems, and the Spirit seals.

Notice how Paul stresses that all this occurs in Christ. Every spiritual blessing is in Christ (1:3). We are chosen in Christ, holy in Christ, and adopted in Christ. Our redemption is in Christ, our forgiveness is in Christ, the purpose of God's will is in Christ, and final cosmic reconciliation is in Christ. Our inheritance is in Christ, our hope is in Christ, and our faith is in Christ. God has blessed us "in the Beloved" (1:6).

What Christ has accomplished for us is now applied to us through our union with him. The Father is the author of salvation, the Son the redeemer, and the Holy Spirit the one who joins people to the Son in salvation. The Father plans salvation, the Son accomplishes it, and the Spirit applies it to believers. The Spirit is thus the person of the Trinity who unites us to Christ. Union with Christ, then, is the Holy Spirit's work of joining believers to Christ, so that all his saving benefits become ours.[28]

The Holy Spirit is our daily help as we live out the realities of our union with Christ. We need a grand goal, proper motivation, and solid content on which to build our lives. But more fundamentally, we need life, which comes from the Spirit's uniting us to Christ. And we need the power that flows from Christ's life, which the Spirit also links to us. The New Testament portrays the power for Christian living in three ways. First, it simply calls it "power." Paul prays for the Ephesians to know the "immeasurable greatness of his power toward us who believe" (1:19). He

---

[28] For more on union with Christ, see Robert A. Peterson, *Salvation Applied by the Spirit: Union with Christ* (Wheaton, IL: Crossway, 2015).

extols this power as that which raised Christ from the dead and which he now exercises at God's right hand, above all things and with everything under his feet (vv. 19–23). It is no wonder that Paul describes God's power as the "working of his great might" (v. 19).[29]

A second way in which Scripture speaks of the power driving the Christian life is as enabling grace. We underestimate God's grace by limiting it to initial saving grace (Eph. 2:8–9), because grace is also our ongoing power to serve God. Paul asserts, "By the grace of God I am what I am" (1 Cor. 15:10). This initial saving grace made Paul, at that time an enemy of Christ, into an apostle. Paul states that he worked harder than any of the other apostles and then clarifies, "though it was not I, but the grace of God that is with me" (15:10). God's enabling grace energized Paul to serve the Lord and bear fruit (15:11). Paul also speaks of enabling grace when he tells of his experience of receiving a thorn in the flesh so that he would not become puffed up (2 Cor. 12:7). Paul asked the Lord three times to remove the thorn, but God denied his requests, explaining, "My grace is sufficient for you, for my power is made perfect in weakness" (12:9). "Grace" is parallel with God's "power," and it is God's grace that fortifies Paul to overcome despite weaknesses. Because of God's enabling grace, the apostle can say: "When I am weak, then I am strong" (12:10).

A third way of viewing the power we need to live for Christ is to speak of the power of the Holy Spirit. The New Testament often associates the Holy Spirit with God's power. The same Spirit who empowered Jesus in his earthly ministry (Acts 10:38) also worked as he made atonement (Heb. 9:14). The same Spirit who raised Jesus from the dead (Rom. 1:4) strengthens us to live for him. The same Spirit who applied salvation to us by enabling us to embrace the gospel (1 Thess. 1:5), regenerating us (Titus 3:5), and justifying us (1 Cor. 6:11), gives us power to serve Christ.

The empowering Holy Spirit works both inside and outside of God's people. He works within to grant spiritual gifts to us (1 Cor. 12:11), enabling us to grow in holiness (Rom. 8:13), to "abound in hope" (15:13), and to gain strength and encouragement (Eph. 3:16). The Spirit also works outside of us to deliver us from difficult circumstances (Phil. 1:19), to empower us for witness (Acts 1:8), and to produce fruit from our evangelistic efforts (Rom. 15:18–19).

The Father providentially guides us as his people through difficult circumstances in order to build holiness into our lives; he disciplines us

---

[29] See John Frame, *Systematic Theology: An Introduction to Christian Belief* (Phillipsburg, NJ: P&R, 2013), 924–32.

"for our good, that we may share his holiness" (Heb. 12:10). In unparalleled love, the Son of God died on the cross to sanctify us: "Christ loved the church and gave himself up for her, that he might sanctify her" (Eph. 5:25–26). As we have seen, the Holy Spirit plays a major role in sanctification: "God chose you as the firstfruits to be saved, through sanctification by the Spirit and belief in the truth" (2 Thess. 2:13). In love, each Trinitarian person works to promote our holiness.

Although God alone initiates salvation due to our spiritual helplessness, it is clear that we have an active role in the Christian life. Jesus exhorts: "Abide in me, and I in you. As the branch cannot bear fruit by itself, unless it abides in the vine, neither can you, unless you abide in me" (John 15:4). Paul urges us "by the mercies of God . . . to present your bodies as a living sacrifice, holy and acceptable to God" (Rom. 12:1). And Peter admonishes: "Above all, keep loving one another earnestly, since love covers a multitude of sins" (1 Pet. 4:8).

Our spirituality, therefore, is the work of the Trinity in and through us. Paul commands us to "work out [our] own salvation with fear and trembling" (Phil. 2:12). But the Christian life is not a self-help project, as Paul's next words show: "For it is God who works in you, both to will and to work for his good pleasure" (v. 13). God is the Lord who saves, keeps, and works in us. Yet we labor for him who saved us by his grace. And we do so by his mighty power, "struggling with all his energy that he powerfully works within [us]" (Col. 1:29).

Christlikeness: The Goal of Our Spirituality

Our triune God breathes spiritual life into us. We who were alienated are now united to Christ, the perfect image of God, and in this union we know and love him. Union with Christ is a legal, judicial, and actual union producing life. In our union with Christ, we echo in our embodied state our purpose to image Christ through worship and devotion, through word and deed. Ivor Davidson notes:

> Responsible Christian talk of salvation is inseparable from responsible Christian talk of God. To speak rightly of God is to speak on the basis of God's initiative in turning towards us; that turning is God's restoration of fellowship with us, his overcoming of the distance that has come to exist between estranged creatures and their creator. The genesis of this movement lies exclusively in God's mercy, in the majestic goodness with which God determines that the alienated should not be forever lost, that those who have chosen death should not perish, that all things should

find their due end in relation to their maker. In the gratuitousness of his outreach, God bestows not mere data but *himself*, enabling us to know him as he is, establishing the conditions within which creaturely apprehension of his character can and does occur.[30]

In our union with Christ, he is at work in and through us to cultivate and change us into people who reflect his character and his ways.

Thus the goal of our Christian life is Christlikeness, and our ambition is to conform to the image of Christ. Romans 8:29 stresses that God's purpose is to conform us to this image of his Son. Second Corinthians 3:18 elaborates: "We all, with unveiled face, beholding the glory of the Lord, are being transformed into the same image from one degree of glory to another. For this comes from the Lord who is the Spirit."

In *The Disciplines of Grace*, Jerry Bridges comments on Romans 8:29 and 2 Corinthians 3:18, unpacking Paul's reference to our being transformed and conformed to Christ and not to the world:

> Both words, *transformed* and *conformed*, have a common root, *form*, meaning a pattern or a mold. "Being transformed" refers to the process; "conformed" refers to the finished product. Jesus is our pattern or mold. We are being transformed so that we will eventually be conformed to the likeness of Jesus. Sanctification or holiness (the words are somewhat interchangeable), then, is conformity to the likeness of Jesus Christ.[31]

Bridges offers a practical test we can employ to determine if we are growing in our transformation: we evaluate Jesus' character against our own actions as we pursue Christlikeness.

Such Christlikeness is immensely practical. God's grace teaches us to "renounce ungodliness and worldly passions" and to pursue "self-controlled, upright, and godly lives" as we await the "appearing of the glory of our great God and Savior Jesus Christ" (Titus 2:11–13). Christlikeness, or godliness, is the goal: "Train yourself for godliness" (1 Tim. 4:7).

Christlikeness is also intensely personal. Indeed, "the fruit of the Spirit is love, joy, peace, patience, kindness, goodness, faithfulness, gentleness, self-control" (Gal. 5:22–23). When the Spirit unites us to Christ, he gives new life, which produces fruit—a display of our new life of goodness. He produces in us Christlikeness/godliness. By connecting us to Jesus' obe-

---

[30] Ivor J. Davidson, "Salvation's Destiny: Heirs of God," in *God of Salvation: Soteriology in Theological Perspective*, ed. Ivor J. Davidson and Murray A. Rae (New York: Ashgate, 2001), 155.
[31] Jerry Bridges, *The Disciplines of Grace: God's Role and Our Role in the Pursuit of Holiness* (Colorado Springs, CO: NavPress, 1994), 98; emphasis original.

dient life, substitutionary death, and bodily resurrection, the Spirit produces the very character of Jesus himself. To be sure, he is always the Creator, and we are always the creatures; he is always the vine, and we are always the branches (John 15). As such, in Christ our lives are increasingly characterized by his character and life: love, joy, peace, patience, kindness, goodness, faithfulness, gentleness, self-control, etc.

Further, Christlikeness is ecclesial. When Paul spoke to the church at Ephesus, he stressed traits that God's people should embody over the totality of their lives. These marks—unity, universality, holiness, truth, love—communicate and reflect God's goodness, which is why such attributes are sometimes called God's communicable attributes. The church bears these marks precisely because the church displays God's goodness in its collective pursuit of Christlikeness. And while God's perfections cannot be fully communicated to or through creatures, through his gracious self-communication and self-condescension the church can still truthfully and genuinely display our great and glorious God.[32]

The marks of God's "display people" characterize both the church as a whole and also the local, visible church. And while the marks already do to some extent characterize the visible church, we are exhorted to maintain unity, to live in accord with holiness, to teach truth, and to embody love. We are to live up to our high calling, and in so doing we showcase God. As such, the marks of the church both display who we are as the church and how we are to live accordingly. Ephesians regularly points to this already/not yet (and indicative-imperative) aspect of the church. As the church, we already are the fullness of Christ (1:23), and yet we long to be filled with the fullness of Christ (3:19) as we seek the measure of the stature of the fullness of Christ (4:13).[33] As the church, we already are the one new humanity (2:14–18), and yet we are to attain unto a mature humanity (4:13) and put on the new humanity (4:20–24). As the church, we already are under our head, Christ (1:22–23), and yet we are to grow up into Christ, who is the head (4:15). As the church, we already are one, united in Christ (2:12–22; 4:1–6), and yet we are to be eager to maintain the unity of the Spirit (4:3). We already are holy (2:19–22), and yet we walk in holiness, put on the new humanity and holiness, become more

---

[32] For more on how the church displays God, see Christopher W. Morgan, "The Church and the Glory of God," in *The Community of Jesus: A Theology of the Church*, ed. Kendell H. Easley and Christopher W. Morgan (Nashville, TN: B&H, 2013), 213–35.

[33] For how the already and not yet relates to the church as temple, see G. K. Beale, *The Temple and the Church's Mission: A Biblical Theology of the Dwelling Place of God*, NSBT, ed. D. A. Carson (Downers Grove, IL: InterVarsity, 2004), 392–93.

and more holy, and one day will be ultimately presented to Christ as holy (4:20–24; 5:2–21, 27). As the church, we already are grounded in truth and built on Christ as the cornerstone, with the apostles and prophets as the foundation (2:19–22), and yet we are to teach truth, speak truth in love, walk in truth, and stand firm as an army with truth (4:5, 11, 14–15, 21; 6:10–18). As the church, we are glorious now, as the fullness of Christ (1:22–23), and yet one day we will be presented to Christ as glorious (5:25–28). Thus, as the church, we are the community of God's people living in the already and not yet. We display God and the realities of the new creation. We are currently marked by godliness—goodness, unity, holiness, truth, and love—and yet we increasingly pursue godliness as well.

Love: The Focus of Our Spirituality

As we have seen, new life in Christ is the beginning of our spirituality, the triune God is the source of our spirituality, and Christlikeness is the goal of our spirituality. Now we turn to the focus of our spirituality: love.[34] In 1 Corinthians 13, Paul points to his readers' highest spiritual aspirations and then turns the tables on them (vv. 1–3). To experience spiritual gifts beyond measure, to have faith that leads to miracles, to know truth as exhaustively as it can be known, to give everything to the poor, or to be willing to die as a martyr for the gospel—to reach all of these, but to do them without "having love," is worthless: "I am nothing" (v. 2); "I gain nothing" (v. 3). Even radical spirituality without love is worthless.

Then, in verses 4–7, Paul points us to true spirituality, which at its core is true Christian love. He does not so much define love as describe and personify it as a person who thinks and acts. And though the content of this passage is indeed suitable for wedding ceremonies and the like, Paul originally wrote this to address real-life problems of the Corinthian church. He warns that the Corinthians' approach to religion is warped and portrays love as what is "central, characteristic, and irreplaceable in biblical Christianity."[35]

Indeed, from the other parts of the letter we find that the clear failure of the Corinthians was their failure to love. Some were impatient and unkind, filled with jealous ambition and egos, and puffed up. They in-

---

[34] For more on love, see Christopher W. Morgan, ed., *The Love of God*, Theology in Community (Wheaton, IL: Crossway, 2016). The comments in this section are shaped by the following works on 1 Corinthians 13: Jonathan Edwards, *Charity and Its Fruits*; D. A. Carson, *Showing the Spirit: A Theological Exposition of 1 Corinthians 12–14* (Grand Rapids, MI: Baker, 1987); Ajith Fernando, *Reclaiming Love: Radical Relationships in a Complex World* (Grand Rapids, MI: Zondervan, 2012); David E. Garland, *1 Corinthians*, BECNT (Grand Rapids, MI: Baker Academic, 2003); Michael Green, *To Corinth with Love* (Dallas: Word, 1988).
[35] Carson, *Showing the Spirit*, 66.

sisted on their own way and were argumentative and resentful. Some rejoiced in wrong rather than in righteousness (chap. 5). Others promoted themselves rather than seeking to promote the good of the overall body. Instead of humbly serving others, they humiliated others. Instead of transcending the social class system, they highlighted it. Instead of following Jesus' example of service, love, and sacrifice for the good of others, they used the symbol of his sacrifice for self-promotion. Instead of viewing their spiritual gifts as a God-given means to strengthen the church, they boasted of their superior knowledge and spirituality. As David Garland notes, "Although the gifts of the Spirit are conspicuous in their assembly, their lack of love is even more conspicuous."[36]

So Paul describes love by its response to others in the church. If we truly love, we will be:

- patient: we will endure suffering and difficult people (6:7);
- kind: we will be tender—Paul often links kindness with forgiveness (Eph. 4:32);
- not jealous/envious: we will want the best for others, not wishing that the successes of others were only ours (1 Cor. 3:3);
- not boasting/vainglorious: we will be unpretentious, not promoting ourselves so that others would praise us (1:17; 2:1);
- not proud/puffed up (4:6, 18, 19; 5:2; 8:1): we will be humble, not arrogant;
- not indecent/shameful/rude (5:1–2): we will be pure, not immoral;
- not insisting on our own way (10:24, 33; cf. Phil. 2:3–4): we will be generous, not self-seeking;
- not irritable: we will be long-suffering, not given to fits of anger;
- not resentful/keeping records of offenses: we will have a forgiving spirit and be not easily offended (1 Cor. 6:7: "Why not suffer wrong?");
- not rejoicing over injustice: we will support justice, not wrongdoing;
- rejoicing in the truth: we will delight in and endorse truth;
- bearing all things: we will put up with all things;
- believing all things: we will be generously trusting, not suspicious or cynical (this does not mean we are gullible);
- hoping all things: we hope for the best and are not pessimistic about others;
- enduring all things: we will persevere in love.

These descriptions show that the particular expressions of our love will vary to meet the needs of the context. In the context of frustrating circumstances and people, our love appears as patience. In the context of the successes of others, love does not allow us to envy but leads us to

---

[36] Garland, *1 Corinthians*, 616–17.

rejoice with those who rejoice. In the context of our own successes, love restrains us from self-promotion and leads to humility. In the context of someone's sin against us, love appears as forgiveness and not as a keeping track of wrongs. The Bible depicts our love for others as expressed also in sharing the gospel, caring for the poor, helping the marginalized, building the faith of others, promoting unity in the church, teaching truth, correcting error, urging repentance, and more.

These descriptions of love in 1 Corinthians 13 affirm the emphasis on love as desiring the good of others and as giving of ourselves for their sake. Such love provides focus and clarity to the trajectory of our spirituality.

The Church: The Community of Our Spirituality

Some of the people we love misunderstand our love, reject it, or even despise it. God uses this to teach us more love, particularly developing our patience, forgiveness, and endurance. Thankfully, though, most in the body of Christ receive our love, appreciate it, return it, and even pass it on by loving others. We can rejoice, knowing not only that the loving God loves us and transforms us by his love into people of love, but also that his very love is extending to us and leading to our love to him as well as to our love for others. The God of love also loves others and transforms them into people of love, and his very love extends out to others and leads to their love for him and even to us as well. God's love has ripple effects. His very love is extending to us through the love of others, and his very love is extending still to others through our love. And on and on it goes, as the God-glorifying process of his self-giving love spirals forward in and through his people!

As such, the church is the community of our spirituality. Herman Bavinck stresses the communal aspect of Christian spirituality, explaining that we are "incorporated in a great whole, taken up into a rich fellowship . . . [as] a member of a new nation and citizen of a spiritual kingdom whose king is glorious in the multitude of his subjects."[37] Dietrich Bonhoeffer speaks similarly: "Christian community is not an ideal we have to realize, but rather a reality created by God in Christ in which we may participate. . . . The ground and strength and promise of all our community is in Jesus Christ alone."[38]

Ephesians helps us see that as the church, we are one new people, a

---

[37] Herman Bavinck, *Our Reasonable Faith* (Grand Rapids, MI: Eerdmans, 1956), 514.
[38] Dietrich Bonhoeffer, *Life Together and Prayerbook of the Bible*, English ed. (Minneapolis: Fortress Press, 2005), 38.

new humanity, a people called to display God to the world.[39] We are the new creation in the image of God, called to reflect Christ and embody God's character (2:14–16; 4:13, 24). As the church, we are composed of believers who were alienated from God and through the saving work of Christ have been united to Christ (2:1–10) and reconciled to each other (2:11–22). As the church, we preach Christ not only to humanity in the verbal proclamation of the gospel but also to the entire cosmos through the visible display of unity (3:9–12). Bryan Chapell explains:

> This grafting of the redeemed is so amazing that it was God's intent to use it to display his wisdom to the heavenly beings. Thus Paul's words create a celestial stage to display the wonders of grace. . . . In union with other sinners made perfect, and as members of one body, we who come from every tribe and nation, people and personality, are on display as a church before the heavenly hosts as a testimony to the wisdom of God. . . . Just as Paul's sin makes the grace of God more apparent, the uniting of sinners in the body of Christ makes the grace of God more brilliant— even to the hosts of heaven. By our unity in Christ's body, the church, we are preaching to the angels about the power, wisdom, and glory of God who made us.
>
> This is the apex of Paul's thought about the church. . . . Here we learn that the church is intended not only to transform the world but also to transfix heaven.[40]

As we showcase God's eternal purpose of cosmic unity to the world, we demonstrate that the kingdom of God has already broken into history. God's eternal purpose of cosmic reconciliation is not perfectly realized yet—sin and injustice still occur. Yet sin will not have the last word; disorder and division will not last forever. Although the present age can still to some extent be characterized as "not the way things are supposed to be,"[41] God will bring about a new creation.

What is so striking is that God's new creation is already underway in the church. The church is the firstfruits of the ultimate new creation still to come. As the firstfruits, we are both the genuine reality of the new creation and also the foretaste of more to come. Thus, as the church, we are the new humanity, new society, new temple—a new creation. We are a foretaste of heaven on earth, a genuine embodiment of the kingdom, a glimpse of the way things are supposed to be, and a glimpse of the way

---

[39] For more on the church, see Easley and Morgan, *The Community of Jesus*.

[40] Bryan Chapell, *Ephesians*, Reformed Expository Commentary (Phillipsburg, NJ: P&R, 2009), 144–45.

[41] Cornelius Plantinga Jr., *Not the Way It's Supposed to Be: A Breviary of Sin* (Grand Rapids, MI: Eerdmans, 1995).

the cosmos ultimately will be; we are a showcase of God's eternal plan of cosmic unity.

Thus, Paul asserts the fundamental unity of the people of God: there is one God, one Lord, one Spirit, one body, one faith, and one baptism (4:4–6). As the one body of Christ, we are to live out our high calling of oneness and to be "eager to maintain the unity of the Spirit in the bond of peace" (4:3). This unity exists amidst a very real diversity: "Grace was given to each one of us according to the measure of Christ's gift" (4:7). Paul elaborates that this means that God has given the church apostles, prophets, evangelists, pastors, and teachers (4:11). He gives people to the church, and he gives the church to people. We are given gifts to serve others, and others are given gifts to serve others, including us. As we serve, others grow and we grow. And as others serve, we grow and they grow. This is the community of our spirituality: life together as the church.

Our life together is guided by the historical and experiential reality of our union with Christ: "We are members one of another" (4:25). Because we are linked together as the community of Jesus, we speak and live truthfully with each other and refuse to nurse anger against each other (4:25–27). We refuse to steal but instead work hard so that we can share with others in the body who have need (4:28). We choose our words carefully because we realize that God gives grace to others through our words (4:29). We put away bitterness, anger, and slander and put on kindness, tenderness, forgiveness, and love (4:31–32). If Jesus loves and forgives us, who are we to detest and hold a grudge against his people? And if Jesus loves and forgives them, who are we to oppose Jesus' people and thus our own spiritual family and body? Life together includes imitating Jesus and embracing his people as our own people (4:32–5:2). Bonhoeffer reminds us of the blessing it is that God gives us the church as the community of our spirituality:

> Let those who until now have had the privilege of living a Christian life together with other Christians praise God's grace from the bottom of their hearts. Let them thank God on their knees and realize: it is grace, nothing but grace, that we are still permitted to live in the community of Christians today.[42]

Ordinary Life: The Context of Our Spirituality

While the church is the community of our spirituality, the normal context of our spirituality is ordinary life. When we think of spirituality, we may

---

[42] Bonhoeffer, *Life Together*, 30.

imagine a pastor's praying for the lost, a believer's retreat of solitude in the mountains, a relief worker's helping the poor in Africa, or a missionary's taking the gospel to unreached peoples. And all of these tasks can be spiritual. But we may forget that our spirituality is also cultivated in, and is manifested in, our rhythms of sleep and rest, our work, our roles as wives and husbands, our roles as children and parents, our physical bodies, and more (e.g., Eph. 4:1–6:9). The context of spirituality is seldom a spiritual retreat center. More often, it includes maintaining joy while driving in congested traffic, living ethically at work, loving our families, cleaning the house, helping children with homework, paying the bills, and forgiving our neighbor.

Such matters seem too ordinary to be significant, too commonplace to be the context of our spirituality. But life—all of life—is where we live out our faith. And since a large portion of our spirituality is forged in everyday normalcy, we must mobilize every effort to see each moment as an opportune time to live in the presence of God for the sake of others. We may miss the importance of the ordinary if we compartmentalize Christ to our Sunday morning gatherings or our quiet times.

Combatting the tendency to sequester Jesus into spiritual arenas as opposed to what are traditionally considered secular arenas requires a robust commitment to the lordship of Christ in all of life. As Vern Poythress states, "If he is Lord of all, he is Lord over business and work and education and science and home life."[43] Our spirituality is an embodied one; we are the on-the-ground expressions of God's ongoing work begun in conversion. Deep down, we are aware that Christ's lordship must be all encompassing in our lives, but we invariably struggle with how to live this out faithfully. At its core, a robust embrace of the lordship of Christ relates directly to a comprehensive obedience to Christ and an overall life of worship (Rom. 12:1–2; Col. 3:1–4:6).

Michael Horton believes that American Christianity provides its own set of challenges to an ordinary Christian life. "American Christianity," he writes, "is a story of perpetual upheavals in churches and individual lives. Starting with the extraordinary conversion experience, our lives are motivated by a constant expectation for The Next Big Thing. We're growing bored with the ordinary means of God's grace, attending church week in and week out."[44] Instead of seeking the next best experience, ordinary

---

[43] Vern Poythress, *The Lordship of Christ* (Wheaton, IL: Crossway, 2016), 31.
[44] Michael Horton, *Ordinary: Sustainable Faith in a Radical, Restless World* (Grand Rapids, MI: Zondervan, 2014), 16.

Christian living should involve our daily dying to self as we seek to fulfill our responsibilities in our families, churches, and vocations; as we seek to love our neighbors with hospitality and presence. The lordship of Christ includes a daily commitment to do all things—yes, ordinary things—for the glory of Christ.

Indwelling Sin and Temptation: Obstacles in Our Spirituality
Ordinary life, as the context of our spirituality, is filled with blessings. God shines in all that is fair; his common grace abounds. The beauty of the sunset, the towering mountains, and a daughter's smile are all gifts from the Lord. But ordinary life is also filled with more danger than we think: the terrain of our trajectory is likened to a spiritual war zone, filled with temptation after temptation:

> In every circumstance of life, every lot, every association, every labor, every pleasure or hardship, there is a possible temptation. There are temptations for the body, for the mind, for the soul. There are temptations to the appetite, to selfishness, dishonesty, to the evasion of duty, the disregard of others' rights, indifference to others' sorrows; pride, sloth, envy, suspicion, taking up an evil report against our neighbor, and the subtle, but even more dangerous, temptations to doubt, to unbelief.[45]

The world around us, however, is not for us but is dead set against us. As David Calhoun cautions, "The world entices us to fit in with, to adjust to, to experiment with, its values."[46]

Ephesians 2 relates three opponent forces at work. Apart from Christ, we are "following the course of this world, following the prince of the power of the air, the spirit that is now at work in the sons of disobedience—among whom we all once lived in the passions of our flesh, carrying out the desires of the body and the mind, and were by nature children of wrath, like the rest of mankind" (Eph. 2:2–3). We were under the domain of two external forces: the course of the world and Satan. And we were under an internal force working in tandem with these external forces: our hearts, which were darkened by sin, under spiritual death, and following the trajectory of the world and Satan.

Thankfully, God intervened: "But God, being rich in mercy, because

---

[45] Clarence Edward Macartney, *The Lord's Prayer* (New York: Revell, 1942), 69. I first read this in David B. Calhoun, "Sin and Temptation," in Morgan and Peterson, *Fallen*, 244.
[46] Calhoun, "Sin and Temptation," 253.

of the great love with which he loved us, even when we were dead in our trespasses, made us alive together with Christ—by grace you have been saved—and raised us up with him and seated us with him in the heavenly places in Christ Jesus" (2:4–6). This salvation is by God's grace and unto our holiness, as we are "created in Christ Jesus for good works, which God prepared beforehand, that we should walk in them" (2:10).

This call to holiness requires a wartime mentality, in which we battle against those forces that held our former allegiance (Eph. 6:10–18). We know who we once were, and we now fight against the sin that so easily mastered us and the indwelling sin that still entangles us (Rom. 6:1–14; Heb. 12:1–2). We long to put off the old self and instead put on the new (Eph. 4:17–24), desiring sanctification, knowing that it is God's will for us (1 Thess. 4:3). Packer puts it wonderfully: "Holiness is in essence obeying God, living to God and for God, imitating God, keeping his law, taking his side against sin, doing righteousness, performing good works, following Christ's teaching and example, worshiping God in Spirit, loving and serving God and men out of reverence for Christ."[47]

This process of putting off/putting on and opposing sin/embracing godliness is continual. Because of this, the book of James urges perseverance and cautions us about the nature of temptation:

> Blessed is the man who remains steadfast under trial, for when he has stood the test he will receive the crown of life, which God has promised to those who love him. Let no one say when he is tempted, "I am being tempted by God," for God cannot be tempted with evil, and he himself tempts no one. But each person is tempted when he is lured and enticed by his own desire. Then desire when it has conceived gives birth to sin, and sin when it is fully grown brings forth death. (James 1:12–15)

God does not tempt us, but external temptation entices our internal desire, and this lust leads to sin, which leads to death (1:13–18; see also Proverbs 5, 7). Sin deceives, entices, conceives, develops, and finishes with death.[48] Temptation masks the fact that sin is destructive. The old adage reflects James's teaching: sin takes us farther than we want to go, keeps us longer than we want to stay, and costs us more than we want to pay. To discover temptation's source, we should look within—at our own evil desires.[49] God

---

[47] J. I. Packer, *Keep in Step with the Spirit* (Grand Rapids, MI: Baker, 1984), 81.

[48] John Owen, "Indwelling Sin," in *Overcoming Sin and Temptation: Three Classic Works by John Owen*, ed. Kelly M. Kapic and Justin Taylor (Wheaton, IL: Crossway, 2006), 295–96.

[49] For more on James and temptation, see Christopher W. Morgan and B. Dale Ellenburg, *James: Wisdom for the Community*, Focus on the Bible Commentaries (Fearn, UK: Christian Focus, 2008), 59–73.

is holy and never the source of temptations. God is not our foe but our covenant Lord. God is for us, not against us.

Here we find our hope: God is the source not of temptation but of "every good gift and every perfect gift," including our holiness (James 1:17). God is our strength against indwelling sin and persistent temptations through the Spirit's ongoing work of mortification. He enables us to fight sin, repent of sin, and walk in holiness, as John Owen explains: "He works upon our understandings, wills, consciences, and affections, agreeably to their own natures; he works in us and with us, not against us or without us; so that his assistance is an encouragement as to the facilitating of the work, and no occasion of neglect as to the work itself."[50]

"Victory over temptation is not gained in the moment of temptation," Calhoun advises. "It is won in the daily living of our redeemed lives. It is won as we 'make every effort to supplement [our] faith with virtue, and virtue with knowledge, and knowledge with self-control, and self-control with steadfastness, and steadfastness with godliness, and godliness with brotherly affection, and brotherly affection with love' (2 Pet. 1:5–7)."[51]

The Already and the Not Yet: Tensions in Our Spirituality

As our experience of indwelling sin reminds us, our spirituality is both "already" (realized) and also "not yet" (fully realized). In definitive sanctification, the Spirit has already set us apart from sin for holiness as saints. But, as we know all too well, we are not yet fully holy. Final sanctification is not yet realized; the ongoing struggle for holiness persists. So we live in between the already and the not yet of our salvation, and this causes us to experience tensions in the meantime. The chapter later in this volume focusing on spirituality according to Paul will address this more thoroughly, but a brief sketch may prove helpful here. From Romans 6–8, we learn that we are both crucified with Christ and alive in Christ (Rom. 6:1–14); we are both slaves and free (6:15–7:7); we are at war but are victorious in it (7:8–8:4); we are both debtors and heirs (8:12–25); we are both persevering and being preserved (8:26–39).

God's sovereignty and man's responsibility also display tensions in our spirituality. God develops our spirituality as the fruit of the Spirit, and yet we confess sin, repent, trust, grow, study, pray, give, witness, and live in community. Similarly, we experience the tension of putting off, being renewed, and putting on. As a result, our spiritual journey

---

[50] Owen, *Overcoming Sin and Temptation*, 62.
[51] Calhoun, "Sin and Temptation," 258.

positively involves pursuing holiness out of love for Christ, yet it also involves negatives—daily turning away from sin out of the same love for Christ. The first of Martin Luther's ninety-five theses states plainly: "When our Lord and Master Jesus Christ said, 'Repent' (Matt. 4:17), he willed the entire life of believers to be one of repentance." Repentance is an "altering of one's habits of thoughts, one's attitudes, outlook, policy, direction, and behavior, just as fully as is needed to get one's life out of the wrong shape and into the right one. Repentance is in truth a spiritual revolution."[52] We are works in progress, still under construction, on the path to spiritual maturity.

Word, Prayer, and Church: Means for Our Spirituality

Paul's language of putting off and putting on (Ephesians 4; Colossians 3) suggests actions we must take and practices we must embrace to fight against the lure of sin and the pervasive manifestations of sin in our world. Dallas Willard clarifies: "Spiritual formation in Christ is an orderly process. Although God can triumph in disorder, that is not his choice. And instead of focusing upon what God *can* do, we must humble ourselves to accept the ways he *has chosen* to work with us."[53] What are the ways of the orderly process?

The Scriptures do not suggest any shortcuts by which we can grow in sanctification. Instead, we are encouraged repeatedly to give ourselves to the time-honored means of Bible reading and meditation (Ps. 1:2; Matt. 4:4; 17:17), prayer (Eph. 6:18; Phil. 4:6), worship (Eph. 5:18–20), witnessing (Matt. 28:19–20), Christian fellowship (Heb. 10:24–25), and self-discipline or self-control (Gal. 5:23; Titus 1:8). Cruise control is a wonderful technology in our automobiles, but there is no such option in the journey of the Christian life. We will not coast into godliness. Writing to Timothy, Paul is upfront about the requirements of spiritual exertion: "Train yourself for godliness" (1 Tim. 4:7).

In his *Spiritual Disciplines for the Christian Life*, Donald Whitney appropriately begins his analysis with two chapters on Bible intake, stating: "No spiritual discipline is more important than the intake of God's Word. Nothing can substitute for it. There simply is no healthy Christian life apart from a diet of the milk and meat of Scripture."[54] Biblical intake

---

[52] J. I. Packer, *Rediscovering Holiness: Know the Fullness of Life with God* (Ventura, CA: Regal, 2009), 110.

[53] Dallas Willard, *Renovation of the Heart: Putting on the Character of Christ* (Colorado Springs, CO: NavPress, 2012), 10; emphases original.

[54] Donald S. Whitney, *Spiritual Disciplines for the Christian Life* (Colorado Springs, CO: NavPress, 1991), n.p.

especially includes reading the Bible. Bible intake also includes meditation on God's Word and carefully studying Scripture to learn about God,
his ways, our sin, Jesus' person and work, our salvation, the church, and
God's grand story of redemption.

Scripture also teaches us the importance of prayer and instructs us in
how to pray, even serving as a source for wording our prayers to God. In
other words, in Bible intake, we immerse ourselves in God's Word and use
it to form our prayers.[55] The apostle Paul models for us the kind of praying
necessary for fighting sin, pursuing holiness, and maintaining a fervency
for spiritual flourishing as he states that we must be "praying at all times
in the Spirit, with all prayer and supplication. To that end, keep alert with
all perseverance, making supplication for all the saints" (Eph. 6:18). In
order for us to pray in all situations, we must include the various senses
in which Scripture portrays prayer. We offer prayers of praise, thanks,
confession, intercession, petition, and more. Our praying encompasses all
seasons, and, because of its frequency, we should fight against every urge
to reduce it to a rote exercise in which we check off the proverbial boxes.
Prayer should be seen as a practice and as a pursuit. As sons and daughters
of God, we are led by the Spirit, even in our prayers (Rom. 8:14–27). Paul's
insistence on prayers for the saints includes the full range of the kinds of
prayers offered to the body of Christ in Scripture. Thus, our prayers for
the saints could include a rejoicing in God's favor and blessing, petitions
for repentance, and strength for the advance of the gospel.

Our Christian discipleship is refined through our dedication to knowing Christ through the spiritual disciplines, but our individual efforts are
only part of the means we have in our spiritual trajectory. On a corporate
level, we lean on God's ordinary means of grace to keep our feet grounded
in the primary ways God works in and through us. Questions 88 and 89 of
the Westminster Shorter Catechism ask two critical questions related to
the means Christ gives his people:[56]

Q. 88. What are the outward and ordinary means whereby Christ communicateth to us the benefits of redemption?

A. The outward and ordinary means whereby Christ communicateth to
us the benefits of redemption, are his ordinances, especially the word,
sacraments, and prayer. . . .

---

[55] Donald S. Whitney, *Praying the Bible* (Wheaton, IL: Crossway, 2015).
[56] Westminster Shorter Catechism, questions 88 and 89.

Q. 89. How is the word made effectual to salvation?

A. The Spirit of God maketh the reading, but especially the preaching, of the word, an effectual means of convincing and converting sinners, and of building them up in holiness and comfort, through faith, unto salvation.

God graciously provides for our sanctification. He not only serves as the source of our spirituality; he also gives us the very means by which we grow.

Reproducing Disciples: The Mission of Our Spirituality

Our spirituality is not only for ourselves but especially for others. Any depiction of Christian spirituality devoid of the pursuit of making disciples is not consistent with the teachings of Jesus. In Matthew, Jesus clarifies true spirituality, which includes being and making disciples.

Jesus launches his public ministry by proclaiming, "Repent, for the kingdom of heaven is at hand" (Matt. 4:17). From the beginning, Jesus stresses a spirituality linked to God's kingdom, which refers to God's rule and reign over us as his people.[57] The kingdom has come into history in the person of Jesus and will finally and ultimately "come at the end of the age in a mighty irruption into history inaugurating the perfect order of the age to come."[58] As the bearer of this kingdom, Jesus demands that we repent, which involves rejecting the present way of the world and embracing God's rule and its corresponding way of life. As such, repentance is the way *into* the kingdom and the way *of* the kingdom, the way of spirituality. As his disciples, we follow Jesus, "the present-in-history king,"[59] and we come under him, walk alongside him, believe his teachings, embrace his way of life, and participate in his mission (4:17–19).

Then, in the Sermon on the Mount, Jesus sets forth his vision of the spirituality and values of his new kingdom community. In the Sermon's beatitudes, Jesus reorients our values and thus spirituality itself. As his people, we are driven not by wealth, power, honor, or comfort but by faith, hope, and love. Our spirituality is linked to our kingdom character. Jesus begins by pronouncing God's blessings upon his kingdom community

---

[57] For more on how spirituality, the church, and mission interrelate, see Anthony L. Chute and Christopher W. Morgan, "Missional Spirituality as Congregational," in *Spirituality for the Sent: Casting a New Vision for the Missional Church*, ed. Nathan A. Finn and Keith S. Whitefield (Downers Grove, IL: InterVarsity Press, 2017), 75–95.

[58] George Eldon Ladd, *The Presence of the Future*, rev. ed. (Grand Rapids, MI: Eerdmans, 1974), 144–49.

[59] Robert W. Yarbrough, "The Kingdom of God in the New Testament: Matthew and Revelation," in *The Kingdom of God*, Theology in Community, ed. Christopher W. Morgan and Robert A. Peterson (Wheaton, IL: Crossway, 2012), 110.

(Matt. 5:3–12). Jesus expressed these blessings in a pattern, first by pronouncing "blessed" people who are marked by particular characteristics:
the poor in spirit, those who mourn, the meek, those who hunger and
thirst for righteousness, the merciful, the pure in heart, the peacemakers,
and the persecuted for righteousness' sake. Jesus here links God's blessing, his kingdom community, and true spirituality. As disciples of Jesus,
we live out a spirituality marked by dependence on God, longing for repentance, humility, desire for true righteousness, integrity, reconciliation
with others, and persecution for faithfully following Christ.

The rest of the Sermon on the Mount expands on the kingdom character of spirituality. In Matthew 5:17–48, Jesus calls us to holistic holiness as he highlights that true righteousness is Word-saturated, internal,
and external (see also Lev. 19:1–18). In Matthew 6:1–18, Jesus calls us to
genuine worship as he stresses that God (not others or ourselves) is to be
the sole audience of our worship (using the examples of three spiritual
disciplines: giving, praying, and fasting) and that living all of life in light
of God's kingdom is the central focus of our prayer. In Matthew 6:19–34,
Jesus sets forth kingdom values as he contrasts earthly treasures with
kingdom significance. In Matthew 7, Jesus focuses on the centrality of
generous love as he overturns judgmentalism and advances the Golden
Rule. Along the way, Jesus clarifies what it means to be his disciple. If
we are Jesus' disciples, we possess true righteousness and live out true
spirituality, which is marked by our kingdom character, holistic holiness,
genuine worship, kingdom values, and generous love.

Jesus then relates the blessings themselves: theirs is the kingdom of
heaven, they shall be comforted, they shall inherit the earth, they shall be
satisfied, they shall receive mercy, they shall see God, they shall be called
the sons of God, and theirs is the kingdom of heaven. The first and last
beatitude also end with the same overarching blessing: "theirs is the kingdom of heaven" (5:3, 10). The six beatitudes in the middle relate future
blessings (note the recurring "shall be" in 5:4–9). God blesses us as Jesus'
people, who are a community of the kingdom now ("theirs is the kingdom") that awaits a fuller, final display of the kingdom ("shall be"). John
Stott puts it well: "The blessing promised . . . is the gloriously comprehensive blessing of God's rule, tasted now and consummated later, including
the inheritance of both earth and heaven, comfort, satisfaction and mercy,
the vision and sonship of God."[60]

---

[60]John R. W. Stott, *The Message of the Sermon on the Mount*, Bible Speaks Today (Downers Grove, IL: Inter-
Varsity Press, 1985), 38.

A community so enthusiastic about the Messiah's arrival and committed to live out such a spirituality might be expected to be self-focused, cloistered, and separated from the rest of society. Jesus, however, interweaves our spirituality with our mission. Indeed, our spirituality fuels our mission. Jesus' call, "Follow me, and I will make you fishers of men" (4:19), reveals that part of being Jesus' disciple is following Jesus. And inherent in following Jesus is becoming "fishers of men" and thus participants in Jesus' own mission. From the beginning of Jesus' ministry, "discipleship and mission are inseparably linked."[61] As his disciples, we are called and sent, called to follow the way of the kingdom and sent to call others to do the same.

Jesus also stresses the inherently missional nature of his kingdom community as he calls us to be the "salt of the earth" (5:13) and the "light of the world" (5:14). These images build on the Beatitudes, in which Jesus associates God's kingdom not with human strength and honor but with our spiritual poverty, crying, meekness, hunger, mercy, peace, and persecution. Fundamental to these images is our distinctiveness as the holy kingdom community (5:3–12). The world is in decay, and we are the salt. The world is in darkness, and we are the light. Both images not only assume the community's distinctiveness but also clarify the community's mission. As the salt of the earth, Jesus' disciples "purify the world by living holy lives and proclaiming the gospel of the kingdom."[62] Further, "Jesus insisted that the disciples' mission of shining in the world, extending salvation to the ends of the earth by proclaiming the gospel of the kingdom, and living transformed lives, is intrinsic to genuine discipleship."[63]

Thus Jesus interweaves his community's spirituality with its mission. Not only does our spirituality fuel our mission, but our mission as Jesus' kingdom community also reproduces spirituality. This is suggested in Matthew 4:17–19, as Jesus calls us to follow him and fish for others who then likewise follow Jesus and presumably fish for others too. It is also suggested in Matthew 5:3–16, as we who are salt and light point others to God through our distinctive goodness, which points to God as our Father. Some persecute us as a result of our strong identification with God (5:10–12), but others glorify God and thus also follow Jesus and too are characterized by righteousness.

---

[61] Eckhard J. Schnabel, *Early Christian Mission: Jesus and the Twelve*, vol. 1 (Downers Grove, IL: InterVarsity Press, 2004), 272–79.

[62] Charles L. Quarles, *A Theology of Matthew*, Explorations in Biblical Theology (Phillipsburg, NJ: P&R, 2013), 80.

[63] Ibid., 86; see also 194–205.

What Jesus teaches in Matthew 4:17 and 5:3–16 is spelled out even more directly in Matthew 28:18–20: our mission as his kingdom community is reproductive spirituality. In Matthew 28:18–20, Jesus issues the Great Commission, asserting that he is the exalted Son who is Lord over all, both in heaven and on earth, including all nations (28:18; see also Dan. 7:14). The universality of the commission is striking: Jesus has all authority, directs us to make disciples of all nations, instructs us to teach all that he has commanded, and charges us to do so "all the days," until the end of the age. The particularity of the commission is also striking: Jesus uniquely is Lord, he alone is worthy of worship by all nations, his teachings have binding authority, and his presence is with us as we participate in his mission.[64]

The essence of Jesus' Great Commission is found in his command to make disciples of all nations. Jesus calls us who are his disciples to make other disciples, who are also expected to follow Jesus, listen to his teaching, and reflect his ways. As his disciples, we live in community, in fellowship with the teacher and with each other as fellow followers of Jesus, the Teacher. Schnabel comments, "The directive to 'make disciples' demonstrates the ecclesiological dimension of the mission of the Twelve: missionary work and church must not be separated, since the very goal and purpose of missionary work is the creation of a community of disciples."[65] Making disciples of all nations expands the mission beyond that of Israel unto all Gentile peoples.[66]

The central command of making disciples is expanded by three participles: *going, baptizing,* and *teaching.* Matthew apparently uses "go" as an introductory circumstantial participle that is rightly translated as coordinate to the main verb—here "Go and make" (cf. 2:8; 9:13; 11:4; 17:27; 28:7).[67] The participle establishes the motion that is necessary for the accomplishment of the command. This makes good sense of the context, since we can make other disciples of all nations only if we go to people who do not yet know Jesus. Jesus calls us to make disciples of all nations also by "baptizing them in the name of the Father and of the Son and of the Holy Spirit" (28:19). We who follow Christ depict our new allegiance to Jesus through baptism. Through baptism, we publicly identify with Christ as Lord, with one another in Jesus' kingdom community, and with

---

[64] Schnabel, *Early Christian Mission,* 353–55.
[65] Ibid., 356.
[66] "Nations" does not refer to a geopolitical nation-state but connotes Gentiles and something akin to peoples, families, clans, and tribes; see Gen. 12:3; Dan. 7:13–14; Matt. 24:14; and Rev. 5:9–10.
[67] David W. Chapman, "The Great Commission as the Conclusion of Matthew's Gospel," *All for Jesus: A Celebration of the Fiftieth Anniversary of Covenant Theological Seminary,* ed. Robert A. Peterson and Sean Michael Lucas (Fearn, UK: Mentor, 2001), 91.

the entire Trinity. Making disciples of all nations also includes "teaching them to observe all that I have commanded you" (28:20). As Jesus' disciples, we do not make our own disciples but point people to become followers of Jesus, the teacher. As such, we do not put forward our own teachings but faithfully pass on the teachings of the teacher. Both believing and practicing Jesus' teachings are required, both by the disciplers and by the new disciples.

Thus Jesus declares that our mission as his kingdom community is disciple making, and as such is reproductive spirituality. We are to be focused on the intentional "multiplication of other faithful followers of the King among the nations."[68] As we follow Jesus, we fish for others who both follow Jesus and likewise fish for others. As we embody true spirituality in our lives, we are salt and light, which leads others to know and follow God too. We have a mission: to make other disciples of all nations. Thus, in and through the community of Jesus, spirituality and mission interweave, each spiraling into the other, each fueling the other, and each increasingly reproducing missional spirituality.

The Glory of God: The Ultimate End of Our Spirituality

What is the ultimate end of our spirituality? Where is the trajectory of our spirituality headed? The ultimate end of our spirituality is neither our spirituality nor the spirituality of others, as important as both are; the ultimate end of our spirituality is the glory of God.

Ephesians is helpful here. From the outset, Paul establishes that God's ultimate end is his glory, and he praises God for his comprehensive blessings of salvation. In his praise, Paul highlights the work of the Trinity in salvation (1:3–14) and explicitly incorporates a refrain: "to the praise of his glorious grace" (v. 6), "to the praise of his glory" (vv. 12, 14). Paul's point is unmistakable: the ultimate end of our salvation is not our salvation, as important as that is. God chose, adopted, redeemed, united, gave an inheritance, and sealed us to the praise of his glory.

Paul continues this emphasis in Ephesians 2. Because of his love and grace, God makes us alive in Christ. What is his ultimate end in saving us? Ephesians 2:7 informs us: "So that in the coming ages he might show the immeasurable riches of his grace in [his] kindness to us in Christ Jesus." That God's glory is his ultimate end is also clear in Ephesians 3:

---

[68] Jeff Lewis, "God's Great Commissions for the Nations," *Discovering the Mission of God: Best Missional Practices for the Twenty-first Century*, ed. Mike Barnett and Robin Martin (Downers Grove, IL: InterVarsity Press, 2012), 104.

> To me, though I am the very least of all the saints, this grace was given, to preach to the Gentiles the unsearchable riches of Christ, and to bring to light for everyone what is the plan of the mystery hidden for ages in God, who created all things, so that through the church the manifold wisdom of God might now be made known to the rulers and authorities in the heavenly places. (Eph. 3:8–10)

Here Paul stresses that his salvation, apostolic calling, and mission to the Gentiles have as their ultimate end the glorious display of God and his wisdom.

The doxology in Ephesians 3:20–21 continues this theme and forcefully declares: "Now to him who is able to do far more abundantly than all that we ask or think, according to the power at work within us, to him be glory in the church and in Christ Jesus throughout all generations, forever and ever. Amen." The prayer and praise of the church is that God will receive glory for all eternity.

Thus God's glory is his ultimate end.[69] But what does this mean? Two aspects stand out in Ephesians. First, God acts unto the praise of his glory, or to the praise of the glory of his grace (1:6, 12, 14). So God's glory as his ultimate end means that God acts unto the reception of worship and praise of his creation, especially his people. Second, God acts to display himself throughout creation. He displays his love, mercy, grace, kindness, creative work, and wisdom (2:4–10; 3:8–10). God's glory as his ultimate end also means that God acts to display himself, and as he displays himself he communicates his greatness and fullness. That in and of itself glorifies him. So, according to Ephesians, God's glory as his ultimate end means that he acts unto the reception of worship and acts to display himself and communicate his greatness.

Remarkably, both relate directly to our identity and purpose as human beings created in the image of God. Sinclair Ferguson explains:

> In Scripture, image and glory are interrelated ideas. As the image of God, man was created to reflect, express and participate in the glory of God, in miniature, creaturely form. Restoration to this is effected through the Spirit's work of sanctification, in which he takes those who have distorted God's image in the shame of sin, and transforms them into those who bear that image in glory. . . .

---

[69] God's glory is the goal of creation; the exodus; Israel; Jesus' ministry, life, death, resurrection, and reign; our salvation; the church; the consummation; and all of salvation history. See Jonathan Edwards, "The End for Which God Created the World," in *God's Passion for His Glory*, ed. John Piper (Wheaton, IL: Crossway, 1998), 125–36.

The mark we were created to reach, but have missed, was glory. We have sinned and failed to attain that destiny. Against this background, the task of the Spirit may be stated simply: to bring us to glory, to create glory within us, and to glorify us together with Christ. The startling significance of this might be plainer if we expressed it thus: the Spirit is given to glorify us; not just to "add" glory as a crown to what we are, but actually to transform the very constitution of our being so that we become glorious. In the New Testament, this glorification is seen to begin already in the present order, in believers. Through the Spirit they are already being changed from glory to glory, as they gaze on/reflect the face of the Lord (2 Cor. 3:17–18). But the consummation of this glorification awaits the eschaton and the Spirit's ministry in the resurrection. Here, too, the pattern of his working is: as in Christ, so in believers and, by implication, in the universe. . . .

The image and image-bearers are one in Spirit to the end, so that when Christ appears in glory image-bearers are one with him in that glory (Col. 3:4). We are raised in Christ, with Christ, by Christ, to be like Christ.[70]

Horton adds, "God did not become human so that humans might become God, or even supernatural, but so that humans who had fallen into sin and death could be redeemed, reconciled, justified, renewed, and glorified as the humanity that we were created to become."[71]

In other words, we were created to be worshipers of God and the display people of God, but we all refused to acknowledge God's glory and instead sought our own glory. Through this we forfeited the glory God intended for us as his image bearers. By his grace and through union with Christ the perfect image, however, God restores us as full image bearers to participate in and reflect the glory we longed for the whole time. Thus we are recipients of glory, are undergoing transformation through glory, and will be sharers of glory. Our salvation, and thus our spirituality, is not merely from sin but is also unto glory. We who exchanged the glory of God for idols, we who rebelled against God's glory, have been, are being, and will be completely transformed by the very glory we despised and rejected (Rom. 1:18–31; 3:23; 8:28–30; 9:23; 2 Cor. 3:18). And through union with Christ, together we are the church, the new humanity (Eph. 2:11–22; 4:11–16; 4:20–24), the firstfruits of the new creation, bearing God's image, displaying how life ought to be, and making known the manifold wisdom of God (Eph. 3:10–11).

---

[70] Sinclair Ferguson, *The Holy Spirit*, Contours of Christian Theology (Downers Grove, IL: InterVarsity Press, 1996), 139–40, 249, 251.

[71] Michael S. Horton, *Covenant and Salvation: Union with Christ* (Louisville, KY: Westminster, 2007), 302.

Even more, we are a part of something far bigger than ourselves. We are a part of the story of the glorious God who graciously and joyfully communicates his fullness, chiefly through his creation, image bearers, providence, and redemptive acts. As his people we respond by glorifying him, and in this God receives glory. Further, through uniting us to the glorious Christ, the perfect image of God, God transforms us and shares his glory with us. And all of this redounds to his glory, as God in his manifold perfections is exhibited, known, rejoiced in, and prized. No wonder Paul exclaims, "From him and through him and to him are all things. To him be glory forever" (Rom. 11:36). Our spirituality is from God, through God, and to God. God is the beginning, middle, and end of our spirituality. Thus his glory is the ultimate end of our spirituality.

The Grace of God: Fuel for Our Journey
Beginning with being created in the image of God and culminating in the glory of God, a trajectory of our spiritual journey has emerged:

- the image of God: created for spirituality
- fallen man: the distortion of our spirituality
- Christ's saving work: the basis of our spirituality
- new life: the beginning of our spirituality
- the triune God: the source of our spirituality
- Christlikeness: the goal of our spirituality
- love: the focus of our spirituality
- the church: the community of our spirituality
- ordinary life: the context of our spirituality
- indwelling sin/temptation: obstacles in our spirituality
- the already and the not yet: tensions in our spirituality
- Word, prayer, and church: means for our spirituality
- reproducing disciples: the mission of our spirituality
- the glory of God: the ultimate end of our spirituality
- the grace of God: fuel for our journey

As we have seen, God is the beginning, middle, and end of our spirituality.
   God's grace begins our spiritual journey (Eph. 2:1–10; Titus 3:4–7). God's grace will complete our spiritual journey (Phil. 1:6; Rom. 8:18–39; 1 Pet. 1:3–5). We will "persevere in holiness because God perseveres in grace."[72]
   And in the meantime, God's grace provides the fuel for our spiritual journey. Charles Spurgeon said it well: "Between here and heaven, every

---

[72] Charles Haddon Spurgeon, *All of Grace*, Read and Reflect with the Classics (repr. Nashville, TN: B&H, 2017), 162.

minute that the Christian lives will be a minute of grace."[73] When we are in need, God's grace gives us boldness: "Let us then with confidence draw near to the throne of grace, that we may receive mercy and find grace to help in time of need" (Heb. 4:16). When we are in sin, God's grace fosters our repentance and promotes our holiness: "The grace of God has appeared, bringing salvation for all people, training us to renounce ungodliness and worldly passions, and to live self-controlled, upright, and godly lives in the present age" (Titus 2:11–12). When we need strength to keep on serving God, God's grace enables us, as Paul testifies: "I worked harder than any of them, though it was not I, but the grace of God that is with me" (1 Cor. 15:10). When we are tired and weak, God's grace fortifies us, as Paul attests: "My grace is sufficient for you, for my power is made perfect in weakness" (2 Cor. 12:9). When we forget who we are in Christ, God's grace reminds us, as Geoffrey Thomas explains:

> God has joined us to Christ. We are no longer standing under what Adam deserves, and I no longer stand under what I deserve, but God has caused us to stand under what Christ deserves. God's grace places us under the eloquence of his blood. He places us under all the adequacy of that sacrifice. God places us in the full deserving of our Lord's obedience and righteousness. He causes us to stand under the total logic of his atonement, so that there is now no condemnation for us who are in Christ Jesus. Your conscience has no right to condemn you, and death has no right to terrorize you, and hell has no right to stand up before you because there is now no condemnation whatsoever. Why? Because you were and are in Christ Jesus. You stand in his merit, and you stand in his righteous obedience in all its glory, because that is what God did when he gave you to his Son Jesus Christ and joined you to him forever. Your life stands under all the implications of how Christ lived and how he died. You stand in the logic of Calvary and the glory of the shed blood. You stand in the righteous life of Christ the blameless Son of God. God has united us to Jesus Christ his Son.[74]

---

[73] Charles Haddon Spurgeon, "The Tenses" (No. 2718), sermon preached May 13, 1880, accessed November 27, 2017, https://www.ccel.org/ccel/spurgeon/sermons47.xi.html.

[74] Geoffrey Thomas, sermon, "But God," preached May 2, 2004, accessed November 27, 2017, http://www.alfredplacechurch.org.uk/index.php/sermons/ephesians/24-7-but-god. I owe this reference to John Mahony, unpublished notes and "Purchased Grace," Christian Ministries Lectures, California Baptist University, February 23, 2016, https://calbaptist.edu/school-of-christian-ministries/lecture-series.

2

SHAPED INTO THE CREATOR'S IMAGE

Spirituality and Spiritual Formation in the Old Testament

PAUL R. HOUSE

Spirituality and spiritual formation have always been part of God's plan for humanity. Having created the heavens and earth and creatures to populate that earth (Gen. 1:1–25), God created men and women in his image and made them stewards of that same earth (1:26–27). He commanded them to multiply and fill the earth with their offspring, blessing them with the physical resources needed to fulfill these tasks (1:28–31). He then designated a day of rest (2:1–3), which at least implies they would need time for reverence, rejuvenation, and learning. The first man and woman related to God immediately, but they had to learn their physical, spiritual, and familial responsibilities (Gen. 2:4–25). Presumably they would teach children born to them how to bear the Creator's image. This instruction would of necessity be a gradual process that would occur as the sons and daughters grew. Thus the need for spiritual formation began at creation. It existed before the sins and consequences Genesis 3:1–24 describes, though sin certainly affects its contours.[1]

As the Old Testament unfolds,[2] God provides the means and resources necessary for those who believe in him to develop traits reflective of his

---

[1] Since I have discussed sin's impact on humanity in another volume in this series, I will not repeat that material here. See Paul R. House, "Sin in the Law," in *Fallen: A Theology of Sin*, Theology in Community, ed. Christopher W. Morgan and Robert A. Peterson (Wheaton, IL: Crossway, 2013), 39–63; and "Sin in the Former and Latter Prophets and Writings," in ibid., 65–81.

[2] In this chapter I use the term *Old Testament* to refer to the Hebrew and Aramaic books in the Protestant canon—in other words, to designate a body of literature, not to separate an era of old covenant from an era of new covenant, since Jesus announces the new covenant in his blood at the Last Supper (Luke 22:20; see Jer. 30:1–31:40). For a study of how Christians came to call the Hebrew and Aramaic Scriptures the "Old Testament" and the Greek Scriptures the "New Testament," see Joshua N. Moon, *Jeremiah's New Covenant: An Augustinian Reading*, Journal of Theological Interpretation Supplements 3 (Winona Lake, IN: Eisenbrauns, 2011): 1–57.

image, as seen in his character, even in a sin-marred world. Biblical writers portray this development in several ways: walking faithfully in God's paths (Psalm 1), growing in wisdom throughout one's life (Proverbs 1–9), loving God wholeheartedly (Deut. 6:4–9), and enjoying friendship with God (Ex. 33:7–11; Isa. 41:8). These and other images contribute to a proper understanding of what it means to learn to serve as God's image bearers in his world, the original purpose for which God created human beings. Taking these descriptions into account, we could say that the Old Testament defines spiritual formation as follows: "Yahweh's developing people made in his image who trust in him into maturing, wise stewards of his world by providing his presence, resources, and practices for their lives in their homes, vocations, and communities." Though spiritual formation begins in homes and communities of faith, it includes learning to reach out to people and places in need of returning to the Creator and his purposes for them.

In this chapter I will attempt to provide a foundation for a biblical theology of spirituality and spiritual formation by outlining its nature and development in the Old Testament canon. I will contend that spiritual formation into God's image requires lifelong learning based on acquisition of truth duly experienced through practice. In other words, spiritual formation basically amounts to growth in biblically defined wisdom. The key to this maturation lies in how Yahweh's followers become like him by developing his character and sharing in his work. By faith his image-bearing children enter into a covenant relationship with him. They then do his work, taking on his redeeming and preserving mission. Fully shaped believers await the fulfillment of his promises, including the promise of a Messiah and the new heavens and earth that he will rule (see Isa. 11:1–9; 65:17–25; 66:22–23). Anna and Simeon, who meet Joseph, Mary, and Jesus in Luke 2:22–28, are striking examples of such image-bearing, mature children of God.

To demonstrate these assertions, I will utilize the following methodology. First, I will approach the Bible as God's written Word to believers for the sake of the world he created. As God's Word, the Bible reflects his character and authority (Ps. 19:7–11; 2 Tim. 3:16a)[3] and is suitable for careful spiritual reflection (Ps. 19:12–14), personal growth (2 Tim. 3:16b–17), and church edification (2 Tim. 4:1–5). The Bible equips believers for mature ministry to other Christians (Eph. 4:12–16) and to

---

[3] For a comprehensive discussion of this view of the authority and inspiration of the Bible, consult Carl F. H. Henry, *Revelation and Authority*, vol. 4 (Waco, TX: Word, 1979).

all peoples on earth (see Isa. 2:1–5; Jonah 1–4; Matt. 28:16–20; Rom. 1:16). It is important to understand this progression from believers to the world. If Christian readers think erroneously that the Bible is written primarily to unbelievers as an evangelistic tool to help them come to faith, then they may consider the Old Testament's instructions as standards that people cannot keep and that make them long for redemption. If Christian readers understand that the Old Testament is written to them (1 Cor. 10:1–16) to help them grow in faith and ministry (see 2 Tim. 3:16–17) and to be salt and light in the world (Matt. 5:13–16), then they will more likely embrace and use its teachings the way Jesus intended (Matt. 5:17–20).

Second, I will examine three key passages that establish growth into God's image as the goal of spiritual formation: Genesis 1:26–2:3; Exodus 34:1–27; and Psalms 110–112. By doing so I adapt Elmer Martens's procedure of using comprehensive passages as the foundation for synthetic biblical-theological work.[4] I also stress the importance of Exodus 34 for understanding Old Testament theology.[5]

Third, I will trace concepts gleaned from these three foundational passages through relevant passages in the Law, Prophets, and Writings, the Old Testament's three main sections. Thus I will utilize a canonical approach like that employed by Brevard Childs, Ronald Clements, John Sailhamer, and Rolf Rendtorff.[6] Each of these writers has put his personal stamp on the method. Yet each sees the value of tracing biblical concepts through the canon much like Jesus does in Matthew 23:29–36 and Luke 24:44–49.

Fourth, at the end of each section I will provide theological syntheses of key themes related to spiritual formation in God's image. Supplying thematic observations fits the pattern of Old Testament theologies penned by Walther Eichrodt, John Goldingay, and Robin Routledge.[7] At

---

[4] See Elmer Martens, *God's Design: A Focus on Old Testament Theology*, 4th ed. (Eugene, OR: Wipf & Stock, 2016), 3–18.

[5] See W. Ross Blackburn, *The God Who Makes Himself Known: The Missionary Heart of the Book of Exodus*, NSBT (Downers Grove, IL: InterVarsity Press, 2012); Graham Cole, "Exodus 34, the Middoth and the Doctrine of God: The Importance of Biblical Theology to Evangelical Systematic Theology," *SBJT* 12.3 (2008): 24–37; Paul R. House, "God's Character and the Wholeness of Scripture," *SBET* 23 (Spring 2005): 4–17.

[6] See Brevard S. Childs, *Introduction to the Old Testament as Scripture* (Minneapolis: Fortress, 1980); Ronald E. Clements, *Old Testament Theology: A Fresh Approach* (London: Marshall, Morgan, & Scott, 1978); John Sailhamer, *Introduction to Old Testament Theology: A Canonical Approach* (Grand Rapids, MI: Zondervan, 1995); Rolf Rendtorff, *The Canonical Hebrew Bible: A Theology of the Old Testament*, trans. David E. Orton (Leiden: Deo, 2005); and Paul R. House, *Old Testament Theology* (Downers Grove, IL: InterVarsity Press, 1998).

[7] Walther Eichrodt, *Theology of the Old Testament*, vol. 1, 6th ed., trans. J. A. Baker (Philadelphia: Westminster Press, 1961); John Goldingay, *Old Testament Theology*, vol. 1, *Israel's Gospel* (Downers Grove, IL: InterVarsity Press, 2003); and Robin Routledge, *Old Testament Theology: A Thematic Approach* (Downers Grove, IL: Inter-

times the synthesis segment will reference New Testament texts to show
the Bible's unity within diverse situations. Instruction in spiritual formation develops as the canon does, through time and situations that enable
later readers to obey God. As history changes, the ways in which people
obey God's instructions in history also change, though the truth itself
does not alter. Of course, the greatest change comes through the incarnation, life, teaching, death, resurrection, commission, and ascension of
Jesus the Messiah. He teaches his disciples how to obey God's law more
thoroughly than do the scribes and Pharisees (Matt. 5:17–20; 5:43–48).

Forming God's Children into God's Character: Genesis 1:26–2:3; Exodus 34:1–27; and Psalms 110–112

As was noted above, spiritual formation is implicit in the Bible's earliest
verses. It is therefore reasonable to begin with the creation accounts. Even
though Genesis 1:26–31 mentions God's "image," the passage does not define the term. It is fairly clear that human beings are to serve as Yahweh's
sub-regents in the world,[8] but determining what traits mark such undershepherds requires further explanation. Therefore, it is helpful to analyze
God's self-revealed personal characteristics detailed in Exodus 34:6–7.
Although it is possible to prioritize other vital passages, none surpasses
this one in thoroughness and usefulness to subsequent biblical writers.[9]
Psalms 110–112 provide the most significant use of Exodus 34 for this
chapter's purposes. As Gordon Wenham observes,[10] Psalms 111–112
are twin psalms that display Yahweh's traits and then state how his followers replicate his characteristics. Together they demonstrate the Old
Testament's emphasis on God's people possessing God's character, which
amounts to reflecting his image in the world.

God's Image and Spiritual Formation: Genesis 1–2

Genesis 1:26–2:3 depicts part of day six and all of day seven of creation.
God has been personally involved in the creation process throughout
Genesis 1:1–25. He has hovered over the waters, spoken the created order
into existence out of nothing, assessed the results of his activity as "good,"
and named and commissioned each major part of what he has created. He

---

Varsity Press, 2008). See also Reinhard Feldmeier and Hermann Spieckermann, *God of the Living: A Biblical Theology*, trans. Mark E. Biddle (Waco, TX: Baylor University Press, 2011).

[8] Craig G. Bartholomew and Michael W. Goheen, *The Drama of Scripture: Finding Our Place in the Biblical Story* (Grand Rapids, MI: Baker Academic, 2004), 36–37.

[9] See fn. 4, above.

[10] Gordon J. Wenham, *Psalms as Torah: Reading Biblical Song Ethically*, Studies in Theological Interpretation (Grand Rapids, MI: Baker Academic, 2012), 158–66.

continues the process in 1:26–31. He makes male and female in his image, blesses them, and commands them to care for the earth as his viceregents. Scholars have offered various interpretations of "our image" (1:26) and "his image" (1:27).[11] All agree that in Genesis 1–2 "image" means that humans can relate positively to God in ways the rest of creation has not been made to do. Only human beings receive God's personal image, blessing, and responsibility for overseeing creation.[12] As Claus Westermann writes, Genesis 1:26–27 "means that the uniqueness of human beings consists in their being God's counterparts. The relationship to God is not something which is added to human existence; humans are created in such a way that their very existence is intended to be their relationship to God."[13]

Furthermore, only human beings are told to exercise "dominion" over the earth (1:26, 28). What *dominion* means here has also sparked a good bit of debate. Karl Barth comments that "in consequence of their divine likeness," humans "are distinguished from all other creatures with autonomous life, by a superior position, by a higher dignity and might, by a greater power of disposal and control."[14] More recently scholars have rightly argued that phrases such as "autonomous life" and "power of disposal and control," however Barth intended, can be taken to mean that people may do with creation whatever they please. Wendell Berry and Ellen Davis have noted that though some authors have interpreted "dominion" this way, the Bible does not.[15] Thus it is important to emphasize that people have more privileges and responsibilities than do God's other creatures. As persons with a special relationship with God and a unique responsibility to him, human beings must exercise their rule in the manner God the Creator has designed. Marsha Wilfong helpfully observes, "If humankind is to carry out the task of dominion as God's representatives on earth, then the exercise of human dominion should imitate God's own dominion over creation, and should have as its goal the fulfillment of God's good purpose for creation. Exploitation of animals or the earth is not appropriate. Autonomous dominion that

---

[11] For the opinions of early church writers, consult Andrew Louth, ed., *Ancient Christian Commentary on Scripture, Old Testament*, vol. 1, *Genesis 1–11* (Downers Grove, IL: InterVarsity Press, 2001), 27–45. For a concise survey of opinions since the Reformation, see Kenneth A. Mathews, *Genesis 1:1–11:26*, NAC 1A (Nashville, TN: B&H, 1996), 126. For a longer summary of key interpretations, consult Claus Westermann, *Genesis 1–11: A Commentary*, trans. John J. Scullion (Minneapolis: Augsburg, 1984), 147–58.
[12] See Bartholomew and Goheen, *The Drama of Scripture*, 36–37.
[13] Westermann, *Genesis 1–11*, 158.
[14] Karl Barth, *Church Dogmatics* III.1, *The Doctrine of Creation*, trans. G.W. Bromiley and T. F. Torrance (Edinburgh, UK: T & T Clark, 1958), 3.
[15] See Wendell Berry, *The Gift of Good Land: Further Essays Cultural and Agricultural* (Berkeley, CA: Counterpoint, 1981), 267–69; and Ellen Davis, *Scripture, Culture, and Agriculture: An Agrarian Reading of the Bible* (Cambridge, UK: Cambridge University Press, 2009), 53–63.

ignores or seeks to overthrow God's ultimate dominion over creation is not appropriate."[16] Thus, appointed stewards may act only in a manner congruent with the Creator. They must reflect his character in order to bear his image properly.

Genesis 2:1–3 highlights God's satisfaction with creation, his kindness, his instructive nature, and his unwillingness to exercise dominion simply because he can do so. Everything has been done well the prior six days. Everything is "good"—that is, appropriate in every way for the purposes for which it has been made. To set an example for his stewards, God rests on the seventh day and sets it apart permanently as a day of rest. God demonstrates his kindness and graciousness by teaching human beings the necessity of rest. He also shows that life does not consist in activity alone.

Though easy to miss among the myriad of other interesting aspects of this passage, God has begun to attend to spiritual formation. This personal teaching continues in Genesis 2:4–25, where God shows Adam and Eve the goodness of place, work, and home. Again, even before sin corrupts humanity and affects creation in Genesis 3:1–24, God personally addresses the first couple's sequential spiritual development.

God's Character and Spiritual Formation: Exodus 34

Exodus 34 states explicitly the image of God that humans are to bear. This great text follows narratives detailing Noah, Abraham, Isaac, Joseph, and their suffering descendants (see Genesis 5–Exodus 2). It also comes after descriptions of Israel and Moses' walk with God during the exodus, the initiation of the Sinai covenant, and the golden calf incident (see Exodus 3–33). At Moses' request, God has forgiven the people, agreed to reinstitute the covenant, and continued to dwell in their midst (33:14). Moses has learned to speak with God face-to-face, as one does with a friend (33:7–11). Therefore he asks for more, requesting to see God's glory (33:19), the fullness of his being. This God will not do, for he cares for Moses (33:20). But he agrees to reveal more about himself (33:21–33), thereby extending Moses' spiritual formation to a new level of understanding.

Yahweh's character has two overarching aspects: he is kind and constantly ready to forgive, and he refuses to clear the guilty. These traits

---

[16] Marsha M. Wilfong, "Human Creation in Canonical Context: Genesis 1:26–31 and Beyond," in *God Who Creates: Essays in Honor of W. Sibley Towner*, ed. William P. Brown and S. Dean McBride (Grand Rapids, MI: Eerdmans, 2000), 45–46.

reflect the rise and continuation of sin that Genesis 3:1–24 first portrays, and also shows that God loves the world and human beings instead of forsaking them.[17] These traits demonstrate that God's character perfectly joins patience and justice. Exodus 34:6 states that he is "compassionate and merciful, slow to anger and plentiful in covenant loyalty and faithfulness."[18] The first two terms occur together eleven times in the Old Testament.[19] In these instances they depict comprehensive sympathy; the first word can describe parental love (see 1 Kings 3:26) and the second the sort of love a merciful king shows to an unworthy subject or the kindness a rich person shows to the poor.[20] Persons with these two traits are of necessity slow to anger and filled with covenant-type loyalty. His patience and loyalty explain his forbearance and ironclad determination that no covenant promise he has made will fail. Over time such patience shows his "faithfulness," a term that includes truthfulness and steady endurance.[21]

Exodus 34:7 reveals that Yahweh's patient ways allow him to be ready at any time to bear with and forgive "iniquity and transgression and sin," words that denote twisting, trespassing, and missing a goal, respectively. Together they summarize "sin."[22] Yahweh forgives those who repent, as his willingness to move past the golden calf incident indicates.

Nonetheless, in his own time Yahweh deals with the wicked, as hardhearted Pharaoh (Exodus 5–15) and some of the Israelite revelers had discovered (see 32:25–29). Indeed, he will judge sin however long it lasts, even if doing so takes three or four generations (34:7). Based on Exodus 20:4–5, these generations "hate" Yahweh, which likely means they choose another god over him (see Mal. 1:2–5). Such choosing rejects relationship with the Creator, the only God.

Since Exodus 34:10–26 reaffirms laws given in Exodus 20–23, Yahweh's character has stood behind his covenant making all along. His command for Moses to write these words signals their enduring validity (34:27). The people may hear or read God's words and learn from them. The many citations of this passage in the rest of the Old Testament (see Num. 14:13–19; Joel 2:12–17; Nah. 1:1–8; etc.) demonstrate its

---

[17] See Davis, *Scripture, Culture, and Agriculture*, 42.

[18] Unless otherwise noted, all Scripture passages in this chapter are the author's translation.

[19] See Mike Butterworth, "rhm," *NIDOTTE*, ed. Willem VanGemeren (Grand Rapids, MI: Zondervan, 1997), 3:1094.

[20] H. J. Stoebe, "hnn," *TLOT*, trans. Mark E. Biddle, ed. Ernst Jenni and Claus Westermann (Peabody, MA: Hendrickson, 1997), 1:442–43; and Robert C. Dentan, "The Literary Affinities of Exodus 34:6f.," *VT* 13 (1963): 42.

[21] See *BDB*, 52–53.

[22] See Paul R. House, "Sin in the Law," 39–63.

foundational importance for the people's spiritual growth.[23] The rest of the Old Testament depends on the people's knowing and displaying this definition of God's character. He rules from these character traits, and his stewards must do so as well.

God's Character and the Imitation of God: Psalms 110–112

Psalms 110–112 pull together Yahweh's covenant promises, character, and goals for believers' spiritual maturation. In 2 Samuel 7, God promises David an enduring, continuous kingdom. This covenant is in continuity with covenants mediated through Noah, Abraham, and Moses (see 7:9–10, 12, and 19).[24] But it extends these covenants by identifying a particular royal lineage (see Gen. 49:10) that will never cease. Like Psalm 2, Psalm 110 builds on this promise. A king-priest will rule the nations, bringing justice to all (110:5–6). This person will operate by Yahweh's power and will be Lord over David, the lord of Israel (110:1).

With these fundamental covenant continuities in place, Psalms 111 and 112 portray the correlation between Yahweh's character and his people's.[25] For example, Psalm 111:3 notes that God's "righteousness endures forever," while Psalm 112:3 amazingly states the same about "the man who fears the LORD" (cf. 112:1). Then Psalm 111:4 quotes Exodus 34:6, declaring Yahweh to be "merciful and gracious," which Psalm 112:4 declares to be true of God's faithful one as well. Psalm 111:7–8 states that God's ways are steady, and Psalm 112:7–8 describes the righteous person's work in the same way. Psalm 111:10 concludes the psalm by declaring, "The fear of the LORD is the beginning of wisdom," and the next psalm begins by describing "the man who fears the LORD" (Ps. 112:1). Thus the chapters connect thematically in the middle (111:10 and 112:1) and correspond virtually verse by verse.

Anchored in Exodus 34, these chapters highlight the connection between Yahweh's Messiah, Yahweh's image, and his people's ways. The person whom Psalm 112 describes embodies God's righteousness, mercy, graciousness, perseverance, and ability to distinguish between the righteous and the wicked (112:8). This person cares for the poor (112:9) and thus shares God's heart for the oppressed (see Exodus 1–2). This person exhibits God's image and thereby stands as an exemplar for a proper steward of God's creation.

---

[23] See fn. 5, above, for studies of the passage's use in the Old Testament.
[24] See Walter C. Kaiser Jr., *The Messiah in the Old Testament*, Studies in Old Testament Biblical Theology (Grand Rapids, MI: Zondervan, 1995), 77–83.
[25] Wenham, *Psalms as Torah*, 158–66.

Synthesis

These key passages provide the origins, definition, and goals of spiritual formation. Genesis 1–2 indicates that spiritual growth through divine revelation and instruction is part of creation's fabric. God is a teacher. Much of the rest of our chapter will deal with how spiritual formation combats sin. Yet the fact that spiritual growth existed before and after sin indicates that formation encompasses more than having one's sins forgiven. Formation is about more than beating back bad habits born of original sin. It encompasses all that stewardship of God's creation entails.

Exodus 34 reveals God's character. This passage shows that God is a perfectly formed person. He balances grace and patience, anger and justice flawlessly. Time reveals how these characteristics operate yet does not alter Yahweh's constantly good motives and deeds. Writers across the canon find these traits relevant. They define Yahweh's nature.

Psalms 110–112 demonstrate that even after Genesis 3, believers in Yahweh can indeed take on his character. They can become transformed into the image of Yahweh (see Rom. 12:2). These chapters prove that Old Testament believers in Yahweh embraced the promise of the Messiah and reflected Yahweh's glory. They did not pine away for the Messiah's appearance, though they looked forward to it. They got on with the important business of serving as God's stewards in his creation by showing the wicked and the righteous his image. They were Yahweh's body on earth, so it is not surprising when Paul uses this image when teaching about the church (see 1 Corinthians 12).

Shaping Priests and Stewards for God's Creation: The Law

Taken as a whole, Genesis–Deuteronomy intends to shape Israel into people who fulfill Yahweh's creation commission. Moses sketches a strategically selective grand narrative that stretches from creation to 1400 BC. Yahweh calls Israel to be stewards of creation by becoming a kingdom of priests (Ex. 19:5–6). This connection is not as strange as it may seem at first, since in the ancient world priests were often agents of preservation of religious customs, moral fidelity, and use of land. They helped to maintain "order in the cosmos."[26] As a kingdom of priests God's people are to oversee a gracious, fruitful, and just society anchored in love (Leviticus 19; Deut. 6:4–9). Land and people will together provide a rooted

---

[26] John H. Walton, *Ancient Near Eastern Thought and the Old Testament: Introducing the Conceptual World of the Hebrew Bible* (Grand Rapids, MI: Baker Academic, 2006), 130.

witness to the world (Leviticus 25). The fact that these vocations (priest and steward) extend into the New Testament (see 1 Pet. 2:9–10; Col. 1:25) indicates their enduring value. The fact that they require growth and maturity underscores the need for spiritual formation tied to creation mandates and covenant instruction. Since two of the three foundational texts introduced above come from the Law, I will focus in this section on three related passages: Exodus 19:5–6; Leviticus 19; and Leviticus 25.

Priests for Yahweh's Creation: Exodus 19

Exodus 19:5–6 explains why Yahweh delivered Israel from slavery in Egypt and provides the basis for the covenant stipulations that follow. Since the days of Noah, Yahweh has sought stewards of creation who will share his redemptive work. Genesis 3–5 describes sin's entry into creation and the ravages it causes. By Genesis 6:5, Yahweh notes sadly that stewardship has devolved into constant violence and corruption. He decides to start fresh with Noah, promising him (and through him all of humanity) that earth and its seasons will endure and demanding that violence end and respect for life ensue (Gen. 8:20–9:17). Sin spreads again in 9:18–11:9, and Yahweh selects Abraham, one of Noah's descendants, as the recipient and agent of his redemptive purposes. Yahweh pledges descendants, land, and the honor of blessing all nations (12:1–9). When Abraham trusts God (15:6), Yahweh reveals to him that his descendants will spend four centuries away from the land (15:13–16). Genesis 16–Exodus 18 details the numerical growth of Abraham's family and its miraculous release from bondage.

Yahweh then declares that this redeemed people will fulfill God's promises to Abraham by serving as a kingdom of priests (Ex. 19:5–6). Ideally, priests in the ancient world believed in their deity and lived by his or her standards. They taught the people, interceded for them, and helped them make appropriate sacrifices. In short, they were supposed to help others walk in the ways of their deity in their daily lives. Priests often lived together in community so they could pass on the practices necessary for maintaining their work across the generations. Israel was to be such a community, yet one dedicated to one another and to the world.[27] Those who served a different god or refused to follow their deity's orders were not considered part of the community. While contemporary readers may marvel that Yahweh simply commissions these people without stating

---

[27] On this subject see Scott W. Hahn, *The Kingdom of God as Liturgical Empire: A Theological Commentary on 1–2 Chronicles* (Grand Rapids, MI: Baker Academic, 2012).

exactly which individuals do and do not believe in him, neither the Old
Testament nor the New Testament spends much time describing the minimum standards for saving faith. Rather, Scripture states the necessity for
belief in and right relationship with Yahweh and states his expectations
and the resources he gives to his people to help them achieve their tasks.

Priests and Stewards in Community for God's Creation: Leviticus 19, 25–26

Exodus 20–31 begins Yahweh's process of instructing his people in their
task. As Allen Ross summarizes, "The worship of devout believers was to
be characterized by praise and thanksgiving at all times (Ps. 33:1; cf. Eph.
5:19–20). Accordingly, the law schedules worship for different hours of
the day, days of the week, months and seasons of the year, and years of
the Jubilee period."[28] This priestly nation was to live as redeemed people
by reverencing God and respecting one another (Ex. 20:1–22:15). They
were to have particular concern for the sojourner, widow, and fatherless
(22:21–27). They were to show courtesy to an enemy (23:4–5). They were
to worship Yahweh alone (20:22–26) and to observe the Sabbath weekly
(23:10–13). Later, Numbers 28:11–15 described rituals for a monthly
new-moon festival.[29]

Three times a year the people were to gather on special occasions
to worship God as one (Ex. 23:14–17). They were to have a central sanctuary and a group of priests within the nation of priests (25–31). Once
in the land (23:20–33), priests would live among the people, teaching
them God's ways in between the times in which they all gather (see Josh.
21:1–42). The sanctuary would be in the midst of the land and the priests
in the midst of the people. Both temple and priesthood represent God's
presence in the midst of the whole people, his kingdom of priests. God
commands the people to offer sacrifices at this tabernacle (Leviticus 1–7).
These sacrifices, offered in faith, would receive God's approval. He would
forgive the people for their sins. On the annual Day of Atonement God
would forgive all sins committed (Lev. 16:1–31). The kingdom of priests
would be cleansed for ongoing ministry.

Children born into this community were thus supposed to be sur-
rounded by instruction for developing into devoted followers of Yahweh. Their parents would teach them in their homes (Deut. 6:4–9). They

---

[28] Allen P. Ross, *Recalling the Hope of Glory: Biblical Worship from the Garden to the New Creation* (Grand Rapids, MI: Kregel, 2006), 228.
[29] Ibid.

would rest and worship with their families and their communities every week and month. They would learn God's great saving deeds through celebration of the Passover (Ex. 12:1–28) and other annual festivals. They would hear God's Word read (see 34:1–27), receive Yahweh's forgiveness (Lev. 16:1–34), learn to pray, and live in a just and gracious society, one that treated non-Israelites in a manner aimed at drawing them to Yahweh. In due time they would become adults ready to take their place in the kingdom of priests. Every aspect of this culture aimed at this goal. Exodus 32:1–6 shows how easily their mentors could forget their teaching role. Nonetheless, foundations for renewed teaching were in place. A believing people constantly growing closer to God and continually fulfilling its role was possible.

Leviticus 19 and 25–26 reveal what such a culture would look like. Here the roles of stewards and priests merge. Leviticus 19:9–18 repeats Yahweh's concern for the disadvantaged. Israel was not to be so greedy as to glean its fields to the edges. Rather, the people were to leave some for the poor and the sojourner (19:9–10). They were never to oppress neighbors or judge unjustly in court (19:11–16). Moreover, they were not even to hate their neighbor in their heart (19:17). Outward compliance would not suffice. In short, they were to love their neighbor as they loved themselves, the point Jesus reiterates in Luke 10:25–38. Doing so would demonstrate their priestly intentions toward all people, foreign and domestic.

Leviticus 25 presents one of the Bible's most radical ideas, the Sabbath year. Every seventh year the people would rest and give the land rest. They would not plant or prune. All levels of society would rest when the land did (25:1–7). Clearly, obeying this standard required extreme faith and competent, confident stewardship. What is more, every fiftieth year there would be a greater Sabbath year. Debts would be forgiven, land restored to original owners, and indentured servants freed (25:8–55). Land and people would find rest from debt, greed, worry, and power.

The key to this radical stewardship lies in one simple fact: the land belongs to Yahweh, not to Israel or anyone else. As Wendell Berry writes, the Sabbath years undercut the "conceit of human ownership."[30] The Creator orders his stewards and priests to rest, restore, rebuild, relearn, and rejoice. Assuming a normal life span, an Israelite would experience this great Sabbath year at least once and the normal Sabbath year many times. Coupled to the practices already noted, they would grow spiritually

---

[30] Berry, *The Gift of Good Land*, 271. See also Craig G. Bartholomew, *Where Mortals Dwell: A Christian View of Place for Today* (Grand Rapids, MI: Baker, 2011), 63.

through the cycles of life and death, work and rest. God's teaching would form them intellectually and physically. They would learn to love their neighbor from the heart (19:17–18) in their bodies. They would learn to love God with heart, life, and strength from their parents and their community, just as Deuteronomy 6:4–9 envisions.

Leviticus 26 includes three sections. First, Leviticus 26:1–13 offers great blessings for an obedient people raised up from slavery by their loving God. They can live in hopeful expectation. Second, Leviticus 26:14–39 depicts sequential consequences for disobedience. Israel must live as a humble people, ever willing to return to their forgiving God. Third, Leviticus 26:40–45 promises that Yahweh will never reject his people, even if he sends them into exile for a time. Deuteronomy 27–28 and 30:1–10 presents these principles to the next generation. This passage teaches God's love in all historical circumstances. When the people fall away from the teachings of Leviticus 19 and 26, they nevertheless still have hope. God remains ready to forgive, as the Day of Atonement ritual in Leviticus 16 clearly shows. He stands ready to place in their hands the tools of stewardship and priesthood once again.

Synthesis

Keeping the conclusions from Genesis 1:26–2:3 and Exodus 34:1–27 in mind, we see the preceding analysis leading to at least three basic observations. Exodus 19:5–6 and Leviticus 25–26 emphasize the shaping of the people into a particular role in a particular place through a particular rhythm of life. When observed, God's instructions shape society from top to bottom, from early age onward, from one generation to the next. Spiritual formation forms a culture, not just an individual.

Exodus 19:5–6 joins Israel's priestly role to mankind's stewardship responsibility. These are connected, not separate, tasks. Priests primarily nourish people. They teach, sacrifice, and serve wherever needed. They depend on others for sustenance. They help establish and sustain a just, forgiving, compassionate community. In short, they help others understand and embody Yahweh's character. Like Moses, they are stewards of God's sacred writings for the sake of others. Over time each Israelite boy and girl can participate in this role so that sojourning boys and girls may as well. Leviticus 19 underscores the fact that these priests can fulfill this role only through self-giving love.

Leviticus 25–26 grounds this priestly ministry in God's land loaned out to God's people. Israel's role takes place in a realm. If priests nourish people, then stewards nourish land. Again, these roles are inseparable, for people live in places. Children grow up in families living in communities, or should do so. They learn what matters from other people. Adults reinforce what matters to one another. Money and endless production do not have ultimate value—loving God and neighbor hold that primary place. Rest reinforces that point, as does forgiving debt and restoring families to home places. Spiritual formation is reflected in how places look, not just in how individuals feel.

Leviticus 25–26 also provides a rhythm of life in which spiritual formation can take place. It thus offers a theological interpretation of time, memory, and concrete history. Cycles of weeks, years, seven-year periods, and fifty-year periods chart a regular instructional schedule. Understanding how Yahweh disciplines people provides meaning to events. Bodily rest that complements normal hard work keeps these spiritual practices from becoming merely abstract. Rest for land and economy would have significant intellectual and physical impact. Over time the people would become a highly functioning "liturgical empire."[31] This empire would become a place where prayer, worship, farming, and commerce intermingled constantly in a just society. Substantive integration of work and spiritual growth would result. Priests and stewards of creation would be formed in rhythm with worship and work.

Shaping Stewards and Priests of God's Word: Spiritual Formation in the Prophets

Prophets in the ancient world carried their deity's or deities' messages. They interceded with these deities on behalf of people. Because they had direct contact with a god or gods, they thought it possible to know the future.[32] Of course, Israel's prophets had a relationship with the only God, the Creator (see Isa. 6:1–13; Jer. 10:1–25; Amos 3:7–8; 4:13; 5:8–9, 9:5–6). Thus they were vocational and genetic direct descendants of Abraham (see Gen. 20:7) and Moses (see Deut. 18:15–22; 34:8–10), two of God's earlier prophets.

Like everyone else, prophets had to grow in spiritual maturity. Their calling did not make them fully formed believers. Yahweh constantly formed them by his Word so that he could deliver his words through them orally and in writing. Many of the prophets left behind few historical records of their deeds, so for this study it is necessary to choose proph-

---

[31] Hahn, *The Kingdom of God as Liturgical Empire*, n.p.
[32] Walton, *Ancient Near Eastern Thought*, 239–63.

ets whose writings reflect their walk with God over some length of time. The narratives of Elijah and Elisha (see 1 Kings 17–2 Kings 13) fall into this category, as do the deeds and words of Isaiah and Habakkuk. This section will focus on three individuals whose spiritual journeys reflect growth forged in the fires of trials, errors, and endurance. Jeremiah and Baruch grow through obedience, questioning, and perseverance. Jonah develops through hard lessons about reflecting God's character beyond Israel's borders. Jeremiah is a priest, and Baruch is a scribe, so both are stewards of God's words. Jonah is a prophet forced to reflect on how he has failed to reflect God's image among foreigners. The existence of his book implies he learned from his experiences with God. These episodes give glimpses into the life of individual believers, just as the Law primarily gives glimpses into community life.

Shaped for Persevering Ministry: Jeremiah and Baruch

Jeremiah and Baruch share a ministry to a dying nation. The accounts of their work together are found mainly in Jeremiah 32–45, which describes events c. 605–586 BC. Before then, Jeremiah served at least from 626 BC (see 1:1–3). When he commissions Jeremiah to his ministry, Yahweh instructs him regarding how difficult his work will be. Since he will preach warnings of approaching disaster, the kings, priests, prophets, and people will oppose him (1:17–19). God does not lie. Jeremiah's life proves exceedingly difficult.

Yahweh provides spiritual resources for this hard walk of faith. First, Jeremiah has the assurance that God has given him this vocation and decided to do so before he was born (1:4–5). Second, Yahweh pledges to give him words to speak (1:9). Some of these words will be in the moment, in a crisis (see 28:1–17). But others will grow out of his extensive knowledge of Scripture (see 2:1–3:5; 7:1–8:3), presumably gained through his work and study as a priest in Anathoth (see 1:1–3). Third, Yahweh promises his unfailing presence. He will "be with" Jeremiah (1:8, 19); God will protect Jeremiah's life and work (1:17–19).

These promises state explicitly what the Law implies. Like Moses and others preceding him, Jeremiah has prayer, Scripture, and divine companionship to see him through the long days ahead. Under better circumstances, the temple ceremonies would be of more help to him (see 7:1–8:3; 26:1–24), as would his friends and family in Anathoth (see 11:18–23). As things stand, he has what he needs, though at times it seems to him like he barely does. For instance, Jeremiah 11–20 depicts at least five instances in which Jeremiah struggles with his walk with God. Often called "Jeremiah's confessions," these passages trace the prophet's growth from surprised newcomer to mature worker.[33]

First, in Jeremiah 11:18–12:17 men from his hometown of Anathoth threaten his life (11:18–23). God keeps his promise to protect him (see 1:17–19), but Jeremiah complains about Yahweh's scales of justice (12:1–4). In response, Yahweh tells him to get tougher, since times will get harder (12:5–6). God also tells him to see things from his perspective. God has much more to lose when Jerusalem falls than does Jeremiah (12:7–13). The lesson over, Yahweh reminds Jeremiah that the future will be bright (12:14–17).

Second, in chapters 13–14 Yahweh sends a drought to discipline the people, as Leviticus 26:19 threatened and Elijah endured (1 Kings 17:1–7). Angry that Yahweh refuses to hear his prayers for relief (see Jer. 11:14; 14:11), Jeremiah complains that he has suffered much while God has done little to help him. Indeed, he compares God to a "deceptive brook" (15:18), one that promises more than it delivers. Yahweh replies that Jeremiah must repent (15:19–21). He must choose between God and worthless, self-serving opinions if he wishes to remain useful. He must reflect God's character, not the people's.

Third, in Jeremiah 17:12–18 Yahweh's rebuke seems to have done its work. Having been given still-harder conditions (16:1–18), Jeremiah turns back to Yahweh. He confesses that Yahweh is his refuge (17:17), persevering in his work (17:16) and trusting God to deliver him when disaster strikes (17:18). Repentance restores the tattered relationship.

Fourth, this growth in trusting Yahweh continues in Jeremiah 18:18–23. After facing another plot against his life, the prophet places himself in God's hands, confident he has fulfilled his commission. By now he has been shaped a bit more in God's image. When Yahweh decides to judge the wicked (see Ex. 34:7; Nah. 1:1–8), Jeremiah agrees with his decision, whatever it costs him personally.

Fifth, Jeremiah 20:7–18 demonstrates that even those who grow in faith face new and troubling situations. After suffering persecution from a fellow priest (20:1–6), Jeremiah states that Yahweh forced him into ministry (20:7a), people scorn him (20:7b–8), and yet he cannot stop speaking Yahweh's words (20:9). God protects him (20:10–12), so he praises God (20:13). Nonetheless, this work makes him wish he had never been

---

[33] See, e.g., J. A. Thompson, *The Book of Jeremiah*, NICOT (Grand Rapids, MI: Eerdmans, 1980), 88–92.

born (20:14–18). Still, he perseveres, trusting Yahweh to have sufficient reason for having him endure such trouble.[34] He grows from complaining egregiously to trusting absolutely, learning to become "slow to anger" (Ex. 34:6), or at least slower to anger, thus allowing Yahweh to shape him into his image.

Baruch is a scribe, a guardian of words. Two connected texts must suffice to show his spiritual maturation. In Jeremiah 36:1–8, Yahweh instructs the prophet to write on a scroll the messages God has given him. Since Jeremiah has been barred from speaking at the temple, Baruch must read the scroll. Jeremiah 45:1–5 reveals Baruch's reaction. He complains that Yahweh has added sorrow to his pain. He may well know that he would risk his reputation among other scribes if he were to read the scroll.[35]

As he did with Jeremiah, Yahweh tells Baruch to realize what God stands to lose. Baruch must not seek great things for himself, though God will indeed spare his life (45:5). Duly chastened, Baruch reads the scroll and suffers the consequences (36:9–26). The king hates the words and burns the scroll (36:20–25). He orders Baruch and Jeremiah seized, but God protects them. Then God orders them to write another scroll, and the duo does so (36:27–32). They learn perseverance and endurance, which is yet another way of saying they learn godly patience. Considering the situation from Yahweh's viewpoint helps them take action reflective of his character. They operate as a good priest and a good steward, respectively.

Shaped for God-Imitating Ministry: Jonah

Jonah receives and merits a good bit of criticism for his unwillingness to preach in Nineveh. His motives for refusing are unclear; Yahweh's motives for sending him are not. Nineveh is an evil place (Jonah 1:2) and faces certain judgment (3:1–4). Therefore, God sends Jonah so that Nineveh will repent. They do so (3:5), and God forgives (3:5–10), which angers Jonah (4:1). He forgets what he prayed in the belly of the whale: "Salvation belongs to the LORD" (2:9). Jonah has obeyed yet has not been sufficiently shaped in God's image. He does not agree with God's decision to be compassionate.

Jonah knows Yahweh is "gracious and merciful, slow to anger, and plentiful in covenant loyalty" and has discovered that Yahweh relents

---

[34] Keith Clements, ed., *Dietrich Bonhoeffer: London, 1933–1935*, vol. 13, *Dietrich Bonhoeffer Works*, trans. Isabel Best (Minneapolis: Fortress, 2007), 351.

[35] See James Muilenburg, "Baruch the Scribe," in *Proclamation and Presence: Old Testament Essays in Honour of Gwynne Henton Davies*, ed. John I. Durham and J. R. Porter (Richmond, VA: John Knox Press, 1970), 228.

from sending disaster (4:2). Whatever Jonah's motives and desires, they do not stem from the truths of Exodus 34:6–7. Yet they must. Yahweh explains patiently that he pities Nineveh's sinful plight (Jonah 4:11). Like Jeremiah and Baruch, Jonah must conform his deeds to God's character. Mere outward obedience has never satisfied God (see Lev. 19:17), for he knows that sin grows from the heart (see Jer. 17:9–10) as surely as love does. Thus he takes the trouble to redeem Nineveh and to take Jonah further along his journey to spiritual maturity.

Synthesis

These short studies hardly scratch the surface of the prophetic books' implications for spiritual formation. Their lives and writings are so profound that Jesus will use them as examples of perseverance and suffering when teaching his disciples in the Sermon on the Mount (see Matt. 5:11–12). He also honors their words in the parable of the rich man and Lazarus, in which Abraham declares that if the rich man's brothers will not listen to Moses and the prophets, then they will not believe even if one rises from the dead (Luke 16:9–31). Still, there are several points worth noting from the preceding analyses. Each builds on the points drawn from the Law.

First, the prophets emphasize God's image shown through his character and the importance of his priests and stewards in his redemptive mission. Yahweh remains gracious, compassionate, and willing to forgive (Jonah 4:2; cf. Joel 2:12–17; Mic. 7:18–20). Jonah and others like him must learn to make reconciliation their primary instinct. No nation can be excluded from this merciful intention. Yahweh also stands ready to judge the guilty, and Jeremiah learns slowly that he must accept this part of Yahweh's character and let it shape his work. Jeremiah and Baruch discover that Yahweh endures much pain when deciding the time has come to punish (Jer. 12:5–13; 45:4–5). Their endurance reflects Yahweh's determination. Prophets were God's special representatives, his ambassadors. It was very important, then, for them to be God's image in the world. Jeremiah was a priest striving to be such a prophet. Baruch's scribal work required him to take care of God's written words (36:1–8, 27–32; 45:1–5) so that later generations could read them. Jonah's lessons about Yahweh's mercy for all still resonate.

Second, the prophets' lives demonstrate that spiritual formation requires patience and endurance even when one embraces the need to be formed into God's character. Jonah was a veteran prophet (see 2 Kings

14:25). Jeremiah served over forty years and Baruch at least twenty. Serving Yahweh in hard times formed Jeremiah and Baruch. Forgiveness and instruction shaped a duly abashed Jonah. Formation takes time; in fact, it takes a lifetime.

Third, the prophetic texts identify resources and practices that Yahweh uses to shape believers. His previous words shaped Jeremiah's subsequent words (see Jer. 2:1–3:5). His new words determined Jeremiah and Baruch's messages and circumstances (36:9–32). His old words reminded Jonah (Jonah 4:2; Ex. 34:6), while his new words chastened him. Yahweh's willingness to converse with his servants sustained them. For all his flaws, Jonah offers a lovely prayer in 2:1–10. Likewise, Jeremiah's honest prayers lead him to know himself by knowing God. Most of all, these messengers experience Yahweh's continual presence (Jer. 1:1–3). Indeed, this presence can seem too near (Jer. 20:7–18; 45:1–5; Jonah 4:3–11). But it is essential. Had the normal rhythms of worship set forth in the Law not been corrupted, they would have presented God's Word, aided prayer, fostered God's presence, and shaped God's people. Jonah's mission work and Jeremiah and Baruch's exile alter these rhythms yet do not remove the fundamental resources. Trouble alone cannot thwart spiritual formation.

Shaping Righteous and Wise Followers of Yahweh: Spiritual Formation in the Writings

The Writings section of the Old Testament is a diverse body of literature that spans Israel's history. These books contain already introduced concepts related to spiritual formation while also presenting new ideas and examples. As noted above, the goal of spiritual formation in the Writings is for Yahweh's followers to reflect his character. Psalms 110–112 demonstrate that the person who reverences God learns to reflect his righteousness, graciousness, compassion, and justice. Perhaps these psalms present a detailed description of the Law's command that God's people be holy because he is holy (Lev. 11:44). Prayer (Psalms 3–7), Scripture (see Psalms 19; 119), and God's presence (see Psalm 23) remain irreplaceable resources for growth. History remains the shaping venue for theological exploration and increasing understanding (see Psalms 78; 89; 104–106). Maturation over time (see Daniel 1–6), faithful priestly obedience (see Ezra 7–10), and dogged stewardship (see Nehemiah) continue to mark the spiritually formed follower. Two concepts summarize these people and their paths: righteousness and wisdom.

Formed into God's Righteous Followers: Psalm 1

Psalm 1 defines God's people as "the righteous" (1:6). Such people have committed their lives to Yahweh. They know him because they believe in him. They have nothing to do with the wicked person's way of life (1:1), for they delight in "the law of the LORD" and think of it inwardly (meditate on it) "day and night" (1:2). Therefore, they have the resources they need and bear fruits of character and, therefore, actions that God desires (1:3–4). He knows them (1:5) and judges between them and "the wicked" (1:6). Writing about Matthew's description of Joseph as a "just man" (Matt. 1:19), Joseph Ratzinger utilizes Psalm 1. He comments, "The flowing waters, from which he draws nourishment, naturally refer to the living word of God, into which he sinks the root of his being. God's will is not a law imposed on him from without, it is a 'joy.' For him the law is simply Gospel, good news, because he reads it with a personal, loving openness to God and in this way learns to understand and live it from deep within."[36] The righteous person reaches this level of loving faith only over a lifetime of walking, standing, and sitting in special intimacy with God.[37] Yet, as William Tyndale noted in the prologue to his exposition of 1 John, such love begins at conversion, for the converted person loves God and thus his law.[38] Believers learn this deep love over time, from youth to weakness and gray hair (see Ps. 71:9, 18). Such people hunger and thirst after righteousness, and Jesus promises that they will be filled (Matt. 5:6, 10, 17–20).

Passages from Psalms that Paul quotes in Romans 3:10–18 are also helpful here, especially when one reads the quoted psalms in context. Paul argues that the gospel is good news for all who believe (Rom. 1:16–17). Then he sets out to prove that Jews and Gentiles both need to believe this news. Speaking as Christ's suffering apostle (Rom. 1:1–6) to believers known to have suffered (Acts 18:2), in Romans 3:9 he claims that Jews and Gentiles have sinned. To buttress his point, he offers biblical evidence from Psalm 14:1–3 or 53:1–3 (see Rom. 3:10–12); Psalm 5:9 (see Rom. 3:13a); Psalm 140:3 (see Rom. 3:13b); Psalm 10:7 (see Rom. 3:14); Proverbs 1:16 and Isaiah 59:7–8 (see Rom. 3:15–17); and Psalm 36:1 (see Rom. 3:18). Representing those who have accepted the good news and thus suffered at the hands of the wicked, Paul cites texts that decry "the wicked" or

---

[36] Joseph Ratzinger, *Jesus of Nazareth: The Infancy Narratives*, trans. Philip J. Whitmore (New York: Image, 2012), 39–40.

[37] Gordon J. Wenham defines Enoch's walk with God in this manner in *Genesis 1–15*, WBC 1 (Waco, TX: Word, 1987), 127.

[38] William Tyndale, *Works of William Tyndale* (1531; repr. Carlisle, PA: Banner of Truth, 2010), 2:136.

"evildoers" (Pss. 14:4; 53:4; 5:4–6; 140:1, 4; 10:3–4; Prov. 1:10; Isa. 59:1–6; 36:1) among all mankind (Ps. 53:2) and among David's foreign and domestic enemies (Pss. 5:8; 140:1–3; 10:2–6; 36:1–4). In short, he identifies wicked Jews and Gentiles who reject God and his people. In every instance he takes the voice of the righteous ones in the texts cited. Finally, in Romans 4:1–24 Paul cites Genesis 15:6 and Psalm 32:1–2 to assert that people are justified by faith. In Romans 12:1–3 he avers that those who trust in Christ do God's will by faith, which conforms them to God's will. Wicked Jews and Gentiles still sin against God and his people.

Thus Paul treats the righteous ones in the Psalms, whose point of view he adopts in Romans 3:10–18, as the justified-by-faith ones he features in Romans 4:1–24; 5:1–5. As Ratzinger puts it, "If we may say that the form of piety in the New Testament can be summed up in the expression 'a believer,' then the Old Testament idea of a whole life lived according to sacred Scripture is summed up in the idea of 'a just man.'"[39] All Paul's letters demonstrate that he could not imagine a justified person who did not live in a righteous way. The righteous ones in Psalms and Paul are not sinless, so their designation does not depend on moral perfection. It depends rather on God's saving grace and their faith that leads to their relational walk with God. So when Paul and the psalmists claim that no one is righteous, they are speaking from the perspective of believers looking at humanity, Gentile and Jew, that persecutes the righteous because they oppose God. The righteous walk with God because they love him. They endure the wrath of those who do not. Paul's willingness to accept beatings and imprisonment proves this point.

Forming Wise Followers of God: Proverbs, Job, and Ruth

Proverbs, Job, and Ruth portray spiritual formation as wise living. Though definitions vary, James Crenshaw rightly stresses wisdom as balanced living that does God's will based on God's Word.[40] The wise person knows Yahweh's teaching (Prov. 1:2–6), fears Yahweh (Prov. 1:7), has Yahweh's Spirit (Prov. 1:23), and stays on Yahweh's paths (Prov. 4:26–27).

Furthermore, wisdom cannot be gained all at once. Proverbs presents wisdom as calling out to the young (Proverbs 7–9), shaping young and veteran community members (Proverbs 10–24), forming leaders (Prov. 25:1–31:9), and identifying a worthy woman (Prov. 31:10–31).[41] Wisdom

---

[39] Ratzinger, *Jesus of Nazareth*, 39.
[40] See James Crenshaw, *Wisdom: An Introduction* (Atlanta: John Knox Press, 1981), 11–24.
[41] See Paul R. House, *Old Testament Survey* (Nashville, TN: B&H, 1992), 222–32.

calls young people to seek her teachings over their whole lives. Only fools choose to stay babes in wisdom (Prov. 1:22). Similarly, Job's faith and wisdom grow through dialogue with his friends. Likewise, Ruth decides to walk with Yahweh spiritually when she converts (Ruth 1:16–18) and physically when she goes with Naomi to Bethlehem (1:19–22). In each book wise patterns of speech, work, family, and community come from God through discipline and hope. There is no fast track. As Leviticus 25 indicates, a just society unfolds in seven- and fifty-year cycles, at the quickest. Jonah, Jeremiah, Baruch, Job, and Ruth would surely agree with Moses and the Wisdom writers on this point.

To conclude this section, I think it appropriate to return briefly to Psalms 111–112. The writer pledges to thank Yahweh in Psalm 111:1 and blesses God and his commands in Psalm 112:1. He calls Yahweh's works great and worthy of universal study in Psalm 111:2 and recognizes the righteous one's mighty deeds in Psalm 112:2. Becoming bolder, in Psalms 111:3 and 112:3 the writer declares that the righteousness of both Yahweh and the one who fears him endures forever, and in Psalms 111:4 and 112:4 he calls both Yahweh and the one who fears him gracious and compassionate. Psalm 112:5–10 describes the righteous person as steady, worthy to be remembered, firm of heart, generous, and confident of victory over the wicked. These traits come from Yahweh's faithfulness, power, trustworthy words, and redeeming ways (112:5–9). All these benefits for the righteous one accrue from reverence for Yahweh, which is the beginning of wisdom (112:10). This passage thereby links Genesis 1:26–2:3; Exodus 34:5–7; and the experienced wisdom of Jeremiah, Baruch, and Jonah.

Synthesis

The Writings continue the Bible's multifaceted description of spiritual formation. As before, only those who know God can move toward maturity. A commitment to faith and thus to relationship begins the process. Until a person fears God, there is no beginning of wisdom, no straight path of righteousness. Once taken, that pathway lasts a lifetime. Given changing situations over long periods of time, wisdom and righteousness develop and shift as faithful priests and stewards learn to reflect God's image. Wendell Berry observes that too often people think jobs are big and time is short, which causes them to take shortcuts and exploit people and places.[42] The Writings reveal that he is correct to argue

---

[42] Wendell Berry, *Standing by Words* (Berkeley, CA: Counterpoint, 1983), 69.

that our lives and jobs are small parts of a greater whole unfolding over a long period of time.[43] Patience and careful work can grow from such transforming wisdom.

Resources for formation do not change in the Writings, but their nature grows clearer. Dozens of prayers teach readers to pray. Further Scripture and uses of previous Scripture offer mature ways of utilizing God's Word. Instruction about stewardship and gratitude for creation's blessing encourage stewardship. Ezra and Nehemiah's lives show how important are the places and rhythms of worship for ongoing spiritual formation, and 1–2 Chronicles demonstrates how vital history is for proper perspective. Daniel and Esther prove how proper devotion to God and his people sustains the wise and righteous in horrific circumstances. Nehemiah 9:38 reminds readers that no matter how much time passes, Yahweh's gracious and merciful character lies behind all truly good work and hopes for a reformed people of God.

Conclusion

Developing mature, wise, just, and loving priests and stewards in God's image challenges even the bravest soul. The task seems so immense, so difficult. After all, there is no instantaneous perpetual wisdom, for life is not static. Spiritual formation is not abstract, an easy math problem, a set of rules or practices alone. It is part of living. Spiritual formation provides no escape from reality or avoidance of home life, for wisdom and righteousness require work made possible and shaped only by faith in God.

Yet nothing gives joy like serious commitments. God calls and shapes through resources he gives. His Word, people, and friendship provide the process with joyful meaning. The fact that human beings can possess and reflect the Creator's character boggles the mind and humbles the heart as it transforms people who follow God. No wonder Paul gave up everything he once held dear to walk a path that led to knowing Christ and the power of his resurrection (Phil. 3:1–10). No wonder Hebrews 11 calls all believers to do the same.

---

[43] Ibid., 70–79.

3

NEW CREATION: SPIRITUALITY ACCORDING TO JESUS

CHARLES L. QUARLES

The supreme authority on spirituality is surely the Lord Jesus. John 3:34 describes Jesus as the one to whom the Father has given the Spirit "without measure."[1] Jesus is uniquely qualified to teach about the life of the Spirit and the effects of the Spirit on a person's conduct and character.

Jesus' teaching presents a robust doctrine of spirituality. He explains the horrifying realities of the sinner's fallen condition as well as the sinner's enormous need for spirituality. He describes his own provision for the spirituality of his disciples. He details the nature and marks of true spirituality. He also teaches frankly about the disciples' need for growth in spirituality and gives clear instructions for how a disciple should pursue this growth. Finally, he describes the essential role the church plays in the spirituality of its members.

Our Fallen Condition and Need for Spirituality

Although most people readily assume that all people are basically good, Jesus holds no such exalted view of humanity. Although he affirms that humans were made by God (Matt. 19:4), and his teaching implies that humans are bearers of the divine image (Mark 12:16),[2] he clearly teaches that

---

[1] Scholars debate whether John 3:34 refers to the Father's bestowal of the Spirit to Jesus or Jesus' impartation of the Spirit to his disciples. For the former view, see Gary Burge, *John*, NIVAC (Grand Rapids, MI: Zondervan, 2000), 123.

[2] Scholars debate whether the reference to "image" in Mark 12:15–17 implies that man was created in the image of God and thus belongs to him. For the view that a reference to the divine image is intended, see David T. Ball, "What Jesus Really Means by 'Render unto Caesar' (It's Not About Taxes)," *Bible Review* 19 (2003): 14–17; James R. Edwards, *The Gospel according to Mark*, Pillar New Testament Commentary (Grand Rapids, MI:

humans are depraved. This depravity makes true spirituality impossible apart from the dramatic intervention of God himself.

Slavery to Sin

In John 8:34 Jesus declares, "Truly, truly, I say to you, everyone who practices sin is a slave to sin." He portrays sin as a master who owns the sinner, holds the sinner in subjection, and forces the slave into his service. Although Jesus' opponents insist that they are free, Jesus adamantly denies their claims to freedom. He teaches that true freedom is possible only as sinners are liberated from their slavery to sin by the truth that Jesus reveals (8:32).

Clearly, the pursuit of spirituality is destined for failure unless the sinner has been set free from his slavery to sin by Jesus. Sin is a master that will tolerate no runaways. The slave wears the master's brand, and his neck is locked in the master's yoke. Escape is impossible. Even if the lost sinner should aspire to any righteous actions or speech, his evil taskmaster will quickly corral any such aspiration. The slave's condition is hopeless unless a liberator more powerful than his present master crushes his tyranny and grants freedom to the slave. Jesus came to bind the strong man and plunder his possessions (Matt. 12:29 par. Mark 3:27). He came to announce the arrival of the Year of Jubilee in which the Anointed One would proclaim liberty to the captives and set at liberty the oppressed (Luke 4:18–19).

Corrupt Heart

The imagery of slavery to sin should not give the impression that sin is merely an external force with which the sinner contends. Sin rules over the sinner because of his own internal condition, his corrupt spiritual nature. In a shockingly grim portrayal of the sinner's spiritual condition, Jesus teaches:

> Are you also still without understanding? Do you not see that whatever goes into the mouth passes into the stomach and is expelled? But what comes out of the mouth proceeds from the heart, and this defiles a person. For out of the heart come evil thoughts, murder, adultery, sexual immorality, theft, false witness, slander. These are what defile a person. (Matt. 15:16–20)

Eerdmans, 2002), 364; R. H. Gundry, *Matthew: A Commentary on His Handbook for a Mixed Church under Persecution*, 2nd ed. (Grand Rapids, MI: Eerdmans, 1994), 443; Michael J. Wilkins, *Matthew*, NIVAC (Grand Rapids, MI: Zondervan, 2004), 722.

Wicked behavior is not prompted merely by external influences such as a decadent culture, peer pressure, poor parenting, or educational systems that promote non-Christian views and ideals. Wicked behavior issues from within. Leon Morris observes: "Jesus is drawing attention to the fact that wickedness takes its origin in our innermost being."[3] Sinful behavior is the necessary by-product of a depraved heart.[4] The rabbis taught that the human heart has two inclinations: a good inclination and an evil one (*m. Ber.* 9:5). Yet when Christ describes the sinner, he makes no reference to righteous behavior's flowing from the good inclination of the heart. Instead, the sinner's heart is merely the source of impurity that defiles his conduct, speech, thoughts, and desires. Christ's view of the sinner's moral nature has far more in common with the anthropology of the Old Testament prophets than with that of the rabbis. After complaining repeatedly about the stubborn, rebellious, evil hearts of the people (Jer. 3:17; 4:14; 5:23; 9:26; 11:8; 13:10), the prophet Jeremiah exclaims, "The heart is deceitful above all things, and desperately sick; who can understand it?" (17:9).

In order to pursue spirituality, the sinner must experience a heart transplant. The corrupt heart must be replaced by the pure heart (Matt. 5:8) that enables the individual to look at last upon God in all of his glory and holiness.

Hard Heart

Jesus teaches that the sinner's heart is not only corrupt; it is also hard. When Jesus discusses the extenuating circumstances that prompted God in the Mosaic Law to permit divorce for sexual immorality, he explains, "Because of your hardness of heart Moses allowed you to divorce your wives, but from from the beginning it was not so" (Matt. 19:8). His statement contrasts humanity's pre-fall and post-fall conditions. Prior to the fall, humans had hearts that were good (Gen. 1:26–27). After the fall, our hearts are corrupt and rebellious—hard (Gen. 6:5). Earlier, in Matthew 13:14–15, Jesus diagnoses the spiritual condition of the people using a quotation from Isaiah 6:9–10 that associates hardness of heart with spiritual blindness, spiritual deafness, insensitivity to God's instruction, and stubborn refusal to repent. Other OT texts, with which Jesus was certainly

---

[3] Leon Morris, *The Gospel according to Matthew*, Pillar New Testament Commentary (Grand Rapids, MI: Eerdmans, 1992), 400.

[4] A marginal note on Matt. 15:16–20 in J. A. Bengel's *German Version of the New Testament* (1753) comments: "The filth of the latrine is not so great as that of a human heart not yet cleansed." See Bengel, *Gnomon of the New Testament*, trans. Charlton T. Lewis and Marvin Vincent (Philadelphia: Perkinpine & Higgins, 1862), 1:200.

familiar, refer to this hard heart (Job 41:24; Ps. 119:70). Later Paul will also indict sinners for their hard and impenitent hearts (Rom. 2:5; Eph. 4:18).

The teachings of Jesus preserved in John's Gospel express this same truth. Jesus insists that spiritual blindness is not merely a symptom of the sinner's inability to see the truth but is also a result of his determined refusal to acknowledge the truth:

> This is the judgment: the light has come into the world, and people loved the darkness rather than the light because their works were evil. For everyone who does wicked things hates the light and does not come to the light, lest his works should be exposed. (John 3:19–20)

Satanic Character

Jesus' most jarring description of the depravity of the sinner identifies unbelievers as children of Satan himself. In John 8:43–45, Jesus asks:

> Why do you not understand what I say? It is because you cannot bear to hear my word. You are of your father the devil, and your will is to do your father's desires. He was a murderer from the beginning, and does not stand in the truth, because there is no truth in him. When he lies, he speaks out of his own character, for he is a liar and the father of lies. But because I tell the truth, you do not believe me.

Jesus thus introduces what may be called the "principle of spiritual genetics." Children naturally bear resemblance to their parents and exhibit characteristics of their parents. Because Satan is the spiritual father of unbelievers, they are like him in remarkable ways. Just as Satan opposes the truth, they oppose the truth. Just as Satan defies the righteous demands of God, they pursue evil desires. They are truly diabolical and manifest the evil nature of the evil one, the very being who epitomizes evil.

Thus the view of humanity taught by Jesus is antithetical to the wildly popular assertion that all people are basically good. Jesus portrays sinners as internally corrupt, inherently depraved, desperately wicked, and shockingly evil. Spirituality is possible only through a radical transformation wrought by Christ through his Spirit.

Christ's Provision for Spirituality

The sinner's desperate spiritual state rules out any possibility of spirituality via attempts at self-improvement. The sinner requires liberation, not self-emancipation. He needs transformation, not mere personal reformation. Jesus offers liberation from slavery to sin through the new exodus. He offers radical transformation through the new covenant, new birth, and the miracle of new creation.

New Exodus

Matthew emphasizes Jesus' resemblance to Moses in many remarkable ways.[5] This emphasis is particularly pronounced in his narrative of Jesus' infancy. Herod's slaughter of the innocents (Matt. 2:16–18) parallels the account of Moses' infancy at several points. In both accounts, an evil pagan king (Pharaoh/Herod) kills male Jewish infants (Hebrews/children of Bethlehem), but God providentially rescues a future deliverer (Moses/Jesus). Other allusions to the Moses narratives confirm Matthew's intention to associate Jesus with Moses. The angel's statement in Matthew 2:20, "Those who sought the child's life are dead," is a conscious allusion to Exodus 4:19, "All the men who were seeking your life are dead." The allusion again associates Herod with Pharaoh and Jesus with Moses. These are only the first of many such parallels in the Gospel of Matthew.[6]

The parallels demonstrate that Jesus is the fulfillment of the well-known "prophet like Moses" prophecy of Deuteronomy 18:15: "The LORD your God will raise up for you a prophet like me from among you, from your brothers—it is to him you shall listen." Although Matthew does not cite this passage using his typical fulfillment formula in order to identify Jesus explicitly as the fulfillment of the prophecy, he instead does something more profound. He shows that the Father himself identifies Jesus as the prophet like Moses. The proclamation of the Father at Jesus' transfiguration is identical to his proclamation at Jesus' baptism: "This is my beloved Son, with whom I am well pleased" (Matt. 3:17; 17:5). However, at the transfiguration, in the context of Jesus' conversation with Moses, the Father adds: "Listen to him." This command is a definite allusion to Deuteronomy 18:15 ("It is to him you shall listen") and marks Jesus unmistakably as the new Moses. Jesus understands this pronouncement, recognizes his own identity, and consciously reenacts features of Moses' ministry in order to confirm his identity as the prophet like Moses.

Jesus' identity as the new Moses is an essential feature of New Testament Christology that has significant implications for soteriology.

---

[5] The classic and most thorough treatment of Jesus' many similarities to Moses is Dale C. Allison Jr., *The New Moses: A Matthean Typology* (Minneapolis: Augsburg Fortress, 1993).

[6] See Charles L. Quarles, *A Theology of Matthew: Jesus Revealed as Deliverer, King, and Incarnate Creator*, Explorations in Biblical Theology (Phillipsburg, NJ: P&R, 2013), 33–46.

Although modern readers may think of Moses primarily as a lawgiver, Jews of the New Testament era thought of him primarily as a savior, redeemer, and deliverer. God acted through Moses to save, redeem, and deliver his people from their slavery in Egypt. The rabbis often insisted that the Messiah would resemble Moses in many ways and would replicate Moses' ministry of redemption. This insistence gave rise to the expression, "As the former redeemer was, so shall the latter redeemer be."[7]

Jesus' identity as the new Moses is related closely to the promise of a new exodus. Both the Pentateuch and the Prophets warned that God would punish the sin of his people by sending them into exile in a foreign land to serve slavishly under the thumb of foreign oppressors. This was comparable to the Egyptian bondage. But they also promised deliverance from this exile, a deliverance often portrayed as a second exodus.[8] Jesus picks up the theme of a new bondage and new exodus. However, he insists that the sinner's greater bondage is to sin and Satan rather than to Roman oppressors, and the greater exodus is liberation from spiritual slavery rather than from Roman occupation.

Jesus teaches that sinners are slaves to sin and insists that only the Son can set them free: "If the Son sets you free, you will be free indeed" (John 8:36). This is very similar to the instruction of the angel to Joseph in Matthew 1:21: "You shall call his name Jesus, for he will save his people from their sins." The promised salvation is described in the broadest terms. It is not merely salvation from the punishment deserved due to sins or the guilt imposed by our sins; it is salvation that snatches Jesus' followers away from sins. The Greek preposition translated "from" (*apo*) clearly expresses separation. In combination with this preposition, the verb "save" describes rescue from one arena and relocation to another, an exodus from the realm in which sins dominate and enslave to a new realm in which we are no longer enslaved. This liberation from captivity to sins frees us to pursue holiness.

New Covenant

During the Last Supper, Jesus holds up the cup and declares, "This cup that is poured out for you is the new covenant in my blood" (Luke 22:20).[9] Jesus' role in inaugurating the new covenant has already been implied by

---

[7] *Qoh. Rab.* 1:9.

[8] For extensive examples from the Old Testament, see Charles L. Quarles, "'Out of Egypt I Called My Son:' Intertextuality and Metalepsis in Matthew 2:15," *Southeastern Theological Review* 8, (Spring 2017): 3–19.

[9] For a treatment of the Lukan form of the Lord's Supper pronouncements that is similar to the treatment here, see I. H. Marshall, *Luke*, NIGTC (Grand Rapids, MI: Eerdmans, 1978), 805–7.

his identity as the prophet like Moses. Just as Moses was the mediator of the old covenant, the new Moses inaugurates the new covenant. In fact, the wording of Jesus' pronouncement in Matthew 26:28, "This is my blood of the covenant," is a clear allusion to Moses' pronouncement in Exodus 24:8, "Behold the blood of the covenant that the LORD has made with you in accordance with all these words."

But Jesus is more than merely the mediator of the new covenant. He is more than one who sprinkles the blood that inaugurates the covenant (Ex. 24:6). He himself is the sacrifice whose blood is shed in order to initiate the new covenant. In all three of the Gospel parallels (Matt. 26:28//Mark 14:24//Luke 22:20), Jesus declares that the blood that inaugurates the new covenant is "*my* blood." The blood that inaugurates the new covenant is not the blood of oxen (Ex. 24:5) but the blood of the mediator, the new Moses himself.

The new covenant inaugurated by Jesus' sacrifice is described in Jeremiah 31:31–34:

> Behold, the days are coming, declares the LORD, when I will make a new covenant with the house of Israel and the house of Judah, not like the covenant that I made with their fathers on the day when I took them by the hand to bring them out of the land of Egypt, my covenant that they broke, though I was their husband, declares the LORD. For this is the covenant that I will make with the house of Israel after those days, declares the LORD: I will put my law within them, and I will write it on their hearts. And I will be their God, and they shall be my people. And no longer shall each one teach his neighbor and each his brother, saying, "Know the LORD," for they shall all know me, from the least of them to the greatest, declares the LORD. For I will forgive their iniquity, and I will remember their sin no more.

This new covenant has several important aspects. First, the covenant promises the complete forgiveness of sin. Iniquity is forgiven and sin forgotten. Second, God causes the covenant beneficiaries to internalize his law so that they naturally and spontaneously fulfill his righteous demands. The old covenant was broken because it was a mere external standard. It told God's people what to do but did not give them the power to do it. However, the new covenant promises that God will transform the sinner from the inside out and thus ensures that the covenant people will not rebel against him. Third, the new covenant establishes a relationship between God and his people that enables his people to know him, not just about him. The sinner who was at enmity with God is reconciled to God. The one who was estranged from him is brought near.[10]

This forgiveness of sin, spiritual transformation, and new relationship with God are the basis for the disciple's spirituality. Without Jesus' establishment of the new covenant, true spirituality would not be possible.

New Birth

Although the phrase "born-again Christian" became something of a cliché in American Christianity in the late twentieth century, few modern church attenders seem to be familiar with the concept of spiritual birth. A survey of over one thousand freshmen at a Christian college found that sixty-five percent could not identify a simple definition of new birth in a multiple-choice question. About half of those who could not define the new birth assumed that it was a reference to reincarnation or transmigration.

Yet the new birth is both an essential doctrine of the Christian gospel and a fundamental component of Christian spirituality. Jesus' clearest explanation of the new birth appears in his discussion with Nicodemus in John 3: "Truly, truly, I say to you, unless one is born again he cannot see the kingdom of God" (John 3:3). When Nicodemus completely misunderstands Jesus' statement and interprets it as if Jesus were referring to a second physical birth, Jesus explains, "That which is born of the flesh is flesh, and that which is born of the Spirit is spirit" (3:6). Jesus' point is that the nature of the parent determines the nature of the offspring.[11] Those given birth by fleshly parents will also be fleshly. Those given birth by the Spirit will be spiritual. The spirituality of those given birth by the Spirit is clarified in John 3:5, as Jesus describes spiritual birth as the process of being "born of water and the Spirit." This reference to water and the Spirit appears to be an allusion to Ezekiel's promise of the new covenant, in which Yahweh declares, "I will sprinkle clean water on you, and you shall be clean from all your uncleannesses," and "I will put my Spirit within you, and cause you to walk in my statutes and be careful to obey my rules" (Ezek. 36:25, 27).

In the new birth, God cleanses the sinner's corruption and causes his own Spirit to indwell him. This transformation results in a lifestyle of obedience to God's commands. Jesus teaches this when he refers to the one

---

[10] See J. A. Thompson, *Jeremiah*, NICOT (Grand Rapids, MI: Eerdmans, 1980), 579–81.
[11] See Craig Keener, *The Gospel of John: A Commentary* (Peabody, MA: Hendrickson, 2003), 552–54.

born of the Spirit as one who "does what is true" and whose "works have been carried out in God" (John 3:21).

New Creation

All four Gospels record John the Baptist's promise that the coming Messiah would baptize sinners with the Holy Spirit (Matt. 3:11; Mark 1:8; Luke 3:16; John 1:33). This spiritual baptism is an allusion to the giving of the Spirit (Ezek. 36:25, 27), which is described as an outpouring of the Spirit in texts such as Isaiah 44:3; Ezekiel 39:29; Joel 2:28–29; and Zechariah 12:10. Throughout the Gospel of John, the Spirit fulfills several different functions. He is paraclete (14:26), a teacher (14:26), and the one who superintends and enables true worship (4:23). Perhaps most importantly, the Spirit is life giver (zōopoioun, "one who creates life or makes alive"; John 6:63). Jesus teaches that the Spirit is the one who imparts new life to Jesus' followers. John 7:39 shows that this life-giving Spirit would be given after Jesus was glorified. This glorification is a reference to Jesus' crucifixion and resurrection.[12] When the Spirit was given, he would indwell believers (14:17: "he will be in you").

John 20:19–22 describes the giving of the Spirit. On the evening of the day of his resurrection, Jesus suddenly appears to his frightened disciples hiding behind locked doors. Twice Jesus pronounces peace on his disciples, both before and after showing the wounds of his crucifixion to the disciples so that they can identify him as the resurrected Lord. Although "peace to you" was the common Hebrew greeting of the day, the repetition of the greeting suggests that it takes on special significance in this context. The double pronouncement signals the fulfillment of the promise of peace in Jesus' earlier teaching (John 14:27; 16:23). It also signals fulfillment of the new covenant, which the prophet Ezekiel described as the "covenant of peace."

The blessings are followed immediately by a commission: "As the Father has sent me, even so I am sending you." This commission is an allusion to the numerous descriptions of Jesus as the one sent from heaven or by the Father.[13]

In John 16:7 Jesus mentions that he will "go away" before sending the Spirit. This is a reference to Jesus' ascension, his return to the Father (John

---

[12] See Andreas Köstenberger, John, BECNT (Grand Rapids, MI: Baker, 2004), 241. Köstenberger noted that glorification in this context was a "Johannine euphemism for the cluster of events centering in the crucifixion." He added, "The present statement thus anticipates the farewell discourse and the commissioning scene in 20:22."
[13] John 4:34; 5:23, 24, 30, 37; 6:39, 44; 7:16, 18, 28, 33; 8:16, 18, 26, 29; 9:4; 12:44, 45, 49; 13:16, 20; 14:24, 26; 15:21; 16:5.

14:2–3; 16:28; 20:17). One's interpretation of the disciples' reception of the Spirit in John 20:19–22 depends largely on how one views Jesus' prerequisite "going away." In the context of John's Gospel, it is difficult to determine confidently whether this going away/return to the Father is a reference to Jesus' bodily ascension or to the departure of Jesus' spirit to heaven during the time between his death and his resurrection.[14] If the anticipated ascension is a spiritual one, then Jesus' promised return to his disciples in texts like John 14:3 may refer to his post-resurrection appearances rather than to the second coming.

Interpreters must also seek to understand how the giving of the Spirit in John 20 is related to the giving of the Spirit at Pentecost several weeks later. Some scholars have suggested that the accounts describe two distinct events in which the Spirit is given, with the events differing mainly in degree or purpose.[15] Several of the early church fathers, including Gregory of Nazianzus, Augustine, and Cyril of Jerusalem, suggested that the giving of the Spirit in John 20 is partial and incomplete, with the bestowal being finalized at Pentecost.[16] Calvin suggested that during the giving of the Spirit in John 20, the disciples "were sprinkled with His grace and not saturated with full power" like they would be later at Pentecost.[17] Calvin added that this first partial endowment of the Spirit anticipates and promises the full blessing of Pentecost: "This breathing should therefore be referred and extended especially to that magnificent sending of the Spirit which He had so often promised."[18] Other scholars have suggested that the Spirit regenerates and indwells the apostles on Easter and grants them power to carry out their mission at Pentecost.[19] Other scholars have argued that the giving of the Spirit

---

[14] For the former view, see Köstenberger, *John*, 574n17. For the latter view, see T. R. Hatina, "John 20,22 in Its Eschatological Context: Promise or Fulfillment?" *Bib* 74 (1993): 196–219.

[15] Although he admits that "the relation of this gift to that made on the day of Pentecost is obscure," Leon Morris points to the diversity of gifts granted by the Spirit in 1 Cor. 12:4 and suggests "the problem is probably to be solved along these lines." See Leon Morris, *The Gospel according to John*, NICNT (Grand Rapids, MI: Eerdmans, 1971), 847.

[16] Thomas C. Oden, ed., *John 11–21*, Ancient Christian Commentary on Scripture 4B (Downers Grove, IL: InterVarsity, 2007), 360–62.

[17] John Calvin, *The Gospel according to St. John 11–21 and the First Epistle of John*, trans. T. H. L. Parker, ed. D. W. Torrance and T. F. Torrance (Grand Rapids, MI: Eerdmans, 1961), 205.

[18] Ibid.

[19] See Brian Neil Peterson, *John's Use of Ezekiel: Understanding the Unique Perspective of the Fourth Gospel* (Minneapolis: Fortress, 2015), 179–82; A. W. Pink, *Exposition of the Gospel of John* (Grand Rapids, MI: Zondervan, 1945), 286–87; Max Turner, *The Holy Spirit and Spiritual Gifts* (Peabody, MA: Hendrickson, 1999), 97–102. Leon Morris likewise writes that this is the occasion on which the Spirit indwells the disciples "bringing both a new creation and life from the dead" (*John*, 846). For a similar view, see B. Lindars, *New Century Bible Commentary* (London: Oliphants, 1972), 611. For the view that John 20:22 is the moment in which the apostles are regenerated, see also James D. G. Dunn, *The Baptism in the Holy Spirit* (Philadelphia: Westminster, 1970), 180. Dunn writes that the apostles "became regenerate . . . only here and not before—only then was the spiritual life (breath) of the new creation communicated to them."

in John 20:22 is symbolic and anticipates the outpouring of the Spirit at Pentecost.[20]

Regardless of their approach to the relationship between John 20 and Acts 2, most scholars recognize that Jesus' act of breathing on the disciples is intended to recall two important Old Testament texts. The verb "breathe" (*emphusaō*) appears in the LXX nine times. The first occurrence is in Genesis 2:7: "The LORD God formed the man of dust from the ground and breathed into his nostrils the breath of life, and the man became a living creature." Philo portrayed the original act of creation as an impartation of the divine spirit: "That which he breathed in [*enephusēsen*] was nothing else than a Divine breath [or Spirit: *pneuma theion*]."[21] Similarly, the author of the Wisdom of Solomon describes why humanity abandoned the worship of the Creator for the worship of idols: "For he did not know the one who formed him and inspired him with an active soul and breathed [*emphusēsanta*] into him a living spirit."[22] Jesus' action seems to be a reenactment of Yahweh's creative work described in these texts.[23] This suggests that Jesus wishes to signal that with the impartation of the Holy Spirit, he is performing an act of new creation. The renewal and restoration of sinful humanity have begun.

More importantly, in Ezekiel's vision of the valley of dry bones, the Lord commands the prophet to summon the breath/spirit (*pneuma*) from the four winds and say, "Breathe [*emphusēsen*] on these slain, that they may live" (Ezek. 37:9). The context shows that the resurrection of the dead pictures the fulfillment of the new covenant in which God places his Spirit in his people and gives them new life (36:27; 37:14). Interestingly, Ezekiel refers to the new covenant as a covenant "of peace" (34:25; 37:26), and Jesus pronounces "peace" on his disciples no less than three times in the

---

[20] This view was affirmed by Theodore of Mopseustia and has more recently been advocated by several evangelical scholars, such as D. A. Carson, *The Gospel according to John*, Pillar New Testament Commentary (Grand Rapids, MI: Eerdmans, 1991), 649–55; Köstenberger, *John*, 573–75; and Thomas R. Schreiner, *New Testament Theology: Magnifying God in Christ* (Grand Rapids, MI: Baker, 2008), 465–66. For recent arguments against the symbolic interpretation, see Gary Burge, *The Anointed Community: The Holy Spirit in the Johannine Tradition* (Grand Rapids, MI: Eerdmans, 1987), 114–49; Hatina, "John 20:22 in Its Eschatological Context," 196–219; R. W. Lyon, "John 20:22 Once More," *Asbury Theological Journal* 43 (1988): 73–85; J. Swetnam, "Bestowal of the Spirit in the Fourth Gospel," *Bib* 74 (1993): 556–76. B. F. Westcott (*The Gospel according to St. John* [1881; repr., Grand Rapids, MI: Eerdmans, 1978], 295) sternly rejected the view: "To regard the words and act as a promise only and a symbol of the future gift is wholly arbitrary and unnatural."
[21] *Creation* 135; LCL, 1.107. Philo of Alexandria was a contemporary of Jesus. He lived from c. 20 BC to AD 50. For a brief introduction, see Craig A. Evans, *Ancient Texts for New Testament Studies: A Guide to the Background Literature* (Grand Rapids, MI: Baker, 2005), 168–73.
[22] Wis. 15:11. Wisdom of Solomon was written sometime between 220 and 100 BC. See David A. deSilva, *Introducing the Apocrypha: Message, Context, and Significance* (Grand Rapids, MI: Baker Academic, 2002), 132–33.
[23] Most commentators acknowledge this. J. Ramsey Michaels's position is a bit baffling: "It is doubtful that this biblical text [Gen. 2:7] is explicitly in view." J. Ramsey Michaels, *The Gospel of John*, NICNT (Grand Rapids, MI: Eerdmans, 2010), 1010.

post-resurrection appearances (John 20:19, 21, 26).[24] The connections between Ezekiel 37 and Jesus' insufflation (breathing out) imply that this is an act of new creation in which Jesus imparts the Spirit to his disciples to fulfill the promise of the new covenant and transform the lives of his followers.

If one thinks in Pauline terms, John 20:22 fulfills the promise of 2 Corinthians 5:17. The disciples are made new creatures. Old things have passed away and the new has come. This dramatic transformation is the basis for the spirituality of Jesus' followers.

The Nature of the Disciple's Spirituality

The most detailed description of the spirituality of the Christian disciple from Jesus' teaching appears in the Sermon on the Mount (Matthew 5–7). The Sermon on the Mount shows that the disciple will be characterized by a righteousness that vastly exceeds even that of the most moral nonbeliever. This righteousness will be expressed through love for other disciples and even bitter enemies by a willingness to forgive and by marital faithfulness, sexual purity, honesty and integrity, and generosity to the needy.[25]

Basic Characteristics of the Disciple

Jesus begins the Sermon on the Mount by pronouncing blessings on his disciples. The future tense of the second clause of the Beatitudes in Matthew 5:4–9 indicates that these blessings are primarily eschatological in nature. Believers will know the full extent of divine comfort, inherit the earth, be satiated with righteousness, and see God face-to-face after the return of Jesus Christ. However, the first clause of each of the Beatitudes describes characteristics manifested in true disciples in the present. Thus the Beatitudes provide a vivid portrait of the disciple and his distinguishing marks.

The phrase "poor in spirit" refers to those who recognize that they are spiritual beggars with nothing to offer God. Their only hope is to depend on God's grace alone for their salvation. Robert Guelich aptly describes the "poor in spirit" as those who stand "without pretense before God, stripped of all self-sufficiency, self-security, and self-righteousness."[26]

---

[24] See Peterson, *John's Use of Ezekiel*, 165–82, esp. 176–79.
[25] This section briefly summarizes material from Charles L. Quarles, *The Sermon on the Mount: Restoring Christ's Message to the Modern Church* (Nashville, TN: B&H Academic, 2011).
[26] Robert Guelich, *The Sermon on the Mount* (Dallas: Word, 1982), 98.

"Those who mourn" are those who are grieved deeply by their sin. They offer to God the broken and humbled heart that David notes will please God more than any ritual act (Ps. 51:16–17). Like John the Baptist (Matt. 3:2), Jesus preaches a gospel that calls sinners to repentance (Matt. 4:17). The first two beatitudes show that Jesus' disciples are truly and deeply repentant.

The "meek" are those who live in submission to God. After recognizing their spiritual poverty and grieving over their past rebellion against God, they submit their lives to God's authority. This beatitude is drawn from Psalm 37, which describes the meek as those who trust in the Lord, delight in the Lord, put their hope in him, and live righteously because the instruction of God is in their heart.

This wholehearted surrender to God prompts an intense longing for righteousness. In first-century Palestine, where both food and water were sometimes scarce, Jesus' hearers would have experienced gnawing stomachs and parched tongues, thus recognizing "hunger and thirst" as vivid metaphors for powerful cravings. Jesus describes his disciples as those who long for righteousness more than a starving man craves his next bite of bread or a dehydrated woman yearns for a sip of water. The consistent use of the term *righteousness* in Matthew shows that this is a reference to imparted, not merely imputed, righteousness. Although disciples will be grateful that they are declared righteous by God on the basis of Jesus' sacrificial death, they still desperately desire to live righteously themselves.

Jesus describes his disciples further as the "merciful." The truly repentant person who is keenly aware of his own faults and astounded by God's great mercy to him will be eager to express mercy to others. The best commentary on this beatitude is the parable of the unforgiving servant, which concludes with the king's indicting question, "Should not you have had mercy on your fellow servant, as I had mercy on you?" (Matt. 18:33). Although the Sermon on the Mount will go on to describe other acts of mercy, such as gifts to the poor (6:2), mercy especially compels Jesus' disciples to offer others gracious forgiveness for their sins.

Although the spiritual hunger described in Matthew 5:6 will not be satisfied fully until a disciple's resurrection and glorification, Jesus nevertheless described his disciples as those who have already experienced a radical spiritual transformation that justifies classifying them as the "pure in heart." This description is an allusion to Psalm 24:4–6. In Psalm 24, purity in heart refers to internal purity associated with moral integrity. The beatitude indicates the new covenant is being fulfilled through Jesus'

ministry. The inscription of the law on the sinner's heart and the indwelling of the Holy Spirit promised in the new covenant result in a changed
life characterized by righteous behavior.

The description of Jesus' disciples as "peacemakers" portrays them as
those eager to seek a reconciliation that brings an end to conflict between
individuals, especially between individual disciples and other people.
Jesus will provide examples of the behavior of a peacemaker later, in Matthew 5:21–48. Disciples will put an end to conflict with others by offering
sincere apologies and restitution to those they have sinned against, by
refusing to seek revenge, by serving their enemies humbly, and by loving
even those who refuse to love in return.

Finally, Jesus' disciples are those who are persecuted both for the
righteous deeds they perform and for their allegiance to Jesus. This attests
to the disciple's faithfulness to Jesus even in the face of hostility, torture,
or martyrdom. True disciples are not fair-weather friends who are loyal
to their master only when such loyalty is easy. They will seek to be true to
Jesus even when the world loathes them just as it detested him.

The new character wrought by Christ in the disciples serves as the
basis for the surpassing righteousness that Jesus describes later in the Sermon on the Mount.

Surpassing Righteousness

Jesus urges his disciples to obey the commandments of the Old Testament
as he interprets them in his teaching. Rabbinic interpreters sometimes
softened the demands of the moral and ethical imperatives of the law or
sought loopholes for evading those demands. Jesus prohibits his followers from relaxing the commandments or encouraging others to do so. His
followers should personally keep the commandments and should teach
others to do the same. Jesus concludes, "Unless your righteousness exceeds that of the scribes and Pharisees, you will never enter the kingdom
of heaven" (Matt. 5:20).

To many modern readers, the Pharisees are little more than notorious
hypocrites. Thus the standard of righteousness established by the Pharisees seems easily surpassed. But Matthew's original readers likely viewed
the Pharisees as paragons of virtue, the most scrupulous observers of the
law in their day. Josephus, a Jewish historian who lived in the first century
AD, described the Pharisees as those who think "they . . . excel others in
the accurate knowledge of the laws of their fathers" (*Life* 191 §38). The
Pharisees were recognized experts in Old Testmament law and the tra-

ditional rules related to it. Josephus described one Pharisee as confessing that he "desired to be a righteous man, and to do all by which he might please God and them, since the Pharisees espouse such convictions" (*Ant.* 13.10.5 §289). The same Pharisee begged other members of the sect to examine his life carefully and, if he did anything wrong or strayed from the path of righteousness in the slightest, to correct him and call him back to righteousness. Josephus seems to express the general opinion of the Pharisees in popular Judaism of the first century AD. Thus, in the original context, Jesus' demand that the righteousness of his disciples must surpass that of the Pharisees likely prompted gasps, startled double takes, and mumbled protests of "Impossible!"

Some theologians have recognized the loftiness of Jesus' demand and have concluded that the surpassing righteousness of Jesus' disciples must be imputed righteousness, the righteousness God credits to the believer's account in justification. However, the context of the Sermon on the Mount makes it quite clear that the surpassing righteousness Jesus demands is *imparted* righteousness rather than mere imputed righteousness. It refers not to a righteous standing before the heavenly Judge but to actual righteous character, behavior, and speech like that described in the next section of Jesus' sermon.

Scholars debate whether the righteousness of the disciple surpasses that of the Pharisees in quantity or in quality. Jesus likely intends no such distinction. He clearly teaches that the righteousness of the disciple is extraordinary in both quantity *and* quality. The parable of the soils seems to stress the amazing quantity of righteous acts performed by the disciple. The yield produced by the seed that falls on fertile ground symbolizes the "fruit," the righteous deeds and words, performed by the true disciple (Matt. 3:8, 10; 7:16–20; 12:33; 21:19, 34, 43). A good harvest in this primitive agricultural age was a sevenfold to fifteenfold harvest. A thirtyfold harvest was a bumper crop. Yields of sixtyfold and one hundredfold were double and more than triple a bumper crop.[27] Through the astonishing abundance of fruit produced by the seed rooted in fertile soil, Jesus depicts the stunning quantity of righteous deeds and words that the disciple produces.

On the other hand, the righteousness of the disciple also surpasses that of the Pharisees in quality. Surpassing righteousness focuses on the spirit of the law and not merely on its letter (15:1–6). It focuses on moral

---

[27] Quarles, *Sermon on the Mount*, 33.

issues and not mere ritual issues (15:10–20; 23:25–28). It focuses on the most important matters of the law rather than obsessing about minor issues (23:23). Surpassing righteousness does more than merely obey God's explicit commands; it expresses the heavenly Father's own character (5:9, 45, esp. 48).

Love

Jesus teaches that the disciple's surpassing righteousness will be manifested in sincere and deep love for God and others. When asked to identify the greatest commandment in the law, Jesus insists that the greatest commandment is Deuteronomy 6:5: "You shall love the LORD your God with all your heart and with all your soul and with all your might." The second greatest commandment is Leviticus 19:18: "You shall love your neighbor as yourself." Jesus argues that these two commandments encapsulate the message of the entire OT: "On these two commandments depend all the Law and the Prophets" (Matt. 22:40). Thus it is no surprise that Jesus views love for others as the essence of this surpassing righteousness (5:43–48).

Some rabbis misinterpreted Leviticus 19:18 by narrowly defining *neighbor* as a fellow Israelite who lived righteously. This reduced the commandment to a weak imperative to love those one would ordinarily love anyway. Jesus counters that the neighbor of Leviticus 19:18 includes even one's personal enemies. Jesus is emphatic that disciples must not merely love those who love them back. Even tax collectors and pagans are capable of this selfishly motivated "love." Disciples are to express this love for their enemies by praying for their persecutors, kindly greeting opponents, and even carrying the burden imposed by a conscription by their Roman oppressors for an extra mile.

Jesus defends this interpretation based on the spiritual principle we have called "the law of spiritual genetics." The principle "like father, like son" is true not only in biology. It applies to spiritual relationships as well (Matt. 5:48). If disciples are truly children of the heavenly Father, they will resemble him in their character and behavior.[28] They will love like he loves. The heavenly Father shows love to his enemies. He displays his compassion by causing his sun to shine and his rain to fall on the crops even of the wicked (v. 45). Because the Father loves people indiscriminately, his true children must as well.

---

[28] The apostle John states this principle very explicitly in 1 John 3:9. John derives this principle from the teaching of Jesus himself.

Jesus also emphasizes the importance of love in John 13:34–35. He offers a "new commandment," ordering his disciples to love each other just as Jesus loves them. The commandment to love others is not new. However, the depth and degree of love required by the command is completely unprecedented. No longer are believers merely to love others like they love themselves. They are to have a love for others matching Christ's own sacrificial love. Jesus identifies this as the hallmark of true disciples. Clearly, true spirituality requires Christlike compassion for others.

Forgiveness

Jesus emphasizes that the surpassing righteousness of the true disciple will be characterized by a willingness to forgive others. This theme is introduced in Jesus' warning against harboring resentment against spiritual brothers (Matt. 5:21–22) and his command to seek reconciliation with those we have harmed (vv. 23–26). The theme is most prominent in the model prayer that lies at the center of the Sermon on the Mount. Jesus teaches his disciples to pray for forgiveness from God "as we also have forgiven our debtors" (6:12). This is the only petition in the model prayer on which Jesus offers immediate commentary (vv. 14–15). Jesus also stresses the necessity of forgiving others in his parable of the unforgiving servant (18:21–35). Although forgiving others does not qualify a person to receive forgiveness from God, it is nevertheless a requirement for receiving God's forgiveness in eschatological judgment. The heavenly Father is characterized by gracious forgiveness of sinners. If professing disciples do not exhibit this forgiveness to others, that failure demonstrates that they do not bear the character of the Father and thus are not his true children (Matt. 5:44–45, 48).

Marital Faithfulness

Jesus teaches that surpassing righteousness involves faithfulness to the covenant of marriage. He recognizes that marital union was established by God, and that union is not to be broken (Matt. 19:6). Many Jewish teachers of his day permitted men to divorce their wives for practically any reason, including the presence of unattractive physical features, failure to perform household chores, failure to offer sexual intimacy frequently enough, or even overcooking a meal. By contrast, Jesus permits divorce only for the innocent spouse in situations in which the other spouse is an unrepentant adulterer whose persistent sexual sin reduces the marriage to a mere legal technicality.

The rarity of commitment to a single spouse for a lifetime causes Jesus' own disciples initially to view the lifelong marriage affirmed by Jesus as a trap that should be avoided altogether (Matt. 19:10). But Jesus explains that radical love and fidelity within marriage are now possible because of the transformation he works in the believer's heart. Moses permitted divorce "because of your hardness of heart." But Jesus reminds his followers that prior to the fall, divorce was not permitted ("Moses allowed you to divorce your wives, but from the beginning it was not so," Matt. 19:8). Prior to the fall, Adam and Eve's hearts were pure and tender so that divorce was neither imagined nor desired. Since Jesus reverses the consequences of the fall and grants his disciples a pure heart (Matt. 5:8), Christian marriage should be like the inseparable bond between Adam and Eve in Eden.

Although many legal experts among the Pharisees excused divorce for the most trivial matters, the righteousness surpassing that of the scribes and Pharisees values the sanctity and honors the permanence of marriage.

Sexual Purity

Jesus teaches that the surpassing righteousness of the Christian disciple exceeds ordinary standards for sexual purity. Although some interpreters defined the adultery prohibited in the seventh commandment narrowly and in the process approved behaviors that the commandment intended to forbid, Jesus allows no such loopholes. He uses the tenth commandment in Exodus 20:17 ("You shall not covet [or lust after] your neighbor's wife") to spell out the full implications of the seventh commandment in Exodus 20:14 ("You shall not commit adultery"). Thus he prohibits lustfully gawking at a woman, since this is the first step toward full-fledged adultery. Jesus calls for the sanctification of the believer's imagination as well as his actions. He urges his disciples to pursue purity in thoughts, desires, and behavior.

Christ presents this purity as such a high priority for the believer that it is worthy of any sacrifice. He bluntly teaches that if the right hand causes the disciple's spiritual downfall, it should be cut off. If the right eye causes the disciple to sin and ultimately be cast into hell, it should be plucked out. Of course, Jesus teaches that sin is caused by an evil heart (Matt. 15:19–20), not eyes or hands. Jesus assumes that it is obvious that literally sacrificing an eye or hand would not purify one's heart or mind. Ascetics who have sought purity through emasculation or other mutilation of the body have confirmed this reality. Nevertheless, Jesus teaches that such a sacrifice would be appropriate if it were effective, for the disciple craves righteousness and desires to enter the kingdom above all else (5:6; 6:33).

Honesty and Integrity

The surpassing righteousness of the Christian disciple expresses itself in honesty and integrity exceeding that of the Pharisees. The Pharisees developed an elaborate system of valid and invalid oaths enabling them to evade the obligation to tell the truth or keep their word due to legal loopholes. The system permitted the Pharisees to deceive those who did not know the system while remaining exempt from the charge of deception. The approach was similar to the childhood concept that it is permissible to lie if one's fingers are crossed behind the back. Jesus condemns this entire system of oaths and vows. He urges his disciples to tell the truth so fully and consistently that they are deemed trustworthy without needing to swear or promise. A simple yes or no should be sufficient. He demands absolute integrity of his disciples in all of their words and dealings.

Generosity and Proper Priorities

Jesus teaches that the surpassing righteousness of his disciples entails putting material wealth in proper perspective and being willing to give generously to meet the needs of fellow disciples. The beatitude "Blessed are the merciful, for they shall receive mercy" (Matt. 5:7) is likely intended to encourage generosity to others, since the key terms in Matthew 5:7 (*eleēmōn, eleeō*) are related to the term for gifts for the needy (*eleēmosunē*, "acts of mercy") in Matthew 6:2.

Naturally, disciples will be most willing to share resources generously with the needy if they value heavenly treasures above earthly wealth (6:19–21), renounce the sin of greed and seek the virtue of generosity (6:22–23), repent of permitting love for money to rival love for God (6:24), trust the gracious providence of God to satisfy their needs (6:25–30), and value the kingdom of God and his righteousness above all else (6:33).

Proper Motivation for Righteous Deeds

Jesus stresses that the surpassing righteousness of his disciples requires not only doing the right thing but also doing the right thing for the right reason. Deeds are not truly righteous unless they are motivated by a desire to please the heavenly Father rather than to impress other people and by a longing for eschatological reward rather than human applause. Good works performed to impress other people are essentially hypocritical (Matt. 6:1–18) and displeasing to God.

The Need for Growth in Spirituality

Although Jesus' teaching indicates that believers have experienced a radical transformation resulting in godly character and behavior, Christ nevertheless insists that the sinner's transformation is not yet complete. He acknowledges that the saint's current state involves struggle with sins, and the saint will sometimes fail in that struggle. Theologians often speak of the tension between the "already" and the "not yet" in Paul's writings. This contrast is based on the observation that believers are not what they once were and yet are still not all that they will ultimately be. That same tension appears in the teaching of Jesus related to the condition and experience of his disciples.

Jesus' Rebukes of Disciples after Their Reception of the Spirit

The narrative following Jesus' resurrection appearance and his impartation of the Spirit shows that the disciples were still not all that they should be. John 20:24–27 records Thomas's continuing doubt, even after the giving of the Spirit. Even though he believes and worships after Jesus appears to him with proofs of his resurrection, Jesus' reply to him sounds like a mild rebuke: "Have you believed because you have seen me? Blessed are those who have not seen and yet have believed" (v. 29). The statement expresses Jesus' dissatisfaction with Thomas's skepticism.

Similarly, Peter receives a mild rebuke after the resurrection. In John 21:18–19, Jesus foretells Peter's arrest and ultimate martyrdom. Peter's immediate reaction is to compare his destiny to that of the other apostles. He points to the beloved disciple and asks, "Lord, what about this man?" The question is motivated by a spirit of competition and driven by an attitude of jealousy. Jesus replies, "If it is my will that he remain until I come, what is that to you? You follow me!"(vv. 21–22). Jesus' retort puts Peter in his place and abruptly commands him to mind his own business. One does not have to read between the lines to see that Jesus regards Peter's attitude as sinful.

The continuing sinfulness of the disciples after John 20:22 is often viewed as evidence that Jesus does not actually impart the Spirit to his disciples on resurrection day. Köstenberger comments: "The disciples' behavior subsequent to the present incident [John 20:22] would also be rather puzzling had they already received the Spirit."[29] Carson more bluntly states: "This fishing expedition and the dialogue that ensues do not read like the lives of men on a Spirit-empowered mission. It is impossible to imagine any of this taking place in Acts, *after Pentecost*."[30] Actually, disciples will be guilty of similar behavior even after Pentecost. Some commentators are convinced that Ananias and Sapphira are true believers whose greed drives them to deception and hypocrisy (Acts 5:1–11).[31] Another Ananias, described by Luke as a "disciple" (9:10), protests a command from the resurrected Lord himself (9:10–17) *after Pentecost*. Believers in Jerusalem lack the faith to believe that God has answered their prayers for a miraculous deliverance of Peter from prison *after Pentecost* (12:6–12). John Mark abandons the missionary team on Paul's first missionary journey (13:13), probably motivated by fear (15:38), *after Pentecost*. Thus not only is it possible that the fear, doubt, and selfishness described in John 20 and 21 occur after the giving of the Spirit; the descriptions of disciples after Pentecost suggest such behavior was even likely to occur. Most readers will be relieved to know that their ongoing struggles with fear, doubt, and selfishness do not necessarily indicate that they have not received the Spirit.

These examples undermine any notion that the transformation wrought by the Spirit has been completed. Disciples have been granted the surpassing righteousness. But they still do not possess perfect righteousness.

The Beatitudes

In the Beatitudes, Jesus describes his disciples as those who hunger and thirst for righteousness. The grammar of the Greek text suggests that disciples are in an ongoing state of spiritual hunger and thirst. The context shows that the ultimate fulfillment of the promise "they will be satisfied"

---

[29] Köstenberger, *John*, 574–75. He points to the fear of the disciples that prompts them to lock the doors (cf. 20:26 and 20:19) and the disciples' return to fishing and failure to catch anything (21:3). See also 589n7: "Had they already received the Spirit, it would be almost inexplicable why Peter went back to fishing so soon after that event."

[30] Carson, *John*, 669.

[31] Craig Keener seems confident that Ananias and Sapphira were not true believers (*Acts: An Exegetical Commentary*, 4 vols. [Grand Rapids, MI: Baker, 2013], 2:1183–85, 1189). Calvin quite bluntly describes the two deceivers as "reprobate" (Calvin, *Acts of the Apostles*, 2 vols., trans. W. J. G. McDonald [Grand Rapids, MI: Eerdmans, 1965], 132–40, esp. 134). However, Darrell Bock seems to suggest that Ananias and Sapphira were disciples: "The passage shows that God knows the hearts of believers" (*Acts*, BECNT [Grand Rapids, MI: Baker, 2007], 219). He also cites with approval Ajith Fernando's view that Luke's report teaches with honesty that "the church is not a place of perfect people" (*Acts*, 227). Fernando writes, "There is nothing to say Ananias and Sapphira were not believers" (*Acts*, NIVAC [Grand Rapids, MI: Zondervan, 1998], 198). The caution of F. F. Bruce (*The Book of Acts*, NICNT, rev. ed. [Grand Rapids, MI: Eerdmans, 1988], 107) seems wise: "There is no point in asking if Ananias and Sapphira were genuine believers or not, because there is no means of answering such a question. On the one hand, they did not behave as if they were genuine believers; on the other hand, it cannot be said for certain that they were not, unless one is prepared to say that no one who commits an act of deliberate deceit can be a genuine believer."

awaits the eschaton.[32] Thus disciples will not be completely satisfied with the righteousness characterizing them in this life. They will yearn constantly for more and greater righteousness. Though their righteousness exceeds that of the scribes and Pharisees, the disciples are not content with it. They crave full Christlike perfection and long to be free of the temptations and spiritual struggles plaguing this life. The spiritual hunger and thirst of the disciple is inconsistent with an overrealized eschatology that assumes believers are perfected in this life.

The Model Prayer

In the model prayer, Jesus teaches his disciples to pray, "Forgive us our debts, as we also have forgiven our debtors" (Matt. 6:12). Jesus commands his disciples to make this request for forgiveness a consistent part of their daily prayers. Thus, repentance is not something the disciple experiences at conversion alone. The disciple continually expresses repentance toward God and acknowledges his absolute dependence on God's grace. This implies that although the disciple has received a pure heart that results in a righteousness surpassing that of the scribes and Pharisees, he succumbs daily to temptation and needs a fresh experience of God's gracious forgiveness. This petition of Jesus' model prayer recognizes that the disciple daily incurs new spiritual debts that prompt his reliance on God's great mercy. Although the believer is no longer a slave to sin, sin remains a stubborn reality. The disciple who has experienced the new exodus is freed from sin but is not sin-free.

The final two petitions of the model prayer also exhibit the limitations of the believer's present spiritual condition. "Lead us not into temptation" (Matt. 6:13) recalls Matthew 4:1, in which Jesus is led by the Spirit into the wilderness to be tempted by the devil. This petition implores God not to lead us into the temptation experience into which he led Jesus, for we would certainly fail in the very situation in which Jesus prevailed. The petition also anticipates Matthew 26:41, in which Jesus urges the disciples in Gethsemane to pray so that they would not "enter into temptation." The petition is a humble admission of the disciple's ongoing spiritual weakness and vulnerability. Similarly, the petition "Deliver us from evil" admits that evil would triumph if the believer sought to resist it on his own. The use of the verb "deliver" (*hruomai*) in the petition indicates that the believer does not need mere assistance in his battle. He needs deliverance,

---

[32] See Quarles, *Sermon on the Mount*, 58–62.

rescue from a fate from which he cannot deliver himself. He must rely completely on another for his victory over sin. His own spiritual resources are insufficient for the challenge.

Thus the transformation experienced by the disciple is obviously not complete. Although the disciple is deeply grateful for the change produced in him by Christ, he longs for greater godliness.

The Disciple's Pursuit of Spirituality

Although Jesus clearly views as a divine gift the surpassing righteousness that is the essence of spirituality, a consequence of new exodus, new covenant, and new creation, he also affirms the importance of the disciple's own initiative in spirituality. Christ never lays out a simple multistep process for growth in godliness. However, several elements of his teaching highlight prerequisites for spiritual growth.

Aligning Priorities

Twice in the Sermon on the Mount Jesus expresses that righteousness will be a top priority for the disciple. In the fourth beatitude, Jesus describes the disciple as one who "hunger[s] and thirst[s] for righteousness" (Matt. 5:6). In an era and climate in which food was often scarce, and a brief period of drought might result in death, hunger and thirst were vivid metaphors for the most intense of cravings. Jesus' point is that the disciple longs for holiness more than his growling stomach longs for his next bite of bread or his parched tongue yearns for its next sip of water. Jesus repeats his description of the disciple's longing for holiness in his discussion of the disciple's priorities in Matthew 6:19–34. The climactic statement of the section is the terse command "Seek first the kingdom of God and his righteousness" (6:33). The disciple should value kingdom righteousness above earthly treasures, food, drink, or clothing. To a certain extent, this set of priorities is a natural expression of the transformation wrought in the disciple's heart by the Spirit. However, the fact that Jesus commands the disciple to seek righteousness above all else indicates that the disciple has some responsibility and must take some initiative in cultivating this set of priorities. Thus growth in godliness entails honest introspection that evaluates one's loves and priorities and seeks to conform these to Jesus' teaching.

Praying for Spiritual Growth

The priorities of the disciple will naturally be exhibited in the petitions he offers God in prayer. Consequently, the one who seeks first the kingdom

of God and his righteousness is commanded to pray for God's kingdom
(Matt. 6:10), the accomplishment of his will (6:10), protection from temptation (6:13), and rescue from the evil one (6:13). The intercession of
Jesus for disciples certainly prevails and ensures that the disciple's faith
will endure (Luke 22:31–32), but the disciple's own faithfulness in prayer
remains essential for victory over temptation (Matt. 26:41).

Remaining in Christ
The illustration of the vine and the branches (John 15:1–17) in Jesus'
Farewell Discourse emphasizes the importance of the believer's spiritual
relationship to Jesus. Only those who are properly related to Jesus will
bear fruit. The branch produces fruit only because of its connection to
the vine that supplies it with life and energy to produce. Similarly, Jesus
supplies the believer with the life and power to produce spiritual fruit.
Just as a vinedresser prunes branches of the vine in order to make the
vine more productive, the Father purifies the believer, removing anything that might hinder the believer's production of spiritual fruit. In
this context, Jesus describes the cleansing of the disciple as already accomplished by the message Jesus has delivered. This message probably
includes the totality of Jesus' teaching (John 14:23).[33] Jesus' teaching earlier in John (13:9–11) shows that the primary cleansing of the disciple
that occurs at conversion must be followed by additional experiences of
cleansing. This continuing work of sanctification increases the believer's fruitfulness.[34] The believer's responsibility is to "remain" in Jesus.
Remaining in Jesus entails obeying his commands (John 15:7, 10; 1 John
3:24) and continuing as his disciple by following his example (John 15:8;
1 John 2:6). The primary command the disciple must obey is the command to love other disciples (John 15:11–17; 1 John 4:16) with the same
sacrificial love Jesus exhibited when he sacrificed his life for his friends
(John 15:13).

The Church's Role in Spirituality
Throughout its history, leading figures in the church have often assumed
wrongly that holiness was to be sought in seclusion from other people,
by withdrawing from society and isolating oneself even from fellow be-

---

[33] Köstenberger, *John*, 453.
[34] Calvin recognized that the cleansing of the feet about which Jesus spoke was "not the forgiveness of sins, but
the renewal by which Christ gradually and continually delivers His followers completely from the desires of the
flesh." Calvin, *The Gospel according to St. John 11–21*, 59.

lievers. On the contrary, Jesus teaches that faithful brothers and sisters are essential allies in the quest for surpassing righteousness. The loving correction by a brother when the disciple sins and the accountability provided by the church serve to promote growth in godliness.

Moral Instruction

Jesus emphasizes the importance of disciples' teaching each other the ways of the Lord. Disciples must affirm the commandments of Jesus, seek to obey those commandments, and encourage others to keep even the least of Jesus' commandments (Matt. 5:19–20). This responsibility is reinforced in the climactic statement of Matthew's Gospel. Jesus' disciples are not merely to teach new disciples what to believe; they are to teach new disciples to observe all that Jesus commands (28:20).

Compassionate Correction

Although Matthew 7:1–5 is often interpreted as prohibiting even the spotting of sin in a brother's life and seeking to help the brother conquer it, Jesus intends merely to prohibit hypocritical judgment in which a disciple is very conscious of lesser sins in the lives of others yet completely blind to his own more heinous sins. The command "First take the log out of your own eye, and then you will see clearly to take the speck out of your brother's eye" shows that loving correction of a brother is necessary under the proper conditions. A brother should seek to assist a brother in dealing with his speck after his own log was removed. If attention is to be given to those with specks in their eyes (relatively minor sins in their lives), how much more do those with logs in the eyes (particularly heinous sins in their lives) require the brother's loving correction?[35]

These implications of Matthew 7:1–6 might be missed if it were not for the very clear instructions in Matthew 18:15–17. There Jesus explicitly commands brothers to confront one another compassionately in hopes of encouraging genuine repentance and restoration. Although the ESV refers to confronting the brother who sins "against you," which suggests that Jesus' instructions apply merely to resolving personal conflict, the oldest extant manuscripts of Matthew 18:15 lack the prepositional phrase "against you."[36] Without the phrase, Jesus' instructions relate to any sin

---

[35] See Quarles, *Sermon on the Mount*, 288–89.

[36] Bruce M. Metzger, *A Textual Commentary on the Greek New Testament* (New York: United Bible Societies, 1994), 36.

that the believer observes in the life of a fellow disciple and not merely sins of which the believer is personally the victim. These instructions immediately follow Jesus' description of a loving shepherd going after a straying sheep and the joy of the shepherd when the sheep is restored to the fold. The mini parable is interpreted by the statement that the heavenly Father does not want even one of his children to be lost. This prelude to Matthew 18:15–17 makes Jesus' intentions even clearer: disciples must not ignore a brother who strays but must go after him, call him to repentance, and seek to restore him to the fold.

Conclusion

The teaching of Jesus precludes any attempt to reduce spirituality to a step-by-step procedure driven by the efforts of the believer. Jesus teaches a view of spirituality that is clearly Christocentric rather than anthropocentric. Spirituality is a by-product of the transformation of the believer wrought by Christ through the Spirit. Our study of spirituality according to Jesus has led to conclusions similar to those reached by David Peterson in his book-length study of holiness in the New Testament:

> As with the offer of salvation in the first place, we are totally dependent on God's grace for transformation, especially as we face the possibility of death. There is no programme of sanctification or glorification we can effect for ourselves. There is no way of hurrying-up God's work in us. We are called to live the sanctified life with faith, repentance and obedience, trusting the Spirit to continue and complete his great work of glorification.[37]

Jesus is emphatic that apart from him, no person can produce good works truly pleasing to God (John 15:5). However, those who rely on Jesus to produce spiritual fruit in them will bear abundant fruit to the glory of the heavenly Father (John 15:8; Matt. 5:16).

Although Christ has already produced a radical change in believers through new birth, new creation, new exodus, and the new covenant, the believer has not been made perfect. He is to hunger and thirst for righteousness and seek it (and the kingdom) above all else. He is to pray for righteousness by petitioning the Father to protect him from temptation

---

[37] David Peterson, *Possessed by God: A New Testament Theology of Sanctification and Holiness*, NSBT 1 (Downers Grove, IL: InterVarsity, 1995), 126. See also the warning on p. 91: "It is possible to be so zealous for 'progress' that one's attention shifts from God's grace to human effort." My study was conducted without reference to Peterson's work. We arrived at similar conclusions independently. For a similar view, see Victor Furnish, *Theology and Ethics in Paul* (Nashville, TN: Abingdon, 1968), 239–40.

and rescue him from the evil one. The church cooperates with Christ in the work of transforming believers by instructing believers in true righteousness and compassionating correctly believers who stray.

These means of producing righteousness in believers ensure that their good character and good works are to the glory of God alone.

4

TENSIONS IN SPIRITUALITY

Spirituality according to Paul

BENJAMIN M. SKAUG AND
CHRISTOPHER W. MORGAN

Do you ever feel like a walking dichotomy, sincerely longing to be holy but struggling with sin, feeling the tensions of experiencing genuine growth with frequent failure?

As God's people, we have taken the name of God upon ourselves and thus are obligated to live in a way that reflects his character. When Israel entered into a covenant relationship with God, they were called to be holy because their God was holy (Leviticus 19). Everything about Israel had to change because of the holiness of their God. Their love for God, love for one another, treatment of and participation in food, thoughts, actions, clothing, crops—even the things they touched—were all subject to legislation because their lives had to reflect the God they served. Anything less was sin. And as the new-covenant people of God, we are in a covenant relationship with the same holy God. Christ has accomplished the requirements of salvation for us because we could not do so on our own. In Christ, we are cleansed, saved, and holy. And in Christ we are called to "be holy in all [our] conduct, since it is written, 'You shall be holy, for I am holy'" (1 Pet. 1:15b–16).

As Christians we desire the things of Christ. We want to obey God; we yearn to please him. Yet we also struggle—with pride, self-absorption, wandering hearts, covetousness, and impatience with others. We love God, but fully? We love others, but as ourselves? We are thankful, some of the time. We are holy, to a degree.

When we sin, are we being hypocritical? Could it not also be the case

that we are sincere Christians struggling to live out our faith in this gap between our initial conversion and our ultimate transformation into Christlikeness, in heaven? We are all works in progress and under construction.
Our salvation has begun and will be completed, but, in the meantime,
we are in the process of growing in holiness, love, and Christlikeness. As
strange as it sounds, we are saints yet are not thoroughly holy in our day-
to-day lives. We are, as Martin Luther stressed five hundred years ago,
simultaneously justified and sinners.

So what are these tensions we experience in the Christian life? How
are we to understand them? And how shall we live amidst such tensions?
The apostle Paul often speaks to such tensions in spirituality. Indeed,
Paul's teachings in Romans 6–8 are particularly helpful as we wrestle with
such tensions; as a result, we will focus on several tensions and dualities
in this essay. As believers, we are both

- crucified and alive (6:1–14)
- slaves and free (6:15–7:7)
- warring and victorious (7:8–8:4)
- volitional and spiritual (8:5–11)
- debtors and heirs (8:12–25)
- persevering and preserved (8:26–39)

The tensions of spirituality in Romans 6–8 emerge from doctrines
explained in Romans 3–5, especially the truth of how God justifies all of
those who have faith in Christ. We are declared righteous not on account
of our own law keeping or obedience but solely on account of Christ's
representative sinless life, substitutionary death, and victorious resurrection on our behalf. While we were ungodly, sinners, and even his enemies,
Christ died for us (5:6–11). Although we were marked by sin, death, and
condemnation in Adam, we now possess righteousness, life, and justification in Christ, the new Adam (5:12–21), who paid the penalty of our sin
and has given us his standing of righteousness (3:21–26). In Christ, we are
forgiven of our sin, recipients of his righteousness, and made alive by his
life. Romans 5:21 also highlights that Jesus is our Lord, our new master
with authority over us, our new king who has delivered us from the kingdom of darkness into his kingdom of light and life. So we stand before
God as justified through Christ, and we have a new identity as followers of
the Lord Jesus. Once we take the name of Christ upon ourselves, we enter
into the glorious responsibility of living according to his character. He is

holy, righteous, loving, merciful, just, gracious, and obedient to God, and so should all of us be who bear his name.

It is precisely at this point that we often feel more than a little deflated. We know that we should live holy lives because God is holy—we know this. The problem is that at this very moment our lives, while somewhat holy, are not completely so. While we show more mercy than we did a year ago, we do not show or display the constant mercy to others that we know we should. In fact, there are times we find ourselves looking more at our faults than at our Christlikeness. How can we be righteous and yet still growing in righteousness, holy and yet still growing in holiness, forgiven and yet still repenting daily? It is in the midst of these tensions that we begin our study.

Tension #1: Crucified and Alive (Romans 6:1–14)

One such tension is that we are both crucified and alive. Crucifixion was one of the most gruesome forms of capital punishment that an ancient government could dispense. Mel Gibson's *The Passion of the Christ* obviously shows Gibson's treatment of Christ's Passion Week, but it also shows his understanding of the awful aspects of the crucifixion. Audience members could almost feel the pain of the nails being driven into Jesus' hands and feet. During the scene in which Jesus dies from crucifixion, many theatergoers cried openly as the lifeless body of Jesus hung from the cross. When we think of crucifixion, we think of what it does: it kills people. It is a horrific means by which someone dies.

When we think of being alive, we may think of vivid colors, fresh mountain air, or the sound of ocean waves crashing on a beach. We think of the people we love and the things we love to do. Being alive is the means by which we get to do the things we love.

What is almost impossible to consider is being both crucified and alive at the same time. To be crucified means to be dead, while to be alive means to be not dead. While it is hard to fathom, Paul says that Christians are both of these things simultaneously. He explains what it means to be crucified and also what it means to be alive. Paul also shows *how* we are crucified and *how* we are alive, holding them as parallel truths in Romans 6:1–14.

Crucified and Dead

Paul begins this section with a question that demands a negative response. He asks, "Are we to continue in sin that grace might abound?" In other words, "Should we desire to see God's grace continue to abound through our continuation in sin?" The response that he gives ensures that such a notion is not merely "impermissible" but an impossibility.[1] Christians are dead to sin, here understood as a power or dominion that, according to Paul, has influence over people (Rom. 5:12–19), rules people (5:21), enslaves people (6:6), and is crucified (6:6).[2] Paul is not referring to an act of sin or asserting sinless perfection (see also Phil. 3:12–15; James 3:2; 1 John 1:10) but is pressing the fact that those of us who are justified and grafted into Christ are not able to return to the powerful domain of sin formerly over us.

Why does Paul state that a return to our previous sinful state is impossible? First, all of us who are in union with Christ have died to the power of sin. Before our union in Christ, we were dead *in* our sin (Eph. 2:1), but after being made alive in Christ, we are now dead *to* sin (Rom. 6:2).[3] Because we are dead to the dominating power of sin, we cannot continue to live under its authority or mastery.

In what way are we dead to sin? Paul describes this death through the gospel and baptism (Rom. 6:3–4). Just as Christ endured death and was buried, so too our old self dies a real death at the moment in which we are born again. Moreover, the power and mastery of sin not only dies at regeneration but also is buried in death, just as the body of Jesus was buried in the tomb.

Just as we were united together with Adam in his sin and fall, so too are we united together with Christ in his crucifixion (6:6), death (6:4), burial (6:4), and resurrection (6:8). Thus, to be baptized into Christ is to be united together with him in the work he accomplishes as the last Adam. Baptism helps us to understand the death and burial of the old self as well as the resurrection of the new life. Every believer has had the chains and shackles of sin's power and authority broken through the victory of Christ (6:7).[4]

Moreover, what we were in Adam has been crucified along with Christ to guarantee that the former self cannot rise up and regain dominance over us (6:6). Since sin has been crucified, destroyed, and buried, there is no conceivable way in which it could ever regain mastery or possession over us. As justified believers, we are truly free from bondage to sin and

---

[1] William Hendriksen, *Exposition of Paul's Epistle to the Romans*, New Testament Commentary (Grand Rapids, MI: Baker, 2007), 195.
[2] Thomas Schreiner, *Romans*, BECNT (Grand Rapids, MI: Baker, 1998), 304. See also James D. G. Dunn, *Romans 1–8*, WBC 38A (Dallas: Word, 1988), 306; Douglas J. Moo, *The Epistle to the Romans*, NICNT (Grand Rapids, MI: Eerdmans, 1996), 357–74.
[3] Leon Morris, *The Epistle to the Romans*, PNTC (Grand Rapids, MI: Eerdmans, 1988), 245.
[4] Robert H. Mounce, *Romans*, NAC (Nashville, TN: B&H, 1995), 150.

what we were in Adam. In short, this is how we as Christians are crucified and dead: we are dead to sin and its dominion, power, and authority over us (6:11). It has been crucified and cannot be resurrected as our master.

Alive

However, we are not freed from the power of sin merely to meander aimlessly in life as antinomians.[5] Just as Jesus was raised from the grave in order to prove that death could not contain him, we too are raised as new creations in Christ, freed from sin's dominion and born anew (6:5) to walk in newness of life (6:4). We are called to consider ourselves dead to sin and alive to God for the purpose of holiness (6:11).[6]

Since sin is crucified, dead, and buried, no longer ruling over us, we are commanded not to allow the former siren song of sin to "hold sway over" us (6:12).[7] We are urged not to allow ourselves to be used as instruments or weapons of sin and the purpose of unrighteousness (6:13).[8] Rather, we are called to present our new selves to God as weapons of righteousness in the pursuit of holiness (6:13): "Having been quickened by the power of God, raised from the death of sin and all its dreadful consequences, they were bound to live unto God."[9] We are freed to live as weapons of righteousness precisely because Christ has accomplished the law of God on our behalf so that our entire regenerated (resurrected) lives are dominated by grace (6:14). This is how we as Christians are alive: we are new creations in Christ who have been raised to a new life in righteousness to God.

Tension #2: Slavery and Freedom (Romans 6:15–7:7)

Paul asserts not only that we as Christians are both crucified and alive, but also that we are slaves and free. When we think about slavery, we often think of a cruel master who owns people as property and forces them to oblige his every demand. When we think of slaves, we think of those in a constant state of involuntary bondage whereby one is in servitude to a master without the possibility of being free. In our normal thinking, to be a slave is to suffer a total lack of freedom.

We may also think that to be in the state of freedom means not to

---

[5] Schreiner, *Romans*, 305.
[6] Charles Hodge, *Romans*, Geneva Series of Commentaries (Carlisle, PA: Banner of Truth, 1986), 195.
[7] Moo, *Romans*, 382.
[8] For a discussion on ὅπλα as "weapon," see Emil Brunner, *The Letter to the Romans* (Philadelphia: Westminster, 1949), 52.
[9] Hodge, *Romans*, 205.

have an owner and thus not to be subject to the hardships of a master. In other words, to be free means to enjoy autonomy and to be able to exercise and carry out one's own desires. We might not think that someone could both be a slave and have freedom at the same time.

Slavery

Paul, however, portrays believers both as slaves subject to a master and also as free. His imagery has its roots in the exodus. The book of Exodus opens as the people of Israel are in bondage and enslaved to Pharaoh and the nation of Egypt. Their persecution begins as Pharaoh commands that they work and toil as slaves, and it increases as their male children are put to death as a means to curb Israel's growth. As the nation cries out to God, he raises up a deliverer who will lead the people out of slavery and bondage to Egypt so that they might become God's people through a covenant agreement.

God accomplishes Israel's emancipation from Pharaoh and Egypt through the Passover event. God brings judgment to the land, including to each home in which there is no slaughtered lamb to stand in for the firstborn son. The death angel brings judgment to each home in Egypt but not to Israel, so that the world would know that there is a distinction between peoples (Ex. 11:7). Pharaoh then releases Israel from her bondage, and Moses leads the people out of slavery toward Sinai, only to have Pharaoh change his mind and pursue Israel. After God destroys Egypt at the Red Sea, the people rejoice and sing songs of praise and devotion to God. Not too long after their emancipation, however, they begin to grumble against God, remembering the "good times" of slavery in Egypt (See Ex. 16:3). This same grumbling is seen again in Numbers 11:5 and grows even more pathetic by Numbers 14:3–4: "'Would it not be better for us to go back to Egypt?' And they said to one another: 'Let us choose a leader and go back to Egypt.'"

"Who on earth would want to turn their backs on God and go back to being slaves?" we ask, scratching our heads. Yet a similar scenario is played out every day in the lives of Christians everywhere. We do not articulate it in this way, but our actions display loyalty to either our former master or our new one, thus revealing our ultimate destination.[10] Either we present ourselves as slaves to sin, which results in death, or we present

---

[10] Moo, *Romans*, 397; Kenneth Boa and William Kruidenier, *Romans*, Holman New Testament Commentary (Nashville, TN: B&H, 2000), 198.

ourselves as slaves to God through obedience, which results in righteousness (Rom. 6:16).

Through the failures of the first Adam, all humanity is in slavery to sin (Rom. 1:18–3:23; 5:12–21). In Romans 6:17 Paul states plainly, "You . . . were once slaves to sin." In this slavery we were not coerced, but we willingly and gladly presented our bodies for corrupt service to our previous master, whom we served with distinction (6:19).[11] We served our previous master well because we were bound also to the law, like one yoked to a spouse by a marital covenant (7:1).[12] This binding marriage lasts as long as both parties are alive and faithful to one another (7:2–3). In our being bound to the law, we were made aware of sin. As we gained further understanding of the law, however, our flesh was awakened and our members stirred into action against the law (7:5).[13] At that time, bodily offerings led us further into lawlessness (6:19b), and we had complete disregard for righteousness (6:20).[14] While we were still held accountable for righteousness to God, we were not concerned with it because it did not have control over us:[15] "Righteousness had no power over you; your service was rendered to another master."[16] That master was the power of sin, and we delighted in carrying out the desires of our owner.

And what type of fruit or benefit did our slavery to sin gain us? First, Paul states that we reaped shame (6:21).[17] The lawless acts into which we gladly entered are now things that bring us deep humiliation. Second, Paul states that all slaves to sin reap the reward of death (6:21; 7:5). This death is not merely the passing away of natural life or the cessation of existence but rather is eternal death[18]—active eternal punishment, banishment, and separation from God.[19] And this is the reward we would have obtained if we had remained slaves to sin. But we have been "reclaimed by God's mercy" and are no longer on the "precipice of death."[20] We are no longer slaves to sin but have been emancipated!

---

[11] Morris, *Romans*, 262; John Calvin, *Commentary on the Epistle of Paul the Apostle to the Romans*, Calvin's Commentaries, vol. 19 (repr., Grand Rapids, MI: Baker, 2003), 239; John Murray, *The Epistle to the Romans*, NICNT (Grand Rapids, MI: Eerdmans, 1968), 234.

[12] Thomas Holland, *Romans: The Divine Marriage* (Eugene, OR: Pickwick, 2011), 227.

[13] Mounce, *Romans*, 162.

[14] Hendriksen, *Romans*, 207, notes that while we were slaves to sin, we were enemies of righteousness.

[15] Mounce, *Romans*, 158.

[16] Hodge, *Romans*, 210.

[17] Murray, *Romans*, 236.

[18] Moo, *Romans*, 407.

[19] Christopher W. Morgan, "Biblical Theology: Three Pictures of Hell," in *Hell under Fire: Modern Scholarship Reinvents Eternal Punishment*, ed. Christopher W. Morgan and Robert A. Peterson (Grand Rapids, MI: Zondervan, 2004).

[20] Calvin, *Romans*, 241–42.

Freedom

Believers are no longer slaves to sin or subject to eternal death. We are no longer under the yoke or lordship of sin but have been delivered from our former master.[21] However, we are not autonomously free. Just like the exodus generation, we have been freed from one master so that we can serve a new one. And just like the exodus generation, our new Master is the one who brought us freedom and delivered us from our former master. This change in ownership did not occur because God saw our goodness or our good works. Rather, this act of deliverance was the gracious work of God through Christ (6:17).[22] Therefore, we are to give thanks to God for freeing us from our former bondage unto death and bringing us into subjection to himself in righteousness (6:17–18).[23] In this way, we are slaves who have been freed, but we are freed to be slaves once again—to our holy, righteous, and good Master.

What does it mean to be a slave to obedience? Just as we obeyed the desires of our former master and were slaves bound to disobedience, so now we are called to carry out the desires, will, and nature of our new Master (6:16, 22). He is holy and righteous, and therefore we are to be holy and righteous. He has given us commands and precepts that reflect who he is, and therefore we are to live in conformity to his will and commands. In other words, we are free to serve God through obedience to his will and desires.[24] This coincides perfectly with the words of Jesus: "Come to me, all who labor and are heavy laden, and I will give you rest. Take my yoke upon you, and learn from me . . . for my yoke is easy and my burden is light" (Matt. 11:28–30). As believers, we are free from sin, but our new Master's yoke is upon us, and he expects us to serve him in obedience (6:22). In this way, we are slaves set free from our former master in order to serve our new Master.

How can we serve our new and good Master? Since believers are new creations through the work of the Spirit, we also have new desires, which yearn to obey God as much or more than our previous desires yearned to serve sin.[25] In this way, we are freed from sin so that we might obey God. Previously, we presented our bodies to serve sin through lawless and impure acts, but now we are to present our bodies as slaves to righteousness

---

[21] Schreiner, *Romans*, 334.
[22] Calvin, *Romans*, 236.
[23] Schreiner, *Romans*, 334, makes this point as he clarifies that both participles in 6:18 (ἐλευθερωθέντες and ἐδουλώθητε) are passive and thus make believers the recipients of God's work of deliverance and redemption.
[24] Moo, *Romans*, 399.
[25] Calvin, *Romans*, 239.

(6:19). Douglas Moo clarifies Paul's meaning: "[Paul] thus makes clear that Christians should serve righteousness with all the single-minded dedication that characterized their pre-Christian service of such 'idols' as self, money, lust, pleasure, and power."[26] In other words, we are called to put forth our members in acts of obedience to God so that we might grow in holiness (6:19).[27] Spirituality is more than not sinning. While not sinning is significant in spirituality, it is not its goal. Rather, we are to be obedient by carrying out the desires and will of our new Master. Any form of spirituality that does not have earnest obedience to God as the goal is shortsighted.

This point is illustrated again in the image of marriage and covenant partnership (7:1–6). Paul states that we as believers are lawfully yoked to Christ in his conquest over death. Thus, through his resurrection from the dead, we are now freed from sin and dead to the law (7:4). Since the law is dead to us, we are no longer bound to it covenantally but are freed from it.[28] The law cannot have any power or authority over us, since its death to us means it cannot continue to be yoked to us.[29] We have a new covenant partner (and master) in Christ, and his victory is our victory. As we are yoked to Christ, our new obligation and desire is to follow him and his will and to reflect his nature as we are now in the newness of the Spirit (7:6).

What is the fruit of being a slave to God? The advantage of being in bondage to God is the free gift of eternal life (6:23). Paul is claiming not that our obedience to God earns us eternal life but that eternal life is the unmerited and undeserved gift of God's grace for all believers yoked to Christ.[30] This free gift is in direct contrast to the wages or earned merits of sin that bring the unbeliever death.[31] Thus, while the unbeliever agonizes in eternal death, justified and sanctified believers delight in the everlasting blessings from God in eternal life.[32]

Tension #3: War and Victory (Romans 7:7–8:4)

Our spiritual journey can feel like a daily and constant battle. It involves spiritual warfare and the ongoing war between our new self and the flesh. Many of us start each day determined to win the battle. There are days

---

[26] Moo, *Romans*, 404.

[27] For a discussion on whether sanctification (ἁγιασμόν) is a process of becoming more and more holy or the state of being holy, see Schreiner, *Romans*, 338; and Murray, *Romans*, 234.

[28] Murray, *Romans*, 241.

[29] Martin Luther, *Commentary on Romans*, trans. J. Theodore Mueller (Grand Rapids, MI: Zondervan, 1954), 109.

[30] Hodge, *Romans*, 211.

[31] Hendriksen, *Romans*, 208.

[32] Calvin, *Romans*, 243.

marked by victory over sin and others that drive us to our knees in repentance. In Romans 7–8, Paul points out both sides of this spiritual tension: we are in a spiritual war, yet we also have victory in Christ.[33]

Law (7:7–13)

Paul starts this section by identifying the nature of the law, asking: "What then shall we say? That the law is sin?" (7:7). This is a reasonable question, as Paul has shown that we have been released from our bondage to the law through the death of Christ.[34] He answers his own question in a strong negative fashion: "By no means!" (μὴ γένοιτο).

Then what is the law? It is not sinful, but what is it? First, the law is not a neutral thing that exists outside of the God who has given it. It is necessarily connected to the one who gives it, and it is to be utilized in the manner he desires. Thus the law itself is holy, righteous, and good (7:12) precisely because it reflects the holy, righteous, and good God who has given it.

Second, the law reveals the character and nature of God the lawgiver.[35] The law that states "You shall not covet" (Ex. 20:17) shows an aspect of God's perfect nature and character in the fact that he needs nothing and does not covet (or desire, חמד). God's *aseity* assures us that he does not lack anything and therefore does not covet. In one sense, to see the law rightly is to see the nature, holiness, and righteousness of God that is revealed by that specific law.

Third, the law not only reflects God and reveals God; it also reveals the will and the holy, righteous, and good standards of God, which are for our good too.[36] It is the law of "You shall not covet" (Ex. 20:17) that demonstrates that anything less than *not coveting* is missing the mark of God's perfect standards. Moreover, this particular law states that while sin can be and is an action, it is primarily a heart matter (see also Matthew 5–7).[37] Long before coveting turns into theft, adultery, or murder, the desiring or longing for something that is not ours is a sin that violates the law and offends our holy God (7:7d). Far from being sinful, God's law is his tool to highlight his nature, character, and standards and, correspondingly, what is sin.

---

[33] Romans 7 is notoriously difficult and debated, and we claim no solution here. While some interpreters will differ on aspects of this section, we do hope that the frequently taught tension of the believer's war and victory will be kept in focus (cf. Galatians 5–6; Ephesians 4–6; Colossians 3–4).

[34] Mounce, *Romans*, 163.

[35] Hodge, *Romans*, 256.

[36] Schreiner, *Romans*, 359.

[37] See Dunn, *Romans*, 380, as he argues that coveting is "the root of all sin," according to Jewish thought.

Fourth, the law, as given by God, does offer life for perfect obedience (Rom. 7:10).[38] Deuteronomy 28 highlights the covenant blessings and life attached to the Mosaic law: "If you faithfully obey the voice of the LORD your God, being careful to do all his commandments that I command you today, the LORD your God will set you high above all the nations of the earth. And all these blessings shall come upon you and overtake you, if you obey the voice of the LORD your God" (Deut. 28:1–2). God's blessings included Israel's residence inside the land of inheritance (Deut. 28:3), the growth of their own offspring as well as their animals' (Deut. 28:4), their produce and sustenance (Deut. 28:5), victory in battle (Deut. 28:7), and the possession of whatever they put their hands on (Deut. 28:8–14). But these covenant blessings and life were available only to those who obeyed the law faithfully.

So if the law is good and holy—and Paul forcefully argues that it is—then why is our death to the law a good thing (7:1–6)? First, Paul has already established that fallen sinners cannot and do not obey God's law (Rom. 3:1–23; Eph. 2:1–10). Second, he states that once we became aware of the law, sin seized the occasion (ἀφορμὴν δὲ λαβοῦσα) to deceive us and produce sin of every kind inside of us (7:8–11). This sin is law breaking and therefore an act of treason against the God who gave the law. Third, since we are lawbreakers, the law that could have led to life brings only death (7:9–10).[39] Thus Paul asserts that sin, as identified through the law, killed him (7:11) precisely because he could not obey God's commandments.

Since Paul could see these truths looking backward, we can do the same. We can look back to see that we were utterly unable to keep any of God's laws. We were in a constant state of law breaking and would have therefore received the wrath of God that stems from sin (Romans 1–2). So, while the law is good and holy as it reflects God, it also brings us an awareness of sin and the death that comes from breaking it.[40] In light of these truths, we confess with Paul that sin (and the death it ensures) is absolutely sinful and something we should despise (7:13).

War (7:13–25)

Thus far we have seen that sin is death that kills us (7:11), that we have been justified by God's grace in Christ at the moment of our helplessness (5:6), that those who are baptized into Christ are dead to sin (6:1–3),

---

[38] Collin G. Kruse, *Paul's Letter to the Romans*, PNTC (Grand Rapids, MI: Eerdmans, 2012), 302.
[39] Moo, *Romans*, 438.
[40] Hodge, *Romans*, 226.

that we are no longer yoked or united to the law (6:22), and that we are enslaved to God (6:22) in order to bear fruit for him (7:4). We know that these things are true, and yet we all still struggle with the very sin that we know is despicable to God. We know that the very sin we have been freed from through Christ is dead and yet still alive in the members of our bodies. How can these things be?

In this debated passage, Paul seems to be writing about such a war. On the one hand, he knows that the law is spiritual (7:14), righteous (7:12), good (7:13), and divine, as it is from God.[41] He also seems to speak as a regenerate man who knows that the law of God is good and right (7:22).[42] Paul, with his mind, truly desires to carry out the law of God (7:25) and knows that Christ has graciously freed him from the body of death (7:25a).[43] All of these truths point toward certain spiritual victory, as Paul is united to Christ.

Paul also explains that he is still flesh, or weak (7:14). Literally, he says, "I am flesh/weak" (ἐγὼ δὲ σάρκινός εἰμι). Thus, the flesh, still living out some of the covenant curses from Adam's failure, is weak and sold into the bondage of sin.[44] Building on Romans 6:1–23, Romans 7–8 seems to reference the common already-but-not-yet tension found in sanctification. In other words, while union with Christ guarantees an ultimate glorification, sanctification is not completed in this earthly life. Instead, in this life we will continue to struggle as regenerate believers united to Christ who are promised and guaranteed victory through him, increasing in sanctification but not obtaining final and full sanctification until glorification, since we are still residing in our vessels of flesh and experiencing the lingering consequences of some of the covenant curses of Adam. For instance, Paul died a physical death. This physical death is one of the curses of the Adamic covenant. In fact, outside of those Christians who are alive at the return of Christ, all believers will die the same physical death, because they are sons of Adam in imperfect flesh and the penalty of his sin.[45]

Paul seems to express the anguish of the internal war. On one hand, he knows that he is fully justified and will see the conclusion of sanctification (Rom. 8:30). On the other hand, he is still residing in the flesh that

---

[41] Kruse, *Romans*, 306.
[42] John Gill, *An Exposition of the New Testament*, Baptist Commentary Series 2 (London: Mathews & Leigh, 1809), 474.
[43] Hodge, *Romans*, 238.
[44] Kruse, *Romans*, 306.
[45] Hendriksen, *Romans*, 231.

maintains its corruption from Adam's fall.[46] Paul does not love or enjoy some of his current actions (7:15a).[47] In fact, he hates some of the things he works in the flesh (7:15b). Yet there is still a part of him that desires the works of the flesh even though he knows that these works are in opposition to the Spirit of God (7:15b). John Calvin explains the complexities of this passage as the internal war of sanctification:

> The godly, . . . in whom the regeneration of God is begun, are so divided, that with the chief desire of the heart they aspire to God, seek celestial righteousness, hate sin, and yet they are drawn down to the earth by the relics of their flesh: and thus, while pulled in two ways, they fight against their own nature, and nature fights against them; and they condemn their sins, not only as being constrained by the judgment of reason, but because they really in their hearts abominate them, and on their account loathe themselves. This is the Christian conflict between the flesh and the spirit, of which Paul speaks in Gal. 5:17.[48]

Although in a different context, in Galatians 5:16–17 Paul speaks of this warring tension between the Spirit and the flesh. In 5:16, he encourages the Galatian believers to walk according to the Spirit so that they will not finish the desires of the flesh. Schreiner notes that believers must acquiesce to the Holy Spirit on a daily basis so that those fleshly desires from Adam are defeated.[49] Herman Ridderbos adds, "He who walks by the Spirit will be able to resist the flesh in the end—resist it, that is, in its wicked desire bent on total domination."[50]

In Galatians 5:17, Paul shows that the Spirit and the flesh are at war and in opposition to one another. The flesh sets its desires against the Spirit, and the Spirit against the flesh. In other words, the flesh, even in those of us who are born again, craves and desires those things that are despised by the Spirit of God. And the Holy Spirit is diametrically opposed to everything that stems from the flesh.[51]

The result of this war is that every thought and action is both supported and hated. Those works according to the flesh are abhorrent to the Spirit of God who indwells us. Furthermore, those works that please God

---

[46] Calvin, *Romans*, 261.
[47] Murray, *Romans*, 261.
[48] Calvin, *Romans*, 263.
[49] Thomas R. Schreiner, *Galatians*, ZECNT (Grand Rapids, MI: Zondervan, 2010), 343.
[50] Herman N. Ridderbos, *The Epistle of Paul to the Churches of Galatia*, NICNT (Grand Rapids, MI: Eerdmans, 1953), 203.
[51] Leon Morris, *Galatians: Paul's Charter of Christian Freedom* (Downers Grove, IL: InterVarsity Press, 1996), 168.

are hated and made difficult by the flesh that lingers until the moment in which our sanctification is completed.[52] So, on one hand, we sometimes do the very works of the flesh that we know are typical of those who will not inherit the kingdom of God (Gal. 5:21). On the other hand, the Spirit of God has empowered us to walk and practice the things of the Spirit. And we will walk in this new way of life, along this direction; we will be characterized by the fruit of the Spirit, not the works of the flesh (Gal. 5:22–25). This transformation is genuine but is also gradual and therefore partial. Accordingly, Paul does not assume that the Christian life continues on autopilot but urges us to act accordingly. We are to "keep in step with the Spirit" and live out the realities of life in the Spirit. This is the already-but-not-yet war continuing inside of everyone in Christ.[53]

Paul may be teaching similarly here in Romans 7:14–25. He hates the practices of the flesh and understands these actions to be contradictory to the law of his mind (7:15–23). He realizes that his flesh is still entrapped by sin and the works of the flesh (7:17). He also knows that this sinful flesh is not a good thing and is at war with his new identity, which desires to obey and please God (7:18; 23).[54] Luther explains:

> Sin remains in the spiritual man, in order that he might exercise himself in grace, put off his pride, and check his arrogance. He who confesses his sins should not believe that he can thereby shake off the burden of sin and quietly live on in sin. But he should know that when he puts off the burden of sin, he enters the warfare for God and takes up a new burden for God against the Devil and his own remaining faults.[55]

What is Paul to do? He desires to please God with his mind and his body, and yet he experiences an internal war (7:23). He expresses his anguish in 7:24, "Wretched/miserable [ταλαίπωρος] man that I am! Who will deliver me from this body of death?" (7:24). This is a cry of maturity, realizing the "conviction of sin; a knowledge of its nature, and a sense of its power over ourselves. Hence the feeling of self-condemnation, of helplessness and misery."[56]

At the same time, Paul believes in the finality of the process of sanctification through Christ: "Thanks be to God through Jesus Christ our Lord!" (7:25). Paul is certain that Christ has provided full justification and

---

[52] Ibid., 169.
[53] Schreiner, *Galatians*, 343–44.
[54] Murray, *Romans*, 267.
[55] Luther, *Romans*, 116.
[56] Hodge, *Romans*, 245.

has promised the completion of sanctification. But the process is still underway, and Paul knows that part of the growth into maturity involves this very struggle. Those of us who are united to Christ know that Christ's victory over sin and death results in our justification. Our justification leads to our sanctification, the process whereby the Spirit develops us in holiness in this life. There will come a time when our sanctification will be completed, but in the meantime, our lives will experience the tensions of war and victory.

Victory (8:1–4)

If Paul has admitted that there is still a portion of him that desires evil, and that he engages in actions that are not pleasing to God, then where does this leave him in light of the law? To break the law of God is to fall under the just punishment of God. Where there is sin, there must, by necessity, be condemnation from the law of God. Does Paul stand condemned by the law? In light of Paul's continual sin from chapter 7, he is guilty of law breaking.[57] He should be condemned by the law and punished by the just and holy God.[58] But in remarkable fashion he declares, "There is therefore now no condemnation for those who are in Christ Jesus" (8:1).

Mention of being "in Christ" draws our attention back to Romans 5:1–21 and all of the benefits for those who are represented by Christ as federal head.[59] Through the life and death of Jesus, the people of God now have peace with God (5:1) and are no longer under his wrath (5:9). This peace was purchased by the work of Christ that brings his people justification rather than condemnation (5:6).[60] Justification is the forensic pronouncement of God that believers possess the perfect righteousness of Christ and find atonement for their sins through the blood of Christ (5:8–10). God's wrath was placed on the person of Christ our substitute so that believers would be saved from it (5:8–9). Thus believers are reconciled back to God and have received eternal life (5:11, 21).

It is in this sense that Paul understands his situation as someone simultaneously justified and sinful. Because he is in Christ, he cannot be condemned. Christ has already been cursed of God for all sins (past, present, and future) of all believers (Gal. 3:10–14) as a sin offering (Rom. 8:3). As the Father sent the Son in the likeness of sinful flesh, the Son is in the

---

[57] The ἄρα νῦν seems to bring Paul's argument from chapter 7 specifically, and from 5–7 generally, to a conclusion; see Morris, *Romans*, 300.
[58] Ibid.
[59] Hodge, *Romans*, 249.
[60] Murray, *Romans*, 274.

unique situation of accomplishing what fallen humanity could not (8:3). Through the incarnation, Christ adds humanity without losing any of his divinity (Phil. 2:5–11). In full humanity, he is in the likeness of sinful flesh but does not have a fallen nature or inherited guilt (Rom. 8:3d). Thus the punishment of condemnation for us has been taken by Christ and cannot now be placed on individual believers.

Christ has not only accomplished the law of God on behalf of those who are in union with him, thus releasing them from the law of sin and death (8:2); the Son has also sent the Holy Spirit as another helper upon all believers (John 14:16) so that the Spirit might aid us in our weakness (8:3; 26). The Spirit applies the life of Christ to every believer so that they are free from the law and are able to walk according to the Spirit rather than the fallen flesh (8:4). Just as Christ has succeeded in his work for us in justification, so too will the Spirit's work in sanctification surely succeed. His work will be finished at the moment of glorification, but he also gives us the ability here and now to live according to God's will and desire and to carry out the function of the law.[61] Under the domain of sin, we could not keep the law, but Jesus came and perfectly obeyed it for us, and now through union with him and the indwelling Spirit he enables us to live out the law partially but truly (see also Rom. 13:8–10; Gal. 5:22–25). This means that we can have victory over sin at this moment. The Spirit empowers us not only to avoid sin but also to please God in obedience. Yes, the flesh still calls to us, but the old self is dead and cannot exercise dominion over us. Moreover, the Spirit is alive in us and is empowering us in our struggle to love and obey God.

Every moment of temptation in our Christian lives is one whereby we are brought to a crossroads. The living and indwelling Spirit has given us the ability to avoid sin and walk in obedience in that moment. We are no longer condemned by the law, but, through the Spirit, we can walk in righteousness (8:1–4). This is an amazing reality. While we were weak and helpless in our flesh, we could not obey the law of God and were therefore under its condemnation of death. But now, for all of us who are in Christ, we cannot be condemned! Christ has already taken our guilt, shame, and punishment of God's wrath as our substitute. The Holy Spirit has also applied Christ's perfect obedience and righteousness to us so that we are set free from the law and can have life. Even more, the Spirit who indwells us enables us now to live in a way that increasingly reflects God, his ways, and the law revealed.

---

[61] We are not espousing a sinless perfection, but that the work of the Spirit in us allows us to love God better, love neighbors better, and carry out the base function of the law.

Tension #4: Volitional and Spiritual (Romans 8:5–11)

As believers united to Christ, we are guaranteed that the law cannot condemn us. We can have real victory over the sin in our life and can live according to the Spirit of God. For most of us, our fight with sin is an all-consuming fight. On our best days, we try not to sin. But sometimes we can think that not sinning equals obedience to God. When this happens, we have allowed the tail to wag the dog. While sin is real and has consequences, our focus should not be on sin. Rather, our focus and attention should be on loving and obeying God. The question is, how can we live in victory and focus on obedience? For Paul, it seems that he begins his spiritual warfare in the mind.

In this section, we will examine the importance and consequences of our mind-set for our spirituality. In Romans 12:2, Paul famously clarifies that believers must be transformed by the renewal of their mind (τοῦ νοὸς). This seems to refer to the change from the natural mind to the regenerate mind.[62] In 8:5–11, Paul focuses on the mind-set (φρονέω), or that upon which we choose to center our minds.[63] He frames his discussion upon God's work in Christ applied by the Spirit as the correct starting point for the right mind-set.[64]

Mind Set on the Flesh (8:5–11)

Paul first describes people who are of the flesh. This group seems to be typified or "idealized" by those who are unregenerate.[65] It is not surprising that Paul maintains that members of this group set their minds upon the things of the flesh. The things of the flesh are "patterned after and controlled by the flesh" and are linked but are not limited to one's general disposition, will, affections, appetites, and feelings.[66] In other words, the fallen and depraved human nature is leading and driving one's life in a manner of the flesh that necessarily leads to death (8:6).[67]

Since the manner of flesh is contrasted with the manner of the Spirit that gives life (8:4), it is consistent for Paul to state that the mind-set of the

---

[62] BDAG, s.v. νοῦς.

[63] BDAG, s.v. φρονέω.

[64] We agree with Carson that spirituality must necessarily begin with the right understanding of God through his Word. See "When Is Spirituality Spiritual?," in D. A. Carson, *The Gagging of God: Christianity Confronts Pluralism* (Grand Rapids, MI: Zondervan, 1996), 555–69.

[65] Dunn, *Romans*, 425. Moo notes, "Paul is contrasting two groups of people: the converted and unconverted" (Moo, *Romans*, 486). Barnhouse adds, "The believer who has passed through all of these wonderful experiences finds that his mind accepts these truths theologically but that in practice the horrible motions of sin are still him." Donald Grey Barnhouse, *God's Heirs: Expositions of Bible Doctrines Taking the Epistle to the Romans as a Point of Departure*, vol. 3 (Grand Rapids, MI: Eerdmans, 1983), 29.

[66] Murray, *Romans*, 285.

[67] Hodge, *Romans*, 255.

flesh results in death (8:6).[68] Again, death in this passage does not reference physical death or annihilationism in eschatological judgment. Rather, it is eternal death, facing God's eternal wrath, that is in direct contrast to the experience of those in the Spirit who will receive God's eternal life (8:6).

Those of the flesh will face God's eternal wrath because their mind-set is at enmity with him (8:7a).[69] Their direction and course of life is driven by their base and depraved desires of the fallen nature, which is at war with God and his law (8:7b). Those whose mind-set is on the flesh cannot submit to or keep God's moral law because they do not possess the ability to do so (8:7c).[70] Since the law reveals God's nature and character, anything that is contrary to God's law is contrary and at war with God, whose holy and righteous nature[71] demands "propitiation."[72]

Finally, Paul takes this argument one step further to deduce that those who do not possess the Spirit of Christ do not belong to Christ (8:9b). In other words, those whose mind-set is directed and controlled by the flesh are those who do not have the Spirit of Christ indwelling them. Thus, if someone does not possess the Spirit of Christ—the Holy Spirit—then that person is not in union with Christ. If such a person is not in union with Christ, then the work of Christ is not applied to that person by the Spirit of God. If the work of Christ is not applied to a person, then that individual is reliant upon his/her own works according to the law for righteousness. However, since those outside of Christ cannot keep the law, all that the law can provide is condemnation and the eschatological wrath of God. In other words, those who do not have the Spirit of Christ indwelling them are not believers.[73]

Mind Set on the Spirit and Life (8:5–11)

Paul then contrasts those controlled by the flesh with those whose mind-set is of the Spirit (8:5b). He assures all true believers that they are in the Spirit and not in the flesh, and therefore have the Spirit of God indwelling them (8:9a). The indwelling of the Spirit applies the work of Christ and guarantees believers that they will not receive the wrath of God but rather will obtain life from God because they are at peace (8:6b) with him through the imputed righteousness of Christ (8:10).

---

[68] Gill, *Romans*, 482.
[69] Schreiner, *Romans*, 412.
[70] Ibid.
[71] Hodge, *Romans*, 256.
[72] Kruse, *Romans*, 331.
[73] Murray, *Romans*, 288.

Moreover, through the indwelling of the Spirit, believers have also been made alive (8:10). Even though this life is one in which we live in corrupted and fallen mortal bodies, Christians have been made alive by the Spirit of God through union with Christ (8:10) and will someday be raised by God to enjoy eternal life.[74]

Until then, we choose to place our minds on the things of the Spirit of God (8:5). Surely this includes a focus on God, his holiness, his righteousness, his will, his kingdom, his people, his mission, and his Word, which we read, meditate on, memorize, and study (see Pss. 1:1–3; 119; Matt. 6:19–34; Phil. 4:8). With our minds on the things of the Spirit, we can focus on loving God and others and on serving God through serving others (Phil. 2:1–11). We can focus on living according to God's character and ways, seeking to obey God, being empowered by his Spirit, and walking according to the Spirit. If we are to have obedience as a way of life, it will flow from choosing a mind-set dedicated to the things of God.

Tension #5: Debtors and Heirs (Romans 8:12–25)

When we think about coming into a massive inheritance, we assume that the inheritance brings increasing freedom, especially from debts. The extra money brings extra freedom to pursue the various activities one enjoys. In this section, however, Paul upholds a tension and duality that might surprise us. He asserts that believers are heirs who will receive an unbelievable inheritance as those who are fellow heirs with Christ. And he adds that we are also under great debt precisely because we are heirs. We are both debtors and heirs. How does this work?

Heirs (8:12–17)

While we were slaves to sin and willingly carried out the deeds of the flesh in obedience to death, we lived as though we were debtors to sin. But Paul reminds us that we are slaves no longer to sin but to God in Christ. The Son of God has delivered us from the condemnation of death so that we no longer live as debtors to the flesh (8:12). The flesh cannot claim us or demand our allegiance, as though we were debtors (ὀφειλέται) in obligation to it and the death it requires (8:13a).[75]

Rather, Christ has purchased and delivered us from the bondage to sin and has taken us to himself. In his blood we have been given the atonement that brings us the forgiveness of our sins. Through his flesh, we have

---

[74] Moo, *Romans*, 492–93.
[75] Morris, *Romans*, 311.

been given his righteousness that allows us into the kingdom of God. But Christ has given us more than redemption and deliverance—he has also given us the title "heirs of God"!

Paul maintains that believers are now sons of God (8:14). When Paul makes this declaration, he is reminding us that human beings are not born naturally into the family of God, as though salvation could be passed down as a family heirloom. Rather, through humanity's union with Adam, we all suffer as the sons of disobedience and are by nature children of God's wrath (Eph. 2:2–3). This is what we are by nature, and thus we must be spiritually reborn through the Spirit's work of regeneration. Once we are regenerated and justified, we are adopted into God's family as sons and daughters through Christ (8:15).[76]

Since we are adopted as sons and daughters of God, we are also given the Spirit of adoption so that we can cry out "Abba! Father!" (8:15). "Abba" is the transliterated Aramaic term of endearment or intimacy[77] used for "Father."[78] This is the same term Jesus uses when praying and calling out to God as his Father (Mark 14:36; Luke 22:42) and the term Jesus teaches his disciples to use in matters of prayer (Matt. 6:9; Luke 11:2). Thus, instead of having a spirit of fear that stems from facing God in his wrath, we who are in Christ have God as our adoptive Father who will hear and answer us in prayer. What an amazing blessing: "See what kind of love the Father has given to us, that we should be called children of God; and so we are" (1 John 3:1).

Not only does Paul make the astounding declaration that believers are adopted sons and daughters of God who can address the Most Holy God as "Father," but he adds that we are coheirs with Christ as heirs of God (8:17). Paul claims that believers are heirs of God (κληρονόμοι θεοῦ), meaning that part of our inheritance as heirs is God himself. Paul is not saying that we possess God, but rather that God is our God, that we are his sons and daughters, and that we will enjoy him thoroughly for eternity.[79]

Since we are coheirs with Christ, we will inherit what he inherits. He is the true seed of Abraham and receives the land and the people God promised him (Gal. 3:16, 29).[80] As coheirs with Christ, we too share in this

---

[76] Ralph P. Martin, "Sonship," in *New Dictionary of Theology*, ed. Sinclair B. Ferguson, David F. Wright, and J. I. Packer (Downers Grove, IL: InterVarsity Press, 1988), 651–53.
[77] Schreiner, *Romans*, 426.
[78] BDAG, s.v. ἀββα.
[79] Schreiner, *Romans*, 428.
[80] Hodge, *Romans*, 268.

inheritance. Our inheritance includes, but is not limited to, God himself, eternal life, the eradication of all covenant curses, glorification, and the new heavens and new earth as our land (see Eph. 1:11; Heb. 1:1–4; 1 Pet. 1:3–7; Revelation 21).

Debtors (8:12–14)

We might think that this inheritance frees us from debts and obligations, but it does not—it does just the opposite. Since all believers are now children of God and will receive an abundant inheritance, we all have an obligation as debtors to live by the Spirit of God who indwells us (8:13b). We are called to the task of putting to death the deeds of the body, or the "mortification of the flesh," by the power of the Spirit.

As we live by the Spirit in obedience, we will, by necessity, be about the task of mortification. We will realize that any thinking or action of the flesh is sin and is at enmity with God and thus is not pleasing to him.[81] Therefore, as slaves to righteousness, we desire to please God through obedience in thought and deed. We are called to hate sin as God hates it and to take every thought captive (2 Cor. 10:5). Martyn Lloyd-Jones skillfully captures Paul's warning: "I want to have nothing more to do with that old life, and therefore I will mortify the deeds of the body which still tend to lead me to live after the flesh. I am going to kill the sin that remains in me, I am going to throttle it, I am going to put it to death."[82] Indeed, we grow in sanctification by loving obedience and hating and denying sin. This action is part of our daily obligation back to God as debtors to him, as John Owen penetratingly reminds: "Do you mortify? Do you make it your daily work? You must always be at it while you live; do not take a day off from this work; always be killing sin or it will be killing you."[83]

Paul then indicates that all heirs of God will suffer in this life (8:17). The author of Hebrews states that Christ, as a Son, learned obedience through suffering (Heb. 5:8). As adopted sons of God united to Christ, we should have a similar expectation: "Those suffer with Christ who suffer as he did, and for his sake. They are thus partakers of the sufferings of Christ. We suffer as Christ suffered, not only when we are subject to the contradiction of sinners, but in the ordinary life in which he, the man of

---

[81] Ibid., 265.

[82] D. Martyn Lloyd-Jones, *Romans: An Exposition of Chapter 8:5–17, The Sons of God* (repr. Carlisle, PA: Banner of Truth, 2015), 107–8.

[83] John Owen, "The Mortification of Sin," *The Treasures of John Owen*, abr. Richard Rushing (Carlisle, PA: Banner of Truth, 2016), 5.

sorrows, so largely shared."[84] He suffered for every believer, and therefore every believer should expect to suffer for him (8:17).[85]

Thankfully, Paul adds that any and all suffering in this life will be worth the cost, since every believer is promised and guaranteed glorification (8:17c–18).[86] Christ suffered, knowing that the Father would vindicate and glorify him, and we too can suffer, knowing that the Father will do the same for us (8:17c). Someday, the Father will raise us from our perishable mortal bodies and give us perfected and sinless bodies in glory (8:18). In this way, we are debtors who are obligated to live by the Spirit and grow through suffering. At the same time, we are adopted sons and daughters of God who are coheirs with Christ and will suffer as a matter of our spirituality. And this suffering is worth it, Paul contends: "I consider that the sufferings of this present time are not worth comparing with the glory that is to be revealed to us" (8:18).

Suffering, Our Inheritance, and Our Hope (8:19–25)

In the age to come, the full realities of our adoption and inheritance as the children of God will be revealed. In the present time, we are merely the firstfruits of the Spirit's resurrection power through regeneration (8:23). However, much as the firstfruit principle of the Old Testament pointed toward the guaranteed completion of God's promises (Deuteronomy 26), so too we can be certain that our adoption will come to fruition,[87] for God has given us the Holy Spirit as the "eschatological pledge" of what is to come (Rom. 8:23; see also Eph. 1:11–14).[88] Therefore, Paul says that we also groan inwardly with anticipation of the age to come and the full redemption of our bodies (Rom. 8:24). In this way, all present sufferings and internal struggles will pale in comparison to what we will be given through Christ by the Spirit in the age to come. In our daily battles of sanctification and spirituality, we can endure moments of suffering and pain, knowing that God will bring it all to a final resolution. There will be a day in which we are fully glorified and the freedom that we will experience at that moment will far surpass the pain of today. While the war of sanctification is painful and momentary, our glorification lasts for eternity.

Paul also reminds us that the creation itself is suffering currently

---

[84] Hodge, *Romans*, 268.
[85] Murray, *Romans*, 298.
[86] We will address glorification in the following section.
[87] Dunn, *Romans*, 473.
[88] Mounce, *Romans*, 185.

under the fall of Adam. When Adam broke the terms of the Edenic covenant, God subjected the creation to futility, or emptiness, by pronouncing a curse upon it (8:20).[89] The creation that was intended to reflect perfectly the majesty and glory of its Creator now does so marred by a curse.[90] The ground brings forth thorns and thistles as it suffers decay and corruption under God's covenant curses (8:21).

But the whole of creation does not groan together in vain (8:22). Rather, it suffers the pains of childbirth, knowing that someday it will be freed and delivered from the bondage of the curse (8:21–22).[91] Thus it eagerly awaits the revealing and glorification of the sons of God so that it too might see a cosmic renewal (8:19).[92] Creation is able to groan under its current suffering of covenant curses because it knows the hope awaiting it. In this way, the groaning of creation serves as an example of our current war in spirituality. The momentary pain is real but worth it because of what awaits us in glorification.

Paul then writes that we are saved in hope (8:24). This hope is not the type of thing that can be physically seen and proven through mathematical theorems. Rather, it is something that cannot be seen, so that the believer desires and anticipates its arrival (8:25). But how is the Christian salvation one of hope? The salvation that has been given to believers is the firstfruits of what is to come (8:23). In this present age, we have received the initial stages of salvation, but the full and final realization of that salvation will be completed in the age to come.[93] And while what we have already received in salvation is gracious beyond comprehension, the promise of that which we will be given as the adopted children of God and coheirs with Christ should make us long for the day of glorification (8:25).

Tension #6: Persevering and Preserved (Romans 8:26–37)

How can Paul be so certain about this hope? Surely the basis for Paul's hope is not merely a human desire for something to happen that may or may not actually happen.[94] Rather, just as he grounded much of his previous thought in sound theology, he now bases our hope of glorification on the sovereignty and character of the triune God who both preserves us and calls us to persevere in our spirituality.

---

[89] Harry Alan Hahne, *The Corruption and Redemption of Creation: Nature in Romans 8:19–22 and Jewish Apocalyptic Literature*, LNTS (New York: T&T Clark, 2006), 207.
[90] C. E. B. Cranfield, *The Epistle to the Romans*, vol. 1 (Edinburgh: T&T Clark, 1975), 414.
[91] Calvin, *Romans*, 306.
[92] Holland, *Romans*, 274.
[93] Hendriksen, *Romans*, 271.
[94] Ibid.

Preserved by God

Our hope, Paul declares, is based on the sovereignty and providence of God. The same God who spoke the creation into existence and subjected it to covenant curses for Adam's failure is the one who works all things according to his ultimate will (8:27b). Thus, under the providence of the sovereign God, all things are working together for good to those who love God and are called according to his purpose (8:28). This calling does not refer to the universal call of the gospel that goes throughout the world as it is preached.[95] Rather, this is the internal call of God that brings forth faith (8:30; 9:11–16).[96] We love God because he first loved us (see 1 John 4:7–12) and knew or chose us ahead of time and called us to himself (8:29). God, who calls those of us foreknown by him, also predestines us to a goal (8:29b). As he is working all things together for our good, he predestines us to be conformed to the image of his Son, so that Christ would be the firstborn among many brothers (8:29c). Notice that God's eternal plan here is not only our salvation but also our spirituality and Jesus' glory. Further, just as Christ was raised and will bring all things to completion according to the will of God, so too are we, as the sons of God in Christ, justified and guaranteed to be brought to our future glorification (8:30).[97] This means that God is preserving, and will continue to preserve, us as his adopted children.

Paul also underlines that God has given the Holy Spirit to all believers (8:26). The Spirit of God has already regenerated, indwelled, and sealed those who are in Christ, but he is also working out God's will of sanctification among all those who love God. At this moment, the Spirit of God is helping us in our weakness as God is moving us forward in his plan of glorification. Just as God's creation and God's people are groaning in anticipation of God's carrying out his plan of redemption, so too is the Spirit of God groaning as he is working and furthering us in holiness (8:26). He is working out the will of God for us in our current state of weakness by interceding for us in prayer because we (Paul included) do not know how to pray rightly (8:26–27).

What does this mean for us and our desire to increase in holiness? Paul is filled with hope, but not because he merely *wants* our spirituality and glorification to happen. Rather, he *knows* that our entire salvation culminates in glorification and is grounded in the perfect work of

---

[95] Morris, *Romans*, 332.
[96] Kruse, *Romans*, 355.
[97] Murray, *Romans*, 321.

the sovereign God who is working all things according to his ultimate purpose. God is working out salvation history so that we are glorified as his adopted children.[98]

What does this mean for us? We must think through our current struggles in our Christian walk in light of the nature and character of God. If we know Christ, we realize that we do so because of God and his grace. Before time began, God foreknew us, loved us, and planned to save us. God then sent his Son to redeem us, called us by his Spirit, and justified and adopted us as we trusted in Christ. But God does not stop with our initial salvation. He made us alive to conform us into the image of Christ, he justified us in Christ, and he is now sanctifying us in Christ. He has been working all things for our good, and he will not stop until that work is completed at glory.

We are on a spiritual journey, one that God planned from eternity past, has accomplished in history in Christ's saving work, is applying to us in history through our union with Christ, and will continue as he preserves us in salvation and conforms us to Christ until he glorifies us in heaven. His preservation means not only that he keeps us saved but also that his power in us has given us the ability to live as sons and daughters of God. Yes, we groan as we await the final resolution, but we groan with hope. We have been crucified to the dominion of sin and are now alive to Christ and can live accordingly. We are no longer slaves to sin but are freed to love and obey God. We are still in a spiritual war, but we live in victory. We are people of the Spirit and can set our minds on the Spirit, which will lead to lives marked by love and holiness. We are adopted by God and heirs of God, now obligated and able to live unto God. We are being preserved, for all this and more—not perfectly, of course, but gradually, partially, and genuinely we can and will grow in holiness. We can and will be conformed to the image of Christ—God's eternal plan guarantees it. He has begun our spiritual journey, he is preserving it, and he will complete it at the day of Christ (see also Phil. 1:6). Indeed, our hope is not seen, but it is certain.

Persevering (8:31–39)

So we are preserved in our spiritual journey, Paul argues. And we are also persevering, which is likewise based on the nature, character, and acts of God. Paul reminds us that the trials and tribulations of this present life are real and should be expected in our war against the flesh. As followers of Christ, we will have enemies and those who will be in opposition to us (8:31).[99] There

---

[98] Schreiner, *Romans*, 448.
[99] Murray, *Romans*, 323.

will be those who will try to condemn us (8:34). We should expect to face real persecution from real enemies. Tribulation, distress, persecution, and armed adversaries are some of the difficulties we will suffer for the name and cause of Christ (8:35). We may also suffer from famines, the lack of basic provision, or even serious dangers in this present life.[100] Such oppositions and evils are a part of all things working together for our good (8:28) and are the means by which we are being conformed to the image of Christ (8:29). Paul quotes Psalm 44:22 (LXX 43:22): "For your sake we are being killed all the day long; we are regarded as sheep to be slaughtered," reminding us that we should expect to suffer unjustly (Rom. 8:36).[101] In the face of this type of opposition, God is actively preserving us, and we are tenaciously persevering.

Since God's plan of redemptive history culminated in the death, burial, and resurrection of the Son, we should expect that we will suffer as Christ suffered (8:17, 32). This difficult truth is consistent with the words Jesus speaks to his disciples in John 15:18–25:

> If the world hates you, know that it has hated me before it hated you. If you were of the world, the world would love you as its own; but because you are not of the world, but I chose you out of the world, therefore the world hates you. Remember the word that I said to you, "A servant is not greater than his master." If they persecuted me, they will also persecute you. If they kept my word, they will also keep yours. But all these things they will do to you on account of my name, because they do not know him who sent me. If I had not come and spoken to them, they would not have been guilty of sin, but now they have no excuse for their sin. Whoever hates me hates my Father also. If I had not done among them the works that no one else did, they would not be guilty of sin; but now they have seen and hated both me and my Father. But the word that is written in their Law must be fulfilled, "They hated me without a cause."

Paul wonderfully explains that these difficulties, while serious and real, cannot separate us from the love of God in Christ (8:39). Since we are children of God, no enemy can be eschatologically victorious over us (8:31). While we might lose our present lives at the hands of our enemies, such enemies cannot stop God's promise of glorification in us (8:32). While we might have many accusers and those who try to condemn us, no charge against God's elect will stand on the day of judgment (8:33). God is the one who has already justified us; our just punishment has al-

---

[100] Hodge, *Romans*, 291.
[101] Moo, *Romans*, 544.

ready been placed upon Christ on the cross, and no guilt remains (8:34): "Not only did Jesus die but he was also raised. His resurrection signified his vindication, indicating that his atoning work was completed."[102] Famine, sickness, or execution do not indicate a lack of faith in God but are expected marks of our adoption. And these sufferings, while arduous, cannot separate us from the love of Jesus Christ (8:35).

We will not only face these hardships; we will conquer them, and then some. We will prevail completely (ὑπερνικῶμεν) against them because of the God who loves us: "In all these things we are more than conquerors through him who loved us" (8:37). God does not take us around the difficulties and opposition but instead gives us abundant grace to preserve us, to enable us to persevere, and even to flourish triumphantly. Indeed, nothing in the present life—not death, angels, earthly rulers, present or future powers, nor anything in this created order—has the authority or the power to separate believers from the electing, justifying, sanctifying, and glorifying love of God displayed and given to us in Jesus Christ (8:39). God is the author and finisher of our faith, and he will bring to completion our glorification and inheritance on the day of Christ (Heb. 12:1–2; Phil. 1:6).

As Christians and legitimate coheirs with Christ, we should expect to suffer, because Jesus suffered. We should expect to be unjustly accused and condemned by the courts of this world, because he endured the same. We should expect to face tribulation and persecution just as our Lord faced them. But we should also expect to endure them successfully, because God has sent us the Holy Spirit to help us in our weakness and to intercede for us in our prayer. We have the mind and life of the Spirit, and the Spirit of sonship as the children of God. He has given us the love and work of Christ the Son, who also intercedes for us. The God who chose us in Christ before the foundation of the world, who works all things together for our ultimate eschatological good, will complete his work and bring us to glory. And he has given us the ability and power through his Spirit to continue in the faith and carry out a victorious life.

Conclusion

Romans 6–8 is a theologically rich section of Scripture that helps us understand the tensions in our spirituality. First, we are both crucified and alive (6:1–14). Just as Christ was crucified and buried, so too have we been crucified and buried. We are no longer obligated to use our bodies

---

[102] Schreiner, *Romans*, 463.

for unrighteousness. Rather, we are alive in and through Christ. As he defeated death through his resurrection, we are new and alive in the Spirit. Because we are alive and empowered by the Spirit, the members of our bodies are instruments to carry out the righteousness of God through obedience. We can be victorious over sin by obeying the Spirit of God.

Second, we are both slaves and free (6:15–7:7). Through our union with Christ, we are no longer slaves to sin as our former master. In that form of bondage, we gladly worked out the desires and will of sin even though we knew that its end is death. But we are now free from sin's rule through Christ. He has broken our spiritual bondage and ensured that sin can no longer have mastery over us. But we are not autonomously free to do as we please. Rather, we are now slaves to God. Just as we served our former master, so now we have the obligation to carry out the will and desire of our new master. His desire is to carry out the plan of redemption in Christ in perfect holiness and righteousness. Thus we are to seek out how we can be the God-ordained means by which his plan comes to fruition. We are to seek to obey our Lord joyously and lovingly through the power and guidance of the Holy Spirit.

Third, we are at war but are victorious in it (7:8–8:4). We are at war with sin, Satan, the world, and our old self. Although our old self is crucified, dead, and buried, we still reside in mortal bodies of flesh. The flesh still desires the works of the flesh and the deeds that bring death and ruin. While we still fall short, we should hate our sin. We should be driven to our knees in repentance when we sin, because we know that God is holy and hates sin. At the same time, God has given us his Holy Spirit to help us walk in victory and carry out the function (not perfection) of the law. In this way, our lives should reflect the character of God. We should live holy lives because God is holy. We should love our neighbors because Christ died for us. In short, a victorious life is one that longs to love and obey God and that rightly reflects his character. Though we are at war, we can have victory.

Fourth, we are volitional and spiritual. We choose the right mind-set of life (8:5–11). In our old self, our mind-set was determined to carry out the deeds of sin. Day after day we sinned, following our former master. Now, as new in Christ, we must choose the mind-set of the life through the Spirit. Each trial and difficulty in life now becomes an opportunity to obey God. Our new mind-set must be one that seeks first the kingdom of God and his righteousness.

Fifth, we are both debtors and heirs (8:12–25). We are adopted sons and daughters of God and can call God "Father." And our Father desires to give us an inheritance that has been earned through Christ. This magnificent inheritance includes the riches of heaven and the privilege of dwelling with God for eternity in the new heavens and the new earth. But our adoption as sons and daughters carries with it an obligation to live as a reflection of his holiness and righteousness.

Sixth, we are both persevering and being preserved (8:26–39). In our obligation back to God, we are called to suffer just as his Son learned obedience through suffering. Each moment of suffering is a moment whereby we can display our devotion to God through persevering in the faith. We can persevere precisely because we know that God is for us and is preserving us. We know that the completion of our spiritual journey is in the capable hands of God. The same God who spoke the universe into existence has chosen us, called us, loved us, and designed us to be his trophies of grace. He has saved us, made us alive, justified us, and started his work of sanctification in us. He is more than capable of completing this task and has promised that he will bring us to full glorification.

So are we walking dichotomies? Not really. But feeling that we are is normal, and certainly not abnormal. As followers of Christ, our lives are marked by both a sincere longing for holiness and a struggle with sin. We live with the tensions related to realizing genuine growth and experiencing frequent failure. We are all works in progress; we are under construction. "He's still working on me" is not just a song for children to sing at church; it is a reality that clarifies our spiritual journey on this side of heaven. Our salvation has begun and will be completed, but, in the meantime, we are in the process of growing in holiness, love, and Christlikeness. As strange as it feels, we are now saints and are also not yet fully holy in our day-to-day lives, though we are increasingly so. We are, as Martin Luther stressed five hundred years ago, simultaneously justified and sinners. Hence the tensions.

One day, though, by God's grace, we will be thoroughly transformed. God's grace has begun our journey, God's grace sustains our journey, and God's grace will lead us home, completing our journey. On that day, we will be completely characterized by holiness and love, and all our current battles with sin will be a distant memory. In the meantime, we can find in Paul's words hope and encouragement to persevere:

If God is for us, who can be against us? (8:31)

Who shall separate us from the love of Christ? (8:35)

In all these things we are more than conquerors through him who loved us. (8:37)

5

INTEGRATED SPIRITUALITY

Spirituality according to James

CHRISTOPHER W. MORGAN

When you hear the word *spiritual*, what comes to mind? Clearing our minds of all distractions? Sitting on a mat? A retreat in the mountains? Journaling? And whom do you associate with being spiritual? Ordained ministers or monks? Contemplatives?

What should come to mind when we think of spirituality?

Written to real-life churches with real-life problems, the epistle of James provides an essential and countercultural vision of spirituality. James's alternative vision is thoroughly grounded in the nature of God and is stubbornly practical. It has its origins in heaven but is geared for God's people on the ground. As a major leader in the Jerusalem church, and therefore of other churches related to that mother church as well, James writes from a pastoral perspective and with pastoral goals. He helps Jewish Christians in local churches experiencing trials (1:2–11) and oppression (2:6; 5:1–11). Some were claiming they had faith, but they had little concern for personal holiness (1:22–25; 4:4) and failed to assist their poor brothers and sisters in Christ (1:26–27; 2:14–17). The congregations also included some who sought influence as teachers but were spiritually unqualified for the role (3:1–18). Many, including some desiring to be teachers, were quarrelsome, bringing friction rather than peace (3:13–4:10). James writes to address such church problems and responds by offering wisdom for consistency in the community.[1]

---

[1] This essay draws from two of my previous works on James, which are more thorough in terms of exegesis, theology, and application: Christopher W. Morgan, *A Theology of James: Wisdom for God's People*, Explorations

137

In doing so, James offers a vision of spirituality, what I call "integrated spirituality." Integrated spirituality is a Christian wholeness,[2] an integrated way of life marked by wisdom, faith, love, self-control, and community. According to James, Christians reject double-mindedness, hypocrisy, and duplicity. Instead, God's people are devoted, sincere, and consistent. They display wisdom and faith even during tough trials; they hear God's Word and obey it; they love God and one another; they have faith in Christ and perform works of love for the poor; they praise God and bless one another with their words.

James relates this integrated spirituality to many situations: suffering, oppression, trials, temptation, poverty, wealth, church, leadership, division, commerce, legal proceedings, sickness, and the sinful wanderings of others. James incorporates multiple virtues and good fruits into this integrated spirituality: faith, wisdom, perseverance, watchfulness, obedience, self-control, holiness, love, mercy, justice, community, meekness, peace, gentleness, sincerity, humility, repentance, submission, patience, steadfastness, hope, and truth. James points to chief means to such integrated spirituality: God's Word, prayer, and life together as the church. And James stresses the active nature of this integrated spirituality: it rejoices, trusts, asks, perseveres, hears, repents, continues, obeys, restrains, visits, guards, honors, fulfills, speaks, believes, gives, serves, bridles, demonstrates, sows, submits, resists, draws, cleanses, weeps, accepts, acknowledges, does, waits, establishes, prays, anoints, confesses, searches, and more.

Let's further explore James's view of integrated spirituality by examining four representative passages.

Integrated Spirituality as Wisdom and Faith amidst Suffering (1:2–8)

James 1:2–4 reveals that James's readers were experiencing various trials. While we do not know exactly what these trials were, the rest of the letter indicates that they likely had to do with poor Christians' being persecuted by rich oppressors. In a manner that sounds audacious to us but stands in continuity with the teachings of Jesus and the other apostles (Matt. 5:10–

---

in Biblical Theology (Phillipsburg, NJ: P&R, 2010); Christopher W. Morgan and B. Dale Ellenburg, *James: Wisdom for the Community*, Focus on the Bible Commentaries (Fearn, Ross-shire, UK: Christian Focus, 2008).
[2] Douglas J. Moo, *The Letter of James*, PNTC (Grand Rapids, MI: Eerdmans, 2000), 43–46. David Dockery notes: "James pictures true piety as the direct application of the implanted word in the life of the believer. The result vertically is the submission to and worship of God. The result horizontally is concern for the poor, widows and orphans in distress. The result relationally is living peaceably with others in the church. The result inwardly is the humility, purity and gentleness of character that comes from heavenly wisdom." David S. Dockery, "True Piety in James: Ethical Admonitions and Theological Implications," *CTR* 1 (Fall 1986): 69.

12; Rom. 5:1–5; 1 Pet. 1:6–7), James charges God's people to count it all joy whenever these trials come. Why? Because God is using such trials for our spiritual formation. Perseverance, completeness, and blamelessness are worthy effects that come as a result of our having faith in the midst of suffering (1:3–4; cf. Rom. 5:1–5; 2 Cor. 1:3–7; 1 Pet. 1:5–8). James urges rejoicing, "for you know that the testing of your faith produces steadfastness" (1:3). James here associates trials with the testing of faith, which is interesting in light of the context. The trials most readily in view were likely brought on by evil, rich landowners. Yet while these oppressors' sins caused the believers' suffering, James asserts that God is at work, using the suffering as a testing of the faith of his people.

What does this testing do? It develops "perseverance." This has also been translated "endurance," "steadfastness," "fortitude," or "patience." Like a muscle that becomes strong when facing resistance from a weight, we develop spiritual strength and stamina through facing trials. It is hard to imagine how perseverance could be developed in any way other than by such resistance, since perseverance presupposes a pressure to endure. So when trials come, James calls us to consider it joy and recognize that God is developing in us perseverance and other good traits. The development of this perseverance is a process. One event does not bring forth enduring character; it is the real-life process of encountering trials and responding to them in faith that produces perseverance.[3] But perseverance is not only an end in our integrated spirituality; it is also a means to further ends: "And let steadfastness have its full effect, that you may be perfect and complete, lacking in nothing" (1:4). The Revised English Bible translates it well: "Let endurance perfect its work in you that you may become perfected."

James teaches that we experience trials because we still live in the present age. The consummation of the ages has not yet occurred; we still await Jesus' coming, last judgment, and complete victory. And while we live in this present age, we are being made mature. Just as the kingdom of God has already come and yet has not been fully realized, so our salvation has come and yet still awaits its full manifestation. James sees the already

---

[3] Peter H. Davids, *The Epistle of James*, NIGTC (Grand Rapids, MI: Eerdmans, 1982), 69. Thanks to my previous co-author Dale Ellenburg for his many insights into this passage. Note also that the importance of persevering through trials is striking (1:3–4, 12). Dan G. McCartney, "Suffering and the Apostles," in *Suffering and the Goodness of God*, ed. Christopher W. Morgan and Robert A. Peterson, Theology in Community (Wheaton, IL: Crossway, 2008), 106: "This chain of life in James 1:12 stands in opposition to a chain of death in 1:13–15, where trials lead to desires which give birth to sin, which brings forth death. Again, this shows that it is not the trial itself that produces maturity and life, for a trial could result in non-endurance, in the giving in to desire, and in the birthing of sin and death."

and not yet of our salvation as intertwined, for God is using trials to produce perfection and completeness in us. We still need to be completed, and this can happen only through the historical process that develops our faith, steadfastness, and maturity. In fact, James links "lacking in nothing" in verse 4 with "if any of you lacks wisdom" in verse 5. We need wisdom because we experience trials, and we also need wisdom because we still "lack." We are not yet "lacking in nothing" (1:4), so we need wisdom to help us become increasingly mature.

James then urges, "If any of you lacks wisdom, let him ask God" (1:5). Here James stands in the Old Testament and Jewish traditions. Proverbs 2:6 states, "The LORD gives wisdom." Proverbs 1:7 clarifies, "The fear of the LORD is the beginning of knowledge; / fools despise wisdom and instruction." Tremper Longman comments on Proverbs 1:7:

> This statement claims there is no knowledge apart from a proper attitude and relationship to Yahweh. Fear of Yahweh is foundational to knowledge. . . . In this way, the book acknowledges the radically relational and theocentric nature of knowledge/wisdom. . . . It is the first thought that makes all other thoughts fall into place. . . . What the prologue makes clear is that the benefits of wisdom are available only to those who have already made a fundamental religious commitment.[4]

So wisdom at its core is theological. It is rightly understanding our place in the cosmos and relating to God accordingly. He is supreme and we are not; therefore, we must fear him and "acknowledge our creaturely dependence upon him."[5] This is basic to James's understanding of wisdom.

James also urges us to ask God for wisdom because of who God is and how God gives. Three truths stand out. First, God gives wisdom *generously* or *singly*. Because God is single-minded and gives singly, we are to ask with single-mindedness, not double-mindedness.[6] Second, God gives wisdom generously *to all*. God is glad to give wisdom. He does not show favoritism or withhold it from people with genuine faith. He is generous in giving wisdom to all people of faith—no matter our age, gender, ethnic-

---

[4] Tremper Longman III, *Proverbs*, Baker Commentary on the Old Testament (Grand Rapids, MI: Baker, 2006), 100–4.

[5] Daniel J. Estes, *Hear, My Son: Teaching and Learning in Proverbs 1–9*, NSBT (Grand Rapids, MI: Eerdmans, 1997), 35–39.

[6] Moo, *James*, 58–60. John Calvin comments on James 1:8: "This sentence may be read by itself, as he speaks generally of hypocrites. It seems, however, to me to be rather the conclusion of the preceding doctrine; and thus there is an implied contrast between the simplicity or liberality of God, mentioned before, and the double-mindedness of man; for as God gives to us with a stretched-out hand, so it behooves us in our turn to open the bosom of our heart." John Calvin, *Commentaries on the Epistle of James*, Calvin's Commentaries, vol. 22 (repr. Grand Rapids, MI: Baker, 1999), 284.

ity, or socioeconomic level. Third, God gives wisdom generously to all *without reproach*. God is a cheerful and ungrudging giver. God desires the best for us, and he knows that what is best for us is dependence upon him.

God is the source of wisdom, but he gives it only to those who will use it rightly. James asserts, "Let him ask in faith" (1:6). Verse 5 warmly exhorts readers to seek wisdom from God, and verse 6 clarifies the stipulation for receiving God's gift of wisdom: faith. Wisdom rightly realizes the sovereignty of God and our subsequent place in the order of things. As such, wisdom is inevitably linked to humility and faith.

James adds, "with no doubting" (1:6), and clarifies the nature and importance of faith. "Doubting" displays a lack of faith. It is to fail to believe, trust, or rely upon God; it is to be divided and drawn in two directions. Verse 8 uses a related word that describes this condition: "double-minded." Those who doubt are like "a wave of the sea that is driven and tossed by the wind," drifting according to external pressures. James warns such doubters not to think they "will receive anything from the Lord" (1:7). God loves to give wisdom to those who ask, indeed to all who ask, and he loves to give it generously and without any desire to hold back. But he gives wisdom only to those who ask in faith. The doubter who asks for wisdom is described again in verse 8. He is a "double-minded man, unstable in all his ways" (1:8). "Double-minded" translates *dipsychos*, a term found in the New Testament only here and in 4:8. Its root is "two-souled" or "divided soul." It is akin to being "two-faced" and indicates covenant unfaithfulness. This expression in James closely resembles Jesus' teaching on hypocrisy. Douglas Moo wonders if James "coined the term to accentuate his concern that believers display a wholehearted, consistent, and integral faith commitment to God."[7] To be double-minded is to have divided loyalties[8] and indicates covenant unfaithfulness. Luke Johnson clarifies, "What makes someone double-minded is precisely the desire to live by both measures at once, to be friends with everyone [the world and God]."[9]

Although the term "double-minded" is unusual, the concept is not, as Moo points out. The Psalms, for example, bless those who follow God with a "whole heart" (Ps. 119:2) but condemn those who display a "double heart" (Ps. 12:2; cf. Hos. 10:2). Jesus himself appeals to Deuteronomy 6:5

---

[7] Moo, *James*, 62.

[8] David DeGraaf suggests that "with no doubt" is an inadequate translation and prefers "without divided loyalties and divisive attitudes." DeGraaf, "Some Doubts about Doubt: The New Testament Use of *Diakrino*," *JETS* 48 (Dec. 2005): 733–55, esp. 741–42.

[9] Luke Timothy Johnson, "Friendship with the World/Friendship with God: A Study of Discipleship in James," in *Discipleship in the New Testament*, ed. Fernando F. Segovia (Philadelphia: Fortress, 1985), 182–83.

and its call to love God holistically: "Love the LORD your God with all your heart and with all your soul and with all your might" (cf. Matt. 22:37–40). He also points to seeking first the kingdom, serving only one master, having a single eye, and avoiding the sin of hypocrisy (Matt. 6:19–34). We cannot have two masters, take two roads, bear two fruits, or lay two foundations (Matt. 7:13–27).

Double-minded living is spiritual wavering, trying to live a double life, seeking to follow a double standard, wanting to please two masters, attempting to walk two paths, or claiming religion without covenant faithfulness. In contrast, for James true spirituality is integrated, embracing purity, single-minded devotion, sincerity, wholeness, and covenant faithfulness. Wisdom, the purpose of which is to enable believers to follow God as a way of life, is a gift God grants only to those who are committed to following him. Why grant it to people who will not use it? Those interested only in dabbling will be disappointed. Peter Davids puts it frankly: "The man who expects to get something from God despite his lack of commitment is simply deluded."[10] Davids later summarizes:

> The author, then, concludes his description of this doubter with a strong condemnation: his divided mind, when it comes to trusting God, indicates a basic disloyalty toward God. Rather than being a single-minded lover of God, he is one whose character and conduct is unstable, even hypocritical. No wonder he should expect nothing from God! He is not in the posture of a trusting child. For James there is no middle ground between faith and no faith; such a one, he will later argue (4:8), needs to repent.[11]

Double-minded spirituality will not do, James asserts. Instead, he calls us to an integrated spirituality, one that seeks wisdom, requires our faith, and leads us into maturity, even in the midst of suffering.

Integrated Spirituality as Holiness and Love for the Poor (1:26–27)
Often considered the center or thesis of the epistle, James 1:26–27 is a striking passage that further clarifies this integrated spirituality: true spirituality integrates holiness with love for the poor. James 1:26–27 flows from the arguments of 1:18–25, which highlight God's Word as central to true spirituality. Just as God's word is his agency throughout the biblical story of creation, election, redemption, and the new creation, God

---

[10] Davids, *James*, 74.
[11] Ibid., 75.

uses his Word holistically in our lives as his people and at the beginning, middle, and end of our spirituality. Through his authoritative and powerful Word, God births us into a new creation (1:18) and brings about our final salvation (1:21). Because of this, we are to be quick to "hear" the Word (1:19), to lay aside sin in preparation to receive the Word (1:21), to receive it with meekness (1:21), and to hear and do it (1:22–25). Those of us who do the Word will be blessed in our doing (1:25). True spirituality is characterized not merely by hearing the Word but by doing it as well. Integrated spirituality is Word-driven, Word-saturated, and Word-centric, as it studies the Word, receives guidance from the Word, perseveres in the Word, acts according to the Word, and is blessed by God accordingly.

James warns that spirituality is more than merely hearing the Word; it integrates the Word into our very lives (1:22–25). Indeed, people of the Word bridle their words (1:26). People of the Word love those whom God loves—the poor and the oppressed (1:27). People of the Word are committed to personal holiness (1:27). Such spirituality is "pure," "undefiled," and acceptable to God. By using purity language and calling true religion "pure and undefiled," James suggests by contrast that the spirituality embraced by some in these churches is impure and defiled. Their so-called worship is evidently unclean, contaminated, and unsuitable for the holy God. By referring to true spirituality as keeping oneself "unstained from the world" (1:27), James suggests that some of them are preoccupied with ritual cleanness without a corresponding interest in moral cleanness or godly values. And by stressing that God accepts true spirituality, he implies that God rejects some of their false approaches. That James calls their efforts at worship "worthless" strengthens the effect. It is worthless because it does not demonstrate love for God or love for others. Indeed, it is worthless because it does not demonstrate love for God *through* love for others.

Martin Luther frequently stressed this very point. Luther complained that believers should not live in monasteries to serve God, for there they were actually only serving themselves. Instead, as Christians we must follow Christ and love and serve our neighbors through our vocations in the world, where our neighbors encounter and need them. Luther argued, "God does not need our good works, but our neighbor does."[12] When we seek to offer our good works to God, we display pride before God and neglect to love our neighbor. Luther contended that in so doing we parade

---

[12] Gustav Wingren, *Luther on Vocation*, trans. Carl C. Rasmussen (repr. Evansville, IN: Ballast, 2004), 2.

ourselves before God and yet fail to do the very thing Jesus commands. In other words, we fail both to love God and to love others. Michael Horton ably captures Luther's point:

> God descends to serve humanity through our vocations, so instead of seeing good works as our works for God, they are now to be seen as God's work for our neighbor, which God performs through us. That is why both orders are upset when we seek to present good works to God as if he needed them. In contrast, when we are overwhelmed by the superabundance of God's gracious gift, we express our gratitude in horizontal works of love and service to the neighbor.[13]

Love is not self-absorbed but genuinely seeks the welfare of others. It is active and outward. Luther is right: religious people often feel noble when they perform external religious acts because they believe they are serving God. But as Solomon Andria suggests, "Rather than serving God, they serve themselves."[14]

Serving others feels far less noble; it often seems only mundane, even insignificant. Yet Jesus washed his disciples' feet and demands that his followers do the same. Jesus' command would not be so burdensome if he merely required that we wash his feet; we could find dignity in helping Jesus. But Jesus demands that we wash one another's feet, which feels not stately but smelly. It reduces us to feeling like unimportant, humble servants. And that is exactly what James stresses: genuine, humble, dependent, loving followers of Jesus will display true spirituality through ministering to others, particularly those in desperation.

Some in James's audience were more concerned with ritual purity than with moral purity, content to express empty words without active compassion for the oppressed. Ironically, some in these congregations stressed the ritual purity taught in Leviticus but failed to notice that Leviticus also stresses moral purity and especially love for the oppressed. It is not by coincidence, in my opinion, that James refers frequently to Leviticus 19 as a basis of his instructions. He takes his audience back to study the very law they claim to be defending.[15] Leviticus 19:2 states, "Be holy, for I the LORD your God am holy." In what ways was Israel to be holy? Commenting on Leviticus 19, Christopher Wright observes:

---

[13] Michael S. Horton, *People and Place: A Covenant Ecclesiology* (Louisville, KY: Westminster John Knox, 2008), 304. I wish to credit Horton for the insights in this paragraph.
[14] Solomon Andria, "James," in *Africa Bible Commentary*, ed. Tokunboh Adeyemo (Grand Rapids, MI: Zondervan, 2006), 1514.
[15] Luke Timothy Johnson, "The Use of Leviticus 19 in the Letter of James," *JBL* 101.3 (1982): 391–402.

We are inclined to think of "holiness" as a matter of personal piety or, in Old Testament terms, of ritual cleanness, proper sacrifices, clean and unclean foods, and the like. Certainly, the rest of Leviticus 19 includes some of these dimensions of Israel's religious life. But the bulk of the chapter shows us that the kind of holiness that reflects God's own holiness is thoroughly practical. It includes generosity to the poor at harvest time, justice for workers, integrity in judicial processes, considerate behavior to other people (especially the disabled), equality before the law for immigrants, honest trading and other very "earthy" social matters. And all throughout the chapters runs the refrain "I am the LORD," as if to say, "Your quality of life must reflect the very heart of my character. This is what I require of you because this is what reflects me."[16]

James operates similarly and instructs that true spirituality is "to visit orphans and widows in their affliction" (1:27), reiterating the teachings of Exodus 22:22 ("You shall not mistreat any widow or fatherless child") and Isaiah 1:10–17 ("Bring justice to the fatherless, / plead the widow's cause"), and also making plain God's requirements for acceptable religion and worship (cf. Deut. 10:16–19; Ps. 69:32–33; Zech. 7:9–14). Together widows and orphans represent those without protection or provision. Ben Witherington III notes, "Our discourse is about a God who is impartial, faithful, righteous, just, merciful—and who requires of his followers the same sort of behavior."[17] Daniel Doriani puts it penetratingly: "Kindness to the needy is God-like. *We* sustain aliens, widows, and orphans because *he* sustains aliens, widows, and orphans (Ps. 146:9)."[18] True spirituality, that which pleases God, is integrated as we reflect God's holiness and love by ministering actively to the poor and oppressed.

Consistent with the many Old Testament teachings and the earliest depictions of the church (cf. Acts 2:42–47; 4:32–37; 5:1–11; 6:1–7; 11:19–30), James instructs the church to assume responsibility for the support of its poor, disadvantaged, and oppressed. Dan McCartney captures the point:

Just as genuine faith endures trials, so a Christian must respond to the suffering of others as a fellow sufferer. Hence he says true religion[19] is to

---

[16] Christopher J. H. Wright, *Old Testament Ethics for the People of God* (Downers Grove, IL: InterVarsity, 2004), 39.

[17] Ben Witherington III, *Letters and Homilies for Jewish Christians: A Socio-Rhetorical Commentary on Hebrews, James and Jude* (Downers Grove, IL: InterVarsity, 2007), 436.

[18] Daniel M. Doriani, *James*, Reformed Expository Commentary (Phillipsburg, NJ: P&R, 2007), 59; emphases original.

[19] McCartney, "Suffering and the Apostles," 107n15 reads, "The term used here for 'religion' (*threskeia*) means not one's overall faith commitments, but religious practice, acts of piety, or cultic activity. By 'true

care for sufferers (James 1:27). Because real faith (2:14–17) is faith that God will exalt the humble (1:9), the works that proceed from true faith will involve showing mercy to those who suffer. Of particular concern to James are the truly destitute, such as "orphans and widows" (1:27), or the man in filthy garments (2:2), who in that social environment were often the most marginalized and powerless people. The church is the community that anticipates the eschatological reversal by caring for and respecting the poor.

Therefore James has little tolerance for those who show favoritism to the rich. This kind of favoritism is offensive first because it violates the law of love and misrepresents the character of God, who cares about the poor. Note that the context of the law of love in Leviticus 19 specifically condemns partiality (Lev. 19:15).[20] Second, partiality belies the eschatological nature of the community, which ought to display in advance God's exaltation of the poor. James 2:1–17 thus teaches us that faithful living does not just pity the poor, it *respects* the poor. This is a difficult concept for most of us who are not poor, especially because suffering, poverty and destitution can make a person appear repulsive, which in turn has the effect of increasing that person's suffering.[21]

In stressing that integrated holiness and love for the poor are fundamental to true spirituality, James reflects the teachings of Jesus, who articulated that our genuine faith in him is integrated with our treatment of the most marginalized of his people ("the least of these my brothers," Matt. 25:31–46).

Integrated Spirituality as Faith in God and Works for Others (2:14–26)

The famous passage in James 2:14–26 also emphasizes that true spirituality is integrated, being driven by faith in God and issuing in corresponding good works for others. In this passage, James probes: "What good is it, my brothers, if someone says he has faith but does not have works? Can that faith save him?" (2:14). James asks, "What good is it?" in order to highlight the utter uselessness of these people's so-called faith. A spirituality that claims faith but is destitute of works is good for nothing because it does not justify the supposed believer and does not help the needy.

---

religion,' therefore, James does not mean 'the essence of true Christian faith' but 'the essence of true Christian religious activity.'"

[20] Ibid. 107n16 reads, "The love command of Lev. 19:18 is shared throughout the New Testament as definitive for Christian life. Its widespread use as the basis of ethics is probably due to the fact that it was promulgated by Jesus himself (Mark 12:29–31 and parallels). James's point is that showing favoritism violates the most basic ethic of God and, hence, violates the whole law."

[21] Ibid., 107; emphasis original.

James illustrates this in 2:15–16, painting the scene of fellow believers in need of basic necessities such as food and clothes.[22] Instead of getting actual help from their loving Christian community, these brothers and sisters in Christ only receive a farewell blessing, "Go in peace, be warmed and filled" (2:16). "Go in peace" is a common Jewish farewell—*shalom* (cf. Judg. 18:6; 1 Sam. 1:17; 20:42; 2 Sam. 15:9). Today it would be like saying, "Goodbye and God bless you." Instead of receiving warm clothes and nourishing food, all they get is religious triteness. Needs are left unmet; only words are offered. And these words speak of grace but fail to minister it. How can they go in peace when in reality they will go hungry and cold? And how do the professing Christians expect God to bless their spiritual family in need? Would it not be natural to think that God intends to bless the poor through others in his family? Even more, how can these professing Christians claim to follow Christ while simultaneously loving their possessions more than their needy brothers and sisters? Jonathan Edwards maintained: "To love our neighbor as ourselves is the sum of the moral law respecting our fellow-creatures; and to help them, and to contribute to their relief, is the most natural expression of this love. It is vain to pretend to a spirit of love to our neighbors, when it is grievous to us to part with anything for their help."[23]

James's illustration in 2:15–16 uncovers the hypocrisy of a spirituality that asserts faith apart from works, of religion apart from love for God's people. Thus James makes his point, "So also faith by itself, if it does not have works, is dead" (2:17). The argument develops as James anticipates another objection, "But someone will say, 'You have faith and I have works'" (2:18). James responds that true spirituality is linked to living faith, which cannot be separated from deeds. He also challenges the hypothetical objector to show his faith in a tangible way (cf. 3:13; Matt. 7:16–17). Such spirituality is orthodox in content but dead in practice. He points out that these church members quote the Shema ("God is one" in 2:19; cf. Deut. 6:4) but fail to carry out its interwoven requirement: "You shall love the LORD your God with all your heart and with all your soul and with all your might" (Deut. 6:5). James sarcastically applauds: "You do well. Even the demons believe—and shudder!" (2:19). How ludicrous it is for people to subscribe to the faith in God required by Deuteronomy 6:4

---

[22] Mariam Kamell, "The Economics of Humility: The Rich and the Humble in James," in *Economic Dimensions of Early Christianity*, ed. Bruce Longenecker and Kelly Liebengood (Grand Rapids, MI: Eerdmans, 2009), 165, observes that James uses the same two illustrations as Deut. 10:18b.

[23] Jonathan Edwards, "Christian Charity: Duty of Charity to the Poor, Explained and Enforced," *The Works of Jonathan Edwards*, rev. Edward Hickman, 2 vols. (Edinburgh, UK: Banner of Truth, 1974), 2:165.

without corresponding love and obedience to the same God prescribed in Deuteronomy 6:5. Such spirituality is bogus. Genuine spirituality is integrated: it has true faith in God that results in genuine works of love for others.

Having illustrated the absurdity of duplicitous spirituality, James shifts his argument to demonstrate that Scripture teaches that obedience flows from true faith. As examples of faith, works, and mercy, James points to Abraham and Rahab—a patriarch and a prostitute, a Jew and a Gentile.[24] God's grace that leads to our initial faith also brings about our continued faith, which is tied to covenant faithfulness. This is sometimes called good works, the obedience of faith, deeds of love, and the fruit of the Spirit. Although the terminology varies, the idea is that our good works are rooted in our faith in Christ, which flows from being birthed by God as a new creation (James 1:18), through union with Christ and his saving work. John Calvin clarifies this relationship between new life, faith, and works:

> Although we may distinguish [justification and sanctification], Christ contains both of them inseparably in himself. Do you wish, then, to attain righteousness in Christ? You must first possess Christ; but you cannot possess him without being made a partaker in his sanctification, because he cannot be divided into pieces [1 Cor. 1:13]. Since, therefore, it is solely by expending himself that the Lord gives us these benefits to enjoy, he bestows both of them at the same time, the one never without the other. Thus it is clear how true it is that we are justified not without works yet not through works, since in our sharing in Christ, which justifies us, sanctification is just as much included as righteousness.[25]

Through the example of Abraham, James emphasizes that faith is always accompanied by works (2:21), is active alongside works (2:22), and is completed by works (2:22), which is tied to Abraham's being counted by God as righteous and called a friend of God (2:23). James then reiterates his conclusion that only people whose faith displays works have real spirituality. Indeed, their consistency shows their genuineness (2:24). John Calvin put it memorably: "Faith alone justifies, but faith that justifies is never alone."[26] Through the example of Rahab, James makes the same point (2:25). Despite her original vocation as a prostitute, she became a heroine of faith in Jewish tradition. Rahab's faith is portrayed in Joshua

---

[24] Mark Proctor, "Faith, Works, and the Christian Religion in James 2:14–26," *EvQ* 69.4 (1997): 322–31.
[25] John Calvin, *Institutes of the Christian Religion*, ed. John T. McNeill, trans. Ford Lewis Battles (Philadelphia: Westminster, 1960), 3.16.1.
[26] Calvin, *James*, 309.

2:11 and confirmed in Hebrews 11:31. She acted on that faith, harboring the Jewish spies who came to her city and sending them out safely. Her deeds of love displayed her heart of faith.[27]

James then concludes, "For as the body apart from the spirit is dead, so also faith apart from works is dead" (2:26). True spirituality is integrated. Creed and conduct cannot be separated any more than can the body from air. Without air, the body is a corpse. Without works, faith is dead. Religious words without accompanying works of love are worthless.

Tim Laato summarizes the basic arguments related to faith and works in James 2:14–26:

1. Faith without works is dead (2:17, 26).
2. Faith itself (not merely the believer) has works (2:17).
3. More broadly, faith without works works nothing (2:20).
4. The faith of Abraham worked with his works (2:22).
5. The faith of Abraham was completed by works (2:22).

Regarding the fifth point, Laato clarifies that works do not supplement faith; rather, in a certain sense works realize the essence of faith.[28] James thus teaches that true faith includes intellectual assent to truths and also includes personal trust. Even more, true faith is manifested in obedience to God as well as in acts of mercy toward others. Orthodox theology is important but insufficient. True spirituality is integrated: genuine followers of Christ hear the Word and do it. We not only claim to have faith; our lives reflect it in our walk with God and our deeds of love for others.

Integrated Spirituality as Wisdom and Words for Church Health (3:1–18)

We see an integrated spirituality again in James 3, in which true wisdom and humility lead to using words for church health. The argument of James 3:1–12 extends into verses 13–18 and relates to those seeking to be teachers.[29] James 3:1–12 begins by emphasizing that not many should

---

[27] This section is especially informed by my previous co-author Dale Ellenburg, as well as by Richard Bauckham, *James: Wisdom of James, Disciple of Jesus the Sage* (London: Routledge, 1999).

[28] Tim Laato, "Justification according to James: A Comparison with Paul," *TJ* 18 (1997): 62–63. James and Paul share much in common related to the doctrine of salvation. Both ground salvation in God's sovereign election (James 2:5–7; Eph. 1:3–14) and new creation in God's gracious initiative (James 1:18; Eph. 2:4–7); and both present new creation/salvation as linked to the effective power of the gospel/word of truth (James 1:18; Eph. 1:13; Rom. 1:16), genuine faith as necessary (James 2:14–26; Eph. 2:8–10), works of love and obedience as an inevitable consequence of genuine faith (James 2:14–26; Eph. 2:10), and final judgment as according to works (James 2:12–26; Rom. 2:6–15). Although the teachings of Paul and James stress distinct truths, their doctrines of salvation are quite compatible. For more on this, see Morgan, *A Theology of James*, 127–43.

[29] Luke Timothy Johnson, "Reading Wisdom Wisely," *Louvain Studies* 28 (2003): 99–112.

presume to be teachers, because they will receive a stricter judgment (3:1). And we find in 3:13–18 that some in these churches supposed themselves to be spiritually wise and worthy of the role. James questions their claims to spirituality and raises the standards. Hopeful teachers in the church should not presume to be worthy but must take seriously the weighty responsibility of the role and the stricter judgment it incurs. Tidball reminds:

> John Chrysostom (347–407) became one of the outstanding pastors of the early church, but he initially resisted the invitation to become a bishop. When asked why he was so reluctant, he argued, with irresistible logic, that no one would consider pulling any old person out of the crowd, turning them into a military dignitary and insisting they head up a great army. It would be stupid. Turning to another illustration, he said they would be foolish to entrust a fully-laden merchant ship into the hands of an inexperienced sea captain like himself, lest I should sink the ship. But in that case, as he points out, the only loss would be a material one. In the church, by contrast, the loss caused by inept or inexperienced handling of people will be eternal. No wonder James writes, "Not many of you should become teachers."[30]

James holds the standard high (indeed, at perfection in 3:2b) but concedes, "We all stumble in many ways" (3:2a). James is quick to admit that all of us sin, himself included (note the use of "we"), but also reminds of the seriousness of controlling our words. To do so he uses six illustrations in this section: a bit (3:3), a rudder (3:4), a fire (3:5–6), a poisonous animal (3:7–8), a spring (3:11), and a fig tree (3:12). Reiterating James 1:26, he urges that we bridle our lives, and our tongues in particular (3:2). Even if no one controls words flawlessly, mature people do exhibit an overall self-control over them (3:2). James then uses two examples of how something small can have a large impact: bits on horses (3:3) and rudders on ships (3:4). The tongue is likened to both the bit and the rudder in that it is small in size yet large in its influence (3:5). The neutral examples give way to negative ones in 3:6–7. The tongue is compared to a destructive fire, a defiler of the whole body,[31] and a world of unrighteousness. By these images, James warns us that the tongue has influence, but too often its influence leads to contamination and destruction rather than blessing and

---

[30] Derek Tidball, *Wisdom from Heaven: The Message of the Letter of James for Today* (Fearn, Ross-shire, UK: Christian Focus, 2003), 102. Tidball refers to John Chrysostom, *On the Priesthood*, Nicene and Post-Nicene Fathers, ed. Philip Schaff (1889; repr. Grand Rapids, MI: Eerdmans, 1997), 3.7, 49.

[31] James reflects Jesus' teaching that "what comes out of the mouth; this defiles a person" (Matt. 15:11).

edification. He also seems to have the church in view with his usage of the word *body*. Ralph Martin concurs, "The implication is that by irresponsible speech the whole body of Christ is stained."[32]

James urges the churches to watch out for those who use words to slander. Such biting words are more destructive than they first appear and more pervasive than we would suppose. Plus, the tongue is "set on fire by hell" (3:6). James Motyer states it well: "The first feature of the tongue was that it was anti-God (the world); the last feature is that it is pro-Satan."[33] Underlining the danger of proud and hypocritical words, James exclaims that the tongue is a "restless evil, full of deadly poison" (3:7–8). Christians should follow not those whose speech is marked by slander and envy but those wise leaders who display love and genuineness.

James warns of inconsistency and how it is displayed in words (3:9–12). He shows that duplicitous words flow from a corrupt heart, whereas a pattern of healthy speech emerges from a genuine heart. Revealing the unstable and deceitful nature of the tongue, James points out that the double-minded use the same tongue to worship God (supposedly) and to slander his people, stating: "With it we bless our Lord and Father, and with it we curse people who are made in the likeness of God. From the same mouth come blessing and cursing. My brothers, these things ought not to be so" (3:9–10). James raises three questions designed to reveal the absurdity of the hypocritical use of the tongue (3:11–12). He asks if one spring supplies both fresh and bitter water, inquires whether a fig tree produces olives, and questions if a vine produces figs. Obviously, good springs produce good water, fig trees produce figs, and vines bring grapes and other fruits but not figs. Thus, following Jesus, James maintains that our words, which come from our heart, reveal much about our heart (cf. Matt. 7:16–20; 12:33–35; Luke 6:43–45). As my friend Dale Ellenburg quips, "What's down in the well comes up in the bucket."[34]

James helps churches to see what good leadership is like by contrasting genuine wisdom with counterfeit wisdom, or, in our terminology, genuine spirituality with counterfeit spirituality. To show that true wisdom (like true faith and true spirituality) is ethical,[35] James highlights realities about false wisdom and true wisdom, distinguishing them by their characteristics, sources, and results. James begins the discussion by

---

[32] Ralph P. Martin, *James*, WBC (Waco, TX: Word, 1988), 115.

[33] Alec Motyer, *The Message of James*, Bible Speaks Today (Downers Grove, IL: InterVarsity Press, 1985), 123.

[34] I wish to thank Dale Ellenburg for his insights into this passage.

[35] Dan G. McCartney, "The Wisdom of James the Just," *SBJT* 4 (Fall 2000): 56.

asking rhetorically, "Who is wise and understanding among you?" (3:13). He then answers his own question, "By his good conduct let him show his works in the meekness of wisdom" (3:13). The point is clear: true, godly wisdom is displayed in consistent Christian behavior, "in the meekness of wisdom."

James then exposes the opposite of true wisdom. Those who long to be viewed as church leaders but exhibit "bitter jealousy and selfish ambition" indicate that they lack real wisdom. God-given wisdom is meek. It is not linked with envy, rivalry, or self-promotion. People characterized by false wisdom seek to "win" against others and in so doing divide churches. Evidently, some even boasted about their wisdom and power over others. James informs them that when they do this, they deny the truth they supposedly teach, and their so-called wisdom "is not the wisdom that comes down from above, but is earthly, unspiritual, demonic" (3:15). Instead of taking pride in their supposed wisdom, those aspiring to be teachers and leaders should examine its actual sources. The source of their wisdom is not from above (God) but at best is earthly and unspiritual and at worst is demonic.

James calls the churches' attention to the results of this spurious wisdom, or false spirituality: "Where jealousy and selfish ambition exist, there will be disorder and every vile practice" (3:16). False wisdom is accompanied by damage to churches. When such "jealousy" and "selfish ambition" are present, the outcome includes "disorder and every vile practice" (3:16). James has used the word for "disorder" twice already (in 1:8 and 3:8) to describe first an unstable person and then a restless tongue. Here he points to the restlessness, disorder, and chaos produced by worldly wisdom. If there is chaos in the church, it is likely associated with people's asserting themselves into leadership while not being spiritually qualified for it. Such people exhibit false wisdom and its cohorts: envy, pride, and self-promotion.[36]

James transitions to discussing the source, characteristics, and result of true wisdom, or true spirituality (3:17). Unlike the fake wisdom just depicted, true wisdom comes from "above," from God. Ralph Martin observes, "Strictly speaking James describes what true wisdom results in rather than what it *is*."[37] In a manner that resembles Jesus' Beatitudes in the Sermon on the Mount (Matt. 5:3–12) or the apostle Paul's depiction of

---

[36] James fostered unity in Acts 15 and 21:18–25. Unity may come from dialogue but also from rebuking sin. See Motyer, *James*, 135.
[37] Martin, *James*, 133.

the fruit of the Spirit (Gal. 5:22–24), James here specifies characteristics of this true wisdom from God that is so vital to the health of these churches: "The wisdom from above is first pure, then peaceable, gentle, open to reason, full of mercy and good fruits, impartial and sincere" (3:17).

The wisdom that God gives is "first pure," free from unmixed motives that mark the double-minded.[38] True wisdom loves peace and is gentle or noncombative. It is also conciliatory, open to reason, not self-seeking, and ready to yield to others (cf. Phil. 2:3). Not surprisingly, it is also "full of mercy and good fruits." Being "full of mercy" suggests one who is eager to help and minister to others (cf. 2:12–17). "Good fruits" speaks of the good works a righteous person will exhibit that flow from a good root (cf. 2:14–26; Matt. 7:17–20). The last two descriptions of this wisdom from God are that it is "impartial" and "sincere." "Impartial" people do not show favoritism but are consistent in the treatment of others because all people matter (cf. 2:1–11). To be "sincere," the opposite of hypocritical, is to be undivided, genuine, integrated.

James concludes this section by pointing to wisdom's results: "A harvest of righteousness is sown in peace by those who make peace" (3:18). That righteousness is related directly to peace comes as no surprise, as James writes to churches divided over pride, slander, and power plays. Those who love peace sow peace, a quality needed in every church. Teachers reveal by their words what kind of wisdom they possess. Not everyone who wants to lead should, because not every leader who claims to have wisdom really does. That more people claim to have true wisdom than actually possess it is obvious from the lack of control over their words and their overall lack of commitment to edify the church. Teachers exist to build up the church, not to harm it. And thus those who are interested more in asserting themselves and having a voice than in the unity of the body display that they value their own egos, ambitions, and agendas more than Christ's church. True wisdom, which is from God, is "pure, then peaceable, gentle, open to reason, full of mercy and good fruits, impartial and sincere" (3:17). It does not exhibit bitter jealousy, selfish ambition, or pride but is shown in peaceable, kind, and meek words (3:13–18). Such wisdom comes from God, is manifested in a person's way of life and speech, and is prerequisite for teachers in Christ's churches. So again, James calls for integrated spirituality, one in which true wisdom leads to grace-filled words that promote church health.

---

[38] Davids, *James*, 154. Davids suitably calls these fruits of wisdom "community-preserving virtues" (54).

Integrated Spirituality

So, when we hear the word *spiritual*, what should come to mind? James sets forth a vision of integrated spirituality for real people in real churches living in the real world. James's portrayals of integrated spirituality are not only ideas, ideals, or methods but are also calls to love God and others in all situations of life. Any so-called spirituality that speaks of a faith in Christ but does not issue in love for others James categorizes as a sham. Such a spirituality is neither integrated nor Christian but double-minded (1:8), deceptive (1:22, 26), impure and defiled (1:27), worthless (1:27), sinful (2:8–13), of no good (2:14–16), useless (2:20), dead (2:26), destructive (3:5–7), poisonous (3:7), inconsistent (3:10–12), earthly, unspiritual, demonic (3:14–16), adulterous toward God (4:4), in friendship with the world, and even at enmity with God (4:4–10).

James clarifies that integrated spirituality is seen when someone is suffering and seeks God's wisdom and perseveringly relies on him in faith, knowing that he is for him or her and present to help (1:2–11). Integrated spirituality is seen in a holiness toward God that takes care of the most vulnerable in our spiritual family (1:26–27). It is expressed in a faith in Christ that issues in good works of love for our neighbors (2:14–26). Such integrated spirituality shines through as we live in community, exuding unity and peace, knowing that loving God and his truth is expressed most clearly in loving his people (3:1–18). While there are as many applications as there are situations, James's message is consistent: true spirituality is an integrated spirituality in which our love for God is expressed in our love for others.

6

HOLINESS IN THE BIBLICAL STORY

GEORGE H. GUTHRIE

In his *Life and Holiness*, Catholic writer Thomas Merton asks, "What is 'holiness'? . . . Are we really seriously supposed to be saints? Can a man even desire such a thing without making a complete fool of himself?"[1] To these, moderns among us might add, "Isn't 'holiness' a primitive holdover from superstition, one that sits uncomfortably with enlightened conceptions of reality and social relationships?"[2] To these questions we answer, "Let me tell you a story."

In recent years, the importance of hearing the Bible as one grand narrative has been ably demonstrated from various quarters.[3] Among other benefits, knowing the biblical story helps us understand our identity, our place in the world, what is wrong with the world—and the solution— as well as where we find ourselves temporally in the unfolding of history.[4] But grasping God's story also tells us how we are to approach life and

---

[1] Thomas Merton, *Life and Holiness* (Garden City, NY: Image Books, 1964), 16.
[2] Pointedly, Thomas Trevethan writes, "God shrinkers have been at work in Western culture, scaling down the Holy One to the measure of the human mind and experience. Shut out of his creation by seventeenth-century deism, silenced, as a matter of method, by eighteenth-century rationalism (Immanuel Kant) and scaled down to the dimension of our religious experiences by nineteenth-century romanticism (Friedrich Schleiermacher), the living God who creates and rules and intrudes in the flow of history to rescue and speak was seriously diminished in the understanding of 'modern' people. The God of the Bible became an embarrassment, a primitive tribal deity in need of radical updating by humankind come of age." Thomas L. Trevethan, *The Beauty of God's Holiness* (Downers Grove, IL: InterVarsity Press, 1995), 34.
[3] E.g., Craig G. Bartholomew and Michael W. Goheen, *The Drama of Scripture: Finding Our Place in the Biblical Story* (London: Society for Promoting Christian Knowledge, 2006); Graeme Goldsworthy, *According to Plan: The Unfolding Revelation of God in the Bible* (Leicester: Inter-Varsity Press, 1991); Michael W. Goheen, *A Light to the Nations: The Missional Church and the Biblical Story* (Grand Rapids, MI: Baker Academic, 2011); Vaughan Roberts, *God's Big Picture: Tracing the Storyline of the Bible* (Downers Grove, IL: InterVarsity Press, 2003). In speaking of the Old Testament story specifically, Christopher Wright notes, "That the Old Testament tells a story needs no defense. My point is much greater however. The Old Testament tells its story as the story or, rather, as part of that ultimate and universal story that will ultimately embrace the whole of creation, time, and humanity within its scope. . . . We live in a storied universe." Christopher J. H. Wright, *The Mission of God: Unlocking the Bible's Grand Narrative* (Downers Grove, IL: IVP Academic, 2006), 71, 73.
[4] Bartholomew and Goheen, *The Drama of Scripture*, 14–15.

what or whom we are to worship. It speaks to us very particularly about how the holiness of God shapes our lives and our worship in accordance with God's desires and for God's mission and glory.[5] In a compelling word picture, Will Herberg writes that

> redemptive history is not merely a recital that we hear and understand. It is also a demand upon us, for out of it comes the voice of God. Faith is responding to the call of God. . . . It is as though we sat witnessing some tremendous epic drama being performed on a vast stage, when suddenly the chief character, who is also its director, steps forward to the front of the stage, fixes his eye upon us, points his finger at us and calls out: "You, you're wanted. Come up here. Take your part!"[6]

In encountering the biblical story at a deep level, therefore, we get invited to play a significant part in the plot line of a story written by God himself, a story that, whatever else it is, is a story about holiness, for it is a story with a holy God at its center.

Defining God's Holiness

Getting our hearts and minds around what we mean by "God's holiness" is no small feat. Since God reveals himself in word and deed in the context of human history, and rarely defines terms he uses of himself, his approach, as Thomas Oden notes, frustrates our "attempts to get God safely boxed into our changing linguistic packages."[7] Indeed, in seeking a clear definition of "holiness," adequate expressions fail us, leaving us silent and in awe before the otherness of a holy God.[8] Accordingly, reflections on the concept of holiness can be profoundly ambiguous, yet most suggest that at the core of the concept, we find something "outside and beyond, removed and distant."[9] This begins to get at what many understand to be

---

[5] When we say that the Bible tells a story, it is not, of course, that the Bible offers an easily discernible, single storyline. In taking up the Scriptures, rather, we find a plurality of "angles on the same subject matter, the profusion and sheer untidiness of narrative materials," which nevertheless work together to form a coherent, overarching story. So states Michael W. Goheen, "The Urgency of Reading the Bible as One Story," *ThTo* 64 (2008): 473, in conversation with Richard Bauckham, *Bible and Mission: Christian Witness in a Postmodern World* (Carlisle; Grand Rapids, MI: Baker Academic, 2003), 92–93. The biblical story, unlike Homer, who invites us away from our own reality for a time, seeks to shape our reality, fitting us for the Real Story of the world. See Erich Auerbach, *Mimesis: the Representation of Reality in Western Literature* (Princeton, NJ: Princeton University Press, 1968), 15, as noted in Goheen, "The Urgency of Reading the Bible as One Story," 471–72.
[6] Will Herberg, *Faith Enacted as History: Essays in Biblical Theology* (Philadelphia: Westminster Press, 1976), 41.
[7] Thomas C. Oden, *Systematic Theology*, vol. 1, *The Living God* (Peabody, MA: Hendrickson, 2006), 41.
[8] Ibid., 99.
[9] As with Muilenberg's beginning ruminations in the *Interpreter's Dictionary of the Bible*. According to Muilenberg, holiness is "the 'given' undergirding and pervading all religion; the distinctive mark and signature of the divine. More than any other term, 'holiness' gives expression to the essential nature of the 'sacred.' It is therefore to be understood, not as one attribute among other attributes, but as the innermost reality to

the most basic association of the Hebrew root קדש—the idea of separation, that God and the things associated with God are set apart, separated from normal, profane human existence. Thus, God's holy mountain (Ps. 2:6), God's people (Ex. 19:6; Lev. 11:44; Deut. 7:6), days (Ex. 16:23), or many things associated with Israel's worship of God (e.g., Ex. 30:10, 29; Lev. 2:3, 10; 5:15–16; 6:17–18, 25) are labeled as "holy," set apart as special for God's purposes in the world.

Nevertheless, all these forms of separateness go back to the very nature of God himself: "Who is like you, O LORD, among the gods? Who is like you, majestic in holiness, awesome in glorious deeds, doing wonders?" (Ex. 15:11). Seen enthroned by Isaiah, God is declared to be superlatively holy: "Holy, holy, holy" (Isa. 6:3). His glory fills the whole earth. Thus, in its most fundamental form, holiness refers to the perfection and otherness of God, his very nature, setting God himself apart from all of creation.[10] In short, then, holiness is near the essence of what marks God off as God, the most basic description of his nature,[11] as reflected in God's name (see Lev. 20:3)[12] and God's confession, "I the LORD your God am holy" (Lev. 19:2). Only God inherently possesses or generates holiness.[13] All other forms of holiness are derived from the holiness of God himself.[14]

Furthermore, holiness refers to God's nature as incomparably good, that is, "that every excellence fitting to the Supreme Being is found in God without blemish or limit," and rather than merely one trait or characteristic among many, holiness "summarizes, unifies, and integrates all the other incomparably good characteristics of the divine life."[15] Perceptively and based on insights from the sacrificial system, Morales suggests that

---

which all others are related . . . a 'something more,' which resists formulation or definition." He continues, suggesting that holiness is marked by an awareness of an undefined and uncanny energy, a sense of the numinous (cf. Latin *numen*), of the imponderable and incomprehensible, an inarticulate feeling of an inviolable potency outside and beyond, removed and distant, yet at the same time near and "fascinating," invading the everyday world of normal experience—what Rudolf Otto has described as the *mysterious tremendous*. See J. Muilenburg, "Holiness," in *The Interpreter's Dictionary of the Bible*, ed. George Arthur Buttrick (Nashville, TN: Abingdon, 1962), 616–17.

[10] Jacob Milgrom, *Leviticus 17–22: A New Translation with Introduction and Commentary*, AB (New York: Doubleday, 2000), 1712.

[11] Thomas L. Trevethan, *The Beauty of God's Holiness* (Downers Grove, IL: InterVarsity Press, 1995), 13.

[12] The Dead Sea Scrolls, for example, can refer to God with the favorite rabbinic title, "The Holy One" (1 QS 10:4; 1QSb 4:28; CD 6:1; 20:22).

[13] Hannah K. Harrington, "Holiness" in *The Eerdmans Dictionary of Early Judaism*, ed. John J. Collins and Daniel C. Harlow (Grand Rapids, MI: Eerdmans, 2010), 749.

[14] Yet can we say, then, that "holiness is another way of saying 'God,'" as with Hannah K. Harrington, *Holiness: Rabbinic Judaism in the Graeco-Roman World* (London: Routledge, 2002), 12? Dozeman, following Milgrom, suggests the answer must be no. Since people are commanded to "be holy," this cannot be equated with them being commanded to "be God." Rather, holiness and God are intimately related, but they are not synonymous. See Thomas B. Dozeman, "Holiness and Ethics," *Wesleyan Theological Journal* 49 (2014): 21.

[15] Oden, *Systematic Theology*, 99–100.

holiness relates directly to God's "fullness of life" or "absolute life."[16] Thus, we might suggest that for human beings to experience God's holiness is to experience the life of God, in relationship to God, benefitting from and reflecting the perfections of God, and resulting in service for God and the worship of God.

This focus on the relationship between holiness and life moves us from holiness conceived primarily and merely as the *absence* of something (e.g., impurity) to holiness in the sense of profound *fullness* or *wholeness* of life, human beings invited to share in the good life of God at the deepest level. Moreover, very near the heart of God's holy life of wholeness, a number of theologians have also discerned another key, interpenetrating aspect of God's nature—love (1 John 4:8).[17] In fact, love and holiness can be considered the two primary aspects of God's character. God's holiness is a loving holiness, and God's love is a holy love.[18] Rather than contradictions or even paradox, God's love and holiness are perfectly integrated, and both in their integration exist as driving forces at the very heart of God's revelation of himself throughout the biblical story. God, through his presence, brings his holy life of love to bear on the world and will do so until all things are made new (Rev. 21:1–5). And, wonder of wonders, in love, and by his presence, and at the heart of the biblical story, he calls people to a relationship of holiness, of wholeness, with himself. The question is, "How does God's holiness then shape us according to that story?" What dynamics can we discern as we take up and read the story of Scripture?

Five Dynamics Associated with God's Holiness in the Biblical Story

In the biblical narrative, there are at least five dynamics associated with God's holiness, driven by holy love, through which human beings are transformed to share in God's holy life, resulting in the worship of God and mission for God in the world. These dynamics are:

---

[16] L. Michael Morales, *Who Shall Ascend the Mountain of the Lord?: A Theology of the Book of Leviticus*, NSBT (Downers Grove, IL: InterVarsity Press, 2015), 31, 157. Muilenberg adds, "The 'life' of Yahweh and his holiness are closely joined. The divine oath: 'As I live,' and the human counterpart: 'As Yahweh lives' (1 Kings 17:12), belong to the same language as does holiness. The living God is a holy God; his 'life' is holy life (Deut. 32:40; Josh. 3:10; Pss. 42:2; 84:2–4; Jer. 10:10)." Muilenburg, "Holiness," 618–19. We will deal with this insight more below.
[17] E.g., James E. Robson, "Forgotten Dimensions of Holiness," *Horizons in Biblical Theology* 33 (2011): 121–46, who understands love as a dimension of God's holiness.
[18] Oden, *Systematic Theology*, 98, who points to Pss. 31:21–24; 146:8; John 3:16; 1 John 2:15; 4:7–21; Rev. 15:4 as examples of passages where the themes of love and holiness intertwine. Donald Bloesch comments, "From my perspective God's love and holiness constitute the inner nature of the living God. These two perfections coalesce in such a way that we may speak of the holy love of God . . . and of his merciful holiness. In the depth of God's love is revealed the beauty of his holiness. In the glory of his holiness is revealed the breadth of his love. . . . His holiness is adorned and crowned by the magnitude of his love." See Donald G. Bloesch, *God, the Almighty: Power, Wisdom, Holiness, Love* (Downers Grove, IL: InterVarsity Press, 1995), 141.

- holy presence
- holy space
- holy time
- holy sacrifice and cleansing
- holy words

We see each of these at the heart of a holy God's interaction with his people in the unfolding of the biblical story. In what follows we briefly trace these dynamics, these holy forces that shape our lives and worship and mission in the world, noting how they develop in the unfolding of the story of Scripture.

Holy Walk: Life in Eden

I love long walks with my wife. In Cambridge, England, there is a neighborhood called Newnham, very near Tyndale House, the world-class research library where we live and work while in that eminently walkable city. And from Newnham you can take a paved path along the Cam River to Grantchester, where you will find The Orchard Tea Room. Enjoying tea and scones while sitting outside among the apple trees offers unique moments of relationship building. Walks too, of course, can be wonderfully relational, and my wife and I have fond memories of walks to and from The Orchard. The pastoral setting, good food both on the table and on the trees, lingering time for talk, or reading, or silence, all contribute to a relational moment. Being "present" with someone, in a special place, on a special walk, can be a profound expression of love and relational wholeness. Thus God seeks to walk with us, to be present among us as human beings, as an expression of his holy love, and this was his pattern from the very beginning.[19]

It is significant that the Bible starts with Adam and Eve knowing God's presence in the garden. The language of God walking with the first couple doesn't appear until Genesis 3:8, the moment of tragedy when human beings stepped off the path. Seduced, they chose to follow their own rebellious way downward and away from God and his garden. Most commentators have understood the image of walking in this passage to be a picture of fellowship with God, for the clause "walked with God" is common in Genesis, speaking of the righteous pattern of life seen in people like Enoch, Noah, or Abraham.[20] Prior to the tragedy, Adam and Eve knew the presence of God in a face-to-face relationship.

---

[19] So, Robson, "Forgotten Dimensions of Holiness," 121.
[20] Kenneth Mathews, *Genesis 1–11:26*, NAC (Nashville, TN: Holman Reference, 1996), 239. "The cool of the day" (literally, "the wind of the day") can be read as referring to the pleasant time of the day for a walk, but

In terms of the garden as holy space, it has become commonplace in recent scholarship to depict Eden functioning as the first sanctuary, having characteristics that foreshadow the tabernacle and the temple, or particularly the Most Holy Place of the tabernacle. Bruce Waltke states plainly, "The garden is a temple from which the heavenly waters flow to the rest of the earth."[21] Like the tabernacle, the garden is a space with only one entrance, guarded by cherubim. It is oriented eastward. Adam *works* and *keeps* the garden (Gen. 2:15), the same two Hebrew terms used to speak of the priests *serving* and *guarding* the tabernacle (Num. 3:7–8; 8:25–26; 1 Chron. 23:32), and the garden is a place of supreme rest.[22] This is holy space.

Here too we see holy time, built into the rhythmic, temporal foundations of the universe as God hallows the seventh day: "So God blessed the seventh day and made it holy, because on it God rested from all his work that he had done in creation" (Gen. 2:3). This temporal rhythm was blessed and given as a blessing to people (Mark 2:27). In some ways, the "space" of this holy time of Sabbath was the fit culmination of creation, a creation that was for the blessing of mankind.[23] But the blessing of the first people was also contingent upon their obedience to God's holy words. When God put Adam in the garden, he commanded him, "You may surely eat of every tree of the garden, but of the tree of the knowledge of good and evil you shall not eat, for in the day that you eat of it you shall surely die" (Gen. 2:16–17). And, of course, Adam and Eve violated this command, these holy words that would have maintained life and wholeness, instead choosing death and decay.

Thus, people's ability to know the presence of a holy God was interrupted when sin entered the world: "the man and his wife hid themselves from the presence of the LORD God" (Gen. 3:8). In the story, their guilt stands in antithesis to God's holiness, and they intuit that their sin has undone them, "undressed" this couple who a few verses earlier "were not

---

others have interpreted this as God coming to the garden in a storm cloud of judgment. See, e.g., Douglas K. Stuart, "'The Cool of the Day' (Gen 3:8) and 'the Way He Should Go' (Prov 22:6)," *BSac* 171 (2014): 259–73.

[21] Bruce K. Waltke and Cathi J. Fredricks, *Genesis: A Commentary* (Grand Rapids, MI: Zondervan, 2001), 101.

[22] E.g., G. K. Beale, *The Temple and the Church's Mission: A Biblical Theology of the Dwelling Place of God*, NSBT (Downers Grove, IL: InterVarsity Press, 2004); John H. Walton, Genesis, NIVAC (Grand Rapids, MI: Zondervan, 2001), 148–49; Lifsa Block Schachter, "The Garden of Eden as God's First Sanctuary," *JBQ* 41 (2013): 73–77; Rachel Elior, "The Garden of Eden is the Holy of Holies and the Dwelling of the Lord," *Studies in Spirituality* 24 (2014), 63–118; J. Daniel Hays, *The Temple and the Tabernacle: A Study of God's Dwelling Places from Genesis to Revelation* (Grand Rapids, MI: Baker, 2016), 20–27. For pushback on this interpretation see, e.g., Daniel Block's comments, "Eden: A Temple? A Reassessment of the Biblical Evidence," in *From Creation to New Creation: Biblical Theology and Exegesis*, ed. Daniel Gurtner and Benjamin L. Gladd (Peabody, MA: Hendrickson, 2013), 20–21.

[23] Gordon J. Wenham, *Genesis 1–15*, WBC (Nashville, TN: Nelson, 1987), 37.

ashamed" (2:25). More straightforwardly, the assertion of Genesis 3:8 reads that they hid themselves "from before the face of the Lord God."[24] When we sin, we cannot look confidently into the face of a holy God (cf. Heb. 10:19). The balance of the biblical story tells how God has worked to reverse this curse, turning our faces back to him, so that in the end we "will see his face" (Rev. 22:3–4).

What then of holy sacrifice and cleansing, and where in this part of the story do we see transformation and mission? At this point in the story, sacrifice and ritual cleansing have not yet appeared and will not do so until they are mentioned later in the Pentateuch (e.g., beginning with the offerings of Cain and Abel in Gen. 4:3–4).[25] The first couple experienced *deformation* in the fall, which necessitated *transformation* as the biblical story develops. Moreover, the mission human beings were given, to "work" and "watch over" the garden, was abdicated as Adam and Eve were driven from the holy space. Holiness—a life of knowing God's presence in holy space and holy time, and attending God's holy words—serves as a foundation for living on God's mission. But in the fall these dynamics of holiness were lost. What did God do? He began the process of renewal by founding a holy people to live in special relationship with him, which eventually would result in the restoration of all things.

A People for God's Holy Presence: The Wilderness Generation

When our first parents sinned in the garden, they were driven out from the presence of the Lord (3:24), mankind becoming murderous and increasingly corrupt, their wickedness widespread, and their thoughts bent on evil (Gen. 4:1–16; 6:3). Migration was eastward, away from the garden and the presence of the Lord (Gen. 11:2). But God came after us as human beings, renewing the vision established in the creation and working out a plan for blessing all the peoples of this cursed world (Gen. 9:1–7; 12:3). In Genesis 12:1–3 God initiated a covenant with Abraham, drawing him into a relationship of trust (Gen. 15:6) and promising him countless descendants and a land in which they would live (Gen. 15:2–7). Then when Abraham was ninety-nine years old, God appeared to him, saying, "Walk before me, and be blameless" (Gen. 17:1); literally, "walk before my face," that is, "live in my presence," God renewing that lost aspect of life in Eden.

---

[24] Bruce Waltke notes that if Adam failed in Paradise, an ideal setting, this sets the tone for a story of failure in terms of keeping faith in relationship with God. People cannot keep God's commands and know his presence; their only hope is for the salvation God can bring them. See Waltke and Fredricks, *Genesis: A Commentary*, 101.
[25] On the error of reading sacrifice into the provision of animal skins for clothing in 3:21, see Walton, *Genesis*, 229.

As we roll history forward to the opening of the Pentateuch's second book, descendants of Abraham had become a vast multitude (Ex. 1:7) and were slaves in Egypt. God kept covenant with Abraham by saving them from slavery. To do so, he drew another man, Moses, to his holy presence in a holy place. Notice the divine humility of God, who came to Moses in a burning bush (Ex. 3:1–4). Bruce Waltke notes, "The Eternal lowers himself into a bush amid the dirt and rocks. . . . Yet, his humility does not compromise his holiness, for none, not even Moses, may enter his presence with dirt on their shoes."[26] Even with shoes off, and like his first ancestors in the garden, Moses "hid his face, for he was afraid to look at God" (Ex. 3:6). But God worked out ways, a system of laws, holy words, by which he would make his people fit to live in the presence of a holy God.

Moses led God's covenant people out of Egypt and brought them to Sinai, a holy space of grace, for the presence of the Lord came "to Sinai to accomplish [God's] salvific purposes (e.g., Deut. 4:10–11; cf. 10:12)."[27] Thus at Sinai God drew his people to his presence and thus to a holy pattern of life by giving them holy words. The law was given both to fit God's people for his presence and to maintain their ability to live in God's presence. For instance, through Sabbath observance, a weekly moment of holy time, the people of God would experience a form of Edenic life in the presence of God, rhythmically entering in a deeper way into the holy presence of the Lord,[28] a pattern of life that was meant to be compelling to those outside of the covenant people.

Laws were given, moreover, for the building of a tabernacle, a mobile holy space for worship. Thus, as a holy space the tabernacle, located at the very center of the Israelite camp, was a primary way for the people of God to experience "the redemptive presence of God."[29] Intimating association with the divine presence, the tabernacle was at times called the "dwelling place" (e.g., Ex. 25:9; 26:1, 6–7, 12–13) but also was referred to as the "tent"

---

[26] Bruce K. Waltke and Charles Yu, *An Old Testament Theology: An Exegetical, Canonical, and Thematic Approach* (Grand Rapids, MI: Zondervan, 2007), 363. Terence Fretheim points out that it is not merely the presence of God that makes a place holy. Rather, the purpose of a place like the burning bush is the key: "There is no holiness inherent in the place as such, no natural sanctity, but that which is not holy now becomes so by virtue of the divine purpose for the place (not just the divine presence). That which is the ordinary part of the divine order, is sanctified, set apart for special use by God." See Terence E. Fretheim, *Exodus*, IBC (Louisville, KY: Westminster John Knox, 2010), 56.

[27] J. Ryan Lister, *The Presence of God: Its Place in the Storyline of Scripture and the Story of Our Lives* (Wheaton, IL: Crossway, 2014), 187.

[28] Morales, *Who Shall Ascend?*, 220. Israel was commanded by God to set apart the Sabbath day as a holy day of rest (Ex 20:8; Deut. 5:12; cf. Ex. 31:15; 35:2). On holy days, feasts, and seasons see J. E. Hartley, "Holy and Holiness, Clean and Unclean" in *Dictionary of the Old Testament: Pentateuch*, ed. T. Desmond Alexander and David W. Baker (Downers Grove, IL: InterVarsity Press, 2003), 424–25.

[29] Lister, *The Presence of God*, 192.

(e.g., Ex. 26:7, 9, 11–14, 36; 27:21). Its status as holy to the Lord was communicated as it was called the "sanctuary" or the "holy place" (Ex. 15:17; 25:8; 30:13, 24; 36:1, 3–4, 6). This, however, was mediated space, a place of curtains and courts that both invited people in, closer and closer to the presence, and put up barriers to keep them out. Such barriers allowed God to be manifested to his people while, at the same time, protecting the people from his holy and consuming presence. Mediation, therefore, is for both the sanctity of God and the security and furtherance of man (e.g., Num. 4:15; 2 Sam. 6:6–7). Even in God's merciful manifestations, fallen humanity is laid bare before a transcendent, holy, and infinite being.[30]

Accordingly, along with the mediation of the priesthood, the structure of the tabernacle was made for drawing near to God in worship, moving from the court to the outer room (the Holy Place) to the Most Holy Place, each place more holy than the one before it. Only the high priest could enter into the very presence of God in the Most Holy Place, once a year on the Day of Atonement (Lev. 16:1–34), a special holy time, a Sabbath of Sabbaths.[31] Through cleansing from sin and drawing near, aspects of life in the garden were renewed. Accordingly, the tabernacle itself was meant to point to Eden, and, as such, it was a holy place of opportunity and transformation, offering the people of God a place to experience holiness and growth in holiness. Through this small space of only 675 square feet, the Israelites' relationship with God and one another could grow, and their role, their mission, in the world could be carried out.[32] The tabernacle served as a sort of launch pad for God's new creation of the world, reversing the curse of the fall. Fretheim comments:

> At this small, lonely place in the midst of the chaos of the wilderness, a new creation comes into being. In the midst of disorder there is order. The tabernacle is the world order as God intended writ small in Israel. . . . The people of Israel carefully encamped around the tabernacle in their midst constitutes the beginnings of God's bringing creation back to what it was originally intended to be. . . . Moreover, this microcosm of creation is the beginning of a macrocosmic effort on God's part. In and through this people, God is on the move to a new creation for all. God's presence in the tabernacle is a statement about God's intended presence in the entire world. The glory manifest there is to stream out into the larger world. The shining of Moses's face in the wake of the experience

---

[30] Ibid., 56.
[31] On the structure and furnishings of the tabernacle, see Hays, *The Temple and the Tabernacle*, 28–62.
[32] Lister, *The Presence of God*, 112.

of the divine glory . . . is to become characteristic of Israel as a whole, a radiating out into the larger world of those glorious effects of God's dwelling among Israel. As a kingdom of priests, . . . they have a role of mediating this glory to the entire cosmos.[33]

Yet to manifest that glory, God's people would have to live out the holy word, "You shall be holy, for I the LORD your God am holy" (Lev. 19:2), and God made it possible for them to do so by giving them other holy words— laws, both ritual and ethical. In the context of tabernacle worship, the priests carried out the sacrificial system. Through a transfer of holiness, the holy sacrifices cleansed the people so that they might be sanctified, able to live with God in their midst; they were "made holy" by the holy God (Lev. 22:16, 32).[34] Moreover, at times people became ceremonially defiled and needed to be ritually cleansed through washing, as when a corpse had been touched (Num. 19:1–13), or when a woman had her monthly period (Lev. 15:19). The ethical or moral laws, moreover, shaped their lives by giving them patterns to live by in relation to one another, the world, and God, keeping them fit for the presence and growing them in holiness.[35]

Through both the presence of God, facilitated by ongoing sacrifices and ceremonial cleansing, and growth in moral character and ethical behavior, God's people were transformed and thus enabled to live out their mission for God in the world. Holy life was foundational for holy mission. Such a life testified "to the living presence of God within God's people" and was "to be such a full and rich human life that the nations of the earth" would be "drawn to it."[36] Thus by living as a holy nation—through holy presence, space, time, sacrifice, and words—transformation of the people of God would take place, and these holy people would function as a kingdom of priests, God's missionaries of blessing and salvific grace to the peoples of the world.[37]

---

[33] Fretheim, *Exodus*, 271–72.
[34] Wright, *The Mission of God*, 336–37. Wright states, "So all of life, then, could be in a state of flux in one of two directions. The effect of sin and pollution was to render the holy profane and the clean unclean. But the blood of sacrifice and other rituals could reverse that process. Sacrificial blood (along with other rituals) would cleanse the unclean and make it clean again (and thereby acceptable to God). And sacrificial blood would be used to sanctify or consecrate the clean to make it holy. The one thing that should never happen is that the opposite ends of the spectrum come in contact—the unclean with the holy. God, the ultimate Holy One of Israel, cannot cohabit with uncleanness."
[35] Ibid., 335. Michael Morales notes the logical progression in Leviticus from ritual cleansing to ethical living: "The progression, then, from cult in the first half of Leviticus to community in the second is not only natural and logical, but also necessary—the purpose of the cult is to sanctify Israel to YHWH. . . . What, however, is not typically appreciated sufficiently is that the holiness of Israel (chs. 17–27) is in fact the goal and programmed consequence of the cultus of Israel (chs. 1–16)." Morales, *Who Shall Ascend?*, 214.
[36] Bartholomew and Goheen, *The Drama of Scripture*, 65–66.
[37] Hartley, "Holy and Holiness," 430.

Holiness Neglected: Of Kings and Kingdoms

Yet the balance of the Old Testament story to a great degree is character-ized by failure in almost every aspect of our five dynamics associated with holiness—holy presence, holy space, holy time, holy sacrifices and cleans-ing, and holy words. We do not have space here to survey such a massive and pervasive failure, but we can illustrate it by focusing on dynamics leading to, found in, and flowing from what perhaps stands as the high point of the Old Testament era—the life and kingship of David.

The prophet Samuel serves as a major hinge figure in the develop-ing Old Testament story, standing at the close of the disastrous era of the judges and the dawn of the united kingdom.[38] Living in a time when God does not speak often to his people (1 Sam. 3:1), for they had not attended his words of the law, Eli and his sons embody the failure of Israel to live out the call to be a holy people: "Now the sons of Eli were worthless men. They did not know the LORD" (1 Sam. 2:12). So God raises up Samuel, but his sons too "turned aside after gain. They took bribes and perverted jus-tice" (1 Sam. 8:3). Consequently, the people ask for a king, which consti-tutes a rejection of God (1 Sam. 8:8): "They have rejected me from being king over them. According to all the deeds that they have done, from the day I brought them up out of Egypt even to this day, forsaking me and serving other gods" (1 Sam. 8:7–8).

Saul is appointed king, but he does not attend to the words of God (holy words); he violates the sacrificial system by offering sacrifice (holy sacri-fice; 1 Sam. 13:8–11) and experiences the absence of the Lord (holy pres-ence), and there is no evidence that ritual cleansing, Sabbath (holy time), or tabernacle (holy space) are significant for him. He ends in utter failure and disgrace: "For rebellion is as the sin of divination, and presumption is as iniquity and idolatry. Because you have rejected the word of the LORD, he has also rejected you from being king" (1 Sam. 15:23). The Spirit of the Lord leaves him (1 Sam. 16:14). But David is found, a man after God's heart (1 Sam. 13:14; Ps. 89:20), and God makes an eternal covenant with him (2 Sam. 7:1–29), a covenant that will serve as a profound backdrop to Jesus' life, ministry, and mission as the fulfillment of messianic hope. David will serve as the paradigm of the consummate King, and his psalms form part of the hymnbook of the people of God, both in the biblical era and throughout church history. God was present with him (2 Sam. 7:9).

But think for a moment about aspects of David's life, aspects that

---

[38] The book of Judges concludes fittingly with, "Everyone did what was right in his own eyes" (Judg. 21:25).

foreshadow the failure generally of Israel to respond to the call to holiness in the old-covenant era. In terms of "holy words," the incident involving the death of Uzzah, who reached out to keep the ark from tumbling to the ground (2 Sam. 6:1–7), demonstrates David's inattention to the ritual laws, for instructions for moving the ark were clearly laid out in God's holy words (Num. 4:15). His adultery with Bathsheba and murder of Uriah (2 Samuel 11) violate two of the ten commandments (Ex. 20:13–14); Nathan the prophet asks, "Why have you *despised the word of the Lord*, to do what is evil in his sight? You have struck down Uriah the Hittite with the sword and have taken his wife to be your wife and have killed him with the sword of the Ammonites" (2 Sam. 12:9). David has a vision for holy space, desiring to build a temple for the Lord, but he is not allowed to do so himself because he is a man of bloodshed (1 Chron. 22:8). David's son Solomon will build the temple, and the glory of God will fill it for a time, but woven into the Solomon narratives is an anticipation of the spiritual collapse of the wisest man in Israel's history (1 Kings 10:14–11:11), and his collapse leads to the division of the kingdom, and ultimately to the destruction of what would become the northern kingdom of Israel.[39]

Thus as the Old Testament story develops, with the exception of brief moments of reform (e.g., 2 Kings 23:4–25), Israel largely rejects God's holy words, failing to practice the sacrificial system faithfully (holy sacrifices) and turning to idols. Israel neglects ritual purification, as well as the holy space of the temple, which will ultimately be abandoned by God and destroyed (Ezek. 10:18; 2 Kings 25:8–12); and Israel neglects holy time (as with Sabbath observance; see e.g., Jer. 17:21–22; Ezek. 22:8; Amos 8:4). In a striking image of God's holy presence being removed from Israel, Jeremiah writes of the ark of the covenant, "It shall not come to mind or be remembered or missed; it shall not be made again" (Jer. 3:16). In the devastation of the exile, the Abrahamic, Sinai, and Davidic covenants seem to have come to utter failure, and the people of Israel have lost any sense of God's mission to the nations.[40] Instead of inculcating holiness into the life of Israel, the law constantly reminds the people of God "of their inability to achieve God's standard of holiness and to love him with all their heart, soul and strength (Deut. 6:5)."[41]

Yet at the darkest point in the story, we also see hope of something

---

[39] On an astute literary analysis of 1 Kings 1–11 see Hays, *The Temple and the Tabernacle*, 63–103.

[40] Jewish scholars still struggle with what seems to be the failure of the Davidic covenant as seen in passages like Ps. 89:39–52. See, e.g., Hayyim Angel, "The Eternal Davidic Covenant in II Samuel Chapter 7 and Its Later Manifestations in the Bible," *JBQ* 44 (2016): 83–90.

[41] Goldsworthy, *According to Plan*, 145–48.

better. The devastation due to the neglect of the holy concerns of God, which we witness, for instance, in Leviticus 26, ultimately leads us to the restoration promised in Ezekiel 34–37 and the prophesied impact of that restoration on all nations.[42] In a continuation of Jeremiah's prophecy of Jeremiah 3, we read of a future time when the presence of the Lord would again come to Jerusalem: "At that time Jerusalem shall be called the throne of the LORD, and all nations shall gather to it, to the presence of the LORD in Jerusalem, and they shall no more stubbornly follow their own evil heart" (3:17). New hearts, brought about by a new covenant, are coming, and it is a covenant in which everyone will know God personally (holy presence), the words of God will be internalized (holy words), and sins will be decisively forgiven (holy sacrifice). The Spirit of God will be poured out in spiritual cleansing and people will experience a holy time of renewal (Jer. 31:31–34; Ezek. 36:16–37:14; Joel 2). Significantly, one will come who will rebuild God's holy space, the temple:

> And say to him, "Thus says the LORD of hosts, 'Behold, the man whose name is the Branch: for he shall branch out from his place, and he shall build the temple of the LORD. It is he who shall build the temple of the LORD and shall bear royal honor, and shall sit and rule on his throne.'" (Zech. 6:12–13a)

This brings us to the next stage in the story.

The Holy One Arrives: Jesus and the Renewal of Holiness

The New Testament has several overt references to Jesus as "holy," or "the Holy One."[43] He was conceived by the Holy Spirit (Matt. 1:18–20) and thus would be called "holy" (Luke 1:35). Both disciples and demons confess him as "the Holy One of God" (Mark 1:24; Luke 4:34; John 6:69), and echoes of this especially messianic title reverberate through the balance of the New Testament (1 John 2:20; Rev. 3:7; and Acts 4:30, which refers to Jesus as "holy servant").[44] Yet it is when we consider the life, ministry, death, resurrection, and exaltation of Jesus, in light of our five dynamics associated with God's holiness, that we see how pervasively Jesus fulfills the vision for holiness found in the Jewish Scriptures.

In terms of the holy presence, we think first, of course, of John 1:14:

---

[42] Wright, *The Mission of God*, 338–39.
[43] Muilenburg, "Holiness," 624.
[44] Notice especially the extensive use of the title "the Holy One" to refer to "the Lord" in Isaiah: 1:4; 5:19, 24; 10:20; 12:6; 17:7; 29:19, 23; 30:11–12, 15; 31:1; 37:23; 40:25; 41:14, 16, 20; 43:3, 14; 45:11; 47:4; 48:17; 49:7; 54:5; 55:5; 60:9, 14; see also Jer. 50:29; 51:5; Ezek. 39:7; Hos. 11:9, 12; Hab. 3:3.

"And the Word became flesh and dwelt among us, and we have seen his glory, glory as of the only Son from the Father, full of grace and truth" (John 1:14). The verb rendered here as "dwelt" (*skēnoō*) has direct lexical associations in the LXX with the tabernacle in the wilderness, and the allusions to the "glory" coming down on the tabernacle are unmistakable in John's euphoric statement (e.g., Ex. 25:8–9; Zech. 2:10). Consequently, "the glory of God, once restricted to the tabernacle (Ex. 40:34), is now visible in Christ (John 1:14b)."[45] As the "tabernacling" God, who walks among his people, it is entirely appropriate, therefore, that Jesus be called "Immanuel," God with us (Isa. 7:14; 8:8; Matt. 1:23). He took on the form of a servant, coming to us as a man, that he might die (Phil. 2:7–8; Heb. 2:14) but not before he had been with his disciples and they with him (Mark 3:14) as he embodied God's holy presence in the world:

> Philip said to him, "Lord, show us the Father, and it is enough for us." Jesus said to him, "Have I been with you so long, and you still do not know me, Philip? Whoever has seen me has seen the Father. How can you say, 'Show us the Father'?" (John 14:8–9)

God himself has stepped onto planet earth, the Creator of the cosmos *present* among the creatures whom he had driven out of the garden at the dawn of creation, and he has come to redeem them, drawing them into the life of holiness, of wholeness, he had planned for his children from the beginning. How did he do this? Through holy words, the crafting of holy space and time, and through holy sacrifice. All of these would be foundational in their own ways for the inauguration of the new covenant and the indwelling of the Spirit.

As "the Word" walked among us, he spoke holy words that put the words of the law through Moses in perspective: "For the law was given through Moses; grace and truth came through Jesus Christ" (John 1:17). At Matthew 5:17–20 Jesus expresses his thoughts on his relationship to the law.[46] The passage begins, "Do not think that I have come to abolish the Law or the Prophets; I have not come to abolish them but to fulfill them. For truly, I say to you, until heaven and earth pass away, not an iota, not a dot, will pass from the Law until all is accomplished" (Matt. 5:17–18). The statement constitutes one of the most controversial passages in biblical studies, as it would have been

---

[45] Gary M. Burge, *John*, NIVAC (Grand Rapids, MI: Zondervan, 2000), 59.
[46] On which see Robert J. Banks, "Matthew's Understanding of the Law: Authenticity and Interpretation in Matthew 5:17–20," *JBL* 93 (1974): 226–42.

controversial among Jesus' contemporaries, especially teachers of the law! Speaking of the authenticity of the statement, as well as Matthew's use of it at this point in his gospel, Robert Banks reflects:

> It, therefore, becomes apparent that it is not so much Jesus' stance towards the Law that [Matthew] is concerned to depict; it is how the Law stands with regard to him, as the one who brings it to fulfillment and to whom all attention must now be directed. For Matthew, then, it is not the question of Jesus' relation to the Law that is in doubt but rather its relation to him!

There were those in Jewish history, both in the Maccabean period and in the Jewish Revolt of the first century, who through assimilation to the surrounding culture sought to "abolish" the law.[47] But this is not Jesus' program. He fulfills the intention of the law, embodying complete obedience to the holy words of God. Moreover, through his words he has the ability to make people holy. At several places in the Jewish Scriptures, God says, "I am the Lord who sanctifies them," speaking of his people (Lev. 20:8; 21:23; 22:9, 16; Ezek. 20:12). In John 17:17 Jesus prays, "Sanctify them in the truth; your word is truth." Christ cleanses his church by the washing of water with the word (Eph. 5:26).

As for holy space and holy time, Jesus, for example, may be understood as reconstituting both the temple and the Sabbath.[48] Herod's temple in Jerusalem, often referred to as "the second temple" (Solomon's, which had been destroyed by the Babylonians, being the first), was understood by Jews of the era to be, quite literally, at the center of the world.[49] The Lord came to his temple (Mal. 3:1) first as a baby, then as a twelve-year-old (Luke 2:27–32, 41–49). As the Lord, Jesus claimed to be greater than the temple (Matt. 12:6), he cleansed the temple (e.g., Matt. 21:12–15; John 2:14–15), and he prophesied about the destruction of the temple (Matt. 24:1–2; Luke 21:5–6), which took place at the hands of the Romans in AD 70. He even associated the temple directly with himself, suggesting that he stands in the place of the temple (John 2:19–22). All of these

---

[47] Matthew Thiessen, "Abolishers of the Law in Early Judaism and Matthew 5:17–20," *Bib* 93 (2012): 543–56.

[48] On Jesus' interactions with the temple see, e.g., Gregory R. Lanier, "Luke's Distinctive Use of the Temple: Portraying the Divine Visitation," *JTS* 65 (2014): 433–62; J. R. Daniel Kirk, "Time for Figs, Temple Destruction, and Houses of Prayer in Mark 11:12–25," *CBQ* 74 (2012): 509–27; Michael Patrick Barber, "Jesus as the Davidic Temple Builder and Peter's Priestly Role in Matthew 16:16–19," *JBL* 132 (2013): 935–53; Rikki E. Watts, "The Lord's House and David's Lord: The Psalms and Mark's Perspective on Jesus and the Temple," *BibInt* 15 (2007): 307–22.

[49] On which see, Oskar Skarsaune, *In the Shadow of the Temple: Jewish Influences on Early Christianity* (Downers Grove, IL: IVP Academic, 2008).

statements should be understood in light of expectations that the Messiah would come and reconstitute the temple system, and, indeed, Jesus' words and actions can be read as him doing away with the sacrificial system at the temple and replacing it with himself![50]

Concerning the Sabbath,[51] Jesus seems to have attended synagogue according to the weekly rhythm (Luke 4:16; cf. Mark 1:21; 3:1; Luke 13:10). However, his concern was that people had become enslaved, boxed in and lessened by Sabbath observance under the traditions of the elders, rather than liberated by it: "The Sabbath was made for man, not man for the Sabbath" (Mark 2:27). The concern stimulated a number of controversies recorded in the Gospels. For instance, he defended his disciples' plucking of grain on the Sabbath (Matt. 12:1–4; Mark 2:23–26; Luke 6:1–4). On three occasions, he healed people on the Sabbath: the man with the withered hand (Mark 3:1–6), a bent-over woman (Luke 13:10–17), and a man with dropsy (Luke 14:1–6). Underlying all of these actions seems to be Jesus' conviction that Sabbath, which had become a time of restriction focused on what one could not do, should rather be a holy time of renewal for people.

As we turn, finally, to holy sacrifice and cleansing, we can consider Jesus' ministry from these two vantage points. First, as noted earlier in the chapter, the old-covenant laws included instructions for dealing with unclean people and things that had become unclean, and in the Gospels, we see Jesus carrying out actions in relation to unclean people. For example, the woman who had a flow of blood in Mark 5:25–34 would have been considered ceremonially unclean, and her uncleanness would have defiled other people and other things that she touched (see Lev. 15:25–30). Yet when she touched Jesus, the opposite happened. Power went out from him, and she was healed, saved, and cleansed (Mark 5:34). In such instances, as well as when Jesus demonstrated what has been called "contagious holiness"[52] in associating with sinners (e.g., Matt. 9:10–13), he showed mercy and grace to those who needed spiritual renewal from the devastation of sin. Contact with Christ led to cleansing.

And then, of course, Jesus made the supreme sacrifice for sins on the cross, replacing the sacrificial system prescribed in the Jewish Scriptures.

[50] Mary Coloe, "Temple Imagery in John," *Int* 63 (2009): 371–72.
[51] On Jesus and the Sabbath see, e.g., Donald A. Carson, "Jesus and the Sabbath in the Four Gospels," in *From Sabbath to Lord's Day: A Biblical, Historical and Theological Investigation* (Grand Rapids, MI: Zondervan, 1982); Donald A. Hagner, "Jesus and the Synoptic Sabbath Controversies," *BBR* 19 (2009): 215–48; Yong-Eui Yang, *Jesus and the Sabbath in Matthew's Gospel*, JSNTSup (Sheffield, UK: Sheffield Academic Press, 1997).
[52] Craig L. Blomberg, *Contagious Holiness: Jesus' Meals with Sinners*, NSBT (Downers Grove, IL: IVP Academic, 2005), 128.

Because of sin, human beings are at enmity with God, condemned and under judgment (Rom. 1:32; 3:9, 19–20; 5:12–14, 16). But there has been a "transformational interchange" effected in the death of Christ (2 Cor. 5:21), the innocent one bearing sin on behalf of the guilty (and Isaiah 53 is the backdrop here, as it is with Heb. 9:28; also 1 Pet. 2:24; 3:18) so that Christ's followers might become righteous, declared to be in right standing with God and in the process of being transformed (Rom. 4:5). God gifts forgiven sinners with life and peace, reconciliation to God, justifying and redeeming them (Rom. 5:1, 10; 2 Cor. 5:15–21). Because of Christ's sacrificial work, we are not condemned (Rom. 5:12; 8:31–34) but, rather, made holy, walking in peace and purpose with the holy God and King of the universe.

Speaking of God's holiness and Christ's sacrifice, Donald Bloesch writes:

> He does not overlook sin but abhors and condemns it. Yet in his gracious mercy and compassion he enters into our sinful world and takes the pain and guilt of our sin upon himself in the life, death and resurrection of his Son, Jesus Christ. He forgives, not because he is lenient or nonjudgmental but because he has dealt with the sin problem once for all in the atoning sacrifice of Jesus Christ. He has taken the retribution that sin carries with it upon himself through an act of love that at once satisfies the demands of his holiness and goes beyond these demands by not only remitting our sin but adopting us into his kingdom as his sons and daughters.[53]

Through that adoption, we become holy people, who carry out a holy mission, and have a holy hope for the future. These come about because Jesus in his earthly ministry, death, resurrection, and exaltation manifested God's holy presence, spoke holy words, redefined holy space and time, and offered both holy sacrifice and cleansing, opening the way for holiness to shape our lives and worship under the new covenant.

The Church: Holy People, Holy Mission

The earliest believers, with whom the church today stands in continuity, understood themselves as a holy people, shaped by the holiness of God and on a holy mission for God in the world (Heb. 9:15–22; 12:18–24; 1 Pet. 1:14–16; 2:9–10). They had received the Holy Spirit (John 20:22; Acts 1:5, 8; 2:4, 38; 8:17; 11:16), are referred to as "saints" (e.g., Acts 9:13,

---

[53] Bloesch, *God, the Almighty*, 158–59.

32; Rom 1:7; 8:27; 15:26; 1 Cor. 1:2; 14:33; 2 Cor. 8:4; Eph. 1:1) who have a "holy calling" (2 Tim. 1:9). They are built upon the holy apostles and prophets (e.g., Acts 3:21; Eph. 3:5) and are given God's words in the "holy Scriptures" (Rom. 1:2).[54] All that we have discussed thus far in this chapter has been moving toward this conclusion: as new-covenant people, we are shaped for a life of holiness, worship, and mission in accordance with five dynamics seen in the grand narrative of Scripture—holy presence, holy space, holy time, holy sacrifice and cleansing, and holy words. Theologically, the foundation is laid in the Jewish Scriptures and brought to fulfillment in the person and work of Christ. We have been both "washed" and "sanctified" by him, the concepts now becoming more conflated in passages such as these:

> And such were some of you. But you were washed, you were sanctified, you were justified in the name of the Lord Jesus Christ and by the Spirit of our God. (1 Cor. 6:11)

> Let us draw near with a true heart in full assurance of faith, with our hearts sprinkled clean from an evil conscience and our bodies washed with pure water. (Heb. 10:22)

> I said to him, "Sir, you know." And he said to me, "These are the ones coming out of the great tribulation. They have washed their robes and made them white in the blood of the Lamb." (Rev. 7:14)

It may be suggested that both the purity laws and the sacrifices for sin have been satisfied in the sacrifice of Christ.[55]

In terms of holy space, when in John 14:1–3 Jesus speaks of the Father's "house" and the "place" he goes to prepare for his disciples, some see an allusion to him building an eschatological temple out of those who would be his new-covenant followers—holy space reframed.[56] At Pentecost the holy presence of God came to indwell this new temple, Jesus sending the Spirit, the holy space comprised of his people made holy by the sacrifice of Jesus. Here lies the backdrop of the temple imagery in passages such as 1 Corinthians 3:16; 6:19; 2 Corinthians 6:16; Ephesians 2:21; 1 Peter 2:5; Revelation 3:12. For example, 1 Peter 2 speaks of believers as "living stones" that are "being built up as a spiritual house" for the Lord.

---

[54] Muilenburg, "Holiness," 624.
[55] David Peterson, *Possessed by God: A New Testament Theology of Sanctification and Holiness* (Leicester, UK: Apollos, 1995), 145.
[56] Coloe, "Temple Imagery in John," 374–78.

We are the dwelling place of the living God, one not confined to a single location in the world. Via the church, the active presence of God, in his new mobile tabernacle, moves through and to the darkest corners of the world, blessing the nations with the gospel.

Further, in a refraction of the word picture, Peter says that believers are a "holy priesthood" offering up "spiritual sacrifices" (1 Pet. 2:5) and also "a chosen race, a royal priesthood, a holy nation, a people for his own possession, that you may proclaim the excellencies of him who called you out of darkness into his marvelous light" (2:9). Holiness serves both as identity and as the foundation for mission. As priests new-covenant believers have free and open access to "draw near"[57] to God in his Most Holy Place (Heb. 10:19–20)—experiencing his holy presence face-to-face—and they offer sacrifices, not for sin but sacrifices of praise, good works, and sharing with others, sacrifices that please God (Heb. 13:15–16).

As to holy time, we can point to two dynamic ways in which the Sabbath of the Jewish Scriptures has been appropriated and adapted. First, Hebrews 4:1–11 encourages perseverance in the faith with the promise of entering God's rest. The "Sabbath rest" that remains "for the people of God" refers to a Day of Atonement rest,[58] in which people by faith have ceased from their own works and have been cleansed from all their sins (Lev. 23:26–28, 32).

> [This] imagery of rest is best understood as a complex symbol for the whole soteriological process that Hebrews never fully articulates, but which involves both personal and corporate dimensions. It is the process of entry into God's presence, the heavenly homeland (11:16), the unshakeable kingdom (12:28), begun at baptism (10:22) and consummated as a whole eschatologically.[59]

The rest rhythm established at the dawn of creation has found its ultimate fulfillment in the salvation work of Christ, and it will be consummated at the end of the age as we enter the very presence of God, who himself is the eschatological sanctuary, in the New Jerusalem (Rev. 21:22).

On the other hand, as believers continue our journey in this world, we live and work in terms of community rhythms, one of which is "the Lord's day" or "the first day of the week" (Acts 20:7; Rev. 1:10). We cannot

---

[57] On the Levitical language of "drawing near" see, e.g., Lev. 9:7–8.
[58] George H. Guthrie, *Hebrews*, NIVAC (Grand Rapids, MI: Zondervan, 1998), 154–55.
[59] Harold W. Attridge, *Hebrews: A Commentary on the Epistle to the Hebrews*, Hermeneia: A Critical and Historical Commentary on the Bible (Minneapolis: Fortress, 1989), 128.

say for sure that all believers in the first century worshipped weekly on "resurrection day," that is on Sunday, but there is evidence that this was a practice among some,[60] and we certainly see a pattern of weekly meetings for worship within the early church. Thus, both in light of the eschatological Sabbath experienced through the gospel, and the rhythmic worship in community experienced weekly, we continue to live in various forms of sacred time.

Thus far, we have discussed ways that holy presence, holy sacrifice and cleansing, holy space, and holy time are embodied in God's new-covenant people, the church. What is left for us to consider is "holy words," and here we focus especially on the call to a life of ethical or moral holiness. We have been decisively forgiven and cleansed in the new covenant because of the sacrifice of Christ (Heb. 10:15–18). Nevertheless, ethical living is mandatory for God's holy people.

At 2 Corinthians 6:16, a passage that includes both holy space imagery (we are the "temple") and language related to holy presence, we read a conflated quotation from Leviticus 26:11–12 and Ezekiel 37:27:

> I will make my dwelling among them and walk among them, and I will be their God, and they shall be my people. (2 Cor. 6:16)

In the context, Paul pleads with the Corinthians to stop inappropriate relationships with those who are not committed to Christ, for such relationships are making them impure. He asks the rhetorical question, "What agreement has the temple of God with idols?" and gives the grounding for his assumed answer, "For we are the temple of the living God" (2 Cor. 6:16a). This reference to God's temple brings to the apostle's mind the OT quotation. God's presence is experienced by his people as they walk in purity. As God's children, they must separate themselves from what is unclean (2 Cor. 6:17–18), and the apostle continues, "Let us cleanse ourselves from every defilement of body and spirit, bringing holiness to completion in the fear of God" (2 Cor. 7:1). Thus, the living out of holiness in community perfects, or brings to full fruition, the positional and transformational holiness decisively given in the sacrifice of Christ. That is, "Social holiness is aimed . . . at completing and thus perfecting the transfer of holiness,"[61] effected by sacrifice, to God's holy people. God's

---

[60] On which see John Laansma, "Lord's Day," in *Dictionary of the Later New Testament and Its Development*, ed. Ralph P. Martin and Peter Davids (Downers Grove, IL: InterVarsity Press, 1997), 679–86.
[61] Dozeman, "Holiness and Ethics," 30–31.

holy people are set apart from the nations in terms of these values, commitments, and patterns of life. In his *Possessed by God: A New Testament Theology of Sanctification and Holiness*, David Peterson writes:

> Just as sanctification in the Old Testament meant being separated from the beliefs and practices of the nations, to be devoted to God and the doing of his will, so sanctification in Christ has to do with a profound re-orientation of values and behaviour. Beginning with the heart and reaching out to touch the life and witness of God's people at every level, God's word and God's Spirit bring change and transformation. In us and through us, something of God's holiness is revealed to the world.[62]

From beginning to end, this is only possible by the work of Christ, through the power of the Holy Spirit.[63] As with the foundation of the people of God in the older covenant, God's intention for new-covenant believers is that their lives would be a compelling testimony to a wholeness of life offered as "good news." The vision for human life established in the garden, in other words, has been rebirthed and reframed in new-covenant church.

Conclusion

In this chapter, we have attempted briefly to address both something of the nature of God's holiness and how that holiness shapes life, worship, and mission. Holiness, this wholeness of life, is integrated profoundly with the love of God and manifests in at least five dynamics seen throughout the grand story of Scripture: holy presence, holy space, holy time, holy words, and holy sacrifice and cleansing. We have seen how all of these come to fruition in the church, the holy people of God, who bear the blessings born in new-covenant holiness to the nations. The end of the Bible's story is not yet, but already we experience realities inaugurated, which will be consummated in the "happy ending." As we have seen, much of the Bible's story is sad, people falling and fallen, running from the presence of the living God. But Christ has turned the story right side up, birthing hope in the world. If we will but look, Christian hope is expressed in our best "legends," expressing our longings for things to be put right in the world. As J. R. R. Tolkien expressed it:

> The Evangelium has not abrogated legends; it has hallowed them, especially the "happy ending." The Christian has still to work, with mind as

---

[62] Peterson, *Possessed by God*, 24.
[63] Ibid., 24.

well as body, to suffer, hope, and die; but he may now perceive that all his bents and faculties have a purpose, which can be redeemed.[64]

Our purpose as human beings, to be holy people who walk in the presence of a holy God, has been redeemed through loving holiness, through the holiness of Christ. We have been transformed, set apart by God, our lives and our worship shaped by God's ongoing work of wholeness in us individually and as an eschatological community, and that shaping fits us for holy mission in the world. Through us, our holy God calls the nations to join us, so that they too may walk in God's glory in the heavenly Jerusalem at the end, that city where nothing that is unholy will ever enter (Rev. 21:26–27).

---

[64] J. R. R. Tolkien, *The Tolkien Reader* (New York: Ballantine, 1966), 73.

7

A HERITAGE OF EVANGELICAL SPIRITUALITY

ANTHONY L. CHUTE

A student once asked which three figures from church history I would want with me if stranded on a deserted island. After giving the question careful thought I replied, "Martin Luther, Charles Spurgeon, and Mark Noll." My reasoning was simple: I wanted Luther and Spurgeon for the entertainment value of their stories, but I wanted Noll there to check for accuracy. Even on a hypothetical island my heroes of the faith would have competing personalities and faulty memories, thereby necessitating the presence of an objective but somewhat sympathetic historian.

The deserted-island question comes in many variations, and therefore no single answer is totally correct, but it does serve the useful purpose of narrowing down the essentials in any given equation. Setting the island imagery aside, from which figures in church history could we learn the essentials of Christian spirituality? The possibilities are nearly endless. Saint Anthony could teach us to fast and pray, while Brother Lawrence could teach us to work and pray; Augustine of Hippo could model loving God with our minds while exercising restraint with our bodies, and Teresa of Avila could inform us of how to meditate on the Lord while our bodies are failing; Francis of Assisi could illustrate dying to self by following Lady Poverty, while Thomas Becket could demonstrate dying itself by challenging King Henry II. Given such endless possibilities, and potential contradictions, it is clear that a narrowing is necessary if there is to be any rationale for choosing models of Christian spirituality.

This book explores Christian spirituality from a decidedly evangelical perspective; therefore, the purpose of this chapter is to promote evangelical spirituality using select figures from church history. The framework for evangelical spirituality is summed up in Titus 2:11–14:

> The grace of God has appeared, bringing salvation for all people, training us to renounce ungodliness and worldly passions, and to live self-controlled, upright, and godly lives in the present age, waiting for our blessed hope, the appearing of the glory of our great God and Savior Jesus Christ, who gave himself for us to redeem us from all lawlessness and to purify for himself a people for his own possession who are zealous for good works.

The path of evangelical spirituality begins with the gospel of grace, by which we are delivered from death and made alive in Christ. We are saved from the penalty of our sins and for service to God and others. Second, evangelical spirituality includes a total reliance on God to deliver us through the trials of this life, faithfully completing what he has begun in us. This reliance includes prayer, by which we increasingly trust our loving and sovereign God to work all things together for our good and his glory. Third, evangelical spirituality involves an ongoing battle against sin in our own lives, the life of the church, and the world at large. Fourth, evangelical spirituality is not a mere resisting of evil but also includes a positive attempt to leave a lasting good in all that we do. Fifth, evangelical spirituality extends to the world to come, which will be free from sin and full of love. This anticipation of a world without end motivates evangelical Christians to long for corporate revival. Sixth, evangelical spirituality includes, at a minimum, the personal and corporate disciplines of prayer (as mentioned above), Bible reading, and active church membership. I have chosen the following as models for this framework:

- Martin Luther, to describe the grace of God;
- John Calvin, to illustrate reliance upon God;
- John Owen, to demonstrate the battle against ongoing sin;
- John Wesley, to stimulate the desire to do good works;
- Jonathan Edwards, to highlight the beauty of heaven; and
- J. C. Ryle, to encourage regular Christian devotion

Selection of these figures might be seen as arbitrary by some, and it is perhaps not likely that these men would last long together even on an imaginary deserted island! But taken together, their contributions provide a fairly comprehensive view of the Christian life that is congruent with

Titus 2:11–14 and consistent with evangelical aims when viewed through the lens of an objective but somewhat sympathetic historian.[1]

The Grace of God Has Appeared Bringing Salvation

Using Titus 2:11 as our guide, we begin our discussion of evangelical spirituality with the gospel of grace, by which we are delivered from death and made alive in Christ. Iain Murray rightly notes:

> If what Christ has done for us is not kept first, *the pursuit of holiness can easily cease to be evangelical.* "Evangelical" means "good news." Any teaching on holiness which puts the main emphasis on the Christian's duty, turns sanctification into a matter of self-effort, a work dependent on ourselves, or an experience we have to seek. If that were the case it would not be good news. Grace would fall into the second place and our works be put before the grace of God.[2]

Grace is therefore central to evangelical spirituality because conversion, or the new birth, is necessary before any attempts at spirituality are acceptable to God.

Martin Luther's lengthy, winding path to discovering a gracious God illustrates this principle well. His promise in a thunderstorm to become a monk should his life be spared led him to an Augustinian monastery, where his daily life was regulated by prayer, study, and obedience. The insecurities he experienced along the way led him to confess every known sin, prompting him also to remain in the confessional admitting sins he had merely *considered* committing. Luther's memorable words, "If any monk ever got to heaven by monkery, then I should have made it," reveal both his sincerity and his despair as a monk. Despite doing more than what was required (according to Roman Catholic teaching at the time), he did not merit favor from God.

---

[1] I use the phrase "sympathetic historian" to indicate that my approach stems from an evangelical perspective while at the same time acknowledging the difficulties associated with ascribing evangelical positions to those who preceded the evangelical movement as we know it. David Bebbington's assertion that evangelicalism began as a recognizable movement in the eighteenth century is generally on the mark but has been refined by others who cite earlier continuities. See David Bebbington, *Evangelicalism in Modern Britain: A History from the 1730s to the 1980s* (New York: Routledge, 1989); and Michael Haykin and Kenneth J. Stewart, eds., *The Advent of Evangelicalism* (Nashville, TN: B&H Academic, 2008). My approach falls in line with Douglas Sweeney, who defines evangelicalism as a "movement that is rooted in classical Christian orthodoxy, shaped by a largely Protestant understanding of the gospel, and distinguished from other such movements by an eighteenth-century twist." Douglas Sweeney, *The American Evangelical Story* (Grand Rapids, MI: Baker Academic, 2005), 23–24. It is therefore not my purpose to argue that Luther, Calvin, or Owen were evangelicals, but only to note contributions that evangelicals have borrowed from them in advancing their understanding of the Christian life.

[2] Iain H. Murray, *Evangelical Holiness and Other Addresses* (Edinburgh: Banner of Truth, 2013), 31.

Actually, Luther's conversion occurred somewhat inconspicuously as he prepared lessons for his students at Wittenberg and came to a "fine syntactical decision about a genitive in Romans."[3] Luther later recalled:

> I had conceived a most unusual, burning desire to understand Paul in his letter to the Romans; thus far there had stood in my way not a cold heart but one single word that is written in the first chapter: "In it the justice of God is revealed" (Rom. 1:17) because I hated that word "justice of God." By the use and custom of all my teachers I had been taught to understand it philosophically as referring to the so-called formal or active justice, that is, justice by which God is just and by which he punishes sinners and the unjust. But I, impeccable monk that I was, stood before God as a sinner with an extremely troubled conscience and I could not be sure that my merit would assuage him.[4]

While this part of his story does not seem as exciting as escaping death by thunderbolt or changing the religious world by nailing ninety-five theses on a church door, it is in fact the most significant moment in Luther's life:

> Then I began to understand the justice of God by which the just person lives by a gift of God, that is by faith. The meaning of this verse started to open up to me: The justice of God is revealed through the gospel but it is a passive justice by which the merciful God justifies us by faith. . . . All at once I had the feeling of being born again and entering into paradise itself through open gates.[5]

On the surface, Luther's experience of saving grace seems to confirm the evangelical narrative of a lengthy struggle that fails to produce either peace within or peace with God, resulting in a brokenness that can trust only in the finished work of Christ for salvation. Modern evangelicals, however, might find Luther's conversion surprisingly different from their own. For one, his preconversion struggles were largely works based, as he attempted to achieve righteousness through obedience to God's commands. Luther was not in bondage to the vices of his day. However, Luther's lengthy experience with unforgiven sin contributed to his theological reflections on the nature of grace. Luther explained this concept best in

---

[3] D. Bruch Hindmarsh, "The Antecedents of Evangelical Conversion Narrative: Spiritual Autobiography and the Christian Tradition," in Haykin and Steward, *The Advent of Evangelicalism*, 331.
[4] Cited in Markus Wriedt, "Luther's Theology," trans. Katharina Gustavs, in Donald McKim, ed., *The Cambridge Companion to Martin Luther* (Cambridge, UK: Cambridge University Press, 2003), 88.
[5] Ibid., 90.

Bondage of the Will, a work "written with a passionate desire to bring the abysmal experience of spiritual trials on the one hand together with the promise of divine mercy and grace on the other."[6] This work served as a corrective treatise against Desiderius Erasmus, who contended that sinful humans retained sufficient moral willpower to work cooperatively with God in pursuit of salvation. Although Luther could have flatly denied Erasmus' position using his own failed attempts to merit God's favor as an example of everyman, he derived his arguments from Scripture instead.[7]

Three of Luther's arguments are pertinent to understanding his views on grace. First, sinful humans are simply unable to obey God. When Erasmus repeated an age-old argument that the commandments of God necessarily imply human ability to perform them, Luther replied that God does taunt humanity with his commandments for the purpose of demonstrating man's inability to perform them:

> Human nature is so blind, so that it does not know its own strength—or, rather, sickness; moreover, being proud, it thinks it knows and can do everything. God can cure this pride and ignorance by no readier remedy than publication of His law. . . . Scripture describes man as corrupted and led captive, and, furthermore, as proudly disdaining to notice, and failing to recognize, his own corruption and captivity; therefore it uses these phrases to goad and rouse him, that he may know by sure experience how unable he is to do any of these things.[8]

Second, if sinful humans could obey God's commands, then Christ died in vain. This issue was particularly repulsive to Luther because it threatened to dislodge the centrality of the cross from the work of redemption. Citing John 1:16, Luther added, "And I wish that the guardians of 'free-will' would be taught by this passage to recognize that when they assert 'free-will' they are denying Christ. For if I obtain the grace of God by my own endeavor, what need have I of the grace of Christ for the receiving of my grace?"[9] If we pursue God's favor through merit instead of by grace, Luther noted, Christ should be approached as a dreadful judge rather than as a sweet mediator.

Third, if sinful humans were required to contribute to their salvation,

---

[6] Ibid., 111.

[7] Luther's methodology is central to his argument. Erasmus had claimed that matters such as freedom of the will remained mysterious and were therefore not worthy of deep exploration. Luther argued that Scripture provides clarity on the subject.

[8] Martin Luther, *The Bondage of the Will*, trans. J. I. Packer and O. R. Johnston (Grand Rapids, MI: Revell, 1957), 153.

[9] Ibid., 305. John 1:16 states, "For from his fullness we have all received, grace upon grace."

then assurance of God's favor is weakened. Recalling his preconversion attempts to please God, Luther throws his hands up with despair at such a thought:

> I frankly confess that, for myself, even if it could be, I should not want "free-will" to be given to me, nor anything to be left in my own hands to enable me to endeavor after salvation; not merely because in face of so many dangers and adversities, and assaults of devils, I could not stand my own ground and hold fast my "free-will" (for one devil is stronger than all men, and on these terms no man could be saved). . . . If I lived and worked to all eternity, my conscience would never reach comfortable certainty as to how much it must do to satisfy God. Whatever work I had done, there would still be a nagging doubt as to whether it pleased God, or whether He required something more. The experience of all who seek righteousness by works proves that; and I learned it well enough myself over a period of many years to my own great hurt.[10]

H. J. Iwand has observed, "Whoever puts this book down without having realized evangelical theology stands or falls with the doctrine of the bondage of the will has read it in vain."[11]

Luther's emphasis on human inability to obey the commands of God naturally raises questions about the role of good works in the Christian life. Luther addressed this issue in a work written five years prior, *The Freedom of the Christian*. Scholars have long recognized Luther's use of paradox to teach that "truth can only be arrived at by way of confrontation with a contrasting truth;"[12] thus it comes as no surprise that his two guiding propositions in *The Freedom of the Christian* would otherwise cancel each other out: "A Christian man is a perfectly free lord of all, subject to none. A Christian man is a perfectly dutiful servant of all, subject to all."[13] As he did with *Bondage of the Will*, Luther maintains in this work that works cannot contribute to one's salvation and in fact may diminish the work Christ performed on our behalf: "Wherefore it ought to be the first concern of every Christian to lay aside all trust in works, and more and more to strengthen faith alone, and through faith to grow in the knowledge, not of works, but of Christ Jesus, who suffered and rose for him."[14] In this sense, Christians have become the "freest of kings" because, spiri-

---

[10] Luther, *Bondage of the Will*, 313–14.
[11] Cited by J. I. Packer in ibid., 58.
[12] Timothy George, *Theology of the Reformers*, rev. ed. (Nashville, TN: B&H, 2013), 62.
[13] Martin Luther, *The Freedom of the Christian*, in *Three Treatises* (Philadelphia: Muhlenberg, 1947), 251.
[14] Ibid., 255.

tually speaking, they have no fear of anything that could separate them from God.

However, Christians are still subject to God and to fellow believers. Thus good works are performed freely to please God and lovingly to serve others. Two of Luther's models are relevant for this discussion. First, he likens the primary motivation of good works, pleasing God, to Adam's work in the garden of Eden:

> Adam was created by God righteous and upright and without sin, so that he had no need of being justified, and made upright through his dressing and keeping the garden, but, that he might not be idle, the Lord gave him a work to do—to cultivate and to protect the garden. These would truly have been the freest of works, done only to please God and not to obtain righteousness, which Adam already had in full measure. . . . Such are the works of a believer. Through his faith he has been restored to Paradise and created anew, has no need of works that he may become or be righteous; but that he might not become idle and may provide for and keep his body, he must do such works freely only to please God.[15]

Second, to illustrate service to others Luther uses Christ's incarnational model in Philippians 2:5–11 as one who truly had all things at his disposal. Although Jesus existed in the form of God, Luther noted, he was not "puffed up," nor did he "lift himself up above us and assume power over us . . . but on the contrary, he so lived, labored, worked, suffered and died . . . for our sake, that all things he accomplished in this form of a servant might become ours."[16] Luther summarizes the role of works in the Christian life accordingly:

> Though I am an unworthy and condemned man, my God has given me in Christ all the riches of righteousness and salvation without any merit on my part, out of pure, free mercy, so that henceforth I need nothing whatever except my faith which believes that this is true. Why should I not therefore freely, joyfully, and with all my heart, and with an eager will, do all things which I know are pleasing and acceptable to such a Father, who has overwhelmed me with his inestimable riches? I will therefore give myself as a Christ to my neighbor, just as Christ offered himself to me; I will do nothing in this life except what I see is necessary, profitable and salutary to my neighbor, since through faith I have an abundance of all good things in Christ.[17]

---

[15] Ibid., 270.
[16] Iibd., 276.
[17] Ibid., 278.

Given Luther's arguments in *Bondage of the Will*, we can state that his contribution to an evangelical understanding of grace is that it is necessary on account of human sinfulness, is glorious on account of Christ's righteousness, and is comforting on account of God's faithfulness. He adds to our understanding of grace through *The Freedom of a Christian* by noting that works, when properly placed after justification, please God, as Adam did prior to the fall, and serve others, as Christ did throughout his life. Evangelical spirituality, then, begins with grace and combines freedom from sin and guilt with the freedom to serve and love.[18]

A People for His Own Possession

Modern evangelicals often describe their faith as a "personal relationship with Jesus," which is helpful in contrasting genuine Christianity with mere ceremonialism or mechanical obedience. Although this phrase falls short on a number of levels, including inadvertently promoting the idea that Christian faith is merely an individual pursuit, it does remind us of the relational nature between God and his people. Paul uses similar relational language in Titus 2:14 as he describes God's redeeming and purifying a "people for his own possession." We should therefore employ such language of relationship without incorporating the false notion of individualism. John Calvin's teaching on providence and prayer is very helpful in this regard. As Elsie McKee notes:

> If one defines spirituality as a person's private relationship with God, which issues in individual holiness, then Calvin manifestly has less to say than some other guides. Even his own very personal conviction of his relationship with God was, in his understanding, predicated on his being engrafted into Christ's body, for he was convinced that no Christian is a Christian apart from the rest of the body. Spirituality for Calvin was therefore never individualistic. It was personal, without question, but it was personal in the context of the community of faith, whether that community was immediately visible or not.[19]

Calvin's explanation of providence provides the foundation for the Christian's ongoing trust in God despite heavy trials in the Christian life.

---

[18] For a fine development of this topic, see John R. W. Stott, *The Contemporary Christian* (Downers Grove, IL: InterVarsity Press, 1992), 46–56. Carl Trueman helpfully reminds evangelicals that Luther further developed his ideas on love and servanthood during his lifetime; consequently, those who use his terminology must be aware of the content of such words as employed by Luther. Carl Trueman, *Luther on the Christian Life: Cross and Freedom*, Theologians on the Christian Life (Wheaton, IL: Crossway, 2015), 159–74.

[19] Elsie Anne McKee, ed., *John Calvin: Writings on Pastoral Piety* (Mahwah, NJ: Paulist Press, 2001), 4.

Timothy George expresses this connection well: "More than any other reformer of the sixteenth century, Calvin was keenly aware of the precarious and utterly contingent character of human life. If Luther was preoccupied with the anxiety of guilt . . . then Calvin was haunted by the specter of the apparently haphazard and meaningless course of existence."[20] Calvin thus projects his discussion on providence against the backdrop of innumerable uncertainties that all humans must face. The body, no matter how strong, is susceptible to "a thousand diseases"; travel, no matter how short, requires but one mishap for death to occur; a stroll through the city streets makes one "subject to as many dangers as there are tiles on the roofs"; and even the comfort of one's home can be disrupted by fire or other similar calamities. "Amid these tribulations," Calvin writes, "must not man be most miserable, since, but half alive in life, he weakly draws his anxious and languid breath, as if he had a sword perpetually hanging over his neck?" Without certainty about God's providence, life would be miserable indeed.[21]

For Calvin, "providence means not that by which God idly observes from heaven what takes place on earth, but that by which, as keeper of the keys, he governs all events."[22] The reference to idleness is an intentional jab against the deistic notion that God created the world to run merely according to natural law. Calvin intends his readers to understand God in more personal terms: "To make God a momentary Creator, who once for all finished his work, would be cold and barren."[23] Moreover, failure to recognize the direct hand of God in the workings of providence is to miss the goodness of his heart:

> If God's governance is so extended to all his works, it is a childish cavil to enclose it within the stream of nature. Indeed, those as much defraud God of his glory as themselves of a most profitable doctrine who confine God's providence to such narrow limits as though he allowed all things by free course to be borne along according to a universal law of nature. For nothing would be more miserable than man if he were exposed to every movement of the sky, air, earth, and waters. Besides, in this way God's particular goodness toward each one would be too unworthily reduced.[24]

---

[20] George, *Theology of the Reformers*, 204.
[21] John Calvin, *Institutes of the Christian Religion*, ed. John T. McNeill, trans. Ford Lewis Battles (Philadelphia: Westminster, 1960), 1.17.10.
[22] Ibid., 202.
[23] Ibid., 197.
[24] Ibid., 200.

Instead, God aims by his providence to draw affection from his creation, as stipulated by Psalm 104:27–28: "These all look to you / to give them their food in due season. / When you give it to them, they gather it up; / when you open your hand, they are filled with good things." The personal nature of providence therefore exceeds bland ideas of fortune or chance because it demonstrates "God's special care, by which alone his fatherly favor is known."[25] Christians in particular can draw comfort from God's providence not because they are protected from the dangers Calvin listed earlier but because they are assured that such trials are ultimately for their good and God's glory:

> Whence Christ, when he declared that not even a tiny sparrow of little worth falls to earth without the Father's will (Matt. 10:29), immediately applies it in this way: that since we are of greater value than sparrows, we ought to realize that God watches over us with all the closer care (Matt. 10:31); and he extends it so far that we may trust that the hairs of our head are numbered (Matt. 10:30). What else can we wish for ourselves, if not even one hair can fall from our head without his will? I speak not only concerning mankind; but, because God has chosen the church to be his dwelling place, there is no doubt that he shows by singular proofs his fatherly care in ruling it.[26]

When providence is understood in relational terms, such as God's goodness and fatherly care, Christians can live in a dangerous world with "gratitude of mind for the favorable outcome of things, patience in adversity, and also incredible freedom from worry about the future."[27] This resulting attitude does not suggest that believers will always understand the mysterious workings of providence; rather, they acknowledge and accept their own limited mental capacities in light of the surpassing wisdom of God.[28]

Calvin did not expect, however, for Christians simply to will themselves to believe in providence. Rather, he instructed believers to pray in order to foster trust in God's good and fatherly care. The fact that he did not view prayer as a subversion of God's providential decrees or a futile practice in light of God's sovereignty is shown by both the attention he gave to and the reasons he provided for prayer.

Calvin's attention to prayer was considerable. The subject of prayer

---

[25] Ibid., 198.
[26] Ibid., 218–19.
[27] Ibid., 219.
[28] Ibid., 232–37.

forms the second-longest chapter in his *Institutes*. He himself prayed in the morning and evening, before and after meals, and prior to his daily work. In Geneva he implemented the Day of Prayer, a two-hour weekly service in which he contributed prayers for public participation and included congregational singing of Psalms, the prayer book of the Bible. In fact, Calvin's longest commentary is on the book of Psalms, of which he declared, "There is no other book in which we are more perfectly taught the right manner of praising God, or in which we are more powerfully stirred up to the performance of this exercise of piety."[29] The psalms were uniquely helpful as a guide to prayer because they contained "all the grief, sorrows, fears, doubts, hopes, cares, perplexities, in short, all the distracting emotions with which the minds of men are wont to be agitated."[30] Calvin's experience with constant criticism, occasional exiles, and failing health enabled him to identify with the psalmists in very personal terms. Consequently, as Bruce Gordon notes, "it was his ability to express in words the emotional responses of the Christian to the Word of God that made him the most powerful of commentators."[31] Calvin also began and ended his lectures and sermons with prayer, the following of which illustrates the connection between divine providence and personal trust:

> We bow ourselves before the majesty of our good God, in acknowledgement of our offenses, asking that He may make us feel them more and more, to be grieved over them and so renounce them, in order to be reclothed with His graces, and to be made participants of the good things we have heard that He promises to His faithful people. And when He presents Himself to be our guide, let us not doubt that He always has a mighty hand to keep us steady; and He will not allow us to fail, but in His power we will rise above all the difficulties that would hinder us from coming to Him. And however we may now have cause to be sorrowful about many things—and some are afflicted in body and others in spirit—that nevertheless this good God will always give us the grace to be led under His hand until, enjoying the fruit of the

---

[29] John Calvin, *Commentary on the Psalms*, in *Calvin's Commentaries*, vol. 4, trans. James Anderson (Grand Rapids, MI: Baker, 1996), *xxxviii–xxxix*.

[30] Ibid., *xxxvii*. Michael Horton points out an added dimension of using the psalms as a guide for prayer: "The Psalms are more than a quarry from which to take our own prayers; through them and in them we find Christ praying with us. These inspired songs not only spoke of Christ, but also were on his heart and on his lips throughout his life. . . . Nobody felt the pains, anxieties, and sorrows of the songs of lament more than Jesus. And no one felt greater joy in the Father's love and will expressed in the songs of praise. It is a remarkable privilege to join our Savior in all of these prayers." Michael Horton, *Calvin on the Christian Life: Glorifying and Enjoying God Forever*, Theologians on the Christian Life (Wheaton, IL: Crossway, 2014), 164–65.

[31] Bruce Gordon, *Calvin* (New Haven, CT: Yale University Press, 2009), 286.

victory He has promised us, we may rejoice fully, singing His praises
with the angels of paradise, when we have been brought forth out of
all weeping.[32]

Thus for Calvin, prayer is predicated upon and fosters the genuine relationship that exists between God and his people: "There is a communion
of men with God by which, having entered the heavenly sanctuary, they
appeal to him in person concerning his promises in order to experience,
where necessity so demands, that what they believed was not vain, although he had promised it in word alone."[33] Yet Calvin is clear that believers are the prime beneficiaries of this relationship, since God ordained
prayer "not so much for his own sake as for ours."[34]

Calvin provides six reasons for prayer, each of which demonstrates
the benefits received by those who commune with God accordingly:
(1) that our hearts may be fired with a zealous and burning desire ever to
seek, love, and serve him, while we become accustomed in every need to
flee to him as to a sacred anchor; (2) that there may enter our hearts no
desire or no wish of which we should be ashamed to make him a witness,
while we learn to set all our wishes before his eyes, and even to pour out
our whole hearts; (3) that we be prepared to receive his benefits with true
gratitude of heart and thanksgiving, benefits that our prayer reminds us
come from his hand; (4) that, having obtained what we were seeking, and
being convinced that he has answered our prayers, we should be led to
meditate upon his kindness more ardently; (5) that at the same time we
embrace with greater delight those things that we acknowledge to be obtained by prayers; and (6) that use and experience may, according to the
measure of our feebleness, confirm his providence, while we understand
not only that he promises never to fail us, and of his own will opens the
way to call upon him at the very point of necessity, but also that he ever
extends his hand to help his own, not wet-nursing them with words but
defending them with present help.[35]

Utilizing prayer as a means of confirming God's providence, as Calvin notes in his sixth reason, is essential because God intentionally "gives
the impression of one sleeping or idling in order that he may thus train

[32] McKee, *John Calvin: Writings on Pastoral Piety*, 229. Calvin concluded his sermon on Isa. 35:8–10 with this prayer.
[33] Calvin, *Institutes*, 3.20.2.
[34] Ibid.
[35] Ibid. Calvin also provides rules for prayer along with an exposition of the Lord's Prayer. This section is given primarily to the relational aspect of prayer between God and his children; the discipline of prayer is discussed later in this chapter with guidance from J. C. Ryle.

us, otherwise idle and lazy, to seek, ask, and entreat him to our great good."[36] The very act of waiting upon the Lord to act in accordance with his promises is designed to prompt believers to shake off their own sluggishness. Prayer thus becomes the antidote to idly waiting or giving up due to discouragement: "If, with minds composed to this obedience, we allow ourselves to be ruled by the laws of divine providence, we shall easily learn to persevere in prayer and, with desires suspended, patiently to wait for the Lord. Then we shall be sure that, even though he does not appear, he is always present to us, and will in his own time declare how he has never had ears deaf to the prayers that in men's eyes he seems to have neglected."[37]

Joel Beeke captures the beauty of Calvin's theology of prayer: "He presents the throne room of God as glorious, holy, and sovereign while also accessible, desirable, and precious in and through Christ. Given the rich blessings accessible to us through prayer, those who refuse to pray 'neglect a treasure, buried and hidden in the earth, after it had been pointed out' to them."[38] Evangelicals can profit from Calvin's teachings on providence and prayer as together they highlight the relational connection between God and his people. The providence of God assures us that our trust is rightly placed in the only sovereign who works all things together for our good, and prayer keeps us tethered by faith to our good and caring heavenly Father who, because he knows our frailties, invites us always to call upon his name.

Training Us to Renounce Ungodliness and Worldly Passions

Even though evangelicals readily affirm that salvation is an act of grace that enables recipients to live in relationship with God, they also realize that sin is an ever-present reality in the world and in their own lives. Luther's famous phrase *semper iustus et peccator*, always righteous and a sinner, underscores the reality that people living in a right relationship with God still commit unrighteous acts in a fallen world. The apostle Paul addresses this dilemma in Titus 2:11–14 by seamlessly connecting justification with sanctification. The same grace that brings salvation also trains Christ's followers "to renounce ungodliness and worldly passions, and to live self-controlled, upright, and godly lives in the present age." Thus the

---

[36] Calvin, *Institutes*, 3.20.3.
[37] Ibid.
[38] Joel Beeke, "John Calvin on Prayer as Communion with God," in *Taking Hold of God: Reformed and Puritan Perspectives on Prayer*, ed. Joel Beeke and Brian G. Najapfour (Grand Rapids, MI: Reformation Heritage, 2011), 41.

saving grace of God includes ethical demands upon the child of God in order for him or her to be conformed to the image of the Son of God. Such grace

> aims to lead the believer to the place where as a definite act he will voluntarily make a double renunciation of the past. He must repudiate and abandon "ungodliness," the impiety and irreverence that characterized his unsaved life, as well as "worldly passions," those cravings characteristic of the world in its estrangement from God. Such an act of renunciation, standing at the beginning of a life of Christian victory, must be maintained in daily self-denial.[39]

Whereas Paul personifies grace in Titus 2:11 as the means by which Christians renounce ungodliness and worldly passions, he elsewhere identifies the person behind such grace, namely, the Holy Spirit who indwells believers and thereby enables them to "put to death the deeds of the body" (Rom. 8:13). This latter text formed the basis of a series of sermons preached by John Owen depicting the role of the Spirit in the work of sanctification. Its 1656 publication under the title *Of the Mortification of Sin in Believers* has since become an evangelical manual for detecting and defeating the root causes of sin.[40]

Owen's treatise may be categorized as evangelical for three reasons. First, by connecting the indwelling Spirit with the command for believers to fight ongoing sin in their own lives, Owen rightly places the call to conversion prior to the duty of sanctification: "I say, then, mortification is not the present business of unregenerate men. God calls them not to it as yet; conversion is their work—conversion of the *whole* soul—not the mortification of this or that particular lust."[41] Second, Owen instructs his readers to uproot sin at its very foundations within the human heart rather than to react to manifestations of sin as they occur. Sinclair Ferguson notes, "This is the difference between legal and evangelical mortification. Legal mortification is concerned with particular sins only when the guilt of them reflects upon the conscience; evangelical mortification is

---

[39] D. Edmond Hiebert, *Titus*, Everyman's Bible Commentary 11, ed. Frank Gaebelein (Grand Rapids, MI: Zondervan, 1978), 440.
[40] John Owen wrote two additional treatises on sin in the life of the believer: *Of Temptation* (1658) and *The Nature, Power, Deceit, and Prevalency of the Remainders of Indwelling Sin in Believers* (1667). Each may be found in vol. 6 of *The Works of John Owen*, ed. William H. Goold, 23 vols. (1850–1855; repr. London: Banner of Truth, 1965–1968). Citations in this chapter are from John Owen, *Overcoming Sin and Temptation*, ed. Kelly Kapic and Justin Taylor (Wheaton, IL: Crossway, 2006). Kapic and Taylor provide an unabridged edition of Owen's three works with updated language.
[41] Owen, *Overcoming Sin and Temptation*, 81.

concerned to deal with sin in any of its manifestations, because it is opposed to the renovation of the image of God."[42]

Third, by following a biblically prescribed pattern for mortification,
Owen rejected contemporaneous practices that merely gave the appearance of pursuing holiness: "The greatest part of [Roman Catholic] religion, of that which looks most like religion in their profession, consists
in mistaken ways and means of mortification. . . . Such as these are their
rough garments, their vows, penances, disciplines, their course of monas-
tical life, and the like; concerning all which God will say, 'In vain do you
worship me, teaching for doctrines the traditions of men.'"[43] The combination of Spirit-empowered and Scripture-sanctioned pursuit of holiness
thus marks a profound break from mere human attempts at pleasing God:
"Mortification from a self-strength, carried on by ways of self-invention,
unto the end of a self-righteousness, is the soul and substance of all false
religion in the world."[44]

Owen's summary of Romans 8:13 is fairly simple: "The choicest believers, who are assuredly freed from the condemning power of sin, ought yet
to make it their business all their days to mortify the indwelling power of
sin."[45] Mortifying sin not only signifies that one has been born of the Spirit
but also ensures that believers will enjoy present, ongoing fellowship with
the Father and Son also, thus challenging faulty evangelical notions that
reduce salvation to a form of "fire insurance."[46] Put more strongly, Owen
states that "the vigor, and power, and comfort of our spiritual life depends
on the mortification of the deeds of the flesh."[47] Given that mortification is
a command to be obeyed with the joy and vigor of one's walk with God at
stake, Owen provides the reader with an injunction that has since become
one of his most recognizable lines: "Make [mortification] your daily work;
be always at it while you live; cease not a day from this work; be killing sin
or it will be killing you."[48]

---

[42] Sinclair Ferguson, *John Owen on the Christian Life* (Carlisle, PA: Banner of Truth, 1987), 72.

[43] Owen, *Overcoming Sin and Temptation*, 58–59. The biblical citation is from Matt. 15:9. Owen also criticized unbiblical practices found in Protestant writings that, as he describes it, "may have become popish devotionists three or four hundred years ago."

[44] Ibid., 47.

[45] Ibid.

[46] The question of the believer's responsibility to keep the commands of God is not new to evangelicals, but the idea of salvation as benefit without cost is surely a truncated view of the gospel message. Owen and his Puritan contemporaries combatted antinomianism, which understands Christian freedom as relaxing the demands of the moral law for believers, individually through numerous treatises and collectively through the Westminster Confession of Faith: "They who upon pretense of Christian liberty, do practice any sin, or cherish any lust, do thereby destroy the end of Christian liberty, which is, that being delivered out of the hands of our enemies, we might serve the Lord without fear, in holiness and righteousness before him, all the days of our life" (WCF 20.3).

[47] Owen, *Overcoming Sin and Temptation*, 49.

[48] Ibid., 50.

What is mortification, and how does one go about it? Owen defined mortification using a mixture of negative and positive assertions. In sum, mortification is neither the utter destruction of sin in one's nature nor an occasional conquest over sin; rather, it is a habitual weakening of sin that consists of frequent successes over such sin. Understood thusly, Owen does not claim to provide a path toward sinless perfection in this lifetime, but he does chart a course for believers to trend toward personal holiness:

> Now, I say, when a man comes to this state and condition, that lust is weakened at the root and principle, that its motions and actions are fewer and weaker than formerly, so that they are not able to hinder his duty nor interrupt his peace—when he can, in a quiet, sedate frame of spirit, find out and fight against sin, and have success against it—then sin is mortified in some considerable measure, and, notwithstanding all its opposition, a man may have peace with God all his days.[49]

In typical Puritan fashion, Owen provides a detailed methodology for mortifying sin. He begins with nine particular directives constituting the preparatory work and concludes with several summary remarks detailing how the death of Christ and the power of the Spirit assure the believer that sin can indeed be mortified. Owen's first directive instructs the believer to come to terms with the depth and power of sin that has reigned unchecked prior to pursuing mortification. To use a modern example, a person who decides to lose weight must realize beforehand that past eating habits are very hard to break and that stricter dietary strategies are necessary in order to shed more than just a few pounds. With regard to unimpeded sin, Owen notes that one's entire being is already so affected that one is likely unaware of the power that sin yet holds: "When a lust has lain long in the heart, corrupting, festering, cankering, it brings the soul to a woeful condition. In such a case an ordinary course of humiliation will not do the work . . . it grows familiar to the mind and conscience, that they do not startle at it as a strange thing."[50] Moreover, a person who has not pursued mortification has likely found easier measures by which to deal with sin, such as placating one's conscience by calling to mind other evidences of God's grace, or denying the reality of sin in one's life only because it has not yet become visible to others. Thus mortification must be understood as a life-altering and lifelong pursuit.

Owen's second directive is to "get a clear and abiding sense upon your

---

[49] Ibid., 77.
[50] Ibid., 90.

mind and conscience of the guilt, danger, and evil of that sin wherewith you are perplexed."[51] Recognizing the guilt of sin goes against the tendency to play down the seriousness of sin either by degrees ("It is only a small sin") or by comparison ("It is not as bad as what others are doing"). The dangers of sin include its hardening effects on the heart, loss of peace and strength in one's walk with God, the possibility of incurring temporal judgment, and even the risk of receiving eternal judgment. The last danger is possible not because salvation can be lost but because those who do not fight against sin may be falsely assured of their right standing before God. Owen also encourages the believer to consider the evils of sin: it grieves the Holy Spirit, it wounds Christ afresh, and it takes away one's usefulness for service.[52]

Third, Owen advises believers to load their consciences with the guilt of sin. He distinguishes this instruction from his previous point by noting that the believer should gain a sense of "the holiness, spirituality, fiery severity, inwardness, [and] absoluteness of the law, and see how you can stand before it."[53] He recognizes that one's conscience may invent ways to deny guilt, but a resolute focus on the law will weaken and ultimately break down such resistance:

> Whatever be the issue, yet the law has a commission from God to seize upon transgressors wherever it find them, and so bring them before his throne, where they are to plead for themselves. This is your present case; the law has found you out, and before God it will bring you. If you can plead a pardon, well and good; if not, the law will do its work.[54]

Owen's fourth admonition flows from the third: believers whose consciences are loaded with the guilt of sin ought to "constantly long and breathe after deliverance from the power of sin."[55] Such a desire is a command and a gift: "Longing, breathing, and panting after deliverance is a grace in itself, that has a mighty power to conform the soul into the likeness of the thing longed after."[56]

Owen's advice takes a slightly different turn at his fifth point. He addresses the possibility that the propensity toward a specific sin could be due to one's personal constitution. Here Owen anticipates the modern

---

[51] Ibid., 97.
[52] Ibid., 98–103.
[53] Ibid., 103.
[54] Ibid., 104.
[55] Ibid., 106.
[56] Ibid.

discussion of genetic predisposition to various addictions and behaviors, but he does not share the conclusion that such persons are innocent before God. Instead, he traces such dispositions to their original source, the first family: "It is from the fall, from the original deprivation of our natures, that the [diseased material] and nourishment of any sin abides in our natural temper. . . . That you are peculiarly inclined unto any sinful distemper is but a particular breaking out of original lust in your nature, which should peculiarly abase and humble you."[57] Rather than comforting those who use their temperament as an excuse to keep on sinning, Owen warns that they must exercise more watchfulness and care over their lives, lest Satan use their weaknesses to his advantage.[58]

Owen's sixth point exhorts all believers to know their own propensity to sin in order to avoid occasions or areas where they are more likely to be tempted: "Consider what ways, what companies, what opportunities, what studies, what businesses, what conditions, have at any time given, or usually do give, advantages to your distempers, and set yourself heedfully against them all."[59] Putting these last two points together, certain believers may struggle with particular sins they are personally prone to commit, but all Christians should proactively avoid company and places where their sins are more likely to occur.

Owen's seventh point builds upon these thoughts: "Rise mightily against the first actings and conceptions of your distemper."[60] In other words, stop the forward movement of sin in its earliest stages. Owen cites James 1:14–15 in this regard: "Each person is tempted when he is lured and enticed by his own desire. Then desire when it has conceived gives birth to sin, and sin when it is fully grown brings forth death." Restraining one's sinful desires before they come to fruition can be accomplished, Owen notes, by considering the deleterious effects of sin as if the sin had been committed: "Rise up with all your strength against it, with no less indignation than if it had fully accomplished what it aims at."[61]

Owen's eighth point directs the believer's attention to the majesty and glory of God as a means of self-abasement.[62] This approach may seem disquieting to evangelicals who affirm the inherent worth of people made in the image of God, but it is consistent with his previous advice to set one's

---

[57] Ibid., 107.
[58] Ibid., 107–8.
[59] Ibid., 109.
[60] Ibid.
[61] Ibid., 110.
[62] Ibid.

sin beside the law in order to gain a proper assessment of the two. Likewise, when believers meditate on the excellency and majesty of God, their boldness to continue sinning is rightly replaced with humility to pursue holiness: "Will not a due apprehension of this inconceivable greatness of God, and that infinite distance wherein we stand from him, fill the soul with a holy and awful fear of him, so as to keep it in a frame unsuited to the thriving or reverential thoughts of God's greatness and omnipresence?"[63]

Owen's final point serves as a warning to those who conclude prematurely that their sin has been mortified: "Do not speak peace to yourself before God speaks it, but hearken to what God says to your soul."[64] Examples of such persons are those who claim repentance but do not genuinely hate their sin; those who find a general promise of forgiveness in Scripture and assume they have received the same from God; and those who claim victory over a particular sin while still harboring other sins in their lives. Owen does not, however, end his treatise with these warnings; rather, he showers the believer with promises that mortification is possible due to the finished work of Christ and the ongoing work of the Spirit. Regarding Christ's work, Owen states, "His blood is the great sovereign remedy for sin-sick souls. Live in this, and you will die a conqueror; yea, you will, through the good providence of God, live to see your lust dead at your feet."[65] Owen reminds the reader that Christ is also a merciful, tender, and kind High Priest who pities those entangled by sin. Believers can finally take comfort in knowing that their conviction of sin and confidence in Christ come not from themselves but through the Spirit, who is particularly active in the work of mortification. It is the Spirit who brings Christ into one's heart with sin-killing power, and it is the Spirit who is the author and finisher of our salvation.[66]

Owen's treatise on the mortification of sin might be dismissed today, as it was by antinomians in his own day, under the guise that it opens the door to legalism in the Christian life. J. I. Packer provides refreshing insight on the matter in "The Puritan Conscience":

> Was all this teaching on Christian conduct a lapse into a new legalism and a curtailing of Christian liberty? Does it mark a decline into pharisaic ways? No; for first, all this ethical teaching was evangelically based, as that of the New Testament is. The supreme ethical motives in

---

[63] Ibid., 118.
[64] Ibid.
[65] Ibid., 131.
[66] Ibid., 138–39.

Puritanism were gratitude for grace received, and a sense of responsibility to walk worthy of one's calling, and there was not the least room in
Puritan teaching for self-righteousness; for not only was it constantly
stressed that the Christian works *from* life, rather than *for* life, but it was
also repeatedly emphasized that our best works are shot through with
sin, and contain something that needs to be forgiven.[67]

Far from being a manual on how to achieve self-righteousness through
self-improvement, Owen's treatise may rightly be received by evangelicals
as a Christ-honoring, Spirit-empowered, Scripture-sanctioned manual on
renouncing ungodliness and worldly passions, thus enabling believers to
enjoy ongoing communion with the Father, Son, and Holy Spirit.

Zealous for Good Works

The emphasis on renouncing ungodliness, however, captures only part
of Paul's admonition in Titus 2:12–14. He also notes that Christ gave his
life to purify a people who are "zealous for good works." Though Owen,
Calvin, and Luther provide their own treatises on good works, it is helpful at this point to consider the contributions of John Wesley, whose life
and legacy paved the remarkable trail of evangelical activism that forms a
quarter of the famous Bebbington quadrilateral.[68] Although the so-called
Rule of Wesley cannot be found in his writings, it certainly resembles
Wesley's life's motto: "Do all you can, by all the means you can, in all the
ways you can, in all the places you can, at all the times you can, to all the
people you can, as long as you ever can." James Gordon writes of Wesley
as an "activist par excellence" when referring to the half-century of works
recorded in his journal: "The narrative throbs with energy and leaves the
reader struggling to keep up with the comings and goings, the doings and
writings, the preaching, teaching, praying, organizing and reorganizing of
the human dynamo at the center of revival."[69] And while it is too much to
claim, as some historians have, that Wesley's Methodist movement pre-
vented England from embracing a secular national identity comparable to
the aftermath of the French Revolution, there is no doubt that his influence led to great social change in Great Britain and North America.[70] Our

---

[67] J. I. Packer, *A Quest for Godliness: The Puritan Vision of the Christian Life* (Wheaton, IL: Crossway, 1990),
118.

[68] Our reference to Luther on good works focused on his placement of works after justification in keeping with
his understanding of grace; this section on Wesley focuses on his drive to improve on good works through his
constant pursuit of loving God and others.

[69] James Gordon, *Evangelical Spirituality: From the Wesleys to John Stott* (London: SPCK, 1991), 11.

[70] This theory was first proposed by Elie Halevy, *The Birth of Methodism in England*, ed. and trans. Bernard
Samuel (Chicago: University of Chicago Press, 1971).

examination of Wesley's activism as an example of evangelical spirituality will proceed with a discussion of zeal that energizes believers for good works, followed by a summary of activities that demonstrate Wesley's zeal on behalf of serving others, and concluding with a critique of Christian perfectionism that forms the theological underpinning of his emphasis on good works.

According to Wesley, zeal is the driving force that motivates believers to serve God and others: "There are few subjects in the whole compass of religion, that are of greater importance than this. For without zeal, it is impossible, either to make any considerable progress in religion ourselves, or to do any considerable service to our neighbor, whether in temporal or spiritual things."[71] Using Galatians 4:18 as his text, Wesley communicates his understanding of how believers should best direct their energies to accomplish the things that matter most to God and that serve to benefit mankind.[72] Wesley notes that the evangelical revivals of his day had produced zeal among many, yet he recognized that such passions could work for evil as well as for good. Unrestrained or misdirected zeal, he notes, resulted in the persecution of believers throughout the history of the church, including Christians' persecuting their own. Wesley therefore argues that genuine Christian zeal must have love as its chief ingredient and good as its ultimate end.

Using the illustration of concentric circles, Wesley begins with love of God and humanity as the centerpiece and target of all other aims. His placement of loving others in the same space as loving God reflects his understanding of the greatest commandment (Luke 10:27) and rejects contemplation or mysticism as the pinnacle of the spiritual life. The circle immediately outside the center consists of "holy tempers," which he defines broadly as the fruit of the Spirit (Gal. 5:22–23). Here again he is mindful of how Christians are to use God-given graces for the welfare of others:

> We should still be more zealous for holy tempers; for planting and promoting, both in our own souls, and in all we have any intercourse with, lowliness of mind, meekness, gentleness, longsuffering, contentedness,

---

[71] I am indebted to the work of Fred Sanders, who highlights this sermon among the many thousands from Wesley's works. See Fred Sanders, *Wesley on the Christian Life: The Heart Renewed in Love*, Theologians on the Christian Life (Wheaton, IL: Crossway, 2013), 95–98. See also John Wesley, "On Zeal," in *Works of John Wesley*, vol. 7 (Grand Rapids, MI: Baker, 2007; repr. from the 1872 edition issued by Wesleyan Methodist Book Room, London), 57–67. The quote above is taken from p. 57.

[72] The text, from the King James Version, reads in part, "But it is good to be zealously affected always in a good thing."

resignation unto the will of God, deadness to the world and the things of the world, as the only means of being alive to God. For these proofs and fruits of living faith we cannot be too zealous. We should "talk of them as we sit in our house," and "when we walk by the way," and "when we lie down," and "when we rise up."[73]

Still moving outward from the center, Wesley cites works of mercy, such as feeding the hungry, clothing the naked, and visiting the sick. Fred Sanders notes that the placement of works of mercy closer to the center than the circle that follows (consisting of works of piety, such as reading the Bible, praying, fasting) is a surprising move, because one might expect spiritual disciplines to have priority over community service.[74] Sanders notes, however, that Wesley insisted on this arrangement in light of the biblical injunction that places mercy over sacrifice (Hos. 6:6; Matt. 9:13). Thus, as Wesley observed, "Whenever, therefore one interferes with the other, works of mercy are to be preferred. Even reading, hearing, and prayer are to be omitted, or to be postponed, 'at charity's almighty call'; when we are called to relieve the distress of our neighbor, whether in body or soul."[75] To clarify, Wesley is not suggesting that personal disciplines do not matter; rather, he reminds us that the Christian life is an active faith that includes the hard work of looking out for the needs of others before resting in the satisfaction that we have completed our own spiritual discipline checklist. Finally, Wesley places the church as the final ring of concentric circles, noting that God has provided the church for believers to grow together in grace and to challenge one another to increase their commitment to spiritual disciplines, good works, holy affections, and love for God and humanity.

Wesley's zeal for doing good works, then, has as its focus serving others while at the same time retaining love of God and humanity as one's ultimate aim. Rather than encouraging those who would be spiritual to remove themselves from the world, Wesley advocated for spiritually minded Christians to get busy working in the world. Timothy Tennent captures this reversal of expectations well:

Wesley understood, for example, that if you really want to be formed spiritually, you should be eager to go out into a place of pain, roll up your sleeves, and get your hands dirty serving the poor. While Wesley

---

[73] Wesley, "On Zeal," 61–62.
[74] Sanders, *Wesley on the Christian Life*, 96.
[75] Wesley, "On Zeal," 61.

was deeply committed to prayer and contemplation, his vision of the church was profoundly missional. Wesley took his new preachers out to the brickyards and into the prisons. Not only was the world his parish, but for Wesley the world is also God's greatest spiritual workshop. It is on the anvil of a suffering world that God shapes and forms his disciples to understand what it means to take up their cross and follow him. Thus the Wesleyan tradition is an active tradition; spiritual formation occurs in the context of active service in the world.[76]

Wesley's commitment to alleviating the effects of sin thus had broad social implications. Ever the organizer, he instructed bands of followers to serve the poor, visit prisoners, feed the hungry, and care for the destitute. He addressed laziness in the lives of Christians, challenging them to sleep less in order to accomplish more; he called upon the rich to get richer in order to give away more; and he preached against vanity in clothing lest believers attempt to be noticed by the world more. National sins also captured his attention, including foreign oppression and slavery. Indeed, the final letter he wrote was addressed to William Wilberforce, who was converted under Wesley's preaching and met the challenge in Wesley's letter to stand against a world that embraced human trafficking.[77]

But the most important contribution he made for the sake of others was preaching the gospel, and he did so tirelessly. He famously preached to people everywhere he could, particularly those who had no intentions of entering a church. On April 2, 1739, Wesley began field preaching, following the model of George Whitefield and overcoming his lifelong sense of church decorum in the process: "I could scarcely reconcile myself at first to this strange way of preaching in the fields of which he set me an example on Sunday. Having been all my life (till very lately) so tenacious of every point relating to decency and order that I should have thought the saving of souls almost a sin if it had not been done in a church."[78] His ministry was never the same from that point forward.[79] Not only did he continue field preaching as a means of bringing the gospel to the nonchurched; he also implemented itinerant preaching for his followers,

---

[76] Timothy Tennent, "Why I am an Evangelical and a Methodist," in *Why We Belong: Evangelical Unity and Denominational Diversity*, ed. Anthony L. Chute, Christopher W. Morgan, and Robert A. Peterson (Wheaton, IL: Crossway, 2013), 144.

[77] For a fine summary of Wesley's views on ethics and society, see Thomas Oden, *John Wesley's Teachings*, vol. 4 (Grand Rapids, MI: Zondervan, 2014).

[78] Wesley, *Journals: 1735–1745*, March 29, 1739, *Works of John Wesley*, vol. 1, 185.

[79] Roy Hattersley comments, "There is hardly a marketplace or village green in England which does not now boast that John Wesley once preached within its boundaries." Roy Hattersley, *The Life of John Wesley: A Brand from the Burning* (New York: Doubleday, 2003), 148.

advising, "You have nothing to do but save souls. Therefore spend and be spent in this work."[80] For his part, it is estimated that Wesley traveled a quarter of a million miles, preached more than forty thousand sermons, and published over four hundred works.[81]

This staggering body of work was made possible by his zeal to serve the Lord well past what is now considered retirement age. His written recollections indicate that the "earnestness of his early years did not become the easy-going pace of an old moderate."[82] Journal entries forty years apart describe him rising at four in the morning to travel nearly eighty miles by horseback or carriage in order to preach several times that day, followed by yet another journey of the same length in order to preach multiple times again. Wesley even attributed his ministerial longevity to evangelical activity:

> This being my birthday, the first day of my seventy-second year, I was considering, How is this, that I find just the same strength as I did thirty years ago? That my sight is considerably better now, and my nerves firmer than they were then? That I have none of the infirmities of old age, and have lost several I had in my youth? The grand cause is, the good pleasure of God, who doth whatsoever pleaseth him. The chief means are, 1, my constantly rising at four, for about fifty years; 2, my generally preaching at five in the morning, one of the most healthy exercises in the world; 3, my never travelling less, by sea or land, than four thousand five hundred miles a year.[83]

Granted, Wesley's productivity is not the normal standard even for committed Christians engaged in full-time ministry. Sanders wisely advises would-be imitators that Wesley was uniquely suited for keeping such a demanding schedule. Nevertheless, he offers application for all: "We should never try to match his productivity! . . . He was in an elite class of healthy, hardworking, high-capacity productive people. What we should imitate, however, are his principles and his attitude toward work, devoting all our time and energy to serving God and man."[84]

If zeal was the driving force behind Wesley's activism, the idea of Christian perfection was its theological underpinning. This was the most

---

[80] John Wesley, "Twelve Rules for Helpers," cited in Sanders, *Wesley on the Christian Life*, 39.
[81] Richard P. Heitzenrater, "Wesley, John," in *Biographical Dictionary of Evangelicals*, ed. Timothy Larsen (Downers Grove, IL: InterVarsity Press, 2003), 715.
[82] Iain Murray, *Wesley and the Men Who Followed* (Edinburgh: Banner of Truth, 2003), 81.
[83] John Wesley, "Tuesday, June 28, 1774," in *Journals from September 19, 1773 to October 24, 1790*, vol. 4, *Works of John Wesley*, ed. Thomas Jackson (1879; repr. Grand Rapids, MI: Baker, n.d.), 20.
[84] Sanders, *Wesley on the Christian Life*, 46.

controversial of Wesley's contributions to the Christian life, in part because opponents found fault with his exegesis and in part because many
who claimed to experience perfection were hardly able to persuade others
of corroborating evidence from their own lives.[85] Understanding Wesley's
position is first in order, but a critique must follow before we can derive a
suitable application.

In *A Plain Account of Christian Perfection*, Wesley described his position as the "loving of God with all our heart, mind, soul, and strength.
This implies that no wrong temper, none contrary to love, remains in the
soul; and that all the thoughts, words and actions, are governed by pure
love."[86] He offered a similar definition in *Brief Thoughts on Christian Perfection:* "By perfection I mean the humble, gentle, patient love of God and
our neighbor, ruling our tempers, words, and actions."[87] Once again love
of God and others is at the center of Wesley's thought. In this context, love
is perfected in the believer such that the desire to sin against God or others has been uprooted. His use of the word *perfection* was based on Matthew 5:48 ("Be ye therefore perfect, even as your Father which is in heaven
is perfect," KJV) and Colossians 1:28 (". . . that we may present every man
perfect in Jesus Christ," KJV), but it was not intended to carry the conno-
tation of being incapable of sin. Rather, Wesley argued that Christians can
attain a state of sanctified maturity whereupon they will not willingly nor
knowingly sin against God or others. This caveat leaves room for sins of
ignorance and recognizes no immunity from future temptation. A person
who has attained Christian perfection, then, is one who loves God as he
should be loved and treats others as they should be treated, yet still has
room for growth in grace and may in fact relapse into a selfish, sinful way
of life.

Wesley's critics have sought to dismantle his teaching on Christian
perfection by pointing to his own irregularities in explaining the doctrine
and by challenging his use of the term *perfection* despite his admission
that such Christians continue to sin, even if inadvertently. More substantive critiques include Wesley's tendency to conflate God's ultimate work
in the believer with promises for the present; his failure to recognize that
even the best of Christians still sin with their eyes wide open; his con-
fusing advice for people to testify they have reached this stage while yet

---

[85] For the role of testimonials in Wesley's understanding and development of this doctrine, see Henry D. Rack, *Reasonable Enthusiast: John Wesley and the Rise of Methodism* (Philadelphia: Trinity Press, 1989), 334–42.
[86] John Wesley, *A Plain Account of Christian Perfection*, vol. 11, *Works of John Wesley*, ed. Thomas Jackson (Grand Rapids, MI: Baker, 2007), 394.
[87] Ibid., 446.

running the risk of pride and self-promotion; and his introduction of an experience subsequent to conversion to be sought by all believers.[88] Even so, those who critique Wesley on this point do so with caution, noting that evangelicals can easily miss Wesley's larger point that loving God and others lies at the heart of Christianity, and therefore believers should continually increase in their desire for both. Iain Murray respectfully reminds, "What is not controversial [in Wesley's teaching] should be underlined."[89] J. I. Packer closes his critical remarks on Wesley's doctrine by heaping high praise on his intentions:

> Yet the nobility of Wesley's ideal of the Christian temper—all joy, thanksgiving, and love—stands as an abiding rebuke to anyone tempted to settle for anything less. And when Wesley's doctrine of total love is heard simply as a witness to what Thomas Chalmers was later to call "the expulsive power of a new affection"—that is, as telling us how love to the Father and Jesus, called forth by the divine love that redeemed us, drives out meanness, bitterness, and pride—it exposes all shallow, self-absorbed and self-indulgent elements in our devotion with devastating force.[90]

John Fletcher, a contemporary of Wesley, skillfully silenced critics with the following observation: "He has generally blown the gospel trumpet, and rode twenty miles, before most of the professors, who despise his labors, have left their downy pillows."[91] Evangelicals can therefore incorporate Wesley's zeal for good works by placing the love of God and others at the center of their energies and affections, with the intent of outwardly serving the church and world for the remainder of their lives while inwardly striving for further growth in grace.

Waiting for Our Blessed Hope

It may seem like an abrupt change of thought to transition from activity to waiting, but in following the flow of Paul's presentation in Titus 2:11–14, such a move is warranted. Paul notes that the grace of God has already appeared visibly in the life of Jesus Christ, yet he also anticipates another

---

[88] See J. I. Packer, *Keep in Step with the Spirit* (Grand Rapids, MI: Revell, 1984), 132–45; and Murray, *Wesley and the Men Who Followed*, 232–46. Fred Sanders provides the best advice for those who still hold to the potential doctrine of Christian perfection: "To do what it did for Wesley, the doctrine must be yoked to an overtly Protestant doctrine of justification, situated in a 1 John framework, ordered toward obeying God's law on the basis of the gospel, and located in a regular use of the means of grace. The whole package worked for Wesley, but may come apart in the hands of less capable practitioners." See Sanders, *Wesley on the Christian Life*, 215.
[89] Murray, *Wesley and the Men Who Followed*, 232.
[90] Packer, *Keep in Step With the Spirit*, 145.
[91] Cited in Murray, *Wesley and the Men Who Followed*, 82.

epiphany, the glory of Jesus Christ upon his return. "Thus the apostle, in this short paragraph of only four verses (11–14), brings together the two termini of the Christian era, that is, the first coming of Christ which inaugurated it and the second coming of Christ which will terminate it. He bids us to look back to the one and on to the other."[92] Given the context of Paul's message, waiting is not synonymous with being idle (he explicitly calls for action) but is an affirmation that the life one has begun in Christ awaits its fulfillment upon the return of Christ. Evangelical spirituality must therefore incorporate an appreciation for the world to come, in which sanctification will give way to glorification and every Christian may truly be deemed perfect in Christ.

Jonathan Edwards is more than capable of helping us to think about heaven as it relates to our spiritual growth. First, he preached about heaven in order to help his congregation see not only the blessings of the world to come but also the benefits of living for that world in this lifetime. His reputation as a fiery preacher, warning sinners about their status before an angry God, has overshadowed his regular preaching that encouraged saints to anticipate eternity with the triune God joyfully. Yet the imagery he used to awaken fear in the mind of the wicked was equally vivid and poignant when employed to speak of the glory of God and the beauty of heaven. Second, Edwards experienced a bit of heaven on earth through the evangelical awakenings of the eighteenth century. His description of and subsequent thoughts on these revivals have bred a desire among evangelicals for the heavens to fall once again.

Of all the sermons Jonathan Edwards preached on heaven, "Heaven, a World of Love" has been singled out as perhaps his best. This was the final sermon in a series entitled *Charity and Its Fruits*, based on 1 Corinthians 13. The connection to heaven comes from the phrase "love never ends" in 1 Corinthians 13:8, leading Edwards to assert that love will continue when other fruits of the Spirit have ceased. The point and time when love will singularly characterize the lives of the saints is when the church is perfected in heaven. Edwards develops his thoughts using five main points. First, heaven is a world of love because God, "the cause and fountain of love," dwells there.[93] Dane Ortlund rightly notes, "The point is not that heaven is a lovely place and God is there too; heaven

---

[92] John Stott, *Guard the Truth: The Message of 1 Timothy and Titus*, Bible Speaks Today (Downers Grove, IL: InterVarsity Press, 1996), 195.
[93] Jonathan Edwards, "Heaven, a World of Love," in *Charity and Its Fruits* (Orlando, FL: Soli Deo Gloria, 2005), 288.

is lovely *because* God is there."[94] Edwards begins with God because God is the source of love in the same way that the sun is the source of light on earth—apart from the former, the latter does not exist. Moreover, Edwards builds anticipation of heaven by highlighting the presence of each person of the Trinity:

> There dwells God the Father, God the Son, and God the Spirit, united as one in infinitely dear, and incomprehensible, mutual, and eternal love. There dwells God the Father, who is the father of mercies, and so the father of love, who so loved the world as to give his only-begotten Son to die for it. There dwells Christ, the Lamb of God, the prince of peace and of love, who so loved the world that he shed his blood and poured out his soul unto death for men. . . . And there dwells the Holy Spirit, the Spirit of divine love, in whom the very essence of God, as it were, flows out and is breathed forth in love, and by whose immediate influence all holy love is shed abroad in the hearts of all the saints on earth and in heaven. There, in heaven, this infinite fountain of love, this eternal Three in One, is set open without any obstacle to hinder access to it, as it flows forever. There this glorious God is manifested, and shines forth in full glory in beams of love. And there this glorious fountain forever flows forth in streams, yea, in rivers of love and delight, and these rivers swell, as it were, to an ocean of love in which the souls of the ransomed may bathe with the sweetest enjoyment, and their hearts, as it were, be deluged with love.[95]

Edwards observes, second, that the objects of heaven are also altogether lovely. Its inhabitants not only are physically free from defects, such as the wearing down of bodies due to advanced aging, but are forever free from moral impurities as well. Moreover, hearts that have been broken due to the death of loved ones will be permanently remedied: "Every gem that death rudely tears away from us here is a glorious jewel forever shining there."[96] Included in this reunion will be people who have never met but belong together in Christ as the church, the people of God: "There we shall have company with the patriarchs, fathers and saints of the Old and New Testaments, and those of whom the world was not worthy, with whom on earth we were only conversant by faith."[97]

Since heaven is the place in which God dwells in his fullness and the

---

[94] Dane Ortlund, *Edwards on the Christian Life: Alive to the Beauty of God*, Theologians on the Christian Life (Wheaton, IL: Crossway, 2014), 171; emphasis original.
[95] Edwards, "Heaven, a World of Love," 289–90.
[96] Ibid., 292–93.
[97] Ibid., 293.

inhabitants therein are altogether lovely, it is also the place where love is experienced and expressed without interruption. Thus, in his third observation, Edwards considers how love is received and reciprocated in heaven. Love originates in God and therefore finds its fullness in him, but it also flows from him to all the inhabitants of heaven, including the angels and the saints. Concurrently, such love is returned to God by the angels and the saints, who also enjoy uninterrupted love from one another:

> His love flows out to his whole church there, and to every individual member of it. And they all with one heart and one soul unite in love to their common Redeemer. Every heart is wedded to this holy and spiritual husband; and all rejoice in him, while the angels join them in their love. And the angels and saints all love each other. All the members of the glorious society of heaven are sincerely united. There is not a single secret or open enemy among them all. Not a heart there that is not full of love, and not a solitary inhabitant that is not fully loved by all the others.[98]

Edwards speaks about the nature of love itself with his fourth point, noting that the love experienced in this world bears only a faint resemblance to the love promised in the world to come. In heaven, love will not be tainted with selfish motives or corrupt desires. The inhabitants of heaven will not resort to jealousy because others are superior in glory, nor will they be looked down upon because they are less glorious. Instead, Edwards notes, "All the members of that blessed society rejoice in each other's happiness, for the love of benevolence is perfect in them all. . . . So the superior prosperity of those who are higher in glory, is so far from being a hindrance to the degree of love felt toward them that it is an addition to it or a part of it."[99] In short, love does not envy nor does it boast; therefore, in a perfect world people are perfectly able to love and to be loved.

Edwards's final point addresses the circumstances in which love shall be expressed and enjoyed in heaven. There will be no flattery in heaven coming from those who profess to love but do not mean it; there will be no feeling that one is unloved; there will be no fear that the love one has encountered will someday cease. The ability to express love for others will have no hindrances such as are common to this world. Lack of words will give way to language that appropriately expresses affection; awkwardness of personality or darkness of heart will give away to comely and pure acts

---

[98] Ibid., 294–95.
[99] Ibid., 296–97.

of love; even distance that normally separates the lover from the beloved will be removed in heaven. Edwards also assures us that the problems that occur on earth between those who love one another shall be entirely absent from heaven, a world of love:

> Nor shall there be any want of full acquaintance to hinder the great-est possible intimacy; much less shall there be any misunderstanding between them, or misinterpreting things that are said or done by each other. There shall be no disunion through difference of temper, man-ners, circumstances, or from various opinions, interests, feelings, or al-liances; but all shall be united in the same interests, all equally allied to the same Savior, and all employed in the same business of serving and glorifying the same God.[100]

In addition to describing heaven in a way that causes us to long for the blessed hope of Christ's return, Edwards provides several points of ap-plication that instruct us in how our longing for heaven should inform our daily living. For example, believers should seek to be at peace with one an-other. Not only is strife foreign to the citizenry of heaven, but those who harbor ill-will toward others will lose assurance of reaching their heavenly destination. Christians should also guard their hearts from becoming too invested in the things of this world. Edwards therefore encourages be-lievers to think on heavenly things, converse with heavenly persons, and pray to God who is in heaven. Finally, he reminds believers that heaven is worth pursuing, even to the point of overcoming obstacles in the way: "That glorious city of light and love is, as it were, on the top of a high hill or mountain; and there is no way to it but by upward and arduous steps. But though the ascent is difficult and the way full of trials, still it is worth your while to meet them all for the sake of coming and dwelling in such a glorious city at last."[101] Living in the light of heaven thus prompts us to seek to be at peace with all people insofar as it is possible, to live as pil-grims passing through this world, and to look at life's difficulties through the eyes of faith, with our gaze fixed on Jesus.

In addition to preaching about heaven, Edwards experienced a bit of heaven on earth during several periods of revival. In *A Faithful Narra-tive of the Surprising Work of God*, Edwards describes seasons in the life of his church and surrounding communities in which people who had grown indifferent to the gospel message suddenly took an interest in the

---

[100] Ibid., 303.
[101] Ibid., 324.

things of God. His depiction of the 1735 revival in Northampton, Massachusetts, seems almost too good to be true, but Edwards was not given to exaggeration:

> The work of God, as it was carried on, and the number of true saints multiplied, soon made a glorious alteration in the town; so that in the spring and summer following, *anno* 1735, the town seemed to be full of the presence of God; it was never so full of love, nor so full of joy; and yet so full of distress, as it was then. There were remarkable tokens of God's presence in almost every house. It was a time of joy in families on account of salvation's being brought unto them; parents rejoicing over their children as newborn, and husbands over their wives, and wives over their husbands. The goings on of God were seen in his sanctuary (Psalm 68:24), God's day was a delight, and his tabernacles were amiable (Psalm 84:1). Our public assemblies were then beautiful; the congregation was alive in God's service, everyone earnestly intent on the public worship, every hearer eager to drink in the words of the minister as they came from his mouth; the assembly in general were, from time to time in tears while the Word was preached; some weeping with sorrow and distress, others with joy and love, others with pity and concern for the souls of their neighbors.[102]

Edwards's narrative was more than a treatise of remarkable information about local awakenings; it created a desire among evangelicals to partake of a similar work in their churches and towns as well. George Marsden notes, "Edwards' astonishing narrative created an immediate stir. It served as an inspiration for revivals in both Scotland and England."[103] To be sure, Edwards did not provide a "how-to" manual regarding revivals, as produced by later evangelicals, but his narrative did prompt contemporaries to look for signs of revival in their own ministries. Just two years after the publication of *A Surprising Narrative*, Edwards began hearing reports of revivals throughout the American colonies, which would culminate in what is now known as the Great Awakening.

Not only did Edwards witness further awakenings; he also continued to examine and publish his thoughts about the revivals from a theological perspective. In *The Distinguishing Marks of a Work of the Spirit of God* (1741), Edwards turned his attention away from describing specific

---

[102] Jonathan Edwards, "A Faithful Narrative of the Surprising Work of God," in *The Works of Jonathan Edwards*, ed. Edward Hickman (Edinburgh: Banner of Truth, 1974), 1:348.
[103] George Marsden, *Jonathan Edwards: A Life* (New Haven, CT: Yale University Press, 2003), 172–73.

revivals to addressing internal problems occurring as a result of misguided notions about revival in general. He discounted claims for and against revival based on the excitement produced by preachers or the emotionalism witnessed by participants, proceeding to lay down clear indicators of how a discerning person could affirm that God was indeed at work: Jesus was exalted, sinners had repented, Scripture was elevated, doctrine was appreciated, and love was demonstrated.

Other works followed, including *Some Thoughts Concerning the Present Revival of Religion in New England* (1742) and *A Treatise Concerning Religious Affections* (1746), both of which provided God-centered insight into the nature of true revival and true conversion. Such writings not only preserved the history of the awakenings but also prompted future generations to consider the possibility and meaning of revivals.[104] Richard Lovelace suggests, "It is possible that the real awakening in America came, not in the firestorm of 1739–1742, but in later years as the church responded to Edwards' critique of the revival."[105] Thus evangelicals who have never experienced the great joys (or distresses) produced by genuine, widespread revival can look to Edwards for narratives that whet the appetite for future revivals and treatises that sharpen the mind to discern the difference between true revival and mere revivalism. Having a taste of heaven on earth and anticipating heaven as a world of love should therefore prompt evangelicals to wait expectantly, not idly, for the glorious appearing of our great God and Savior, Jesus Christ.

Godly Lives in the Present Age

Stephen Nichols offers an important observation regarding Edwards's overall view of revival that may come as a surprise to evangelicals today. He notes:

> Revivalists, and those seeking revival, look for the quick fix, the immediate result, genuine or not as the case may be. Edwards learned that it's the long haul that matters. The experience of true religion is week in and week out. It is in the daily task and in the ordinary, rather

---

[104] Indeed, Edwards continued to keep the reality of future revivals before his congregation and ministerial colleagues, as evidenced in the 1747 publication of *A Humble Attempt to Promote an Explicit Agreement and Visible Union of God's People through the World, in Extraordinary Prayer, for the Revival of Religion, and the Advancement of Christ's Kingdom on Earth, Pursuant to Scripture Promises and concerning the Last Time*. Iain Murray notes, "It is arguable that no such tract on the hidden source of all true evangelistic success, namely, prayer for the Spirit of God, has ever been so widely used as this one." See Iain Murray, *Jonathan Edwards: A New Biography* (Edinburgh: Banner of Truth, 1987), 299.

[105] Richard Lovelace, *Dynamics of Spiritual Life: An Evangelical Theology of Renewal* (Downers Grove, IL: InterVarsity Press, 1979), 43.

than simply a passing fad that loses its appeal as soon as the excitement wears thin.[106]

Without discounting the appropriate longing for heaven or revival, Nichols correctly finds in Edwards the need to stay grounded in our spirituality. Of course, this discovery was not new with Edwards, as Paul himself called upon believers to live "godly lives in the present age" (Titus 2:12). Thus there is a certain quality of life that Christians are to pursue as they wait for the blessed hope. How, then, can Christians live godly lives in this present age?

John Charles Ryle addressed this question while confronting defections from the evangelical movement to Roman Catholicism and also correcting misunderstandings of sanctification stemming from branches of the Holiness movement. The former advocated baptismal regeneration, whereas the latter promoted instant sanctification. Neither approach was biblical and therefore did not qualify as evangelical religion, which Ryle described using five principles: (1) the absolute supremacy it assigns to the Holy Scriptures as the only rule of faith and practice; (2) the depth and prominence it assigns to the doctrine of human sinfulness and corruption; (3) the paramount importance it attaches to the work and office of our Lord Jesus Christ; (4) the high place it assigns to the work of the Holy Spirit in the heart of man; and (5) the importance it attaches to the outward and visible work of the Holy Spirit in the life of a man.[107] Although his firm stance on these issues brought criticism from those he critiqued as well as from those within his Anglican communion, Ryle staked his ministry and reputation on the belief that evangelical religion is a "fully coherent and demonstrably correct understanding of what is central in the Bible."[108]

Ryle's definition of sanctification is not original to him, but the final clause illustrates his main contribution to the topic:

> Sanctification is that inward spiritual work which the Lord Jesus Christ works in a man by the Holy Ghost, when he calls him to be a true believer. He not only washes him from his sins in His own blood, but He also separates him from his natural love of sin and the world, puts a new principle in his heart, and makes him practically godly in life.[109]

---

[106] Stephen Nichols, *Jonathan Edwards: A Guided Tour of His Life and Thought* (Phillipsburg, NJ: P&R, 2001), 105.

[107] J. C. Ryle, *Knots Untied: Being Plain Statements on Disputed Points in Religion, From the Standpoint of an Evangelical Churchman* (Edinburgh: Banner of Truth, 2016), 4–7.

[108] J. I. Packer, *Faithfulness and Holiness: The Witness of J. C. Ryle* (Wheaton, IL: Crossway, 2002), 33.

[109] J. C. Ryle, *Holiness* (Edinburgh: Banner of Truth, 2014), 22.

Ryle's emphasis on godly living was practical indeed, as any claim to be spiritual must also be visible: "The true grace of God is a thing that will always make itself manifest in the conduct, behavior, tastes, ways, choices and habits of him who has it. It is not a dormant thing. . . . Where there is nothing *seen*, there is nothing possessed."[110] Again, "The very idea of a man being 'sanctified,' while no holiness can be seen in his life, is flat nonsense and a misuse of words."[111] Since holiness must be internalized in the heart before it can become externally evident, Ryle advocated for the use of scriptural means that believers must use in order to grow in grace. Included in this list are some of the most basic disciplines of the Christian life: private prayer, Bible reading, regular attendance of public worship, regular hearing of God's Word, and regular reception of the Lord's Supper.

For Ryle, private prayer stands as the forefront of Christian disciplines because it is necessary for salvation. A person can be saved without first reading the Bible but not without calling upon the Lord. Consequently, those who call upon the Lord for salvation will continue to seek the Lord in prayer. This is, Ryle states, one of the surest marks of a true Christian. There is great encouragement in prayer because Christ serves as advocate and intercessor: "The bank note without a signature at the bottom is nothing but a worthless piece of paper. A few strokes of a pen confer on it all its value. The prayer of a poor child of Adam is a feeble thing in itself, but once endorsed by the hand of the Lord Jesus it availeth much."[112] Time must be set aside for prayer because it is so easy to neglect. Ryle therefore encourages believers to allot time for daily prayer just as they would make time for eating, working, or sleeping: "Whatever else you make a business of, make a business of prayer."[113] Moreover, those who neglect private prayer risk returning to the ways of the world: "We may be sure that men fall in private long before they fall in public. They are backsliders on their knees long before they backslide openly in the eyes of the world."[114] He avers that believers should persevere in prayer, remain earnest in prayer, be bold in prayer, and pray with faith. Above all, believers must be watchful in prayer: "Prayer is that point of all others in religion at which you must be on your guard. Here it is that true religion begins: here it flour-

---

[110] Ryle, *Knots Untied*, 7–8; emphasis original.
[111] Ryle, *Holiness*, 26.
[112] Ryle, *Practical Religion: Being Plain Papers on the Daily Duties, Experiences, Dangers, and Privileges of Professing Christians* (Edinburgh: Banner of Truth, 2013), 67.
[113] Ibid., 82.
[114] Ibid., 73.

ishes, and here it decays. Tell me what a man's prayers are, and I will soon tell you the state of his soul."[115]

Reading the Bible is another indispensable contribution to Christian growth. Ryle notes that the Bible itself is unique because, being inspired by God, it is fully perfect from beginning to end. The Bible provides us with God's plan of salvation; informs us of the life, death, and resurrection of Jesus Christ; surrounds us with people both good and bad as examples to follow and to avoid; and gives us hope in the face of suffering. It was the Word of God that enabled the early church to withstand its persecutors and that prompted the Reformers to recover the gospel. Scripture is the book that has been loved by saints in the past and is the book that brings comfort to the dying at their last breath: "There is but one fountain of comfort for a man drawing near to his end, and that is his Bible. Chapters out of the Bible, texts out of the Bible, statements of truth taken out of the Bible, books containing matter drawn from the Bible—these are a man's only chance of comfort when he comes to die."[116] Christians should read their Bible each and every day, with a desire to understand it, a humility to receive it, and the intent to submit to it.

Attending church services, hearing the Word preached, and partaking of the Lord's Supper are all public means of grace that Ryle considered necessary for genuine Christian growth. Worship is a reminder that Christians are separate from the world. Belonging to the family of God is a special privilege, because its members have the same Father and the same Savior; they also share the same family characteristics:

> They all hate sin and love God. They all rest their hope of salvation on Christ, and have no confidence in themselves. They all endeavor to "come out and be separate" from the ways of the world, and to set their affections on things above.... They all have the same inward experience. Repentance, faith, hope, charity, humility, inward conflict, are things with which they are all more or less acquainted. No wonder they are called a "family."[117]

Thus the public gatherings for worship are essentially family reunions in which brothers and sisters rejoice together in their common salvation. For this reason, their regular times of worship should never descend to mere formality: "The very familiarity . . . is apt to make us careless. The

---

[115] Ibid., 88.
[116] Ibid., 118; punctuation modernized.
[117] Ibid., 353.

regular return of the same voice, and the same kind of words, and the same ceremonies, is likely to make us sleepy, and callous, and unfeeling. If we would grow, we must be on our guard here."[118] More importantly, God rejects any form of worship that does not come from the heart: "When the heart is wrong, all is wrong in God's sight. Many right things may be done. The forms and ordinances may seem to be honored. But so long as the heart is at fault God is not pleased. He will have man's heart or nothing."[119]

Church leaders bear the responsibility of distinguishing between believers and nonbelievers, even in worship. Although unbelievers can attend a church service and hear the preaching of the Word, they should not be allowed to participate in the Lord's Supper: "It does not work like medicine, independently of the state of mind of those who receive it. The teaching of those who press all their congregation to come to the Lord's table, as if the coming must necessarily do everyone good, is entirely without warrant in Scripture."[120] Conversely, "true-hearted" communicants have much to gain as often as they observe the ordinance in remembrance of the Lord. Over time they can expect to receive "clearer views of Christ and his atonement, clearer views of all the offices which Christ fills as Mediator and Advocate, clearer views of the complete redemption Christ has obtained for us by his vicarious death on the cross, clearer views of our full and perfect acceptance in Christ before God, fresh reasons for deep repentance for sin, [and] fresh reasons for lively faith."[121] The Lord's Supper also acts as a means of grace in that it impresses believers with a greater sense of accountability before the Lord: "The man that goes regularly and intelligently to the Lord's table finds it increasingly hard to yield to sin and conform to the world."[122]

The fact that these means of grace are nothing more than basic disciplines of the Christian life does not diminish their importance or effectiveness: "I lay it down as a simple matter of fact, that no one who is careless about such things must ever expect to make much progress in sanctification. I can find no record of any eminent saint who ever neglected them."[123] Ryle's reference to history is important. His conviction that evangelical religion provides the most biblical pattern for living godly

---

[118] Ryle, *Holiness*, 125–26.
[119] Ryle, *Practical Religion*, 253.
[120] Ibid., 136.
[121] Ibid., 141–42.
[122] Ibid., 143.
[123] Ryle, *Holiness*, 28.

lives in the present age came about in part because he studied the lives of Christians in the past and wanted his generation to emulate those who lived so faithfully for the Lord.[124] Thus his approach to evangelical religion was neither new nor trendy; it stood the test of time because it stemmed from the Word of God:

> To avow attachment to Evangelical views, in some quarters, is to provoke a sneer, and to bring on yourself the reproach of being an "unlearned and ignorant man." But none of these things move me. I am not ashamed of my opinions. After forty years of Bible reading and praying, meditation and theological study, I find myself clinging more tightly than ever to "Evangelical" religion, and more than ever satisfied with it. It wears well: it stands the fire. I know no system of religion which is better. In the faith of it I have lived for the third of a century, and in the faith of it I hope to die.[125]

Conclusion

Titus 2:11–14 provides an excellent framework for evangelical spirituality. We may even stipulate that evangelicals, on the whole, are familiar with the ideas contained therein: gratitude for grace, trust in providence, battle against sin, zeal through life, hope for heaven, and growth in godliness. Viewing such truths through the lives of those who embody these aspects, however, adds yet another dimension to evangelical spirituality: ideas become more personal and our growth becomes more tangible. Hence we are reminded by Luther that grace is a gift no sinner deserves and no saint can earn. We find in Calvin a confidence in God's sovereignty that fosters a childlike trust in the Father's care. We learn from Owen that wrestling with ongoing sin is not a sign of weakness but one of strength in the Lord. We take issue with Wesley's idea of perfection but appreciate his emphasis on loving God and others. We hear from Edwards about a place that we have never been but are longing to call home. And we get back to the basics with Ryle's pattern of spiritual growth that continues to stand the test of time.

---

[124] See J. C. Ryle, *Light from Old Times* (Edinburgh: Banner of Truth, 2015).
[125] Ryle, *Practical Religion, viii.*

8

SPIRITUALITIES IN THE CHRISTIAN TRADITION

NATHAN A. FINN

Take my life and let it be
consecrated, Lord, to thee.
Take my moments and my days;
let them flow in endless praise,
let them flow in endless praise.

Frances Ridley Havergal (1836–1879) was a prolific poet and hymnist in nineteenth-century England. Frances was the daughter of Rev. William Havergal, an Anglican evangelical who served as rector of numerous English parishes in Astley, Worcester, and Leamington, as well as a parish church in Swansea, Wales. Following her conversion in her mid-teens, Frances became a woman of deep piety who shared her father's evangelical faith. She never married, serving as a governess for several years before moving back in with her father and stepmother to care for them in their later years. Frances would remain unknown to us today were it not for her poetry and especially her hymns, which numbered over fifty, the most famous of which include "Like a River Glorious" and "Take My Life and Let It Be." The words at the beginning of this chapter comprise the first stanza of the latter hymn. They reflect what traditionally has been an important theme in the Christian life: the pursuit of holiness.[1]

---

[1] For more on Havergal and her hymns, see David B. Calhoun, "Frances Ridley Havergal (1836–1879): 'Always, Only for My King,'" *Knowing and Doing*, C. S. Lewis Institute (Spring 2014), accessed December 20, 2016, http://www.cslewisinstitute.org/webfm_send/2943.

While nearly every Christian tradition values the importance of holiness, in past generations evangelicals frequently gave special attention to this topic. For example, J. I. Packer writes:

> There was a time when all Christians laid great emphasis on the reality of God's call to holiness and spoke with deep insight about His enabling of us for it. Evangelical Protestants, in particular, offered endless variations on the themes of what God's holiness requires of us, what our holiness involves for us, by what means through what disciplines the Holy Spirit sanctifies us, and the ways in which holiness increases our assurance and joy and usefulness to God.[2]

In particular, evangelical pastors, evangelists, and others in positions of spiritual leadership emphasized the importance of holiness. In his influential study *Evangelicalism in Modern Britain*, historian David Bebbington writes, "The summons to holiness was constantly heard in the Evangelical pulpit."[3] The famous English Methodist leader John Wesley once argued, "Give me one hundred preachers who fear nothing but sin and desire nothing but God, and I care not a straw whether they be clergymen or laymen, such alone will shake the gates of hell and set up the kingdom of heaven upon earth."[4] The great Scotch Presbyterian pastor Robert Murray M'Cheyne once said, "But, oh! Study universal holiness of life. Your whole usefulness depends on this. Your sermon on Sabbath lasts but an hour or two; your life preaches all the week."[5] Contemporary evangelicals would do well to recover the burden for holiness that so often characterized our spiritual forebears.

This is a book about biblical spirituality, or what the Scriptures and the best of the Christian tradition teach about the pursuit of holiness. The question I hope to answer, at least in an introductory manner, is "How have various Christian traditions approached holiness?" Much of this survey is historical in nature. I focus upon the two broad streams of Christian spirituality in the West: Roman Catholicism and Protestantism. These streams are certainly not exhaustive, but they address the most common variations of Christian spirituality found in the English-speaking world

---

[2] J. I. Packer, *Rediscovering Holiness: Know the Life of Fullness with God*, 2nd ed. (Ventura, CA: Regal, 2009), 12.
[3] David Bebbington, *Evangelicalism in Modern Britain: A History from the 1730s to the 1980s*, 2nd ed. (London: Routledge, 1993), 63.
[4] Quoted in Luke Tyerman, *The Life and Times of the Rev. John Wesley*, 3 vols. (London: Hodder & Stoughton, 1871), 3:632.
[5] Robert Murray M'Cheyne, *The Works of the Late Robert Murray M'Cheyne*, 2 vols. (New York: Robert Carter, 1847), 2:68.

since the time of the Reformation.[6] Since this is a book written by evangelicals, and for a primarily evangelical readership, I turn my attention in the second half of the chapter to three varieties of evangelical spirituality.[7]

Catholic Holiness: Sacramental, Liturgical, Devotional

Roman Catholics have a deep sense of their history, as church authorities have interpreted it, along with a commitment to the abiding authority of their tradition. Catholics believe the Church of Rome is the institutional continuation of the movement founded by Christ and his apostles. In fact, the church is the ongoing incarnation of the ascended Christ, what Gregg Allison calls the "Christ-Church interconnection" of Catholicism.[8] Thus, the Catholic Church is the purest expression of Christianity on earth, and though Catholics affirm that believers in other "communities" are authentically Christian, true unity "subsists" in the Catholic Church alone.[9] Therefore, all believers should be reconciled with the Catholic Church. Because of this understanding of their church's identity and history, modern Roman Catholic spirituality continues to be informed by emphases and practices that stretch back centuries, though they have been refined in response to challenges introduced since the Reformation era.

Though all Catholics in theory affirm the inspiration and authority of Scripture and the church's magisterial tradition as interpreted by the pope and other higher clergy, modern Catholicism is remarkably diverse. For this reason, there are many Catholic approaches to spirituality. Nevertheless, at the heart of the Catholic pursuit of holiness lie three oft-related themes: (1) the sacramental nature of the Christian experience, (2) the importance of the liturgy for one's spiritual journey, and (3) Marian devotion.[10] Each contributes to the final goal of the Catholic vision of the Christian life: progress toward more intimate union with Christ, a concept that Catholics understand primarily in mystical terms rather than as

---

[6] Space precludes a treatment of Eastern Orthodoxy, with its rich emphasis on the sacramental and liturgical life as the pathway to holiness. For accessible introductions, see John Chryssavgis, *Light through Darkness: The Orthodox Tradition, Traditions of Christian Spirituality* (Maryknoll, NY: Orbis, 2004); and Bradley Nassif, "Orthodox Spirituality: The Quest for Transfigured Humanity," in *Four Views on Christian Spirituality*, Counterpoint, ed. Bruce Demarest (Grand Rapids, MI: Zondervan, 2012), 27–55.

[7] Readers interested in book-length treatments of the material I discuss should consult the following works, each of which covers Christian spirituality from the Patristic era to the present day: Bradley P. Holt, *Thirsty for God: A Brief History of Christian Spirituality*, 2nd ed. (Minneapolis: Fortress, 2005); Gordon Mursell, ed., *The Story of Christian Spirituality: Two Thousand Years from East to West* (Oxford, UK: Lion, 2001); Gerald L. Sittser, *Water from a Deep Well: Christian Spirituality from Early Martyrs to Modern Missionaries* (Downers Grove, IL: IVP Academic, 2007).

[8] Gregg R. Allison, *Roman Catholic Theology and Practice: An Evangelical Assessment* (Wheaton, IL: Crossway, 2014), 46.

[9] *Catechism of the Catholic Church*, 2nd ed. (Vatican: Libreria Editrice Vaticana, 1997), 1.3.817, 820.

[10] Alistair E. McGrath, *Christian Spirituality* (Oxford, UK: Blackwell, 1999), 14–15.

a theological category. Progress in holiness is evidenced by more perfect charity (Christian love), which is attained over time as the believer mortifies sin and cultivates godly virtues.[11]

Since the medieval era, the Catholic Church has affirmed seven sacraments.[12] These sacraments are considered channels of grace in the Christian's life. They are efficacious *ex opera operato* (by the fact of their being administered), though one can choose to abandon faith and no longer receive the benefits of the sacraments. The first three are considered sacraments of initiation. Baptism marks one's entrance into the church, washes away the effects of original sin, begins the process of regeneration, and is applied to both infants and new believers. Confirmation takes place at the age of discretion when a Catholic is able to profess faith for oneself. The confirmed is anointed with oil, sealed with the Spirit, and strengthened in the grace of his earlier baptism. Once confirmed, a Catholic can participate in the sacrament of the Eucharist. The Eucharist, also called the "Mass," is the celebration of the Lord's Supper. The Eucharist makes present to believers the body and blood of Jesus Christ, of which more will be said below. The Eucharist is the most important of the sacraments, and the sacraments of initiation as a whole are more foundational to Catholic spirituality than the remaining four sacraments.

Penance, also called "confession," is the first of the two sacraments of healing. In particular, penance provides reconciliation (spiritual healing) between God and a believer when the latter has committed post-baptismal sins. Penance includes contrition (sincere repentance), confession to and absolution by a priest, and satisfaction, or acts of service or piety that demonstrate the sincerity of one's contrition. The anointing of the sick is the other sacrament of healing. The priest anoints the gravely ill with oil and offers prayers for healing. Those for whom death seems imminent receive last rites (also called "extreme unction"), which include anointing, penance, and reception of the Eucharist to prepare the sick for a faithful death. The two sacraments of service are holy orders and matrimony. Holy orders, which is the Catholic understanding of ordination to the clergy, is a sacrament limited to single men who dedicate their lives to service of God and church. Matrimony, which is a Church-sanctioned marriage, is a

---

[11] *Catechism of the Catholic Church*, 3.4.2013–15.

[12] The sacraments receive extensive treatment in part 2 of the *Catechism of the Catholic Church*, which includes three chapters. For an accessible Catholic introduction to the sacraments, see Stratford Caldecott, *The Seven Sacraments: Entering the Mysteries* (New York: Crossroad, 2006). Part 2 of Gregg Allison's evangelical summary and critique of Catholicism is dedicated to the sacraments, following the outline of the *Catechism of the Catholic Church*. See Allison, *Roman Catholic Theology and Practice*, 227–387.

sacrament reserved for believing heterosexual couples; it is considered a permanent bond. In the cases of these sacraments of service, most Catholics receive one or the other, but none receives both.

Roman Catholic spirituality also emphasizes that holiness is attained through liturgy. In the Catholic context, liturgy and sacrament overlap in the celebration of the Mass, which is the culmination of Christian public worship.[13] For Catholics, as for most Christian traditions, the Lord's Supper is an act of faithful remembrance of Christ's sacrifice and a forward-looking proclamation of the kingdom of God. But in the Catholic tradition, the Eucharist is characterized by the mystery of transubstantiation, through which the substance of the bread and wine are transformed into the body and blood of Christ, who is then really physically present in those elements. The Mass is a sacramental sacrifice that re-presents the historical sacrifice of Christ, and wherein the ongoing effects of the atonement are made continually efficacious in the life of the believer. The faithful reception of Christ's body and blood is the means through which believers receive the grace that is necessary to continue in the Christian life. Devotion to the Mass is a defining characteristic of Catholic piety, resulting in a history of Eucharist hymnody, liturgical prayers related to the Mass, and festive traditions, most notably the Feast of Corpus Christi (the body of Christ). At times, Eucharistic spirituality has tended toward superstitious, even quasi-magical understandings of the Mass. This was a common critique of Eucharistic devotion in the late-medieval era and remains a concern today, particularly in those parts of the world where nominal Catholicism is part of the warp and woof of the culture.

Marian devotion marks a third key theme in Catholic spirituality.[14] In the Roman Catholic tradition, the saints include all the faithful dead who are in heaven—the "communion of saints," as stated in the Apostles' Creed. Certain saints are considered exemplars of the faith, and as such these saints, as well as relics and places associated with them, are subjects of veneration (though not worship) by Catholics, a practice with roots stretching back to the martyrs of the Patristic era. Because of their

---

[13] For brief introductions to the Catholic understanding of the Eucharist, see Gabriel O'Donnel and Robin Maas, "The Eucharist and the Continual Remembrance of God," in *Spiritual Traditions for the Contemporary Church*, ed. Gabriel O'Donnel and Robin Maas (Nashville, TN: Abingdon, 1990), 419–27; and Lawrence S. Cunningham and Keith J. Egan, *Christian Spirituality: Themes from the Tradition* (Mahwah, NJ: Paulist Press, 1996), 183–200. See also Allison, *Roman Catholic Theology and Practice*, 299–325.

[14] For an introduction to Marian devotion, see Eamon R. Carroll, "Marian Spirituality," in *Spiritual Traditions for the Contemporary Church*, 365–79. For a historical treatment of various Christian views of Mary, see Jaroslav Pelikan, *Mary through the Centuries: Her Place in the History of Culture* (New Haven, CT: Yale University Press, 1996).

exemplary faith, heavenly saints intercede for living believers. By far, the most important of the saints is Mary. She is the mother of God because she gave birth to the incarnate Lord, Jesus Christ. Catholics believe Mary was immaculately conceived without original sin, she remained a virgin perpetually, she was the most faithful disciple of her Son, and at the end of her life her body was assumed into heaven without experiencing physical death. A substantial piety has developed around Mary, most notably the Hail Mary prayer and countless musical settings of the Magnificat (both drawing from Luke 1:26–56). Catholics pray for Mary to intercede on their behalf, and Mary is the patron saint of more professions, places, and activities than any other member of the communion of saints. At times, Marian piety has been distanced from, or has even competed with, devotion to Christ. Medieval concepts of Mary as comediatrix with her Son and superstitious repetitions of the Hail Mary serve as examples. However, official Catholic doctrine makes clear that Jesus alone is Lord and that Mary is simply one of his most faithful servants, worthy of our honor because of her faithfulness.

These three themes of the sacramental economy, liturgy, and Marian piety transcend the various Catholic subtraditions. Through the centuries, some have approached these emphases from the standpoint of monasticism.[15] Each of the monastic orders developed their own traditions and emphases, thus evolving into distinct streams of spirituality within Catholicism. Today, monastic orders remain an important part of Catholicism. Even many Protestants are drawn to aspects of the monastic way, though typically not without reframing the monastic commitment to celibacy as including sexual fidelity among the married.[16] Other Catholics—clergy, monastics, and laity—have been inspired by these spiritual themes to embrace a life dedicated to acts of mercy, advocacy for social justice, and dedication to the poor and needy. Twentieth-century figures such as Dorothy Day, Oscar Romero, and Mother Teresa are examples of a distinctively Catholic activist spirituality.[17] Many Catholics in the past and today have also embraced various forms of mysticism as ways to cultivate pronounced experiences with God through prayer and medita-

---

[15] For an accessible introduction to monasticism written for an evangelical audience, see Greg Peters, *The Story of Monasticism: Retrieving an Ancient Tradition for Contemporary Spirituality* (Downers Grove, IL: IVP Academic, 2015).

[16] See Dennis Okholm, *Monk Habits for Everyday People: Benedictine Spirituality for Protestants* (Grand Rapids, MI: Brazos, 2007); and Jonathan Wilson-Hartgrove, *New Monasticism: What It Has to Say to Today's Church* (Grand Rapids, MI: Brazos, 2008).

[17] See Mae Elise Cannon, *Just Spirituality: How Faith Practices Fuel Social Action* (Downers Grove, IL: InterVarsity Press, 2013).

tion (often called "contemplative prayer"). Thomas Merton is one famous twentieth-century Catholic mystic whose best-known work, *The Seven-Storey Mountain* (1948), appealed even to many Protestants.[18] The Centering Prayer movement, rooted in both Catholic and Eastern Orthodox contemplative practices, has also had a wide appeal beyond the confines of contemporary Catholicism.[19]

Protestant Holiness: *Sola* Spiritualities

Protestantism traces its roots to the various European reform movements that critiqued and eventually rejected late-medieval Catholicism during the course of the sixteenth century. Contrary to popular imagination, there was no such thing as a monolithic Protestant Reformation.[20] The Magisterial Protestant traditions, including the Lutherans, Reformed churches, and the Church of England, fought among themselves over such matters as the presence of Christ in the Eucharist, the precise relationship between church and state, predestination, church polity, and the enduring role of ecclesiastical tradition. The various Anabaptist sects focused their critique elsewhere, rejecting the validity of both state churches and infant baptism. By 1700, these diverse reform movements had gradually hardened into denominational families, each with their own approach to faith and practice.

Nevertheless, despite their differences, especially over ecclesiology and the sacraments, the various reformational movements did share several emphases that came to define Protestantism over against Catholicism. These distinctive principles have sometimes been called the "five *solas*" of the Reformation, taken from the Latin for "alone" or "only."[21] *Sola Scriptura*, "Scripture alone," was the conviction that the Bible is the sole inspired and sufficient authority for faith and practice. This principle provided the theological foundation for reformational critiques of late-medieval Catholicism. The other four emphases all spoke directly to the doctrine of salvation. *Sola fide*, "faith alone," was the belief that justification is by faith alone and that works play no role in one's right standing with God. *Sola gratia*, "grace alone," was the

---

[18] Thomas Merton, *The Seven Storey Mountain* (New York: Houghton Mifflin, 1999).
[19] See Thomas Keating, *Intimacy with God: An Introduction to Centering Prayer*, 3rd ed. (New York: Crossroad, 2009); and Basil Pennington, *Centering Prayer: Renewing an Ancient Christian Prayer Form* (New York: Image, 2001).
[20] Carter Lindberg, *The European Reformations*, 2nd ed. (Oxford, UK: Blackwell, 2009).
[21] For a compelling treatment of the five *solas* by a leading evangelical theologian, see Kevin J. Vanhoozer, *Biblical Authority after Babel: Retrieving the* Solas *in the Spirit of Mere Protestant Christianity* (Grand Rapids, MI: Brazos, 2016).

belief that human salvation from beginning to end is an act of God's pure grace, even though most Protestants agreed that faithful works play a part in one's sanctification. *Solus Christus*, "Christ alone," was the belief that the saving work of Christ alone accomplishes our salvation. *Soli Deo gloria*, "God's glory alone," spoke to the ultimate end of our salvation—to glorify the one who created us and has redeemed us. Taken together, these five principles represented a direct challenge to the spiritual vision of late-medieval Catholicism.

Different Protestant traditions put their own unique spin on these principles, which directly influenced their respective spiritualities. The Lutheran tradition focused upon the centrality of forensic justification, with sanctification assumed as the inevitable and ultimately eschatological result of justification. Lutherans retained the sacraments of baptism and the Lord's Supper, with the former contributing grace toward regeneration and the latter maintaining a form of Christ's real presence. However, the true sacrament was the written Word read and preached, in faith, because it made present the incarnate Word, the Lord Jesus Christ. The faithful reception of the proclaimed Word ensured the efficacy of baptism and the Lord's Supper.[22]

The Pietist movements of the seventeenth and eighteenth centuries primarily arose in response to Lutheran scholasticism, which Pietists believed to have overemphasized the objective nature of justification at the expense of the subjective reality of sanctification. The Pietists emphasized personal conversion, devotional prayer and Bible study, faith-inspired activism, and what we might today call small groups or cell groups within local congregations. As a general rule, Pietists placed greater emphasis on lived Christianity and the pursuit of spiritual maturity than they did the doctrinal categories that described the Christian life.[23]

The Reformed churches also strongly emphasized *sola fide* but gave greater attention to sanctification as a progressive reality that flowed from one's justification. The sufficiency of Scripture for faith and practice became a signal emphasis among the Reformed, who argued for a close connection between Word and Spirit. Baptism was a covenant sign for Christians and their families, while the Lord's Supper enabled com-

---

[22] See Bengt Hoffman, "Lutheran Spirituality," in *Exploring Christian Spirituality: An Ecumenical Reader*, ed. Kenneth J. Collins (Grand Rapids, MI: Baker, 2000), 122–37; and Bradley Hanson, *Grace That Frees: The Lutheran Tradition*, Traditions of Christian Spirituality (Maryknoll, NY: Orbis, 2004).

[23] See John Weborg, "Pietism: 'The Fire of God Which . . . Flames in the Heart of Germany,'" in *Protestant Spiritual Traditions*, ed. Frank C. Senn (repr. Eugene, OR: Wipf & Stock, 2000), 183–216; and Douglas H. Shantz, *An Introduction to German Pietism: Protestant Renewal at the Dawn of Modern Europe* (Baltimore, MD: Johns Hopkins University Press, 2013).

munion with Christ, through the Spirit, as believers feasted on Christ by faith. The law, though valued for its convicting power by Lutherans, played a more active role in moral formation among the Reformed.[24]

In the English-speaking world, Puritanism became the dominant form of Reformed Christianity from the late 1500s until around 1700. The Puritans were the Reformed counterparts to the mostly Lutheran Pietists, though in this case responding to allegedly Catholic tendencies within the Church of England rather than supposed dead orthodoxy in Lutheranism. Some Puritans remained within the Church of England, while others withdrew to form various sorts of independent churches. The Puritans emphasized both personal conversion and what they called "experimental" Christianity, which was shorthand for the ongoing experience of progressive sanctification. However, the Puritans maintained more concrete doctrinal commitments than their Pietist counterparts and continued to embrace the assumptions of Reformed theology as eventually expressed in the Presbyterian Westminster Confession of Faith (1646) and other confessional standards it inspired among Congregationalists and some Baptists. Puritanism spread to North America through colonization, where it was eventually influenced by the evangelical revivals of the 1700s, as exemplified in figures such as Jonathan Edwards and, to varying degrees, among American Presbyterians.[25]

The Church of England was the most spiritually diverse of the Protestant movements, embracing a spirituality that was informed by its Lutheran and especially Reformed predecessors, but which also continued to draw upon various Catholic sensibilities. Anglicans affirmed the reformational *solas*, though they combined this Protestant view of Scripture and soteriology with a robustly liturgical understanding of worship and, among some, a more sacramental account of baptism and Eucharist. This attempt to balance Protestant doctrine with a deeper catholicity than was always apparent among the Lutherans and the Reformed led to tensions within the Church of England. Some, like the Puritans, wished to more intentionally prioritize reformational emphases, while others preferred to highlight continuity between the Church of England and both Patristic and medieval traditions. Moderates desired a church that could

---

[24] See Howard G. Hageman, "Reformed Spirituality," in *Exploring Christian Spirituality*, 138–57; and David Cornick, *Letting God Be God: The Reformed Tradition*, Traditions of Christian Spirituality (Maryknoll, NY: Orbis, 2008).

[25] See Joel Beeke, *Puritan Reformed Spirituality: A Practical Biblical Study from Reformed and Puritan Heritage* (Darlington, UK: Evangelical Press, 2006); and J. I. Packer, *A Quest for Godliness: The Puritan Vision of the Christian Life* (Wheaton, IL: Crossway, 1994).

encompass both trajectories through common submission to the authority of bishops and use of the *Book of Common Prayer* in worship.[26]

In the 1730s, a significant renewal movement arose within the Church of England among the followers of John Wesley and George Whitefield. The Methodists were appreciative of Puritan spirituality and even some medieval spiritual writers such as Thomas à Kempis, but they were especially influenced by Pietist emphases. Influences notwithstanding, Methodist spirituality was filtered through the experience of the trans-Atlantic revivals of the era. John Wesley taught that one's sanctification could be almost fully realized in this life, a concept that is addressed later in greater detail. By 1800, Methodists had withdrawn from the Church of England, were arguably the most dynamic denomination in America, and had become a mostly Arminian tradition as most of Whitefield's followers gravitated toward Calvinist denominations.[27]

The Anabaptists proved to be the most radical of the reformers, preferring to restore New Testament Christianity, as they understood it, rather than reforming the existing church, which they believed to have become apostate. Anabaptists affirmed a purely symbolic understanding of the sacraments, championed personal conversion rather than gradual nurture into belief, and were committed to the importance of discipleship. The line between justification and sanctification was less apparent among Anabaptists than the mainline reformers, while greater attention was given to a life of faithful obedience to and witness for Christ, even unto death. The Anabaptists championed religious liberty for all and denounced any persecution on account of one's religious sentiments. The Anabaptists themselves were fiercely persecuted, which led to a spirituality that anticipated the likelihood and even ultimate benefit of martyrdom, similar to the Patristic era, though without venerating martyred saints.[28]

In the early 1600s, the Baptist tradition began in the English-speaking world. Though possessing many of the same ecclesial emphases as the Anabaptists, the Baptists' roots were found in radical English Puritanism. The Baptists valued the role of Scripture in the Christian life, emphasized believer's baptism and a regenerate church membership, and championed

---

[26] See Harvey H. Guthrie, "Anglican Spirituality," in *Exploring Christian Spirituality*, 158–71, and Alan Barlett, *A Passionate Balance: The Anglican Tradition*, Traditions of Christian Spirituality (Maryknoll, NY: Orbis, 2007).

[27] See David Lowes Watson, "Methodist Spirituality," in *Exploring Christian Spirituality*, 172–213; and Gordon Mursell, *English Spirituality: From 1700 to the Present Day* (Louisville, KY: Westminster John Knox, 2001), 20–30, 86–103.

[28] See Peter C. Erb, "Anabaptist Spirituality," in *Protestant Spiritual Traditions*, 80–124, and C. Arnold Snyder, *Following in the Footsteps of Christ: The Anabaptist Tradition*, Traditions of Christian Spirituality (Maryknoll, NY: Orbis, 2004).

religious freedom over against state churches. Following the advent of the evangelical revivals, Baptists became an intensely missionary movement that focused on evangelism and church planting. Like Anabaptists, Baptist spirituality was communal and emphasized conversion and discipleship. Unlike the Anabaptists, the Baptists were more influenced by the English Reformed tradition in their doctrinal assumptions, especially about Scripture, justification, and sanctification. Also, the Baptist understanding of religious liberty normally did not entail pacifism or the rejection of Christians serving as civil servants, as was the norm among Anabaptists. In the English-speaking world, the threat of persecution informed Baptist spirituality less and less as the English-speaking became increasingly tolerant of religious pluralism.[29]

These Reformation and post-Reformation traditions took root in North America, where Protestantism took on a decidedly evangelical flavor. The eighteenth century was an era of intellectual enlightenment, religious revival, and political revolution, all of which contributed to the evangelical ethos of American Protestantism.[30] David Bebbington's widely cited "quadrilateral" of biblicism, conversionism, crucicentrism (cross-centeredness), and activism certainly characterized American evangelicalism, but unlike in the British Isles, American evangelicals came of age in the context of religious disestablishment and political democracy during the Early Republic era.[31] This republican atmosphere led to what some have called a "religious free market" wherein different denominations competed with each other for adherents, and new sects were formed on a regular basis.[32] Furthermore, the new nation was located on a vast continent that had hardly been touched by Europeans beyond the Eastern Seaboard. As Americans moved westward, their republican virtues and evangelical sentiments traveled with them. By the beginning of the nineteenth century, evangelical Protestantism comprised what historian Martin Marty has called a "righteous empire," a de facto religious establishment at the heart of American culture and civil religion.[33]

---

[29] See Stanley J. Grenz, "Maintaining the Balanced Life: The Baptist Vision of Spirituality," in *Perspectives in Religious Studies* 18 (Spring 1991): 59–68; Glenn Hinson, "Baptist Approaches to Spirituality," *Baptist History and Heritage* 37 (Spring 2002): 6–31; Paul S. Fiddes, ed., *Under the Rule of Christ: Dimensions of Baptist Spirituality* (Macon, GA: Smyth & Helwys, 2008).

[30] See Thomas S. Kidd, *The Great Awakening: The Roots of Evangelical Christianity in Colonial America* (New Haven, CT: Yale University Press, 2007).

[31] Bebbington, *Evangelicalism in Modern Britain*, 3–19.

[32] See Nathan O. Hatch, *The Democratization of American Christianity* (New Haven, CT: Yale University Press, 1991); and Roger Finke and Rodney Stark, *The Churching of America, 1776–2005: Winners and Losers in Our Religious Economy* (New Brunswick, NJ: Rutgers University Press, 2006), 25–116.

[33] Martin E. Marty, *Protestantism in the United States: Righteous Empire*, 2nd ed. (New York: Scribner's, 1986).

Evangelical Holiness: Born Again

Methodists, Baptists, and Presbyterians were the largest evangelical groups in nineteenth-century America, though they were hardly alone on the American religious scene. New quasi-evangelical groups were established during the Second Great Awakening, most notably the Churches of Christ and the various Adventist movements. More anti-revivalist Protestants such as Lutherans, most Episcopals, and some Reformed churches thrived in cities and among immigrant groups. Sectarian movements, including heretical groups such as the Latter-Day Saints, competed with mainstream denominations. Other outliers included Jews, mostly located on the East Coast, and rationalist movements such as Unitarians and Universalists. After the Civil War, Catholic immigrants poured into the country in large numbers, coalescing in the more industrial urban centers in the North. African Americans, the overwhelming majority of whom descended from slaves, developed their own spiritual traditions that included elements of their inherited denominations with emphases unique to the experience of enslavement. After the Civil War, African Americans formed their own denominations, furthering a "black church" tradition that was both mainstream and marginal, conversionist and committed to social justice.[34] But religious diversity notwithstanding, for most American believers evangelicalism was the default setting.

During the first half of the twentieth century, evangelical Protestantism waned in its influence in American public life. The fundamentalist-modernist controversies of the 1920s and 1930s resulted in more progressive forces gaining control of the mainline denominations while most evangelicals retreated into their own network of parachurch ministries or resided in then-regional denominations such as the Southern Baptist Convention.[35] By mid-century, self-confessed fundamentalists had separated from self-described evangelicals over issues ranging from interdenominational cooperation to strategic disagreements over education, political engagement, and mass evangelism. Postwar evangelicals fought to become culturally mainstream once again, hoping they might play a role in bringing about a Third Great Awakening in American culture. They retained their historic emphases on biblical authority, basic

---

[34] See James Phelps, "Black Spirituality," in *Spiritual Traditions for the Contemporary Church*, ed. Robin Maas and Gabriel O'Donnell (Nashville, TN: Abingdon, 1990), 332–51; and Flora Wilson Bridges, *Resurrection Song: African-American Spirituality* (Maryknoll, NY: Orbis, 2001).

[35] My basic narrative for twentieth-century evangelicalism relies heavily upon George M. Marsden, *Fundamentalism and American Culture*, new ed. (New York: Oxford University Press, 2006); and Joel A. Carpenter, *Revive Us Again: The Reawakening of American Fundamentalism* (New York: Oxford University Press, 1999).

Protestant orthodoxy, personal conversion, and the importance of evangelism and missions. But they remained diverse, divided over the issues that had traditionally separated various Protestant groups (e.g., predestination, polity, baptism), as well as newly emerging differences such as biblical inerrancy, gender roles in the home and church, and ongoing debates about how best to faithfully engage culture. For better and worse, by the final decades of the twentieth century the right wing of evangelicalism became increasingly known for its influence in electoral politics and the conservative theological positions it staked out in the various intra-evangelical debates.[36] But where did all these twentieth-century tensions and transitions leave evangelical spirituality?

The Power of the Spirit: Evangelical Holiness Traditions

In recent decades, three broad streams of spirituality have dominated American evangelicalism. Though all three of these streams are evangelical in their affirmations, each approaches the pursuit of holiness from a different perspective. The first spiritual tradition is actually comprised of a cluster of related emphases that became popular in the mid-nineteenth century, but the roots date even further back to John Wesley himself. Wesley argued for what he called *Christian perfection*, which he suggested was perfect love toward God and other people, resulting in a deliverance from inward and outward sin—even the very desire to sin. This perfection was normally a second work of grace, received from the Holy Spirit by faith. Though the Christian is perfected in his or her dispositions, sin is still possible due to ignorance, mistakes, temptations, and other shortcomings that are part of human nature. But the desire to sin is gone through a transforming work of the Holy Spirit. Though Wesley did not deny progressive sanctification, he and especially his followers emphasized the importance of Christian perfection as God's desire for all believers.[37]

In America, Wesley's view was often called "entire sanctification" and was tied to the baptism of the Holy Spirit, which was considered a second work of grace separate from and subsequent to conversion. Famed evangelist and later pioneering educator Charles Finney helped popularize entire sanctification among Arminian evangelicals who were dissatisfied

---

[36] See Steven P. Miller, *The Age of Evangelicalism: America's Born-Again Years* (New York: Oxford University Press, 2014); and Molly Worthen, *Apostles of Reason: The Crisis of Authority in American Evangelicalism* (New York: Oxford University Press, 2013).

[37] See John Wesley, *A Plain Account of Christian Perfection* (1777), accessed January 13, 2017, http://wesley.nnu .edu/john-wesley/a-plain-account-of-christian-perfection/. For a helpful interpretation of Wesley's views, see Kenneth J. Collins, *The Theology of John Wesley: Holy Love and the Shape of Grace* (Nashville, TN: Abingdon, 2007), 279–312.

with the traditionally Reformed understanding of progressive sanctification. Another key voice was Phoebe Palmer, a poet and preacher who wrote an influential treatise titled *The Way of Holiness* (1843). Eventually, advocates of entire sanctification came to be called the "Holiness movement" because of their emphasis on this doctrine. Holiness ideas were promulgated through hymns, publications, and camp meetings devoted to preaching the message of entire sanctification. Holiness evangelicals were also numbered among the great social activists of the nineteenth century, advocating temperance, abolition of slavery, and women's suffrage.[38] Eventually, several denominational traditions formed around Holiness views, including the Church of God, the Nazarene Church, and the Salvation Army.

Some evangelicals were influenced by Holiness views but rejected the overt Arminianism of the more Wesleyan and Finneyite advocates of entire sanctification. These evangelicals came to be called the Higher Life movement, named for William Boardman's *The Higher Life* (1858), or the Keswick movement, named for the English resort town where British adherents gathered for annual conferences. While also emphasizing a second baptism of the Holy Spirit, or in some cases ongoing fillings of the Spirit, Higher Life evangelicals never fully abandoned progressive sanctification. Rather than teaching entire sanctification, the Higher Life movement focused on surrendering oneself to the Holy Spirit's control—sometimes summarized as "let go and let God." The Higher Life movement was far more popular across the English-speaking world than the older Holiness movement, which was confined mostly to America. American advocates of the Higher Life included Hannah Whitall Smith, author of *The Christian's Secret of a Happy Life* (1875), evangelist D. L. Moody, evangelist and educator R. A. Torrey, and A. B. Simpson, founder of the Christian and Mission Alliance. In part through the influence of Moody and Torrey, Higher Life views became popular among some dispensationalists who also affirmed premillennialism and the imminent rapture of the church.[39]

During the first decade of the twentieth century, Christians all over the world began to experience what they considered "Pentecostal outpourings," evidenced in miraculous gifts such as divine healing,

---

[38] See Timothy L. Smith, *Revivalism and Social Reform: American Protestantism on the Eve of the Civil War* (Nashville, TN: Abingdon, 1957); and Donald W. Dayton and Douglas M. Strong, *Rediscovering an Evangelical Heritage: A Tradition and Trajectory of Integrating Piety and Justice*, 2nd ed. (Grand Rapids, MI: Baker Academic, 2014).
[39] See Benjamin B. Warfield, *Studies in Perfectionism* (Phillipsburg, NJ: Presbyterian & Reformed, 1958); and Andrew David Naselli, *Let Go and Let God? A Survey and Analysis of Keswick Theology* (Bellingham, WA: Lexham Press, 2013).

prophecy, and especially *glossolalia*—speaking in unknown tongues.[40]
The origins of the American version of this movement cannot be pre-
cisely dated, but most date it to the Azusa Street Revival of 1906, led
by an African American Holiness preacher named William Seymour.
Early on, the Pentecostal movement overlaps considerably with the
Holiness movement, identifying *glossolalia* as evidence one has been
baptized with the Holy Spirit. New denominations were formed, such
as the Assemblies of God, the Pentecostal-Holiness Church, and the
Church of God in Christ, while some older Holiness groups, like the
Church of God, embrace Pentecostalism. First-generation Pentecostals were mostly poor, were far more racially diverse than other evangelical denominations, and were fiercely dedicated to foreign missions.
Around 1960, non-Pentecostal evangelicals, some mainline Protestants,
and even Roman Catholics began to embrace miraculous gifts. This self-
proclaimed Charismatic movement differed from the older Pentecostalism in that it was more interdenominational, downplayed the Holiness
tendencies of Pentecostalism, and did not always identify speaking in
tongues with a second baptism of the Holy Spirit. Both Pentecostals and
Charismatics (the lines are not always absolutely clear) have been susceptible to the so-called prosperity gospel that identifies physical healing with the atonement, and promises material blessings to believers
who have enough faith.[41]

Beginning among some faculty members at Fuller Theological Seminary, a so-called third wave of miraculous gifts influenced evangelicals
in the 1980s, further popularizing *glossolalia*, prophecy, and divine healing. This third wave strongly influenced the modern "praise and worship"
movement, directly affecting evangelical liturgy and worship postures.
For example, it is now common for evangelicals to clap along and even
raise their hands while singing, regardless of their convictions about miraculous gifts. Though many evangelicals are *cessationists* who deny that
miraculous gifts are available today, most seem to be *continuationists*
who are at least open to the continuation of such gifts in certain contexts.
Worldwide, evangelical Christianity is mostly continuationist, especially
in the global south. Though Holiness tendencies toward perfectionism

---

[40] See Grant Wacker, *Heaven Below: Early Pentecostals and American Culture* (Cambridge, MA: Harvard University Press, 2003); and Vinson Synan, *The Holiness-Pentecostal Tradition: Charismatic Movements in the
Twentieth Century*, 2nd ed. (Grand Rapids, MI: Eerdmans, 1997).
[41] See David W. Jones and Russell S. Woodbridge, *Health, Wealth, and Happiness: Has the Prosperity Gospel
Overshadowed the Gospel of Christ?* (Grand Rapids, MI: Kregel, 2010); and Kate Bowler, *Blessed: A History of
the American Prosperity Gospel* (New York: Oxford University Press, 2013).

remain confined to historically Wesleyan denominations, millions of Christians across denominational lines embrace a spirituality that is open, perhaps even driven by the expectation that God is still working miracles all the time. Global revival in the twentieth century was largely continuationist in its character.[42]

Celebrating the Disciplines: Spiritual Formation and Holiness

A second stream of spirituality began in the 1970s as evangelicals began to pay closer attention to conversations that other Christian traditions were having about spirituality.[43] During the mid-twentieth century, mainline Protestants increasingly emphasized the devotional reading of spiritual writings as one helpful way to mature in one's Christian life. Some of these writings were spiritual classics from Christian history, especially pre-Reformation history, while others were the works of modern writers such as the Quaker Thomas Kelly, the Catholic Thomas Merton, the German Lutheran Dietrich Bonhoeffer, or the English Anglo-Catholic Evelyn Underhill. For their part, Roman Catholics following Vatican II reemphasized the importance of devotional reading of the Bible and spiritual classics, as well as the practice of spiritual disciplines mined from Scripture and Christian history.[44] Catholics especially began to emphasize the importance of these practices in seminary education for the sake of preparing men for the priesthood, a process they came to call *spiritual formation*. Many evangelicals adopted this language to describe the growing interest in their own circles on practicing spiritual disciplines and reading spiritual classics for the sake of progress in holiness.

As was the case with Catholics, spiritual formation had a significant influence on evangelical higher education and theological education.[45]

---

[42] See Philip Jenkins, *The Next Christendom: The Coming of Global Christianity*, 3rd ed. (New York: Oxford University Press, 2011); and Mark R. Shaw, *Global Awakening: How 20th-Century Revivals Triggered a Christian Revolution* (Downers Grove, IL: IVP Academic, 2010). For a general survey of continuationist spirituality, broadly defined, see Mark J. Cartledge, *Encountering the Spirit: The Charismatic Tradition*, Traditions of Christian Spirituality (Maryknoll, NY: Orbis, 2007).

[43] The remainder of this chapter draws closely upon material previously published in Nathan A. Finn and Keith Whitfield, "The Missional Church and Spiritual Formation," in *Spirituality for the Sent: A New Vision for the Missional Church*, ed. Nathan A. Finn and Keith Whitfield (Downers Grove, IL: IVP Academic, 2017), 17–27; and Nathan A. Finn, "Contours of a Healthy Baptist Spirituality," *CTR* 12 (Fall 2014): 3–8. However, the material has been adapted for this chapter.

[44] See Gregg Allison's chapter for an evangelical account of spiritual disciplines.

[45] See Glenn T. Miller, *Piety and Plurality: Theological Education since 1960* (Eugene, OR: Wipf & Stock, 2014), 58–61; *CCCU Report on Spiritual Formation* (Washington, DC: Council of Christian Colleges and Universities, 2011), accessed January 20, 2017, https://www.cccu.org/~/media/filefolder/CCCU-SpiritualFormation_Booklet.pdf; Linda M. Cannell, "Theology, Spiritual Formation and Theological Education: Reflections toward Application," in *Life in the Spirit: Spiritual Formation in Theological Perspective*, ed. Jeffrey P. Greenman and George Kalantzis (Downers Grove, IL: IVP Academic, 2010), 229–49.

However, the leading voices in the evangelical spiritual formation movement were a cluster of authors who wrote about spiritual disciplines and spiritual classics for an evangelical readership, adapting these concepts into an idiom that appealed to late-twentieth-century evangelicals. One early voice was Richard Lovelace, who taught church history at Gordon-Conwell Theological Seminary. In 1973, Lovelace identified an evangelical "sanctification gap" in a widely cited journal article.[46] In 1979, he followed up with a book-length work on evangelical spirituality that drew upon both the Bible and Christian history.[47] The early leaders of the evangelical spiritual formation movement agreed with Lovelace's diagnosis of a sanctification gap and believed that the "dismal failure of American evangelicals to mature spiritually" resulted from unhealthy tendencies that evangelicalism had carried over from fundamentalism.[48]

Four key authors shaped the spiritual formation movement among evangelicals. Richard Foster, an evangelical Quaker, was the most important. Foster's best-selling book *Celebration of Discipline* (1978) could be considered the symbolic beginning of the spiritual formation movement among evangelicals.[49] In 2000, *Christianity Today* listed *Celebration of Discipline* as one of the ten books that had most shaped Christian thought during the twentieth century. Six years later, the magazine listed Foster's book as one of the fifty titles that had most influenced evangelicals.[50] Foster's book was an evangelical apology for adopting the classical spiritual disciplines as a means of progressing in holiness. Foster drew upon diverse movements, including Puritanism, Pietism, the Quakers, Pentecostals, Roman Catholicism, and Eastern Orthodoxy. He practiced a "hermeneutic of charity" when it came to learning from past authors, assuming they were faithful Christians and that modern evangelicals could learn from them. Foster contributed other influential books, including *Prayer: Finding the Heart's True Home* (1992), *Streams of Living Water: Celebrating the Great Traditions of Christian Faith* (1998), and two coedited volumes:

---

[46] Richard Lovelace, "The Sanctification Gap," *ThTo* 29 (January 1973): 363–69.
[47] Richard Lovelace, *Dynamics of Spiritual Life: An Evangelical Theology of Renewal* (Downers Grove, IL: InterVarsity, 1979).
[48] Chris Armstrong, "The Rise, Frustration, and Revival of Evangelical Spiritual *Ressourcement*," *Journal of Spiritual Formation and Soul Care* 2.1 (2009): 114.
[49] Foster's book, which has sold more than one million copies, is currently in its third edition. See Richard J. Foster, *Celebration of Discipline: The Path to Spiritual Growth*, 3rd ed. (San Francisco: HarperSanFrancisco, 2002).
[50] See "Books of the Century," *Christianity Today*, April 24, 2000, accessed January 20, 2017, http://www.christianitytoday.com/ct/2000/april24/5.92.html; and "The Top 50 Books that Have Shaped Evangelicals," *Christianity Today*, October 6, 2006, accessed January 20, 2017, http://www.christianitytoday.com/ct/2006/october/23.51.html.

Devotional Classics (1990) and *Spiritual Classics* (2000).[51] In 1988, Foster
founded Renovaré as a retreat and training ministry to promote spiritual
formation among evangelicals and other interested Christians.[52] Renovaré
is easily the most influential evangelical parachurch ministry devoted to
spiritual formation.

A second key author was Foster's close friend Dallas Willard, a longtime philosopher at the University of Southern California. Willard was
raised as a Southern Baptist, though in the 1970s he attended the Wood-
lake Avenue Friends Church in Canoga Park, California, where Foster
was his pastor. Early in his career, Willard focused his attention on scholarly publications in his discipline, but by the late-1980s he was becoming more recognizable outside the academy because of his popular books
and articles on spiritual formation. His *The Spirit of the Disciplines: Understanding How God Changes Lives* (1988) and *The Divine Conspiracy:
Rediscovering Your Hidden Life in God* (1998) were both award-winning
books that shaped the spiritual formation movement, along with Willard's
numerous other popular writings.[53] Willard and Foster also helped co-
edit the *Renovaré Spiritual Formation Bible* (2006), a resource that included both evangelical and mainline contributors. Willard maintained a
close relationship with Renovaré until his death in 2013. As a scholar who
taught at a state university, Willard brought academic credibility to the
sort of approach to spirituality Foster had first popularized.

A third author was James Houston, an Oxford University geologist
who was influenced by C. S. Lewis and who for many years was involved
in InterVarsity Christian Fellowship in the UK. In 1970, Houston relo-
cated to Canada to become the founding principal of Regent College in
Vancouver. Houston taught spiritual theology at Regent for many years.
Spiritual theology as conceived by Houston was a more academic approach to spiritual formation that was informed by insights from the
disciplines of systematic theology and especially church history. Unlike
Foster and Willard, Houston did not write an influential book about spiritual disciplines in the 1970s or 1980s. Instead, he dedicated his energies
to republishing updated editions of spiritual classics by historical authors

---

[51] For a list of all of Foster's books related to spiritual formation, see https://renovare.org/people/richard-foster
/books.
[52] See https://www.renovare.org/.
[53] Willard's former personal website continues to be updated and includes a full list of his books and essays. See
http://www.dwillard.org/defaultNew14.asp. For a helpful exposition of the major themes in Willard's spirituality, see Steven L. Porter, "The Willardian Corpus," *Journal of Spiritual Formation and Soul Care* 3 (Fall 2010):
239–66. For a more general introduction to Willard's thought, see Gary Black Jr., *The Theology of Dallas Willard: Discovering Protoevangelical Faith* (Eugene, OR: Wipf & Stock, 2013).

such as Juan de Valdés, John Owen, Blaise Pascal, Jonathan Edwards, and William Wilberforce.[54] Through Houston's influence, Regent became an academic hub for evangelicals interested in spiritual formation.

The final author was Eugene Peterson, a longtime pastor who later spent twenty-five years on the faculty of Regent College. Though most famous for his biblical paraphrase *The Message: The Bible in Contemporary Language* (2002), Peterson also wrote dozens of books that closely tied spiritual formation to the life of the modern pastor. His better-known works include *A Long Obedience in the Same Direction: Discipleship in an Instant Society* (1980), *The Contemplative Pastor: Returning to the Art of Spiritual Direction* (1980), as well as an award-winning five-volume series on spiritual theology published by Eerdmans (2005–2010).[55] In his later years, Peterson, like Willard, was frequently called upon to give a more academic voice to the spiritual formation movement through published essays and public lectures.

Today, the spiritual formation movement is still identified with these authors—especially Foster and Willard. But it is also known through dozens of lesser-known authors (both scholarly and popular), ministries such as Renovaré and the more ecumenical Academy for Spiritual Formation, and academic centers such as the Dallas Willard Center for Christian Spiritual Formation at Westmont College and the Institute for Spiritual Formation at Biola University. Biola has become especially important for evangelicals interested in the academic study of spiritual formation, whether for scholars or practitioners. Through the Institute for Spiritual Formation, the university offers multiple programs related to spiritual formation and publishes *The Journal for Spiritual Formation and Soul Care*. Several evangelical publishing houses have also given attention to publishing works related to evangelical spiritual formation, especially InterVarsity, Baker, Eerdmans, and NavPress, as have some more mainstream publishers such as HarperCollins.

The spiritual formation movement is theologically eclectic, ecumenical, and tends to be more egalitarian in its view of gender roles. A Quaker-Wesleyan emphasis on experiencing God permeates the movement, as does a similarly rooted commitment to social justice. Perhaps for this

---

[54] Following his retirement, Houston wrote more himself, authoring or coauthoring numerous books related to spirituality. For a partial list of Houston's published works, see his faculty website at Regent College, accessed January 21, 2017, http://www.regent-college.edu/faculty/retired/james-houston. See also Aram Haroutunian, "No One Closer: A Conversation with James Houston," *Mars Hill Review* 1 (Fall 1996): 51–66, accessed January 21, 2017, http://www.leaderu.com/marshill/mhr06/houston1.html.

[55] For a partial list of Peterson's published works, see his faculty website at Regent College, accessed September 26, 2007, http://www.regent-college.edu/faculty/retired/eugene-peterson.

reason, many charismatics and Pentecostals resonate with the Renovaré approach to spiritual formation. Authors from this perspective tend to be more descriptive in their use of church tradition, drawing upon many nonevangelical sources, though always engaging them from a broadly evangelical perspective. For these reasons, some evangelicals have criticized the spiritual formation movement. For example, some negatively associate practices such as contemplative prayer with the Roman Catholic Church, the occult, or the new age movement. In response, advocates of evangelical spiritual formation have in recent years more frequently critiqued spiritual practices that fall short of the biblical witness, while at the same time pushing back against accusations that any spiritual practice with roots among ancient or medieval believers is inherently mystical, and thus presumably sub-Christian.[56] Still other evangelicals resonate with the spiritual formation movement in principle, but have framed their approach somewhat differently than early shapers such as Foster, Willard, and Peterson.[57]

Gospel-Centered Spirituality: Recovering Reformational Holiness

A third stream of spirituality, which is small but growing, is often associated with the so-called New Calvinist movement within evangelicalism.[58] To be sure, not everyone who might be identified with the New Calvinism is a consistent Calvinist in the Dortian sense of the term. For many, the New Calvinism seems to be less about the so-called five points of Calvinism, or even historically Reformed confessions and denominations, and more about identification with certain parachurch ministries such as The Gospel Coalition, Together for the Gospel, the Cross Conference, Ligonier Ministries, and Desiring God Ministries. Those who identify with this vision of spirituality talk far more about what they call "gospel-centeredness" than they do Reformed theology, emphasizing classic reformational emphases such as justification by faith alone, penal substitutionary atonement, and progressive sanctification. These doctrines are considered key aspects of the gospel, which many in this movement be-

---

[56] See Tom Schwanda, "'To Gaze on the Beauty of the Lord': The Evangelical Resistance and Retrieval of Contemplation," *Journal of Spiritual Formation and Soul Care* 7 (Spring 2014): 62–84; and John Coe, "The Historical Controversy over Contemplation and Contemplative Prayer: A Historical, Theological, and Biblical Resolution," *Journal of Spiritual Formation and Soul Care* 7 (Spring 2014): 140–53.

[57] For example, see Bruce Demarest, *Satisfy Your Soul: Restoring the Heart of Christian Spirituality* (Colorado Springs, CO: NavPress, 1999); and Donald G. Bloesch, *Spirituality Old and New: Recovering Authentic Spiritual Life* (Downers Grove, IL: IVP Academic, 2007), both of which are more overtly theological than most works in the spiritual formation movement.

[58] The language of "New Calvinism" is taken from Collin Hansen, *Young, Restless, Reformed: A Journalist's Journey with the New Calvinists* (Wheaton, IL: Crossway, 2008).

lieve has been undermined, downplayed, or sometimes even abandoned among too many evangelicals.

On the whole, there is a decidedly doctrinal flavor to the gospel-centered movement that has sometimes been lacking in the older spiritual formation movement. As a rule, the gospel-centered movement is non-Arminian (if not always overtly Calvinist), staunchly committed to biblical inerrancy, and affirms a complementarian understanding of gender roles. Despite its identification with parachurch movements and conferences, an emphasis on the primacy of local churches permeates the movement, perhaps because of the preponderance of Reformed and Baptist influence within the movement. The gospel-centered movement places greater importance on evangelism than social justice, though the latter is also valued. Authors from this perspective tend to be more judicious in their use of church tradition, focusing more on Reformed and classical evangelical sources, especially the Puritans, and being less open to insights from medieval Catholic writers. Crossway, Moody, and explicitly Reformed presses such as Reformation Heritage, Evangelical Press, and P&R tend to be the publishers of choice for authors who resonate with this stream of evangelical spirituality.

Some of the better-known advocates of a more gospel-centered approach to spirituality include J. I. Packer, Jerry Bridges, John Piper, and Donald Whitney. Packer's books *Knowing God* (1973), *A Quest for Godliness: The Puritan Vision of the Christian Life* (1990), and *Rediscovering Holiness* (1992) were shaped by the Reformed and especially Puritan spiritual traditions. He is also a longtime critic of the older Keswick view of holiness, within which tradition he was nurtured early in his Christian life.[59] Though Packer's ministry long predates the "gospel-centered" language—he is better known as a key advocate of Reformed theology within evangelicalism—his works on spirituality significantly shaped many of the figures that later became identified with the gospel-centered movement. That Packer taught for many years at Regent College also meant he was situated at one of the centers for the evangelical spiritual formation movement, which both informed his own writings and provided Packer with a counterpoint as he offered a more consistently Reformed alternative.

Jerry Bridges was a longtime staff member with the Navigators, a discipleship ministry found on many college campuses in the USA. Bridges' books *The Pursuit of Holiness* (1988) and *The Discipline of Grace: God's*

---

[59] See Packer's seminal article "'Keswick' and the Reformed Doctrine of Sanctification," *EvQ* 27 (July 1955): 153–67.

Role and Our Role in the Pursuit of Holiness (1994) focused more on the traditional language of holiness than the newer language of spiritual formation, which is a common practice in the gospel-centered movement. A primary concern of Bridges was that the pursuit of holiness can become unintentionally legalistic when it is divorced from the gospel, which Bridges identified closely with justification by faith and penal substitution. Justification is the foundation for sanctification; indicative comes before imperative. As a Presbyterian, Bridges' works were implicitly Reformed, though not always dogmatically so, since he was writing for a general audience.

Longtime pastor John Piper also wrote much about how the gospel ought to shape spirituality, albeit from a more robustly Calvinistic perspective. His seminal work was *Desiring God: Meditations of a Christian Hedonist* (1986), which was a manifesto for Piper's "Christian hedonism." This terminology has proven controversial, with some Reformed critics rejecting it because of the seeming incompatibility of Christianity and hedonism.[60] Piper simply means that we are motivated by our desires, and the more we desire God, the more God shapes all of our desires. Drawing upon the insights of Jonathan Edwards and C. S. Lewis, Piper tweaked the first question in the Westminster Shorter Catechism, arguing, "The chief end of man is to glorify God *by* enjoying him forever."[61] Christian hedonism also informed Piper's other writings, notably *A Hunger for God: Desiring God Through Fasting and Prayer* (1997) and *When I Don't Desire God: How to Fight for Joy* (2004).

Donald Whitney is former pastor and current professor at Southern Baptist Theological Seminary. Whitney is author of numerous books related to spiritual formation, but from a gospel-centered perspective. His *Spiritual Disciplines of the Christian Life* (1991) represented a more Reformed or even neo-Puritan take on the spiritual disciplines, while his *Spiritual Disciplines within the Church* (1996) is an example of the gospel-centered movement's emphasis on the local church. A more recent book, *Praying the Bible* (2015), is an example of how the gospel-centered movement also seeks to be a Word-centered movement, much like the Reformation to which it so often looks for inspiration. In many ways, Whitney

---

[60] Piper responds to one prominent critic, the Reformed philosopher Richard Mouw, in John Piper, "A Response to Richard Mouw's Treatment of Christian Hedonism in 'The God Who Commands,'" Desiring God Ministries, May 28, 1993, accessed January 21, 2017, http://www.desiringgod.org/articles/a-response-to-richard-mouws-treatment-of-christian-hedonism-in-the-god-who-commands.

[61] John Piper, *Desiring God: Meditations of a Christian Hedonist*, rev. ed. (Colorado Springs, CO: Multnomah, 2004), 18.

functions as the gospel-centered alternative to Foster and Willard, and in more Reformed contexts, Whitney's books are often recommended instead of similar works written by the more famous spiritual formation authors. It is noteworthy that Whitney teaches at Southern Seminary. Like Biola, Southern has become an academic hub for the study of spiritual formation, though the seminary prefers the term *Biblical Spirituality*, perhaps to signal its greater emphasis on biblical and theological prescription over historical description. At Southern, students can earn several master's degrees and two doctoral degrees in biblical spirituality. The PhD at Southern is currently the only terminal academic degree in the discipline of spirituality offered by an evangelical institution.[62]

Conclusion

As this brief survey has shown, nearly all Christians care about holiness, even if different traditions dispute the best way to define it and pursue it. Descriptively speaking, we live in a world of many different Christian spiritualities—even among evangelicals. Everyone believes their approach to holiness is at least informed by Scripture, and all parties see value in the insights of at least parts of the Christian tradition. I will close with a biblical command that should resonate with all believers who desire to grow in holiness: "As obedient children, do not be conformed to the passions of your former ignorance, but as he who called you is holy, you also be holy in all your conduct, since it is written, 'You shall be holy, for I am holy'" (1 Pet 1:14–16). God is holy. He has called us to reflect his holy character. This is the essence of Christian spirituality.

---

[62] See Jeff Robinson, "SBTS Appoints Renowned Early Church Scholar to Faculty," *Southern News*, May 14, 2007, accessed January 20, 2017, http://news.sbts.edu/2007/05/14/sbts-appoints-renowned-early-church-scholar-to-faculty/.

9

SPIRITUAL AND EMBODIED DISCIPLINES

GREGG R. ALLISON

If I were to pose the question "How do spiritual and embodied disciplines promote spirituality?" to the members of my church and to the students whom I teach, the vast majority of them would counter quickly and easily, "Spiritual disciplines promote spirituality by nourishing our relationship with God, but I don't think embodied disciplines have anything to do with spirituality. And, by the way, what are 'embodied disciplines' anyway?" This response underscores the great divide, one that has been with us for a very long time: spirit versus body, immaterial versus material, heaven versus earth, good versus evil. Spiritual disciplines nourish our spirit and contribute to our spiritual relationship with God, which will last forever. Embodied disciplines strengthen our body and contribute to our embodied existence, which is coming to an end. So goes our typical thinking.

The Great Divide

To drive this point home further, think of the sermons that you've heard over the last few months, even years. How many of them or their applications had something to do with praying more consistently, reading the Bible more regularly, meditating on and memorizing Scripture more steadily, and the like? How many of them or their applications had something to do with sleeping more consistently, working out at the fitness club more regularly, eating nutritious meals more steadily, and the like? Do you have no entries in the second column? I thought so. I still recall teaching a Sunday school class on gluttony. One participant actually stood up after five minutes of my presentation and told me to stop talking about the topic because it was too convicting. Besides, he said, a matter like gluttony, dealing as it does with our body, is not a topic that should be addressed in church.

Reasons for the Divide

Four centuries before Jesus Christ, the Greek philosopher Plato set forth a worldview that emphasized the mind and spiritual matters over the body and physical matters. On a societal level, Plato distinguished between three classes of people: the ruling class (the guardians), the soldier/warrior class (the auxiliaries), and the working class (the producers/artisans). Interestingly, Plato asserted that these three social classes correspond with the three-part structure of human nature: reason, spirit, and body/appetite. For the proper and just functioning of society, the guardians must rule, the warriors must support the rulers, and the workers must produce. Similarly, for the proper and just functioning of a human being, her reason must rule, her spirit must support her reason, and her body/appetite must follow the lead of her reason.[1] Plato especially underscored the inherent goodness of spiritual reality and denigrated as inherently evil material reality. For example, he considered salvation to be the soul's escape from its imprisonment in the body.[2]

Tragically, this Platonic philosophy favoring the mind and spiritual matters over the body and physical matters infiltrated the early church. In an extreme form, it reared its ugly head in the various movements called Gnosticism. Key tenets included (1) a dichotomy between the evil god of the Old Testament, who created the evil, physical world, and the good god of the New Testament, who saves people spiritually through Jesus Christ; and (2) a salvation that comes through secret knowledge (*gnōsis*, hence *Gnos*ticism), the study of philosophy and aesthetics, and the practice of asceticism, which denies the body any physical pleasures. Whereas the early church knew Gnosticism was wrong, it struggled to combat it. The church pointed to the physical creation as being "very good," the incarnation—the embodiment—of the Son of God, his physical resurrection, the future physical resurrection of believers, and the promise of the new heaven and new earth—a physical place—as evidence for the goodness of physical things. At the same time, the church elevated spiritual character-

---

[1] Plato, *The Republic*, bks. 2–4.
[2] For further discussion, see Frank Bottomley, *Attitudes to the Body in Western Christendom* (London: Lepus, 1979), 20.

istics (humility, sober reasoning), spiritual practices (prayer, meditation, ecstatic experience), spiritual relationships (while never denouncing marriage, the church celebrated virginity), and more. Monasticism, originally constructed as an escape from the world in order to focus on spiritual pursuits leading to purity, and the withdrawal of church leaders (the clergy) from ordinary physical work so they could concentrate on full-time spiritual ministry, are further evidences of the church's capitulation to the great divide between spirit and body, between spiritual and physical.

Some Things Never Change

Contemporary evangelicalism still suffers from the great divide. Evangelical Christians engage in spiritual disciplines, promote their spiritual life, offer spiritual solutions to spiritual problems, and evangelize to "save souls." At the same time, medical and sociological statistics bear witness to the fact that of all the religious traditions, conservative Protestants are the most overweight, with Southern Baptists claiming the top spot on the obesity scale. Contributors to this plight include poor nutrition, overconsumption of food, absent or irregular physical exercise, lack of rest and leisure, poor sleep patterns, and more. And it is these infamous habits on which the church is largely, if not completely, silent.[3]

The great divide will not be easily overcome, nor will it be reversed by focusing attention on embodied disciplines while neglecting spiritual disciplines. Indeed, Paul links them together: "Train yourself for godliness; for while bodily training is of some value, godliness is of value in every way, as it holds promise for the present life and also for the life to come" (1 Tim. 4:7–8). Disciplining ourselves for godliness entails rigorous training so as to mature in the faith, become more and more Christlike, honor God in doing his will, bear the fruit of the Holy Spirit, and more. Elements of this training are those spiritual disciplines with which we are very familiar: reading, memorizing, studying, meditating on, and applying Scripture; praying for ourselves, our family and friends, our church, nonbelievers, and our society; worshiping with other Christians; and more. Such discipline for godliness is valuable both now, as maturity in Christ pleases God and furthers his work in this world, and later, when such holiness will be rewarded.

---

[3] Ken Ferraro, "Study Finds Some Faithful Less Likely to Pass the Plate," *Purdue University News*, August 24, 2006, http://www.purdue.edu/uns/html4ever/2006/060824.Ferraro.obesity.html; Wendy Ashley, "Obesity in the Body of Christ," *SBC Life: Journal of the Southern Baptist Convention*, January 2007, http://www.sbclife .net/Articles/2007/01/sla8.

Yet another training is valuable: embodied discipline. Disciplining ourselves bodily entails rigorous physical training so as to be in proper shape, cultivate good health, stave off many illnesses associated with poor physical care, be responsive to God's will and be able to carry it out, and more. Elements of this training include good nutrition, regular exercise, proper rest and sleep, and avoidance of abuse of our body. Unlike discipline for godliness, such discipline for embodied health is valuable only now, during our earthly existence. It will not be beneficial in the intermediate state, when we are disembodied, or in the new heaven and new earth, when we in our glorified bodies will not need physical training.

In accordance with this twofold disciplinary emphasis, I will address how both types of discipline—spiritual and physical—contribute to our spirituality. Because far greater familiarity exists in regard to spiritual disciplines, I will give more attention to embodied disciplines. Before addressing specific disciplines, I need to underscore an important yet often overlooked fact about discipline itself: all discipline is purposeful.

Discipline Is Purposeful

All discipline, of whatever variety, is purposeful and never an end in itself. Discipline is always directed at some purpose, aim, or goal. The very title of this volume indicates the purpose for spiritual and embodied disciplines: the promotion of spirituality. Specifically, Scripture presents at least two aims for Christians to engage in disciplining themselves. The first is progress in sanctification, or holiness. The following apostolic prayer expresses this goal: "Now may the God of peace himself sanctify you completely, and may your whole spirit and soul and body be kept blameless at the coming of our Lord Jesus Christ" (1 Thess. 5:23). As we Christians engage in the discipline of prayer, we request that the God with whom we enjoy a personal relationship renew us through and through. This completeness permeates every aspect of our being. Certainly (and as we would expect), it includes our spirit and soul, the immaterial element that is manifested in proper thinking about God and his ways, appropriate feelings such as righteous anger and godly jealousy, God-honoring decisions, upright motivations, and more. Additionally (and importantly for our discussion), this completeness includes our body, the material element that expresses itself in the proper use of the tongue (for blessing God and edifying rather than cursing others; James 3:1–12), hard work to provide for oneself and others (Eph. 4:28; 1 Tim. 5:8), fitting actions such as giving to the poor and worshiping the Lord together with other believers, virtuous habits, and more. Discipline (in this case, engagement in prayer) is purposeful, aiming toward progress in holiness.

A second aim of discipline is to complete the marathon of the Christian ministry and reap its promised rewards. Paul's self-discipline underscores this goal. After explaining his practice of "becom[ing] all things to all people, that by all means I might save some" (1 Cor. 9:22), he highlights the purpose for his personal contextualization: "I do it all for the sake of the gospel, that I may share with them in its blessings" (1 Cor. 9:23). As Paul preaches the gospel, plants churches, and fans the flames of the nascent Christian movement, he engages in this ministry like he would run a marathon, intending to complete the race and receive the prize at its conclusion.

By means of analogy to training for the ancient Isthmian games (which featured both running and boxing), he expresses the aim of his self-discipline:

> Do you not know that in a race all the runners run, but only one receives the prize? So run that you may obtain it. Every athlete exercises self-control in all things. They do it to receive a perishable wreath, but we an imperishable. So I do not run aimlessly; I do not box as one beating the air. But I discipline my body and keep it under control, lest after preaching to others I myself should be disqualified. (1 Cor. 9:24–27)

The contrast is strong: the self-control exercised by an athlete in training and competing is in view of receiving a perishable reward, whereas the self-control exercised by Christians in living and ministering is in view of receiving an imperishable reward. By way of application (vv. 26–27), Paul does not run without purpose, and he does not box without purpose, affirming that his self-control is aimed at moving him toward and preparing him for the goal. Indeed, he disciplines his body and keeps it under control lest, after preaching to others (that is, engaging in ministry to start off people on the race and to encourage Christians to run the race so as to receive the prize) he himself should be disqualified (that is, he should fail to exercise the proper self-control, break the rules of the game so as to be disqualified, and thus fail to obtain the prize at the end of the race). Discipline is purposeful, aimed at completing the marathon of the Christian ministry and reaping its promised rewards.

Accordingly, all discipline, of whatever variety, is purposeful. I emphasize this point to challenge Christians who are rightly involved in discipline but engage in it as an end in itself, or who have lost sight of the goal of their discipline. For example, we fast, but we don't fast for fasting's sake; that would be nonsensical (though it may be very beneficial). Additionally, we don't fast because Scripture commands us to fast. Though it is indeed the case that Scripture commands fasting, the imperative to fast and the reason for fasting are two different matters. In obedience to God's will expressed in Scripture, we fast for specific purposes, which we will see below.

Spiritual Disciplines

To cover a vast amount of material in a brief amount of time and space, I will approach this presentation of spiritual disciplines by following the structure (but not necessarily the content) of Richard Foster's *Celebration of Discipline*. It organizes the spiritual disciplines in three categories:[4]

1. The *inward disciplines* consist of meditation, prayer, fasting, and study. *Meditation* involves contemplation of Scripture, reading and re-reading it, praying and applying it, even memorizing it. Scripture meditation is in accordance with such biblical instruction as, "Like newborn infants, long for the pure spiritual milk, that by it you may grow up into salvation" (1 Pet. 2:2), and illustrated by the man whose "delight is in the law of the LORD, / and on his law he meditates day and night" (Ps. 1:2). Meditation is a sustained reflection on the Word of God by which we develop a deep familiarity with its commands, promises, warnings, affirmations, and the like. Meditation readies us for recalling Scripture when we face personal trials and temptations and when others need words of comfort, exhortation, rebuke, and more.

Prayer is "the act of communicating with God as an expression of trust in him," with several elements as part of that act.[5] Prayers of *praise* honor God for his greatness and goodness and adore him for his mighty works of creation, providence, redemption, and the like. Prayers of *thanksgiving* express gratitude for God's gracious granting of favor and blessing. Prayers of *confession* are the admission of sin and guiltiness, together with reception of divine forgiveness. As sin is committed, we sincerely acknowledge the wrongness of that attitude or action and the guilt it brings before God. We also express faith in God's provision by recognizing and embracing

---

[4] Richard J. Foster, *Celebration of Discipline: The Path to Spiritual Growth*, special 20th anniversary ed. (San Francisco: HarperSanFrancisco, 1998). Another popular book in this field is Dallas Willard, *The Spirit of the Disciplines* (San Francisco: Harper & Row, 1988).

[5] Gregg R. Allison, *The Baker Compact Dictionary of Theological Terms* (Grand Rapids, MI: Baker, 2016), s.v. "prayer." See also s.v. "praise," "thanksgiving," "confession," and "intercession."

the forgiveness of that sin through the work of Christ. Prayers of *petition* are requests made for oneself, imploring God to sanctify us, empower us, guide us, discipline us, fill us with his Spirit, and the like. Prayers of *intercession* are requests made for and on behalf of others, pleading with God to convict them, save them, heal them, embolden them, protect them, send them, and more.

Combining the first two spiritual disciplines, praying the Bible, that is, pausing when one is reading it and addressing God in prayer (e.g., praise, confession, intercession) in accordance with his Word, fosters both meditation on Scripture and communication with him.[6]

Fasting is the "voluntary abstinence from food for spiritual purposes."[7] Jesus assumes his disciples will fast by giving us instructions about fasting: "And when you fast, do not look gloomy like the hypocrites, for they disfigure their faces that their fasting may be seen by others. Truly, I say to you, they have received their reward. But when you fast, anoint your head and wash your face, that your fasting may not be seen by others but by your Father who is in secret. And your Father who sees in secret will reward you" (Matt. 6:16–18; cf. 9:14–15). Specific elements of fasting include: (1) We don't appear to be fasting so as to draw attention to ourselves and our (alleged) religious superiority. (2) We hide from others the fact of our fasting so that we have only one—and the proper—audience: God. (3) We stop eating for a time, and this abstinence from food often results in intense hunger, stomach cramps, withdrawal symptoms, tiredness, dizziness and fainting, and more. But it also results in a deepened dependence on God and a heightening of our spiritual senses. (4) We embrace the promise that God will reward our fasting.

In terms of this last aspect, God may give us this reward in terms of manifesting his presence in a deeper, more intimate way. He may answer our passionate and ongoing prayers in the case of particularly important matters. He may vividly guide us when we (or others for whom we are praying during our fast) urgently need his direction. God may restore us after deep confession and repentance of prevailing sins. He may protect us from brutal enemies and evil circumstances that threaten to undo us. He may raise us up after we have humbled ourselves and renounced our prideful ways. God may answer our intercession on behalf of others who are desperately in need. He may renew and freshly empower us for a pioneering or heightened ministry. He may tangibly communicate his sense

---

[6] For how to engage in this practice, see Donald S. Whitney, *Praying the Bible* (Wheaton, IL: Crossway, 2015).
[7] Donald S. Whitney, *Spiritual Disciplines for the Christian Life* (Colorado Springs, CO: NavPress, 1991), 152.

of pleasure for us being his children, his worshipers, his servants. These rewards correspond to the many reasons for fasting. As explained earlier and included in the definition of fasting, this discipline, like all other disciplines, is purposeful.

Study is the intellectual examination of Scripture that focuses on researching, analyzing, and interpreting it. Similar to meditation in that both involve the Bible, study is a more profound engagement with Scripture. It seeks to understand biblical passages in their redemptive-historical context (creation, fall, redemption, consummation), according to their covenantal framework, by means of a grammatical-historical hermeneutic, and with attention to their genre (e.g., narrative, prophecy, letter, song). Engagement with biblical scholars may play an important role in our study of Scripture. Studying for theological formulation is another important aspect of this discipline. Beyond Scripture, we may study other significant books like Augustine's *On the Trinity* and John Calvin's *Institutes of the Christian Religion*.

2. The second category, *outward disciplines*, consists of simplicity, solitude, submission, and service. *Simplicity* involves freedom from materialism, consumerism, workaholism, and similar domineering ideologies and practices. Though its invitation is often muffled, Scripture calls believers to simplicity.

When asked to be an arbiter in the matter of a division of wealth among family members, Jesus said to them, "Take care, and be on your guard against all covetousness, for one's life does not consist in the abundance of his possessions" (Luke 12:15). He followed this warning with a parable of a rich man who amassed a great quantity of grain and possessions, only to die unexpectedly (12:16–20). Jesus' lesson: "So is the one who lays up treasure for himself and is not rich toward God" (12:21). In the following section Jesus urges his disciples to avoid anxiety about the things of this world and to be characterized by faith instead, concluding: "Do not seek what you are to eat and what you are to drink, nor be worried. For all the nations of the world seek after these things, and your Father knows that you need them. Instead, seek his kingdom, and these things will be added to you" (Luke 12:29–31). When Mary "sat at the Lord's [Jesus'] feet and listened to his teaching," and "Martha was distracted with much serving," Jesus said, "Martha, Martha, you are anxious and troubled about many things, but one thing is necessary. Mary has chosen the good portion, which will not be taken away from her" (Luke 10:39–42).

We are called to a single focus: not to live with clutter and anxiety but faithfully and peacefully under the rule and reign of God, choosing Jesus above all else. Everything else—family, schooling, job, money, relaxation, home, and life itself—is a secondary matter. Living in this way is to embrace simplicity.

Solitude is the discipline of savoring aloneness. It is not loneliness, which is a state imposed on us by others (through intentional avoidance or unintentional neglect), but a self-imposed state of seclusion from others. Like other disciplines, solitude is not an end in itself, but purposeful, aimed at connecting intimately with God.

Jesus himself modeled solitude by his habit of withdrawing from the crowds pressing on him and isolating himself for the purpose of prayer to and communion with his Father (e.g., Matt. 14:13, 23; Mark 1:35; Luke 5:16; 6:12). He invited his disciples to do the same (Mark 6:31). As his disciples today, we intentionally isolate ourselves from others, from our work, from our responsibilities, from social media, and from our normal commitments. Removed from these everyday matters, we seek the Lord through prayer, meditation, study, listening, silence, and the like. The fruit of solitude is often personal renewal, the deepening of our relationship with God, and clarity for our next steps.

Submission is the "act of yielding to those in authority."[8] Ultimately, Christians submit to God, even when human authorities prescribe actions that contradict his will (e.g., Acts 5:27–32). Specifically, Christians obey the commands and prohibitions of Scripture; in this way, they submit to the authority of God, who reveals his will through his written Word. In the family, relationships between husband, wife, and children are framed in terms of authority and submission (e.g., Col. 3:18–21; Eph. 5:22–6:4). In the church, members submit to their pastors: "Obey your leaders and submit to them, for they are keeping watch over your souls, as those who will have to give an account. Let them do this with joy and not with groaning, for that would be of no advantage to you" (Heb. 13:17). These leaders, for their part, lead in submission to Christ, the head of the church (Eph. 1:19–23). Leaders are undershepherds obeying their chief Shepherd (1 Pet. 5:1–5). Last but not least, being filled with the Spirit, and in reverence of Christ, members submit to one another (Eph. 5:21).

Our contemporary society lends no aid whatsoever in encouraging and modeling submission to authority. Indeed, anti-authority characterizes

---

[8] Allison, *Baker Compact Dictionary*, s.v. "submission."

our culture, making it doubly hard for Christians to understand the nature of submission and engage in it. Tragically, even our churches balk at authority, both for its unpopularity in society and for its abuses of ecclesial authority (e.g., church disciplinary action that is carried out for wrong reasons and/or in wrong ways).

Thankfully, the ultimate model of authority is a divine one, illustrated in the submission of the Son of God to the Father in becoming incarnate and carrying out his mission of salvation. The eternally generated Son, submitting to the authoritative sending of his Father, obeyed fully the will of God: the Son became incarnate as Jesus of Nazareth, submitted himself to the law in all matters, suffered the cruelty of crucifixion and the punishment of divine wrath, died as the innocent and sinless God-man, was buried, rose again the third day, and ascended back to his Father. His obedience through submission is the model after which we Christians are to pattern our lives (1 Pet. 2:21–25).

Service is gospel-centered ministry directed to the expansion of God's glory, the growth of the church, the fulfillment of the Great Commission, and the extension of mercy to the poor and marginalized.[9] It is not some type of generic service that is so commonplace today: paying it forward, giving back to the neighborhood, charitable benevolence, helping others so as to assuage one's feelings of guilt for being comfortable and successful, giving so that God is obligated to extravagantly reward such faith, doing good to others so as to merit God's favor, or other such notions of service.

Clearly, the goal of the above-listed acts of service is to draw attention to, or to help, the one who engages in them. Typical service, in other words, is about attaining prestige in the eyes of others, spreading one's own fame, and/or aiding one's own cause. Even Jesus' own disciples were infected with this self-oriented disease:

> James and John, the sons of Zebedee, came up to him [Jesus] and said to him, "Teacher, we want you to do for us whatever we ask of you." And he said to them, "What do you want me to do for you?" And they said to him, "Grant us to sit, one at your right hand and one at your left, in your glory." Jesus said to them, "You do not know what you are asking. Are you able to drink the cup that I drink, or to be baptized with the baptism with which I am baptized?" And they said to him, "We are able." (Mark 10:35–39)

---

[9] The following material is adapted from Gregg R. Allison, *NorthStar Theology*, unpublished book developed for Sojourn Community Church, Louisville, KY. Used with permission.

These two disciples of Jesus showed their true colors: though professing to be able to serve their master, their real motivation for serving Jesus was so that they could use him. Of course, they did not grasp the gravity of the service to which Jesus was calling them—self-sacrifice to the point of death—but their tragi-comic profession of ability to so serve revealed their true goal: to get Jesus to grant them positions of fame in his coming kingdom. They would serve Jesus so that he would give them glory.

Genuine service for Jesus is the polar opposite of such self-centered glory grabbing. Oriented away from themselves, Christians pray, "To him [God] be glory in the church and in Christ Jesus throughout all generations, forever and ever. Amen" (Eph. 3:21). Church members operate according to the following commands: "As each has received a gift, use it to serve one another, as good stewards of God's varied grace: whoever speaks, as one who speaks oracles of God; whoever serves, as one who serves by the strength that God supplies—in order that in everything God may be glorified through Jesus Christ" (1 Pet. 4:10–11). Indeed, when the church serves as it should in light of the gospel—and the following example is the service of giving—wonderful fruit is produced: "For the ministry of this service is not only supplying the needs of the saints but is also overflowing in many thanksgivings to God. By their [the recipients of the church's giving] approval of this service, they will glorify God because of your submission that comes from your confession of the gospel of Christ" (2 Cor. 9:12–13). Accordingly, genuine service is oriented toward, and redounds to, the glory of God.

In their service, Christians follow the example of their King who, in his inauguration of the kingdom of God, took on the role of a servant to his subjects (John 13:4–17). Loving his disciples with unconditional love, Jesus displayed selfless, sacrificial service for their sake. Though rightly acknowledged as their Lord and teacher, he stooped to the lowest level of slave labor and washed his disciples' feet, providing an example of humble, even humiliating, service for them to imitate. Servants are certainly not greater than their master; if Jesus served his disciples, they are expected to serve others similarly. Furthermore, they are promised the blessing of God if they so serve. As Michael Card underscores, "In the upside-down kingdom, true greatness is found in the servant's kneeling with the basin and the towel."[10]

---

[10] Michael Card, *Scribbling in the Sand: Christ and Creativity* (Downers Grove, IL: InterVarsity Press, 2002), 85.

3. The third category, *corporate disciplines*, consists of confession, worship, guidance, and celebration.

Confession includes two elements: "The admission of sin and guiltiness, and the expression of belief. In the first sense, confession follows an act of sin and is the sincere acknowledgment of the wrongness of that act and the guilt that it brings before God."[11] As a personal discipline, Christians are to confess their sins as soon as they become aware of them, according to this command and promise: "If we confess our sins, he is faithful and just to forgive us our sins and to cleanse us from all unrighteousness" (1 John 1:9). Confession involves admitting our sins, agreeing with God that they are wrong and heinous before him, acknowledging that Christ's death has atoned for those sins, and appropriating his forgiveness.

As a corporate discipline, confession involves admitting our sins to one another, according to the command and promise: "Confess your sins to one another and pray for one another, that you may be healed" (James 5:16). As a church becomes a recognized safe haven in which its members can be vulnerable with one another without fear of rejection and retribution, an atmosphere of grace and acceptance fosters transparency with sins and openness in confessing them.

"In the second sense, confession is . . . the verbalization of the faith, or what the church believes about God, Christ, salvation, the Holy Spirit, and more (e.g., recitation of the Apostles' Creed)."[12] Participating in this corporate discipline, members articulate "the faith that was once for all delivered to the saints" (Jude 3). Indeed, they join their verbal confession with that of the church from its inception: the early Christian creed inscripturated in 1 Timothy 3:16, the early church's canon of truth and rule of faith, and the ecumenical creeds of Nicaea, Constantinople, and Chalcedon.

In terms of benefits of this practice, this corporate discipline has been and continues to be an important element of the church as a confessional community. When contemporary churches engage in confession of the faith, they stand in continuity, and express their unity, with believers throughout the entire Christian era. "Corporate confession of the faith by the church is also beneficial for providing personal assurance that the faith that its members confess is indeed the true Christian faith. . . . A confession of faith also contributes to the cohesiveness of the members of a church. . . . Corporate confession also fosters a deepening of trust in the

---

[11] Allison, *Baker Compact Dictionary*, s.v. "confession."
[12] Ibid.

faith and personal commitment to it, because of 'the self-involving nature of confession.'"[13]

Worship is "an act of acknowledging and acclaiming the majestic greatness of God in ways that he prescribes."[14] In terms of a corporate discipline, worship entails Christians regularly gathering together for what is commonly called a "worship service."

> This corporate act consists in ascribing honor to God through praise of his nature and mighty works by singing and praying; reading, preaching, and hearing the Word of God, with responses of obedience and faithfulness to covenant responsibilities (e.g., giving money, confessing sin, edifying one another, sending missionaries); and the administration of the new covenant ordinances of baptism and the Lord's Supper.[15]

The corporate discipline of worship brings Christians together to bless God and experience his blessing, carry out the biblical "one anothers" (e.g., love one another, John 13:34–35; live in harmony with one another, Rom. 12:16; instruct one another, Rom. 15:14; comfort and agree with one another, 2 Cor. 13:11; serve one another, Gal. 5:13; forgive one another, Eph. 4:32), be nourished and sanctified by the Word of God (Col. 3:16), participate in Christ and his saving benefits through the celebration of the Lord's Supper (1 Cor. 10:16), and much more.

Guidance is God's leading through his Spirit and Word. While commonly embraced as an individual experience, corporate guidance refers to divine leading of the church as the body of Christ. Two examples illustrate this discipline.

1. While the prophets and teachers of the church of Antioch "were worshiping the Lord and fasting, the Holy Spirit said, 'Set apart for me Barnabas and Saul for the work to which I have called them.' Then after fasting and praying they laid their hands on them and sent them off" (Acts 13:2–3). This guidance through the Spirit resulted in the first of several missionary journeys and the planting of scores of churches.

2. The Jerusalem council (Acts 15), held at the church of Jerusalem with representatives from several other churches, deliberated about the requirements for Gentiles to embrace salvation in Jesus Christ. Pivotal in the decision of the Council to "not trouble those of the Gentiles who

---

[13] Gregg R. Allison, *Sojourners and Strangers: The Doctrine of the Church* (Wheaton, IL: Crossway, 2012), 138–39. The concluding citation is from Richard S. Briggs, *Words in Action: Speech-Act Theory and Biblical Interpretation: Hermeneutic of Self-Involvement* (Edinburgh: T & T Clark, 2001), 214–15.

[14] Allison, *Baker Compact Dictionary*, s.v. "worship."

[15] Ibid. See also Allison, *Sojourners and Strangers*, 424–33.

turn to God" (Acts 15:19) by requiring circumcision and obedience to the law of Moses, were "the words of the prophets," specifically those of Amos (Acts 15:15–18; the citation is from Amos 9:11–12). God guided his people through his Word.

Accordingly, the church engages in this discipline by intentionally, fervently, and expectantly seeking God's guidance. Concrete acts in this discipline include (1) meditating on Scripture that particularly addresses the matters for which the church is seeking guidance; (2) being filled with the Spirit (Eph. 5:18–21) and sensing his leading; (3) fasting for the purpose of intensely seeking the will of God; (4) asking for and receiving divine wisdom (James 1:5); and (5) inviting leaders and members alike to answer the question, "What is the mind of the Lord for our church?"

Celebration is the festivity associated with worship and community life. In regards to the first association, worship can be defined as "the celebration of being in covenant fellowship with the sovereign and holy triune God."[16] For some, the word *celebration* conjures up visions of debauched partying and worldly reveling. "The word itself does not necessarily carry a sense of emotionalism; indeed, some types of celebrations may be somber expressions of rejoicing and thanksgiving."[17] The grounds of the church's celebratory worship include the divine election of its members, the accomplishment of salvation by Jesus Christ, the communication of the gospel, the application of salvation through the Word and Spirit, and the glorious future to which the church is called in the consummation.

As for the second association, "Specific celebrations that build community life and foster discipleship should be a regular part of the church's rhythm." For example, "the church celebrates births, marriages, and important career milestones"; the latter includes "national holidays, school graduations, promotions at work, retirements, significant social/political/military/educational achievements, and the like."[18] Member/congregational meetings seem particularly appropriate for such community celebrations.

In conclusion, following Richard Foster's three categories, I have explored twelve spiritual disciplines: (1) the *inward disciplines* of meditation, prayer, fasting, and study; (2) the *outward disciplines* of simplicity,

---

[16] Allen P. Ross, *Recalling the Hope of Glory: Biblical Worship from the Garden to the New Creation* (Grand Rapids, MI: Kregel, 2006), 67–68.

[17] Allison, *Sojourners and Strangers*, 426.

[18] Ibid., 444–45. The church's celebration of these milestones must be circumspect, taking into consideration the diversity of views among its members. For example, non-Americans in a church celebrating American national holidays feel excluded by those celebrations.

solitude, submission, and service; and (3) the *corporate disciplines* of confession, worship, guidance, and celebration.

Embodied Disciplines

Leaving spiritual disciplines with which we are most familiar, I turn now to embodied disciplines. These corporeal habits focus on physical training so as to be in proper shape, cultivate good health, stave off many illnesses associated with poor physical care, be responsive to God's will and be able to carry it out, and more. Elements of this training include regular exercise, good nutrition, proper rest and sleep, and avoidance of abuse of our body.

Regular Exercise[19]

Anyone living in our contemporary American society is aware of the importance of regular exercise.[20] From home exercise equipment to local fitness gyms to yoga, we are offered a myriad of choices for keeping in shape physically. One element of embodied discipline for Christians is regular exercise.

As Christians our motivation to exercise comes not from the cultural idols of thinness, looking good, feeling good, or feeling attractive. Rather the goal of our regular exercise is fitness, which can be defined in two ways: (1) our body's ability to utilize and facilitate the uptake of oxygen into our circulatory system; and (2) the absence of disease. Exercise promotes the proper functioning of our cardio-respiratory system and strengthens our muscular system. Benefits of exercise leading to fitness can be broken down into two general categories: reduction of diseases that lead to death and promotion of good health.

1. All causes of mortality are reduced:

    - the risk of cardiovascular disease mortality in general, and coronary heart diseases in particular, is lowered
    - hypertension is prevented or lowered (inactive people are 35–52 percent at greater risk for hypertension than those who exercise regularly; exercise reduces blood pressure)

---

[19] The following discussion incorporates material taught in my theology of human embodiment classes over many years by exercise physiologists Rebecca Adams, Renee Stubbs, Janet Spear, Roberto Pelayo, and Lainey Greer.

[20] Ken Hutchins defines exercise as the following: "Exercise is a process whereby the body performs work of a demanding nature, in accordance with muscle and joint function, in a clinically-controlled environment, within the constructs of safety, meaningfully loading the muscular structures to inroad their strength levels to stimulate a growth mechanism within minimum time." Ken Hutchins, "The First Definition of Exercise," http://www.ren-ex.com/the-first-definition-of-exercise/.

- the risk of disease associated with cholesterol is lowered (exercise increases the "good" cholesterol [HDL] and reduces the "bad" cholesterol [LDL])
- the risk of non-insulin-dependent diabetes mellitus is lowered (exercise eases blood sugar regulation)
- the risk of cancer is lowered (demonstrated for colon cancer; potentially applicable to breast and prostate cancers)
- the symptoms of depression and anxiety are relieved (fitness can contribute to improved mood)

2. Health is increased:

- muscle strength and endurance is increased
- bone strength is increased
- the metabolic, endocrine, and immune systems are benefitted
- one's overall good sense of health is raised

These many benefits are not reserved for athletes or exercise fanatics, but accrue to most who engage in regular exercise.

As embodied human beings and bearers of the renewed image of God, Christians should aim at fitness through the physical discipline of regular exercise. Most exercise physiologists suggest some type of thirty-minute workout at least five days a week. People who have not exercised regularly for a long time should begin slowly and increase their workout gradually. Those who do currently engage in exercise may increase the intensity and/or duration of their workout for greater health benefit. In either case, they should consult with their doctor before embarking on or increasing physical training.[21]

Good Nutrition[22]

When Americans hear the expression "good nutrition," we often think of the food pyramid or its latest permutation, the pyramid plus. This pyramid-shaped guide illustrates how much food from five major food groups we should eat each day. Starting from the bottom and working to the top, the pyramid directs us to consume six to eleven servings of breads and cereals, three to five servings of vegetables, two to four servings of fruits, two to three servings of milk and milk products, and two to three servings of meat and meat alternatives.

---

[21] For further discussion, see "Physical Activity and Health: A Report of the Surgeon General," 1994, https://www.cdc.gov/nccdphp/sgr/.

[22] The following discussion incorporates material taught in my theology of human embodiment classes over many years by nutritionists Marsha Hilgeford, Julianna Crider, and Lainey Greer.

Alternatively, given that most Americans don't follow the "pyramid plus" but eat unhealthily, we often associate good nutrition with dieting. Far more often than not, dieting consists of good intentions to lose weight, the expenditure of significant amounts of money to go on a crash-diet program, the initial and immediate success of weight loss, hitting a plateau and being frustrated with the lack of ongoing success, binging on junk food, the loss of discipline in eating, and gaining all the initial weight lost and more beyond that. Tragically, weight-loss programs such as Weight Watchers, Jenny Craig, and Nutrisystem are notoriously unsuccessful. But they are big business: the American diet industry earns about twenty billion dollars annually.

Christians even have their own weight-loss programs, with catchy titles such as Overeaters Victorious, the Faithfully Fit Program, the Daniel Plan, and the Maker's Diet. Books offer help as well: *I Prayed Myself Slim*; *Devotions for Dieters*; *The Fat Is in Your Head*; *God's Answer to Fat*; *The Devil Wants Me Fat*; *Slim for Him*; *The Weigh Down Diet*; *The Jesus Diet* (the final "t" is in the shape of a cross); *Taste for Truth*; *The Eden Diet*; and *Bod4God*. We seem to equate good nutrition with dieting. But such is not the case, and dieting can be both a failure and dangerous.

Briefly, nutrition is the act or process of providing or obtaining food and drink for the energy necessary for metabolism, health, growth, and repair. Nutrients come in six classes: carbohydrates, proteins, fats, vitamins, minerals, and water. The proper intake of these nutrients and water constitutes good nutrition. The physical discipline of good nutrition includes the following elements:[23]

1. Eating smaller meals over the course of the day (for example, five small portions every three hours), beginning with breakfast, which should not be skipped

2. Drinking at least eight ounces of water eight times a day, avoiding carbonated beverages like soda/pop and high-sugar fruit juices

3. Consuming complex carbohydrates rather than simple carbohydrates by choosing, for example, whole-grain foods rather than refined grains

4. Eating at home rather than regularly eating out, to avoid the large portions served at restaurants with their large amount of calories

---

[23] This list is adapted from Lainey Greer, "The Christian's Role in the Obesity Epidemic," unpublished ThM thesis, Dallas Theological Seminary.

5. Increasing fiber intake by eating whole-grain foods, nuts, oats, beans, and many vegetables

6. Avoiding foods with hydrogenated oil/trans fat, saturated fat, enriched wheat flour, sugar, and high fructose corn syrup (when these items appear among the first five ingredients in the ingredient list, their quantity is too high and they should not be consumed)

As embodied human beings and bearers of the renewed image of God, Christians should aim at good health through the physical discipline of eating properly. Most nutritionists suggest beginning slowly to adopt new eating patterns. They also underscore that we take weeks if not months to establish good nutrition habits. Slowly reducing caloric intake, occasionally introducing new, more nutritional foodstuffs, and always avoiding frustration when progress seems fleeting or nonexistent, are other good counsels to follow.

Proper Rest and Sleep

A case can be made for, and I will adopt, the position that rest is a creation ordinance.[24] In other words, the normal pattern of our week, consisting of seven twenty-four-hour days, is six days of work and one day of rest. Accordingly, weekly rest is proper and right. It was established as a normative pattern for humanity at the conclusion of the divine work of creation (Gen. 2:1–4). Additional revelation came later, providing details concerning its observance (e.g., old-covenant Sabbath regulations; Ex. 20:1–17; Deut. 5:6–21). The New Testament changes those details while confirming rest as a creation ordinance to be observed by the new-covenant church (e.g., Matt. 12:9–14; Mark 2:27; Acts 20:27; 1 Cor. 16:2).

As a physical discipline, rest may take some or all of the following forms. In terms of what to avoid:

1. Activity that is similar to our usual work (the infamous "busman's holiday")

2. Activity that stimulates worry and anxiety such as making major purchases, paying bills, filling out tax forms, planning our schedule for the coming week, and engaging with people who are likely to provoke anger and frustration

---

[24] See John English Lee, "There Remains a Sabbath Rest for the People of God: A Biblical, Theological, and Historical Defense of Sabbath Rest as a Creation Ordinance," PhD diss., Southern Baptist Theological Seminary, 2018. See also D. A. Carson, ed., *From Sabbath to Lord's Day: A Biblical, Historical, and Theological Investigation* (Grand Rapids, MI: Zondervan, 1982).

3. Activity that we should have completed during our work phase of the week but failed to finish because of hectic pace, laziness, poor planning, procrastination, and the like

4. If our day of rest corresponds with Sunday, avoid filling Sunday afternoons with church committee meetings and other nonessential "religious" activity

In terms of what to do:

1. Spend time with loved ones and enjoy being together

2. Nap, read, listen to music, work out, reflect, take a walk, paint

3. Visit shut-ins, talk with people who are lonely, extend mercy

4. If our day of rest corresponds with Sunday, gather together with other believers for worship

Rest as a discipline requires developing new rhythms, fighting against the idol of workaholism, overcoming the prideful belief that we are indispensable to the accomplishment of God's will in this world, and engaging in rest as an activity (different from our normal work) rather than as stagnation or loafing around. Pastors, who do a significant part of their work on Sundays, need help to take a day off other than Sunday.

In addition to rest, we need proper sleep. Apparently, Americans wrestle with getting enough sleep and getting peaceful sleep. Statistics show that tens of millions suffer from scores of sleep disorders and spend billions of dollars on sleeping pills and other sleeping aids. While there are many causes of insomnia or fitful sleep, one reason for Christians is our erroneous sense that God's kingdom may not come, and his will may not be done, unless we forgo sleep and do more than what is normal.

Importantly, God created Eve out of Adam's side (Gen. 2:21) and unilaterally established his covenant with Abraham (Gen. 15:12) while the two men were sleeping. God communicated dreams and visions to people while they were sleeping (e.g., Gen. 20:3). He instructs his people, "It is in vain that you rise up early / and go late to rest, / eating the bread of anxious toil; / for he gives to his beloved sleep" (Ps. 127:2). If God is the giver of sleep, and he remains sovereign and accomplishes all of his good will while his people are asleep, we can surely discipline ourselves to sleep properly.

The physical discipline of sleep includes the following elements:

1. Avoid eating and drinking (especially things that contain caffeine and nicotine) for several hours before going to bed

2. Try to go to sleep about the same time each day

3. Take a hot bath or shower before going to bed

4. Avoid exercising, watching television, and engaging in emotionally charged issues for several hours before bedtime

5. Avoid high-intensity elements such as lights, noise, temperature changes, and more

Avoidance of Abuse of Our Body

The first three elements of physical discipline are largely positive in their orientation: exercising regularly, eating and drinking rightly for good nutrition, and resting and sleeping properly. The fourth element, on which I will spend a significant amount of time, is largely negative in its orientation: wrestling with or overcoming three sins of the body: lust, gluttony, and sloth.[25] Traditionally, these three sins are included in the list of seven deadly sins: pride, covetousness, gluttony, lust, sloth, envy, and anger.[26]

The Sexual Body and Overcoming Lust

The first of our deadly sins against the body is lust. Before addressing that problem, however, it behooves us to set our discussion in the broader context of a biblical theology of the sexual body.

God created human beings as male and female and told them to "be fruitful and multiply and fill the earth" (Gen. 1:28). This universal command means that the majority of human beings will be married. Sexual intercourse is to be enjoyed within the bounds of this covenant and is designed for several purposes, including pleasure, procreation, and unity.

Tragically, the fall into sin has wrought havoc with sexuality, but Scrip-

---

[25] Some of the following is adapted from Gregg R. Allison, "Toward a Theology of Human Embodiment," *SBJT* 13 (Summer 2009): 4–17, used with permission; also Gregg R. Allison, "Am I Lustful, Gluttonous, or Slothful?," christianitytoday.com, March 29, 2011, http://www.christianitytoday.com/biblestudies/articles/spiritual formation/lustfulgluttonousslothful.html.

[26] John Cassian developed a list of eight *principal* sins; as principal sins, they lead to all other sins. John Cassian, *Third Conference of Abbot Theonas*, 11, 16, in *A Select Library of Nicene and Post-Nicene Fathers of the Christian Church*, 2nd series, ed. Philip Schaff and Henry Wace, vol. 11, *Sulpitius Severus, Vincent of Lerins, John Cassian* (repr. Grand Rapids, MI: Eerdmans, 1983), 525. Thomas Aquinas enumerated seven *capital* sins, from the Latin *caput*, or head; as capital sins, they direct to other sins. Thomas Aquinas, *Summa Theologica*, pt. 1, pt. 2, q. 84.

ture helps us overcome temptation and failure in this area. For example, Paul denounces sexual immorality (1 Cor. 6:12–20), placing it into a category by itself when he writes that "every other sin a person commits is outside the body, but the sexually immoral person sins against his own body" (6:18). This heinous sin wrenches away one's body, which "is not meant for sexual immorality, but for the Lord, and the Lord for the body" (6:13), from its rightful membership with Christ and, if married, with one's spouse, and unites it with the body of someone other than one's spouse. The result is that "the two will become one flesh" (6:16), which is a tragic disorientation of the body. In no uncertain terms, Paul warns against sexual immorality, reminding Christians "that [their] body is a temple of the Holy Spirit" and urging them to "glorify God in your body" (6:19–20).

The apostle echoes this alert in 1 Thessalonians 4:3–8, urging married people to engage in sexual activity in a God-honoring and spouse-respecting manner (4:4–5). Tragically, Christian men were committing adultery with the wives of other Christians, so Paul also warns the church "that no one transgress and wrong his brother in this matter" (4:6). The close relationships that church members enjoy with one another should never be allowed to cross these lines of morality.

The apostle also issues instructions (1 Cor. 7:1–9) to ascetically minded Christians, telling them they cannot pursue holiness before God by refusing to engage in sexual intercourse if they are married. Paul concedes—not commands (7:6)—that regular sexual activity may be interrupted for a time if the two mutually agree, if there is a good purpose, and if they reengage after the period is complete. This abstinence, however, does not make them more holy but can instead lead to disastrous results if not treated properly (7:5).

In this discussion of marriage, Paul also addresses singleness (7:7–9). This state, like that of marriage, is a gift of God. Paul's preference is that "the unmarried and the widows . . . remain single," as he is, for celibacy offers many advantages, including avoidance of worldly troubles, freedom from anxieties, and undivided devotion to the Lord (1 Cor. 7:25–40). The advantages of singleness are many, yet only those to whom this gift is given should remain single. Those with the gift of celibacy are not asexual beings lacking sexual desire, but they are able to control those urges by channeling them in God-honoring ways. Lacking such self-control, people should pursue getting married so they are not overwhelmed by sexual desire and thus fall into immorality.

We are all aware of the many troubles Christians encounter in this area: rampant immorality, adultery, homosexuality, sexual abuse of children and women, "sexting," pornography, "friends with benefits," and other problems. Lust, with its many expressions, is a deadly sin. Cognizant of these many challenges, we should never lose sight of the fact that sexual intercourse between married couples is a gift from God that should be celebrated and enjoyed. And the specter of pitfalls in this area should never be allowed to chill the commands to love one another (e.g., John 13:34) and to relate to one another as family (e.g., 1 Tim. 5:1–2).

Having addressed the broader context of a biblical theology of the sexual body, we turn now to lust, the deadly sin of strong desire that contradicts and wages war against our sexual body. What can we do to avoid lust, to express God-given sexual desires in God-honoring ways, and to overcome the rampant, tragic sins in this area?

1. Develop a vision of Jesus and his many saving benefits that so enthralls us that lustful enticements fade in comparison.

2. Engage in sexual activity in an appropriate manner (pleasures enjoyed by husband and wife have the mutual consent of both and are not considered shameful or entered into unwillingly by either one).

3. Teach adolescents about the wonders of sexual desire and intercourse while explaining the biblically prescribed boundaries not as killjoys but as protections and preparations for sexual flourishing.

4. Make use of accountability structures such as close friends who help us with our struggles in this area, Internet accountability programs such as Covenant Eyes, restrictions on television shows, movies, pictures, and more.

5. Encourage repentance and confession when sexual failures occur.

6. Act graciously and ruthlessly to rescue those who have fallen into persistent sexual sin (counseling, redemption groups dealing with sexual addictions, and the like).

7. Practice church discipline for sexual sins for which there is no repentance.

Though a deadly sin, lust can be overcome.

The Properly Nourished Body and Overcoming Gluttony

This second sin of the body is closely connected to the above discussion of good nutrition: life in the body demands physical discipline and wrestling to overcome the deadly sin of gluttony. But what is this sin, and what Scripture supports its being considered as such a serious failure?

"Gluttony is the immoderate consumption of food arising from the unchecked appetite for something more than, or other than, what the Lord has provided and is therefore judged a sin by God."[27] Gluttony is often associated with drunkenness: "Be not among drunkards / or among gluttonous eaters of meat, / for the drunkard and the glutton will come to poverty, / and slumber will clothe them with rags" (Prov. 23:20–21). So drunkenness is to the overconsumption of alcohol as gluttony is to the overconsumption of food.

Biblical portrayals of gluttonous people help us to understand various aspects of this sin. Esau (Gen. 25:29–34, with Heb. 12:16–17) came in from the field and saw his brother Jacob cooking stew. Esau claimed to be exhausted, famished to the point of exaggeration: "I am about to die." Accordingly, he demanded to devour the red stew being prepared by his brother (colloquially, he insisted that Jacob let him stuff his mouth with that red stuff). Esau's profane appetite was so out of control that it resulted in his engaging in a stupid, even immoral, act: the selling of his birthright. Being a slave to his appetite and to the moment, he forfeited his birthright and lost the opportunity to play a crucial role in Israel's election. Gluttony so consumed him that he could not even repent of the evil he had committed.

The sons of Eli (1 Sam. 2:12–17), characterized as "worthless men . . . [who] did not know the LORD," further illustrate the sin of gluttony. The custom in Israel was that when a person brought an animal to a priest for an offering, the priest's servant would take some of the meat while it was boiling and reserve it for the priest. By this means, the priests were well provided for in terms of nourishment. Eli's sons, however, were not content with this provision. They demanded raw, not boiled, meat, because they preferred to roast it. If their immediate demand was refused, they threatened violence: "No, you must give it now, and if not, I will take it by force." Their insistence on raw meat for roasting rather than boiled meat underscores an important aspect of gluttony: the unchecked appetite for something more than, or other than, what the Lord has provided.

As the people of Israel journeyed through the wilderness (Num. 11:4–10, with Ps. 78:18), the conspicuous lack of food prompted them to complain and crave. Their complaint focused on the abundance and diversity

---

[27] Jeff Olson, ThM thesis, Western Seminary, Portland, Oregon.

of food they had enjoyed in Egypt, a lavishness and variety they currently lacked in the wilderness. Consequently, they pined for "the good old days" when they had fish, cucumbers, melons, leeks, onions, and garlic in Egypt, despite the fact that they had been slaves in that land. Their craving focused on their rejection of God's good provision for their nourishment—manna— and their wish for another type of provision: "Oh that we had meat to eat!" (Num. 11:4). Their intemperate appetite, an aspect of gluttony, led to them lusting for something more than, or other than, what the Lord had pro- vided. Rejecting God's provision, which was designed to develop their daily trust in him, they sought to be satisfied by something—really, someone— other than God. Gluttony led the people to put God to the test and to speak against him, prompting God's furious anger to blaze against them.

Gluttony is a deadly sin.

Biblical passages and illustrations emphasize that gluttony consists of several interrelated elements. At the heart of gluttony is an unchecked appetite, the absence or loss of self-control. Moderation in one's appetite for food is lost; then it becomes a matter of eating to excess. As Frederica Mathewes-Green explains, "Gluttony is not wrong because it makes you fat; it's wrong because it is the fruit of self-indulgence."[28] Manifestations of gluttony as the fruit of intemperance include finicky eating (e.g., de- manding that food be cooked in a certain way and served piping hot), restricting one's eating to sumptuous foods (e.g., steak, lobster, caviar, and other costly food), speedy eating (e.g., gulping down food without enjoy- ing its taste and without consideration for the pace of others who are also eating), and being obsessed with food (e.g., planning one's day so that it revolves around meals and snacks).[29]

Gluttony is a serious problem for believers. It is not only evidenced by excessive weight; indeed, one may be pencil thin and yet gluttonous. Chris- tians who cannot pass a fast-food place without pulling into the drive-thru and ordering a burger and fries, even though their nutritional needs are more than satisfied, commit the sin of gluttony. While we may boast about the im-

---

[28] Frederica Mathewes-Green, "To Hell on a Cream Puff," *Christianity Today* (November 13, 1995), 45. Avail- able at http://frederica.com/writings/to-hell-on-a-cream-puff.html.

[29] According to Thomas Aquinas, "gluttony denotes inordinate concupiscence in eating. Now two things are to be considered in eating, namely the food we eat, and the eating thereof. Accordingly, the inordinate con- cupiscence may be considered in two ways. First, with regard to the food consumed: and thus, as regards the substance or species of food a man seeks 'sumptuous'—i.e., costly food; as regards its quality, he seeks food prepared too nicely—i.e., 'daintily;' and as regards quantity, he exceeds by eating 'too much.' Secondly, the inordinate concupiscence is considered as to the consumption of food: either because one forestalls the proper time for eating, which is to eat 'hastily,' or one fails to observe the due manner of eating, by eating 'greedily.'" Thomas Aquinas, *Summa Theologica*, pt. 2, q. 148, art. 4. As William Backus described it, gluttony is eating "too soon, too expensively, too much, too eagerly, or with too much finicky fussing about your food." *What Your Counselor Never Told You* (Minneapolis: Bethany, 2000), 191.

mense quantities of greasy food at church potlucks and joke about deacon Bob serving up his third heaping plate of it, gluttony is not a laughing matter.

What can we do to avoid gluttony, to express our God-given appetite in God-honoring ways, and to overcome the rampant, tragic sins in this area?

1. Develop self-control through the power of the Spirit (Gal. 5:22–23), which means that proper eating is not an end in itself, but a means to flourish for the sake of the Lord and his purposes in this world (and not, as is so commonly the case, to conform to the cultural idol of thinness).

2. Eat at meal times and avoid snacking when one's appetite rages for satisfaction.

3. Eat with moderation, not hastily or impatiently, with the goal of providing the necessary nourishment for one's physical wellness.

4. Be aware of factors that can contribute to gluttony (e.g., a chemical imbalance that leads to craving food, a genetic propensity toward obesity, poor parental or family guidance in the area of nutrition, and compulsive eating triggered by forces beyond one's knowledge or control) and, while not using them as excuses, take special precaution so as not to fall prey to them.

5. Be thankful for God's provision (1 Tim. 4:4–5), with keen awareness of the unsatisfied nutritional needs of others throughout the world (Gal. 2:10).[30]

6. Seek help from, and be accountable to, others when gluttony is beyond our ability to control.

Though a deadly sin, gluttony can be overcome.

The Productive Body and Overcoming Sloth

This third sin of the body is sloth. Before addressing that problem, however, it behooves us to set our discussion in the broader context of a biblical theology of the productive body.

Created in the divine image, all human beings have been charged with and equipped to carry out the mandate to exercise dominion over the rest of the created order (Gen. 1:28). The initial fulfillment of this divine

---

[30] John Milton associated gluttony with thanklessness (*Comus*, line 776): "Swinish gluttony Ne'er looks to heav'n amidst his gorgeous feast, But with besotted base ingratitude Crams, and blasphemes his feeder."

mandate is narrated in Genesis 4: Abel tended sheep and Cain worked the ground (4:2), Enoch built a city (4:17), Jabal attended to livestock, Jubal played musical instruments, and Tubal-cain forged bronze and iron tools (4:2, 17–22). To contemporize this point, we build civilization by employing our God-given abilities and skills to work in areas such as education, medicine, construction, government, farming, business, and the arts to promote human flourishing.

With this as the divine design for human beings, failure to engage in work is the third deadly sin—sloth. But what is this sin, and what Scripture supports its being considered such a serious failure?

Sloth is psychological indifference and physical weariness toward the work that God has provided for one to accomplish.[31] It may involve and be masked by frantic yet misdirected activity. It is a conscious neglect of doing what is humanly possible and required. One possesses the requisite (mental, emotional, physical) abilities, educational degree(s), technical skill(s), and the like, as well as a job or opportunity for it, but the slothful person does not engage properly in the work. Mentally, sloth is characterized by affectlessness, the lack of any feeling about self, others, and God that gives rise to boredom, apathy, and inertia. Occasionally, sloth is due to Christians so emphasizing God's providential care for them and his promise to meet all their needs that they neglect the important element of their human responsibility to use their God-given abilities to engage in vocation for civilization building.

Such sloth results in the lack of resources for living: "How long will you lie there, O sluggard? / When will you arise from your sleep? / A little sleep, a little slumber, a little folding of the hands to rest, / and poverty will come upon you like a robber, / and want like an armed man" (Prov. 6:9–11; cf. 13:4; 20:4). The slothful person refuses to work, even inventing the most absurd excuses for not doing so, and ends up finding every endeavor wearisome while considering himself wise: "The sluggard says, 'There is a lion in the road! / There is a lion in the streets!' / As a door turns on its hinges, / so does a sluggard on his bed. / The sluggard buries his hand in the dish; / it wears him out to bring it back to his mouth. / The sluggard is wiser in his own eyes / than seven men who can can answer sensibly" (Prov. 26:13–16). Contrast this portrait of the sluggard with the description of the diligent wife of Proverbs 31: Her husband has no lack of

---

[31] Adapted from Solomon Schimmel, *The Seven Deadly Sins: Jewish, Christian, and Classical Reflections on Human Psychology* (Oxford, UK: Oxford University Press, 1997), 193.

gain (31:11) because she works with willing hands (31:13). She rises early while it is yet night and works hard (31:15–19), avoiding idleness (31:27).

Sloth is a serious problem for believers. Paul denounced idleness for Christians: "If anyone is not willing to work, let him not eat. For we hear that some among you walk in idleness, not busy at work, but busybodies. Now such persons we command and encourage in the Lord Jesus Christ to do their work quietly and to earn their own living" (2 Thess. 3:10–12). Furthermore, Christians are expected both to provide for their families and to give sacrificially to the church and to the poor (e.g., 2 Corinthians 8–9); failure to do so means that one "has denied the faith and is worse than an unbeliever" (1 Tim. 5:8). Sloth is a deadly sin.

What can we do to avoid sloth, to express our God-given gifts and abilities in God-honoring ways, and to overcome the rampant, tragic sins in this area?

1. Acknowledge God's explicit will for human beings to work to build civilization as the divine purpose for humanity.

2. Affirm that God has equipped us to do some kind of work ("God has provided the requisite abilities for me to engage in work").

3. If our slothfulness is particularly tied to poor personal management skills, work in a field that is highly structured so that our schedule is established by someone else and not left up to us.

4. Identify the source of our psychological indifference toward work (e.g., poor example of slothful parent[s], belittling criticism that makes us feel incapable of achievement) and seek the help of others to overcome it.

5. Ensure that our physical weariness is not due to some correctable medical problem or lack of proper nutrition, exercise, and/or rest.

6. Seek personal accountability from a trusted friend(s).

7. Embrace the joy of obeying God through working hard so as to be able to provide for our own needs, the needs of our family, and the needs of our church and the poor.

Though a deadly sin, sloth can be overcome.

In conclusion, I have explored a number of embodied disciplines. These corporeal habits focus on physical training and include regular exercise, good nutrition, proper rest and sleep, and avoidance of abuse of our body in terms of lust, gluttony, and sloth.

Conclusion: Undivided in Discipline

As holistically created, embodied human beings and image bearers of God, we are called to engage in spiritual and embodied disciplines for the promotion of spirituality. This chapter has presented both kinds of disciplines, providing guidance in most cases how to engage in them. Importantly, though we can divide these disciplines into these two discreet categories, we engage in them not as divided people, with our immaterial aspect—our soul or spirit—meditating, praying, submitting, serving, worshiping, and celebrating, and our material aspect—our body—eating, exercising, resting, avoiding lust, overcoming gluttony, and battling sloth. We are not compartmentalized people, and we cannot easily compartmentalize our disciplines according to the headings "spiritual" and "physical."

Let us pursue both spiritual and embodied disciplines for progress in spirituality.

10

SPIRITUALITY AND OUR WORK

GREGORY C. COCHRAN

According to the *Organisation for Economic Co-Operation and Development* (OECD), the average worker in the United States is actively on her job for 38.6 hours each week. This number is slightly higher than the OECD average worldwide (36.8 hours per week). Given that there are 168 hours in a week—about forty-nine of which are spent sleeping—most Americans spend roughly one-third of their waking hours at work. In contrast, Christians who regularly attend worship services invest little time in formal worship. Even the most committed Christians spend fifteen times longer at work each week than in formal worship. What kind of pressure does this dynamic force on people of faith? Time is undeniably on the side of the workplace. Money is produced by the workplace. The sacred commodities of time and money are anchored outside of the gathered church, and Christians often struggle to integrate work and worship.

The Struggle for Spirituality at Work

The struggle to make sense of work and worship is serious. John Knapp, a researcher and theologian who helps Christians understand their daily work in relation to faith, interviewed hundreds of Roman Catholic and Protestant Christians across the country. He found that

> an overwhelming majority reported that the church had done little or nothing to equip them for faithful living at work. They mostly perceived the church and its clergy as preoccupied with the private sphere of life . . . and disinterested in the spiritual and ethical stresses of weekday work.[1]

---

[1] John C. Knapp, *How the Church Fails Businesspeople (And What Can Be Done about It)* (Grand Rapids, MI: Eerdmans, 2012), *xii.*

Knapp's concern is that Christians have responded to the tension between work and worship by adopting a "privatized" faith—faith that belongs to the personal sphere but does not connect well to the workplace. Knapp asserts that the privatization of faith has proved disastrous because it has ceded significant aspects of life to non-Christian (or even anti-Christian) authorities: "The moral terrain of our work lives is mostly defined by law and economics rather than theology, leaving us with an uninspired ethical pragmatism lacking in wisdom and heart."[2]

Christians are being pushed into accepting a divide between public interactions at work and the private exercise of faith for an hour on Sunday. Through many different forces at work in the world, Christians are expected to keep their Christianity secluded. As a result, a serious problem erupts as believers are tempted to suppress their identities on every day but Sunday. Greg Forster of the Oikonomia Network laments this problem, noting, "In America today, millions of churchgoers are 'Christians' for only a few hours a week. For them, Christianity is a leisure-time activity rather than a way of life."[3]

Other Christians have simply chosen to embrace this privatized faith. Ray Kroc, who made McDonald's a household name, famously remarked, "My priorities are God first, family second, and McDonald's hamburgers third. And when I go to work on Monday morning, that order reverses."[4]

The driving force behind this divorcing of public and private lives is dualism. Within Christianity—and particularly in conversations about Christians at work—dualism imposes categories such as the "spiritual" life versus the "secular" life. Paul Helm explains this dualism in his helpful book *The Callings*:

> Christians have become accustomed to think of themselves as having a "spiritual life" which is sharply distinct from the every-day life in the family, and from work and leisure. A "spiritual life" is a life of prayer and watchfulness, of Bible-reading and church-going. As a result of this distortion, instead of the Christian life being thought of as an integrated

---

[2] Ibid.

[3] Greg Forster, *Theology That Works: Making Disciples Who Practice Fruitful Work and Economic Wisdom in Modern America*, Oikonomia Network (2013), http://oikonomianetwork.org/wp-content/uploads/2014/02/Theology-that-Works-v2-FINAL.pdf.

[4] As quoted in Scott B. Rae, *Moral Choices: An Introduction to Ethics* (Grand Rapids, MI: Zondervan, 2009), 343. See also Margaret J. King, "Empires of Popular Culture: McDonald's and Disney," *Journal of American Culture* 1 (June 7, 2004): 424–37.

whole, it is [artificially] broken up into compartments which have little or nothing to do with one another. The "vertical" dimension of a person's life with God seems unrelated and unrelatable to the "horizontal" dimension of his life on planet Earth.[5]

The Spirituality of Work in Church History

The problem of dualistic thinking is current but not new. To some in church history, for example, the "spiritual life" was the monastic ideal, a life of quiet contemplation, daily work, and withdrawal from society. Reformers such as Martin Luther and John Calvin pushed back against such ideas, offering valuable counsel on work that can help us live a single, undivided life of faith. According to these Reformers, Christians are called by God to a unified life. Whatever our office or station in life, we are to serve God and one another in that work. Luther and Calvin stress that God blesses us with work so that we might bless others through it. Michael Horton summarizes the Reformation concept of vocation: "Every Lord's day is like a gathering of children in the living room on Christmas morning to receive and exchange gifts. From this ministry a host of spiritual gifts arise that circulate among all the members, who then love and serve neighbors in the world through ordinary vocations."[6] Horton also shows how this Reformation approach to work flows from its view of salvation linked to true piety:

> Biblical piety, according to Calvin, directs our faith toward God and our love toward our neighbor. The Christian life is therefore extrospective: that is, looking outside ourselves. . . . The striving for an inner sanctity that will withstand God's judgment keeps you focused on yourself, ignoring both Christ and others. No one is helped by this sort of piety. It is a fool's errand that incurs God's wrath, avoids our neighbor, and, as it turns out, doesn't even help us.
>
> Like that of other magisterial Reformers, Calvin's piety is marked by two emphases: (1) All good gifts come down to us from God; before God, we are only receivers (Acts 17:25–26; Rom. 11:35–36; James 1:17); (2) Not only does God love and serve us, but also through us he loves and serves our neighbors by means of our callings; before others, we are givers. So we bring only faith to God and good works to our neighbors. Our callings—as children, spouses, parents, volunteers, employers, and employees—are the channels through which these good works flow

---

[5] Paul Helm, *The Callings: The Gospel in the World* (Carlisle, PA: Banner of Truth, 1987), x.

[6] Michael Horton, *Calvin on the Christian Life: Glorifying and Enjoying God Forever*, Theologians on the Christian Life (Wheaton, IL: Crossway, 2014), 228. I am indebted to Chris Morgan for pointing to this section of Horton's research.

from God to others. And we're engaged simultaneously in many different vocations. So it's more of a gift ethic than a work ethic.[7]

Horton points out that although Luther and Calvin had a high view
of ministry, they did not hold a dualistic view. In God's design, the calling is not the holy thing. The *people* of God are holy. Thus, Horton
concludes:

> *We* are holy—set apart—even if the *callings* themselves are common.
> There is no such thing as Christian farming, holy medicine, or kingdom
> art, even though believers engaged in these callings alongside unbeliev-
> ers are holy citizens of his kingdom. The service that a janitor, home-
> maker, doctor, or business person provides is part of God's providential
> care of his creatures. It requires no further justification.[8]

Horton captures Luther's concept of calling. Technically, Luther used
the language of *office* (not *calling*) to convey the notion that Christians
have a vocation in the world. Luther's concern was ultimately not vocation per se but the gospel itself. His burden was nothing less than the
health of the gospel and the good of the church. Thus, when he spoke
against the kind of dualism proffered by the pope and his bishops, Luther
was hoping to free the church from erroneous thinking. In 1520, Luther
wrote his *Open Letter to the Christian Nobility of the German Nation
Concerning the Reform of the Christian Estate*. In this letter, Luther argued
against three "walls" the pope had constructed to prevent meaningful critique. The first wall Luther thought needed to go was the wall between
the temporal and the spiritual (which, of course, is similar to what today
is called the secular and the spiritual). Luther did not think much of such
a dividing of reality:

> It is a pure invention that pope, bishops, priests, and monks are to be
> called the "spiritual estate"; princes, lords, artisans, and farmers the
> "temporal estate." That is indeed a fine bit of lying and hypocrisy. Yet no
> one should be frightened by it; and for this reason—viz., that all Chris-
> tians are truly of the "spiritual estate," and there is among them no differ-
> ence at all but that of office, as Paul says in 1 Corinthians 12:12.[9]

---

[7] Ibid., 228.
[8] Ibid., emphasis original.
[9] Martin Luther, *Open Letter to the Christian Nobility of the German Nation Concerning the Reform of the
Christian Estate*, https://web.stanford.edu/~jsabol/certainty/readings/Luther-ChristianNobility.pdf. For a
thorough consideration of Luther's concept of office in relation to vocation, see Karlfried Froehlich, "Luther
on Vocation," *LQ* 13 (1999): 195–207.

Like Luther, Calvin expected Christians to live an integrated spiritual life, whether at work or at leisure. In some ways, Calvin's concerns were more concrete than Luther's. Luther was taking aim at the papacy and ecclesiastical powers, while Calvin was working with a particular church in Geneva to put into practice what the Scriptures teach. In 1562 Calvin produced a practical prayer for Christians to use each day before engaging in their labors. This popular prayer was often included in later editions of the Geneva Bible. Commenting on this prayer, David Hall and Matthew Burton note:

> Calvin prayed that workers would care for the indigent and that the prosperous would not become conceited. He prayed that God would diminish prosperity if he knew the people needed a dose of poverty to return them to their senses. Far from callousness toward the less fortunate, Calvin prayed that workers would "not fall into mistrust," would "wait patiently" on God to provide, and would rest with entire assurance in [God's] pure goodness.[10]

Thus the Reformers understood that work is a gift of God that meets the needs of others and blesses us too. Not to be divided into sacred and secular, our work is a means by which God blesses us and our neighbors through us. And others' work is a means by which God blesses them and us through them.

The Spirituality of Work in Jesus

Jesus himself especially clarifies and personifies the value of all work. Consider one of Jesus' remarkable encounters in his hometown (Matt. 13:53–58). In this episode, Jesus returns home after having taught many parables and performed many miracles, the kind of work many today call "spiritual." But the residents of Nazareth do not think much of Jesus or his miracles. They are actually offended by him because "Jesus received no rabbinic training, and it was inconceivable that a mere commoner could say and do such things."[11] In other words, Jesus—God incarnate—did not seem spiritual enough!

For more than two decades, Jesus lived among the citizens of Nazareth and worked with his hands in such a way that he was considered as nothing more than a worker. As Grant Osborne explains, "The people of

---

[10] David Hall and Matthew Burton, *Calvin and Commerce: The Transforming Power of Calvinism in Market Economics*, Calvin 500 Series (Phillipsburg, NJ: P&R, 2009), 28.
[11] Grant Osborne, *Matthew*, ZECNT (Grand Rapids, MI: Zondervan, 2010), 550.

Nazareth know Jesus' family and his occupation and cannot accept that he is now the great rabbi . . . and miracle worker all Galilee is talking about. That goes against over thirty years of watching him in a very small town."[12] One of the most noticeable aspects of the life of Jesus is how remarkably unworthy of notice most of it was. Jesus—the most spiritual man who ever lived—was known first and most often as a carpenter: "Jesus was never known as a miracle worker but first as the son of the carpenter Joseph and later, after Joseph died, as the village carpenter."[13] The life of Jesus allowed no secular/spiritual divide.

Jesus was a daily worker and set an example for his followers to see all work as significant:

> The view that all work is honorable set the early Christians apart not only in their rejecting the Greco-Roman attitude that despised manual work but also because they prospered economically as a result of their strong work ethic. Their prosperity was sometimes an additional reason that the Romans saw them as undesirable people, resulting in their persecution.[14]

Like Jesus, most Christians work with their hands day after day, building houses, repairing cars, performing surgeries, mowing lawns, cleaning pools, catching fish, writing computer code, planting corn, sending emails, or harvesting grain. The living God who took on flesh came to the earth and lived as the village carpenter:

> Through Jesus' natural involvement in his trade and business, the Incarnation gives divine approval to and redeems human economic culture from all the powers of evil that seek to claim it. Just as the person of Christ as a truly human being redeems our human essence and the essence of creation . . . it also redeems the essence of human work and business in cultural economic form."[15]

Therefore, Christians can and should engage in so-called secular work without any sense of inferiority. Unless we are willing to say that for most of his life Jesus performed meaningless work, we must admit that the Bible dignifies and extols honest labor. Jesus was more than a carpenter, but he was, in fact, a carpenter.

---

[12] Ibid., 551.
[13] Ibid., 550.
[14] Alvin J. Schmidt, *How Christianity Changed the World* (Grand Rapids, MI: Zondervan, 2004), 196.
[15] John Schneider, *The Good of Affluence: Seeking God in a Culture of Wealth* (Grand Rapids, MI: Eerdmans, 2002), 129.

The rest of this chapter falls in two parts. The first synthesizes what has been said thus far, attempting to apply the synthesis practically for Christians at work. The remainder of the chapter presents a broader collection of biblical principles for living an integrated spirituality at work and in all of life.

Synthesis

First, God blesses us with work so that we might bless others through work. All (nonsinful) work is good. No matter how seemingly small is our contribution, the result is God's blessing of others through us. Gene Veith summarizes Luther's theology of vocation and illustrates how God uses our work in his love for others:

> When we pray the Lord's Prayer, observed Luther, we ask God to give us this day our daily bread. And He does give us our daily bread. He does it by means of the farmer who planted and harvested the grain, the baker who made the flour into bread, the person who prepared our meal. We might today add the truck drivers who hauled the produce, the factory workers in the food processing plant. . . . Also playing their part are the bankers, futures investors, advertisers. . . . All of these were instrumental in enabling you to eat your morning bagel.[16]

In the integrated way Veith describes, God is blessing us through each other's work.

Second, as we live out our faith, we may face trials at work. More and more, Christians are under pressure to "privatize" faith. Over the past decade, a push has been underway to redefine religious liberty in this way. The US Department of Justice has argued for two alterations to the historic understanding of religious liberty. In one alteration, this federal agency asked that religious rights be diminished in the "public" marketplace. In other words, people of faith can believe as they wish, but those beliefs must not be practiced in commercial exchanges. This position has led to many lawsuits from florists, bakers, and Christian-owned businesses such as Hobby Lobby. Another alteration to religious liberty was the Department of Justice's insistence that religious liberty ought to extend only to houses of worship—not to individual citizens. The law would protect freedom to worship for ninety minutes on Sunday, but not to express faith and practice it openly at work on Monday.

---

[16] Gene Edward Veith Jr., *God at Work: Your Christian Vocation in All of Life* (Wheaton, IL: Crossway, 2002), 14.

The temptation to segregate faith from work is significant, and we must not only embrace a biblical view of work but also live it out in an increasingly hostile environment.[17]

Third, we should guard against compartmentalizing our faith into the dualistic categories of spiritual and secular. Gordon Fee comments on 1 Corinthians 10:31 and reminds us of how our faith is integrated into all of life: "God is to be blessed because everything is his and thus to his glory. . . . One's whole life must be to God's glory."[18] Indeed, our first calling as a Christian is the call to belong completely to Christ.

Fourth, the call to a vocation—to be a plumber, teacher, electrician, computer programmer, administrative assistant, or CEO—is a secondary call for the Christian. The primary call of the Christian is to be Christian. Again, Paul Helm's *The Callings* is helpful:

> Nowadays, the idea of a calling or vocation, where it is used at all, is limited to special occupations such as nursing or social work. But the biblical view is that any lawful occupation may be a calling and more than this, that the whole of a person's life is a calling from God. God is in it. It has His blessing. It is the product of His providential ruling. And the Christian is to live his life in the belief that God continues to call him to be where he is, to use his gifts to the full.[19]

Callings such as that of the pastor, missionary, or evangelist are also subordinate to the primary call of being a Christian. Some Christians are missionaries; others are radiologists. All are equally Christian and thus equally faithful before God. Moreover, because each person's calling is a whole-life calling, no one should equate his own job with God's ultimate will. God's will for the Christian is greater than any vocation the Christian chooses to pursue. God's will is for us to be set apart daily in holiness and for service to God and others. Or, more accurately, Christians are holy by calling. Paul declares, "This is the will of God, your sanctification" (1 Thess. 4:3). Paul spells out further what sanctification means when he instructs Christians to abstain from sexual immorality, honor the rights of others, love other Christians, seek to live quietly, and mind their own business. So God's will does not lead the Christian to a single vocation; rather, God's will leads the Christian to a singular devotion to Christ. The

---

[17] See Gregory C. Cochran, *Christians in the Crosshairs: Persecution in the Bible and Around the World Today* (Wooster, OH: Weaver, 2016).

[18] Gordon Fee, *The First Epistle to the Corinthians*, NICNT (Grand Rapids, MI: Eerdmans, 1987), 488.

[19] Helm, *The Callings*, xiii.

Christian's vocation—whatever it is—leads to God's will, which is holiness, sanctification, and usefulness for God's redemptive purposes.

Fifth, as Christians we are integrated, unified persons whose faith in Christ is an indispensable part of our identity. The apostle Paul in 1 Corinthians 7 develops a helpful principle that applies here, namely, that to remain in the life station we occupied when we were saved is the default setting for Christians. We are to be Christians wherever we are—twenty-four hours per day, seven days per week. Our primary calling—the calling around which all of our lives ought to be organized—is the calling to belong to Christ. Scott Rae states this biblical truth plainly: "The Bible is very clear that we are to live all our lives under the lordship of Christ, that he is the boss over every aspect of our lives. No part of our lives is to be exempt from his scrutiny and direction. Following Christ is not something that we reserve for the weekend—it is a full-time vocation (Matt. 6:33; 1 Cor. 10:31; Col. 3:17)."[20]

Applying the Spirituality of Work to Our Work

Thus understanding the nature of life and work as an integrated whole, Christians should digest biblical instruction with the aim of growing in godliness through work. How can work build up the believer spiritually? And how can the believer's faith supply nutrients necessary to sustain good work Monday through Saturday? Thinking through Scripture, we see a few basic principles standing out, along with some practical ramifications of these principles.

Principle 1: Honor All Work as Valuable before the Lord

Work is an aspect of God's goodness in creation; it is not a result of the fall. The fall increased the frustration of work (Gen. 3:17–19), but work was instituted before the fall (1:28), and work will continue after Christ's return. Primary among the work that Christians will perform will be the functions of serving and reigning (see Rev. 22:3–5). From Eden to the full redemption of the new heavens and new earth, humans have work to do.

Work, then, is honorable before God. Ethicist Scott Rae suggests there are at least three reasons work is valuable before the Lord. Work is valuable because it was an aspect of God's good creation in Eden before the fall. Work is valuable because it is God's ordained means by which human beings participate in further life-giving, productive work. And

---

[20] Rae, *Moral Choices*, 343.

work is valuable because "God is a worker, and human beings are workers by virtue of being made in God's image."[21] Thus, unless the work involves going against God's will (that is, unless it is sinful), all work is good. God blesses us with work that we might bless others through work.

The principle that all work is honorable before the Lord is a foundational aspect of Tim Keller's book *Every Good Endeavor*. In this work, Keller unfolds a dramatic tale of an artist named Niggle. The name Niggle signifies how the artist spends an inordinate amount of time on every little detail. The tale of Niggle turns out to be autobiographical, written by J. R. R. Tolkien to help him believe again that his own work had value. Niggle (like Tolkien) often found himself bogged down in details or interrupted by others he desired to help. In the story, the artist Niggle works his whole life attempting to paint a tree he had imagined against the backdrop of a perfect forest scene. This scene would be his masterpiece. Each leaf of the tree needed to be perfect. Niggle constructed a very large canvas on which the perfect tree might be stretched out for others to view. Niggle started with a single leaf. And he died before anything else could be completed. After his death, "Niggle was assured that the tree he had 'felt and guessed' was 'a true part of creation' and that even the small bit of it he had unveiled to people on earth had been a vision of the True. Tolkien was very comforted by his own story. It helped 'exorcise some of Tolkien's fear, and to get him to work again.'"[22]

Realizing that work has value beyond our own lifetime is a powerful antidote to despair. Work has value and is a blessing to ourselves and to others. Several practical consequences follow from this first principle:

- We work knowing that our labor is a good gift from God.
- We work because work in itself is good and not just a means to get money.
- We work to serve God and others. We ought to consider how our particular jobs help other people.
- We work realizing that our work and faith in God are interrelated.

Principle 2: Expect God's Blessings on Our Work

If work is a gift from God, and we do it with all our might as unto the Lord, why would we not experience God's blessings? God delights to give good gifts to his children (Matt. 7:11). The Bible is filled with example after example of God's faithful people being rewarded for their steadfast faith

---

[21] Ibid., 335.

[22] Timothy Keller with Katherine Leary Alsdorf, *Every Good Endeavor: Connecting Your Work to God's Work* (New York: Riverhead, 2012), 13.

and daily labor. We can think of Abraham, Isaac, and Jacob. Later, Joseph rose to the highest ranks of the Egyptian government even though he was betrayed by his own family. Boaz in the days of the judges flourished and thus was able to bless others. Daniel, in a time of exile from the Promised Land, was elevated time after time by different pagan kings because of his faithful labor. God blesses his faithful people.

The book of Deuteronomy prepared God's people for the blessing of the Promised Land. God ordered the way for them to live, and his people confidently agreed to obey. Thus God promised every blessing to their faith, including blessings so that their families would multiply and their work would produce good fruit. God forewarned them that curses would follow disobedience, but even with such disobedience, God offered this hope and assurance:

> The LORD your God will make you abundantly prosperous in all the work of your hand, in the fruit of your womb and in the fruit of your cattle and in the fruit of your ground. For the LORD will again take delight in prospering you, as he took delight in your fathers, when you obey the voice of the LORD your God, to keep his commandments and his statutes that are written in this Book of the Law, when you turn to the LORD your God with all your heart and with all your soul. (Deut. 30:9–10)

The same God who delighted to bless Israel still delights to bless his children. The reality of the fall, the potential of persecution, and the vagaries of various circumstances mean that hard work might not "pay off" in the sense of financial prosperity. However, hard work does usually unleash good rewards (see Proverbs for dozens of such examples). This principle, then, leads to several practical outcomes:

- We expect God's blessings as we work faithfully unto him.
- We do not fear blessings—including monetary ones. If our labor is rewarded by our employer, we should accept such for what it is—a blessing from God. God is blessing the company in such a way that there is more money available to give. And God is giving us favor in the sight of our employer so that he or she desires to give that extra money to us. We can be thankful and encouraged by God's blessing.
- We should be grateful and not feel guilty about prospering in our labor. When God's people follow God's way, good results often flow. This might include promotions, special recognition, and financial bonuses.
- We should rejoice when God blesses others through their work.

Principle 3: Esteem Others in Our Work

If work is good, then it should be good both for us when we do it and also for others who might benefit by it. All Christians should think of their work as ministry. Some Christians are in the nursing ministry.[23] Others have an elementary teaching ministry. Still other Christians may have a tire or automotive maintenance ministry. Several members of my family work in the paper industry. They have a paper ministry. How many, including those reading this book, have benefited from paper? Working in a paper mill is a ministry, a service to the glory of God and good of others. From coloring books and newspapers to cardboard boxes and school textbooks, paper mills serve hundreds of millions of people each year. Calling work *ministry* is one way to keep God and others in mind as we labor.

Another aspect of esteeming others in our work is related to how we carry out our responsibilities. If we are lazy or idle, we esteem ourselves above others—the opposite of the biblical expectation (Phil. 2:1–4). Puritans such as Richard Baxter viewed idleness as a sin not to be tolerated by Christians, for it robbed God and others of honor.[24] The idle person does no service to God and thus is of no use to others. Idleness violates the truth that God blesses us with work so that we can bless others through work. Baxter took seriously the command of 2 Thessalonians 3:10: "If anyone is not willing to work, let him not eat." More recently, Leon Morris has commented on this passage: "These people had existed on the bounty of others. They are urged to exist on the fruits of their own labors."[25]

A few clarifications may prove helpful. First, this command focuses on an unwillingness to work, not on an inability to work. Situations arise, such as illnesses, injuries, economic downturns, or urgent responsibilities, that may create an inability to work. Second, no justification (not even a theological one, like the return of Christ) is adequate to allow Christians to be idle. Christians must be willing to work to serve God and others. Several ramifications follow from this truth:

- We must consider how to meet the needs of others in our work. How can our work serve our colleagues and supervisors?
- We must let others—Christians or non-Christians—know how valuable

---

[23] I am indebted to Scott Rae, who offered the ministry title to common vocations in a lecture he delivered at Southeastern Baptist Theological Seminary.

[24] Richard Baxter, *A Christian Directory: Or a Body of Practical Divinity and Cases of Conscience* (London: Richard Edwards, 1825).

[25] Leon Morris, *The First and Second Epistles to the Thessalonians*, rev. ed., NICNT (Grand Rapids, MI: Eerdmans, 1991), 258.

their work is. When the non-Christian is productive, he is manifesting God's common grace. As Tim Keller puts it, "Through his common grace God blesses all people, so that Christians can benefit from, and cooperate with, non-Christians."[26]

- We must desire to work.
- We must concern ourselves with meeting the needs of our families (1 Tim. 5:8).

Principle 4: Avoid the Vanity and Futility of Work

As noted above, work is an aspect of our being made in the image of God (Gen. 1:26–30). The God who is always working (John 5:17) has created us that we might, in a sense, be colaborers with him as he accomplishes his redemptive purposes through us (1 Cor. 3:9; 2 Cor. 6:1). When we work as unto the Lord, our labor is never in vain (1 Cor. 15:58). Yet vain labor remains a possibility.

Nowhere in Scripture is the vanity of work considered more painstakingly than through the mouth of the preacher of Ecclesiastes. Two key words in Ecclesiastes are *work* and *vanity*. Given these words' frequency, one might expect the preacher to conclude that all work is vanity. In fact, he comes very close to saying just that. In Ecclesiastes 2:20–21, the preacher concludes, "I turned about and gave my heart up to despair over all the toil of my labors under the sun, because sometimes a person who has toiled with wisdom and knowledge and skill must leave everything to be enjoyed by someone who did not toil for it. This also is vanity and a great evil." This man of wisdom had been very productive but has realized that life (as James will say later) is a mere "mist" (James 4:14). Who knows, the person who inherits everything from us might squander it all away!

Nevertheless, even the preacher of Ecclesiastes sees value in labor. The preacher writes in chapter 3, for instance, "I perceived that there is nothing better for them than to be joyful and to do good as long as they live; also that everyone should eat and drink and take pleasure in all his toil—this is God's gift to man. I perceived that whatever God does endures forever; nothing can be added to it, nor anything taken from it. God has done it, so that people fear before him" (Eccles. 3:12–14). In short, the distinction between vanity and fruitful labor concerns whether one works for himself or for the Lord. Is work a means for self-aggrandizement, or is it a gift from God to be received in joy? All self-aggrandizing work is vanity, striving after the wind. In Ecclesiastes, the preacher is "advocating the

---

quiet acceptance of whatever God gives to man."[27] Labor is not necessarily undertaken in vain. We avoid vanity in several ways:

- By accepting all work—even difficult work—as a gift from God to be received and completed by faith
- By avoiding working primarily for money, promotions, recognition, or other perks, for self-aggrandizing work will lead to vanity
- By avoiding equating one's rewards with one's own merit, lest we fall like Nebuchadnezzar when he took pride in all that he had built (Dan. 4:28ff.)
- By allowing ourselves ample time to rest, recognizing that rest demonstrates faith in a sovereign God and understanding that, while God allows us to participate in work, he is the one ultimately who accomplishes his purposes through our work, and so we must trust him enough to rest in his care
- By allowing others—especially younger employees—to learn from us, thus developing future leaders who will be able to fill our positions someday
- By working for the good of others—our spouses, children, colleagues, community, and network of customers, students, and other people whom our work affects

We must strive to be integrated, unified Christians who work as unto the Lord. We must receive our working life as an aspect of our whole life in Christ. We should recognize that God has blessed us with the work we do so that we may bless others through it. We should be grateful that God blesses others through our work. God serves others through our work, and he serves us through their work as well.

---

[27] R. N. Whybray, *Ecclesiastes*, Old Testament Guides (repr. Sheffield, UK: Sheffield Academic Press, 1997), 73.

SELECTED BIBLIOGRAPHY

Barrett, Matthew, and Michael A. G. Haykin. *Owen on the Christian Life: Living for the Glory of God in Christ.* Theologians on the Christian Life. Wheaton, IL: Crossway, 2015.

Baxter, Richard. *A Christian Directory: Or a Body of Practical Divinity and Cases of Conscience.* London: Richard Edwards, 1825.

Beeke, Joel. *Puritan Reformed Spirituality: A Practical Biblical Study from Reformed and Puritan Heritage.* Darlington, UK: Evangelical Press, 2006.

Beeke, Joel, and Brian G. Najapfour, eds. *Taking Hold of God: Reformed and Puritan Perspectives on Prayer.* Grand Rapids, MI: Reformation Heritage, 2011.

Bloesch, Donald A. *Spirituality Old & New: Recovering Authentic Spiritual Life.* Downers Grove, IL: IVP Academic, 2007.

Bolt, John. *Bavinck on the Christian Life: Following Jesus in Faithful Service.* Theologians on the Christian Life. Wheaton, IL: Crossway, 2015.

Bonhoeffer, Dietrich. *Life Together* and *Prayerbook of the Bible.* Dietrich Bonhoeffer Works 5. English edition. Minneapolis: Fortress, 2005.

Bray, Gerald. *Augustine on the Christian Life: Transformed by the Power of God.* Theologians on the Christian Life. Wheaton, IL: Crossway, 2015.

Bridges, Jerry. *The Disciplines of Grace: God's Role and Our Role in the Pursuit of Holiness.* Colorado Springs, CO: NavPress, 1994.

Burns, Lanier. *The Nearness of God: His Presence with His People.* Explorations in Biblical Theology. Phillipsburg, NJ: P&R, 2009.

Calvin, John. *Institutes of the Christian Religion.* Translated by Ford Lewis Battles. Edited by John T. McNeill. Philadelphia: Westminster, 1960.

Cannon, Mae Elise. *Just Spirituality: How Faith Practices Fuel Social Action.* Downers Grove, IL: InterVarsity, 2013.

Carson, D. A. *Showing the Spirit: A Theological Exposition of 1 Corinthians 12–14.* Grand Rapids, MI: Baker, 1987.

_____. "When Is Spirituality Spiritual? Reflections on Some Problems of Definition." *JETS* 37 (September 1994): 381–94.

Chapell, Bryan. *Holiness by Grace: Delighting in the Joy That Is Our Strength.* Wheaton, IL: Crossway, 2001.

Collins, Kenneth J., ed. *Exploring Christian Spirituality: An Ecumenical Reader.* Grand Rapids, MI: Baker, 2000.

CCCU Report on Spiritual Formation. Washington, DC: Council of Christian Colleges and Universities, 2011. https://www.cccu.org/~/media/filefolder/CCCU-SpiritualFormation_Booklet.pdf. Accessed January 20, 2017.

Demarest, Bruce, ed. *Four Views on Christian Spirituality.* Counterpoints. Grand Rapids, MI: Zondervan, 2012.

_____. *Satisfy Your Soul: Restoring the Heart of Christian Spirituality.* Colorado Springs, CO: NavPress, 1999.

Dockery, David S. "True Piety in James: Ethical Admonitions and Theological Implications." *Criswell Theological Review* 1 (Fall 1986): 51–70.

Easley, Kendell H., and Christopher W. Morgan, eds. *The Community of Jesus: A Theology of the Church.* Nashville, TN: B&H, 2013.

Edgar, William. *Schaeffer on the Christian Life: Countercultural Spirituality.* Theologians on the Christian Life. Wheaton, IL: Crossway, 2013.

Edwards, Jonathan. *Charity and Its Fruits.* Carlisle, PA: Banner of Truth, 1969.

_____. *Freedom of the Will.* New Haven, CT: Yale University Press, 1957.

Ferguson, Sinclair. *The Holy Spirit.* Contours of Christian Theology. Downers Grove, IL: InterVarsity, 1996.

_____. *John Owen on the Christian Life.* Carlisle, PA: Banner of Truth, 1987.

Fernando, Ajith. *Reclaiming Love: Radical Relationships in a Complex World.* Grand Rapids, MI: Zondervan, 2012.

Finn, Nathan A., and Keith Whitfield, eds. *Spirituality for the Sent: Casting a New Vision for the Missional Church.* Downers Grove, IL: IVP Academic, 2017.

Foster, Richard J. *Celebration of Discipline: The Path to Spiritual Growth.* 3rd ed. San Francisco: HarperSanFrancisco, 2002.

Gordon, James. *Evangelical Spirituality: From the Wesleys to John Stott.* London: SPCK, 1991.

Greenman, Jeffrey P., and George Kalantzis, eds. *Life in the Spirit: Spiritual Formation in Theological Perspective.* Downers Grove, IL: IVP Academic, 2010.

Haykin, Michael A. G. *The Reformers and Puritans as Spiritual Mentors: Hope Is Kindled.* Kitchener, ON: Joshua Press, 2012.

Hoekema, Anthony A. *Created in God's Image.* Grand Rapids, MI: Eerdmans, 1986.

_____. *Saved by Grace.* Grand Rapids, MI: Eerdmans, 1989.

Holt, Bradley P. *Thirsty for God: A Brief History of Christian Spirituality.* 2nd ed. Minneapolis: Fortress, 2005.

Horton, Michael. *Calvin on the Christian Life: Glorifying and Enjoying God Forever.* Theologians on the Christian Life. Wheaton, IL: Crossway, 2014.

_____. *Ordinary: Sustainable Faith in a Radical, Restless World.* Grand Rapids, MI: Zondervan, 2014.

House, Paul R. "God's Character and the Wholeness of Scripture." *SBET* 23.1 (Spring 2005): 4–17.

Hughes, Philip E. *The True Image: The Origin and Destiny of Man in Christ.* Grand Rapids, MI: Eerdmans, 1989.

Keller, Timothy, with Katherine Leary Alsdorf. *Every Good Endeavor: Connecting Your Work to God's Work.* New York: Riverhead, 2012.

Lovelace, Richard. *Dynamics of Spiritual Life: An Evangelical Theology of Renewal.* Downers Grove, IL: InterVarsity, 1979.

Lundgaard, Kris. *The Enemy Within: Straight Talk about the Power and Defeat of Sin.* Phillipsburg, NJ: P&R, 1998.

Luther, Martin. *The Bondage of the Will.* Translated by J. I. Packer and O. R. Johnston. Old Tappan, NJ: Revell, 1957.

_____. *Commentary on Romans.* Translated by J. Theodore Mueller. Grand Rapids, MI: Zondervan, 1954.

_____. "The Freedom of a Christian." In *Three Treatises.* Philadelphia: Muhlenberg, 1947.

Merton, Thomas. *Life and Holiness.* Garden City, NY: Image Books, 1964.

Meyer, Jason. *Lloyd-Jones on the Christian Life: Doctrine and Life as Fuel and Fire*. Theologians on the Christian Life. Wheaton, IL: Crossway, 2018.

Morgan, Christopher W., ed. *The Love of God*. Theology in Community 7. Wheaton, IL: Crossway, 2016.

_____. *A Theology of James: Wisdom for God's People*. Explorations in Biblical Theology. Phillipsburg, NJ: P&R, 2010.

Morgan, Christopher W., and Robert A. Peterson, eds. *Fallen: A Theology of Sin*. Theology in Community 5. Wheaton, IL: Crossway, 2013.

_____. *Suffering and the Goodness of God*. Theology in Community 1. Wheaton, IL: Crossway, 2008.

Murray, Iain H. *Evangelical Holiness and Other Addresses*. Edinburgh, UK: Banner of Truth, 2013.

Naselli, Andrew David. *Let Go and Let God? A Survey and Analysis of Keswick Theology*. Bellingham, WA: Lexham Press, 2013.

Nichols, Stephen J. *Bonhoeffer on the Christian Life: From the Cross, for the World*. Theologians on the Christian Life. Wheaton, IL: Crossway, 2013.

Ortlund, Dane. *Edwards on the Christian Life: Alive to the Beauty of God*. Theologians on the Christian Life. Wheaton, IL: Crossway, 2014.

Owen, John. "The Mortification of Sin." In *The Treasures of John Owen*. Carlisle, PA: Banner of Truth, 2016.

_____. *Overcoming Sin and Temptation*. Edited by Kelly Kapic and Justin Taylor. Wheaton, IL: Crossway, 2006.

Packer, J. I. *Keep in Step with the Spirit*. Grand Rapids, MI: Baker, 1984.

_____. *Knowing God*. Downers Grove, IL: InterVarsity, 1973.

_____. *A Quest for Godliness: The Puritan Vision of the Christian Life*. Wheaton, IL: Crossway, 1990.

_____. *Rediscovering Holiness: Know the Fullness of Life with God*. Ventura, CA: Regal, 2009.

Peterson, David. *Possessed by God: A New Testament Theology of Sanctification and Holiness*. New Studies in Biblical Theology. Downers Grove, IL: InterVarsity, 1995.

Peterson, Robert A. *Salvation Applied by the Spirit: Union with Christ*. Wheaton, IL: Crossway, 2015.

Piper, John. *Desiring God: Meditations of a Christian Hedonist*. Revised edition. Colorado Springs, CO: Multnomah, 2004.

Plantinga, Cornelius, Jr. *Not the Way It's Supposed to Be: A Breviary of Sin*. Grand Rapids, MI: Eerdmans, 1995.

Poythress, Vern. *The Lordship of Christ: Serving Our Savior All of the Time, in All of Life, with All of Our Heart*. Wheaton, IL: Crossway, 2016.

Reeves, Michael. *Spurgeon on the Christian Life: Alive in Christ*. Theologians on the Christian Life. Wheaton, IL: Crossway, 2018.

Ross, Allen P. *Recalling the Hope of Glory: Biblical Worship from the Garden to the New Creation*. Grand Rapids, MI: Kregel, 2006.

Sanders, Fred. *Wesley on the Christian Life: The Heart Renewed in Love*. Theologians on the Christian Life. Wheaton, IL: Crossway, 2013.

Schreiner, Thomas R. *New Testament Theology: Magnifying God in Christ*. Grand Rapids, MI: Baker Academic, 2008.

Scorgie, Glen G., ed. *Dictionary of Christian Spirituality*. Grand Rapids, MI: Zondervan, 2011.

Senn, Frank C., ed. *Protestant Spiritual Traditions*. Mahwah, NJ: Paulist, 1986; reprint, Eugene, OR: Wipf & Stock, 2000.

Sittser, Gerald L. *Water from a Deep Well: Christian Spirituality from Early Martyrs to Modern Missionaries*. Downers Grove, IL: IVP Academic, 2007.

Storms, Sam. *Packer on the Christian Life: Knowing God in Christ, Walking by the Spirit*. Theologians on the Christian Life. Wheaton, IL: Crossway, 2015.

_____. *Pleasures Evermore*. Colorado Springs, CO: NavPress, 2000.

Thorson, Don. *Pocket Dictionary of Christian Spirituality*. Downers Grove, IL: InterVarsity, 2018.

Tidball, Derek. *The Message of Holiness*. Bible Speaks Today. Downers Grove, IL: InterVarsity, 2010.

Trueman, Carl R. *Luther on the Christian Life: Cross and Freedom*. Theologians on the Christian Life. Wheaton, IL: Crossway, 2015.

Venning, Ralph. *The Sinfulness of Sin*. Edinburgh, UK: Banner of Truth, 1993.

Warfield, Benjamin B. *Studies in Perfectionism*. Phillipsburg, NJ: Presbyterian and Reformed, 1958.

Wenham, Gordon J. *Psalms as Torah: Reading Biblical Song Ethically*. Studies in Theological Interpretation. Grand Rapids, MI: Baker Academic, 2012.

Wesley, John. *The Works of John Wesley*. Grand Rapids, MI: Baker, 2007; reprinted from the 1872 edition issued by Wesleyan Methodist Book Room, London.

Whitney, Donald S. *Praying the Bible*. Wheaton, IL: Crossway, 2015.

_____. *Spiritual Disciplines for the Christian Life*. Colorado Springs, CO: NavPress, 1991.

Willard, Dallas. *Renovation of the Heart: Putting on the Character of Christ*. Colorado Springs, CO: NavPress, 2012.

_____. *The Spirit of the Disciplines*. San Francisco: Harper & Row, 1988.

Wright, Christopher J. H. *Old Testament Ethics for the People of God*. Downers Grove, IL: InterVarsity, 2004.

Zaspel, Fred G. *Warfield on the Christian Life: Living Life in Light of the Gospel*. Theologians on the Christian Life. Wheaton, IL: Crossway, 2012.

NAME INDEX

Abraham, 148, 277; covenant with, 64, 161–62

Adam: condemnation in, 108; fall of, 119, 129; sin of, 25–26; union with, 110–11; walk with God in the garden, 159–60

Allison, Gregg, 217

Ananias and Sapphira, 99

Ananias (disciple), 99

Andria, Solomon, 144

Anna, 56

Augustine, 88, 177, 246

Backus, William, 262n29

Banks, Robert, 169

Barnhouse, Donald Grey, 123n65

Barth, Karl, 59

Bascal, Blaise, 233

Bavinck, Herman, 36

Baxter, Richard, 278

Bebbington, David, 179n1, 196, 216, 225

Becket, Thomas, 177

Beeke, Joel, 189

Berry, Wendell, 59, 66, 76

Bloesch, Donald, 158n18, 171

Boardman, William, 228

Boaz, 277

Bock, Darrell, 99n31

Bonhoeffer, Dietrich, 38, 230

Bridges, Jerry, 32, 235–36

Brother Lawrence, 177

Bruce, F. F., 99n31

Burton, Matthew, 271

Calhoun, David, 40, 42

Calvin, John, 88, 99n31, 102n34, 119, 140n6, 148, 178, 184–89, 213, 246, 269–71

Card, Michael, 249

Carson, D. A., 19–20, 89n20, 99, 123n64

Chapell, Bryan, 37

Childs, Brevard, 57

Chrysostom, John, 150

Clements, Ronald, 57

Collins, C. John, 24

Cyril of Jerusalem, 88

Daniel, 77, 277

David, kingship of, 165

Davidson, Ivor, 31–32

Davids, Peter, 142

Davis, Ellen, 59

Day, Dorothy, 220

DeGraf, David, 141n8

Demarest, Bruce, 19

de Valdés, Juan, 233

Dockery, David, 138n2

Doriani, Daniel, 145

Dunn, James D. G., 88n19

Edwards, Jonathan, 147, 178, 203–8, 213, 223, 233, 236

Eichrodt, Walter, 57

Ellenburg, Dale, 151

Erasmus, Desiderius, 181

Esther, 77

Ezra, 77

Ferguson, Sinclair, 50–51

Fernando, Ajith, 99n31

Finney, Charles, 227

Fletcher, John, 202

Forster, Greg, 268

Foster, Richard, 231, 233, 234, 244, 252

Francis of Assisi, 177

Freitheim, Terence, 162n26, 163–64

SUBJECT INDEX

SCRIPTURE INDEX

THEOLOGY IN COMMUNITY

FIRST-RATE EVANGELICAL SCHOLARS
take a multidisciplinary approach
to key Christian doctrines

OTHER BOOKS IN THE SERIES

For more information, visit **www.crossway.org**.